Called to
SERVE

Called to
SERVE
The Shaping of a Servant

Carmen L. Lewis

Rev. date: 02/26/2013

To order additional copies of this book, contact:
Xlibris Corporation
1-888-795-4274
www.Xlibris.com
Orders@Xlibris.com
117754

This manuscript is dedicated to Mom, Clara Pauline Smith Beasley, who passed away in 1990 and to Dad, Gerald Austin Beasley, who currently lives and still preaches at the age of ninety-two in Geary, Oklahoma. Both dedicated their lives to serving God and have been great Christian examples to their six children, grandchildren, and great-grandchildren. They have influenced hundreds of friends and family members to live moral and active lives in the service of Christ our Lord.

I also dedicate this to my brother, Hoyt Terrell Beasley, who went to be with God in September of 2012. He preached for many years until his health prevented him from working full time. He continued to preach pro bono at the church of Christ in Depew, Oklahoma, when his health permitted.

PREFACE

Mom, Clara Pauline (Smith), and Dad, Gerald Austin Beasley, grew up in humble circumstances working hard on farm(s) in Oklahoma with their respective families; and both lived through the depression years of the 1920s. After World War II, Dad and Mom spent forty-four years preaching and teaching the Gospel in various congregations of the churches of Christ across the central United States in Oklahoma, Kansas, Texas, and Montana. Dad has continued to serve the Lord in Geary, Oklahoma, since Mom's death in 1990. Altogether, Dad has spent approximately seventy years as a Gospel preacher. During his life, he has influenced thousands of souls, including his wife and their six children: Hoyt Terrell, Sheba Beth, Reba Nell, Carmen Lee, Neva Ann, and Treva Kay.

Dad was never famous as a politician, great artist, or musician (actually, he was a pretty good clarinet player and musician). He never published a book, made millions of dollars, or became a national celebrity. Worldly accomplishments and admonitions may have tickled his ambitions; but his interest, concern, and dedication has been to serve the Lord. He was, and is, a great man of God who answered the call by saying, "Here I am, Lord! Send me!" There is no greater legacy.

As we six Beasley children were growing up, Dad and Mom often told stories of their childhood and adolescence. Dad would repeat stories of his military service experiences during World War II. He also repeated fictional short stories, puns, and some tales he had made up. He used many of these stories as illustrations in his sermons or sometimes just to amuse us. We encouraged both of Mom and Dad to write their remembrances so they would be recorded and not forgotten. Before she died, Mom did write down some remembrances of growing up on her family's farm, but Dad chose to talk about them. So I took it upon myself to assemble the following book of Mom and Dad's early lives and stories.

Even without this collection of stories, Dad and Mom have found a place in history, in the hearts of family and friends, and in the heart of our Lord and Savior.

Over their lifetime, Mom and Dad always remembered family and friends. The world became small as our family traveled throughout the Midwest visiting and revisiting Dad and Mom's family and friends. Even today as Dad travels, he is still mindful to look in a telephone book for the name, phone number, and address of a relative or old acquaintance and then pay a visit.

I have tried to be as factual and accurate as possible about the people, places, and events in Mom and Dad's lives. Information was gathered from several sources:

1. I spent many hours interviewing and audio-taping Dad (after Mom's death) as he answered my questions and related his memories.
2. Mom had made copies of old pictures of great-grandparents, grandparents, aunts and uncles, nieces and nephews. On the backs of these pictures she had written names, dates of birth, places, and relationships. The information, though overwhelming, was very useful. Some of these pictures have been included in the text.
3. Mom had also done a genealogy study of the Smith and Beasley families gathered by word-of-mouth from relatives and friends, personal documents, various city and county documents, and actual visits to cemeteries and homestead locations. She wrote the information down and assembled it in two three-ring notebooks (and some loose papers).

These were a bit confusing but quite helpful. From Genealogy.com, I was able to validate and organize some of her data and add additional information.

4. Mom had found and kept some writings in notebooks that Maggie (Herring) Smith, her mother, had written as a girl.

5. Mom also had written a diary beginning January 1, 1945, during the year that Dad was in Europe participating in World War II.

6. Dad had begun a journal "somewhere on the Atlantic" as he headed overseas to engage on the European conflict. In the journal, he expressed his thoughts, feelings, impressions of war, and of his fellow soldiers. After returning home, he continued a recording of baptisms and names of people he knew and taught in various churches. Biblical verses he included in his journal were from the King James Version.

7. Over several years, Mom wrote rough drafts of some remembrances and events from her childhood. She called these "Writings from an Ignorant Bend, Sand Hill, Elkview Lass."

8. Historical information was gleaned from the following:

    a. An old set of the *New Standard Encyclopedia* (which I no longer have)

    b. An old college textbook of Mom's titled *Our Oklahoma* by Muriel H. Write, copyright date of 1939, Co-Operative Publishing Company

    c. *Life in the Oil Fields*, by Roger M. Olien and Diana Davis Olien, Texas Monthly Press, 1986

    d. *American Colonies*, by Alan Taylor, Penguin Books, copyright 2001

    e. *Texas: An Album of History*, by James L. Haley, Doubleday and Company, Inc., Garden City, New York, 1985

    f. Various websites on the Internet

g. I corresponded with Robert Habercorn, one of Dad's former fellow military band members during World War II. Robert provided me a list of still living, retired, military band members that he had remained in touch with. From this list, I wrote to and received back some information from several of these musicians from the AAATC band. Some of their responses are included.

h. Biblical scriptures I quoted were from the New International Version; published by Zondervan Bible Publishers; Grand Rapids, Michigan; copyrighted 1973, 1978, 1984 by International Bible Society (text may be quoted up to one thousand verses (1000) without written permission from the publisher).

I embellished and fictionalized some stories and events, but most of the events are accurate and true. Some names have been changed, but most names are accurate and true, taken from word-of-mouth or written documents from Dad and Mom.

Carmen Lee (Beasley) Lewis

ACKNOWLEDGMENTS

Special thanks to John Free, a teacher, who read and edited my first manuscript back in 2004. He carefully reviewed historical information included in the text, made some corrections and suggestions. I followed his suggestion to eliminate some excessive historical information within the text. As I deleted, hopefully, I still retained historical integrity. Perhaps, I still retained too much.

Special thanks goes to my dad, Gerald Beasley, who tolerated long interview sessions and questions over the phone which provided many recollections of people, places, and events in his and Mom's lives.

Special thanks also goes to my brother and sisters who answered questions, verbally shared and wrote personal remembrances.

PART ONE

Remembrances

CHAPTER ONE

A kindhearted woman gains respect.
—Proverbs 11:16

A Good Woman

It was a warm spring day in Sapulpa, Oklahoma, in the year of 1918. The one-room country school just north of Sapulpa was about to be dismissed for the day. Outside, budded trees were beginning to awaken, grasses were greening, congregations of insects swarmed aimlessly, and birds spoke their return.

The slender brown-haired, green-eyed twenty-one-year-old teacher, Ms. Hallie Morris, was liked by all her students but was having a difficult time keeping her students focused on their lessons. Usually, because she always praised and encouraged her students for their ingenuity and creativity, they wanted to do their best to please her. But not this day. The children, ranging in ages from six to fifteen, were restless and distracted; they gazed out the window wishing to be outside climbing trees, swinging on the tree swing, fishing at the creek, riding horses—anything but sitting at a school desk.

Lena was the only student working; she so wanted to please Ms. Morris. She admired Ms. Morris and thought she was the best teacher in the whole world. She wished to emulate her teacher's quiet independence, patience, kindness, and positive approach to learning.

Eight-year-old Lena remained on task as she concentrated on her writing assignment hoping to finish before dismissal. Uncle Edgar, her father's youngest brother, was to pick her up from school and take her home. She knew he would not want to wait for her.

Finally, Ms. Morris clanged the dismissal bell hung outside the door and then stepped aside as the eager children ran out of the school building whooping and hollering, glad to leave the confining walls and mind exercises to romp freely in the alluring spring air.

When twenty-one-year-old Uncle Edgar arrived and saw that his niece had not come out, he impatiently got out of his recently purchased used Model-T and stomped inside to hasten her along.

"Lena, hurry! I've got to get you home so I can get back to work," he exclaimed. He was actually meeting some fellows in the basement of the drug store to play billiards, but Lena did not need to know that.

Lena responded, "Okay, I'm coming."

Turning quickly to go back outside, Edgar bumped into and almost knocked down Ms. Morris. "Oh, I'm sorry! Are you okay?" he asked as he steadied her and gave her a look of puzzlement, then of recognition.

"I'm fine. I just came over to tell Lena she can finish her assignment tomorrow," Ms. Morris replied as she tilted her head. She looked at him inquisitively, then, asked. "Don't I know you?"

"Yeah! We were in school together a few years back. You were gone for a while, but I've seen you around town recently," Edgar responded.

After completing only elementary grade school, Edgar had discontinued school to work on the farm with his dad. Hallie had gone on to finish junior high school; then, she went to Clarendon, Oklahoma, to study and receive teaching credentials. Now she was back in Sapulpa, a relatively small city with many surrounding farms, where everybody was bound to know everybody else, or at least to have heard about them.

Lena smiled as she stood looking up at Uncle Edgar and her teacher watching the sparks fly as they renewed their acquaintance.

It was the first night of the Creek County Fair in Sapulpa. An Indian summer was holding winter in its closet, and the September fall weather was perfect for the occasion with a slight chill in the air, the leaves barely turning yellow, brown, and orange. At the fair, there would be something for everybody to do: the adolescents and the young at heart could dance, the women could attend to the bake sale where they could gossip, the men could attend the rodeo, and all, including the children, could view the entries or play the carnival games in the midway.

Stomping her feet impatiently on the farmhouse porch, Lena waited for the rest of her family to finish getting ready. "Let's go! Hurry, we're going to be late!" she exclaimed.

"Lena! Calm down! We'll get there soon enough," her mother, Cordelia, emphatically ordered.

When the Robert Beasleys were ready, Lena, the youngest of six; Harl, her brother; and Grace, her sister, jumped into the back of the gig eager to hit the road. Cordelia handed a covered baked good to each child. "Hold them carefully! I don't want them crumbled or dumped," Mom warned.

Many friends and family would be at the fair. In fact, most of the Beasley clan would be there, and that must be half the population in the Sapulpa area: Grandpa Samuel and Grandma Lavina Beasley, Robert and Cordelia Beasley's family, Aunt Betty's family, Uncle Richard and Aunt Nancy Yokum's family, Uncle Jim Beasley's family, Uncle Tom Beasley's family, Uncle Carl Beasley's family, and Uncle Edgar Beasley, not to name the many children in each family.

The Beasley gig lined up on the dirt road leading to the fairgrounds along with other family gigs full of eager children.

Friends and relatives waved and hollered, "Hi." Those few folks who owned a motorized vehicle honked their noisy car horns, which frightened the horses pulling the drawn gigs, making it necessary for the drivers to pull on the reins and speak reassuringly to calm the animals. The many turning wheels stirred up the dust as the slow caravan moved toward the fairgrounds.

Finally arriving, Lena, Harl, and Grace wiggled impatiently as they waited to hand off the goods, but Cordelia commanded, "Don't run off just yet! You're going to help me carry these to the tent."

"Oh, Mom, all the other kids are already on the midway playing!" They complained.

"I don't care. I labored all day cooking. The least you can do is help me," Cordy stated.

The children grudgingly but obediently carried the goods and followed their mom into the tent where many ladies had already begun to assemble, along with a great number of the Beasley clan.

After setting the baked goods down, Lena and her siblings turned and readied to dash off when Ms. Morris and Uncle Edgar enter the tent together. Lena ran to her teacher. "Ms. Morris, I didn't know you would be here with Uncle Edgar! It's so good to see you! Come meet my family!" Lena grabbed the hand of her mentor and led her over to the clan.

"I didn't know you had so many relatives living around Sapulpa!" Ms. Morris exclaimed after the many introductions and then asked, "Lena, why don't you come with us to the midway?" Hallie glanced toward Edgar as he nodded his approval.

"Well, if that's okay. That would be great!" she answered.

And so, the Beasley clan met and gave their approval of the courtship of Uncle Edgar Beasley and Ms. Hallie Elizabeth Morris. Lena liked to think of herself as their matchmaker.

Edgar and Hallie continued their courtship as World War I was coming to an end.

(See appendage for Beasley and Morris Genealogy.)

CHAPTER TWO

Each man should have his own wife,
and each woman her own husband.
— 1 Corinthians 7:2

Early Remembrances of a Sand Springs, Oklahoma, Lad

I remember Mom, Hallie Elizabeth (Morris) Beasley, talking about her families' move from Missouri to Oklahoma. She was the youngest, about four years old, but she remembered the change of the landscape as they left Missouri and came into Oklahoma. There were green hills and lots of trees where she had grown up as a little girl in Missouri, but she marveled at the extent of the yellow drier Oklahoma plains.

After finishing eighth grade in Sapulpa, Oklahoma, Mom went through a "teaching normal," a training program for elementary school teachers over at a campus in Claremore, Oklahoma, just north of Tulsa. (That particular campus has since been a military school and several different kinds of establishments.) Mom probably began teaching when she was only seventeen or eighteen.

Both Mom and Dad had a lot of relatives living near the Sapulpa, Sand Springs, and Tulsa area.

I remember visiting Uncle Robert and Cordelia (everybody called her Cordy) Beasley on a farm just outside of Sapulpa. They had a large family of six children: Harl, Grace, Lena, Alvin,

Marvin, and Jerome. (Over the years, I've kept in contact with Marvin.)

Great-Uncle George (brother to my grandfather, Samuel) and his wife, Mary (Acru) Beasley, lived with their many children on a farm northwest of Sapulpa.

Uncle Jim Beasley lived with his good-sized family in the country northeast of Sand Springs. Uncle Jim was a hard guy to figure out. I never knew just how to respond to him. He made me a little uncomfortable. He was pleasant enough but seemed somewhat aloof in the way he looked and the way he conducted himself. (One of his daughters later lived in San Antonio, Texas. Another descendant of one of Jim's boys later moved in Illinois. In 1987, or thereabouts, this female descendant corresponded with the scattered Beasleys about having a reunion in Illinois around the big pond on their property. Those who attended said the reunion was very nice.)

(By the way, many descendants of Nathaniel Beasley and his cousin, William Beasley, mentioned in the Beasley genealogy, had remained in Illinois since the early 1800s.)

Uncle Tom Beasley and his family also farmed in the Sapulpa area.

Aunt Nancy (Beasley), married to Richard Yokum, also had a large family and lived near Sapulpa.

Dad's father, Samuel Beasley, lived near Sapulpa.

The Beasley Boys: Top from left to right: Tom, Carl, and Edgar. Bottom from left to right: Robert and Jim

Hallie's sister, Aunt Floyd (Morris), and her husband, E. H. Berry, lived in Sand Springs. They had four daughters: Louise, Maurine, and the twins, Madeline and Marjorie.

Mom's parents, George and Francis Morris, also lived near Sapulpa.

Dad's brothers were a jovial bunch of Good Ole Boys, a fun-loving, well-liked clan. However, they could be quite vain and sometimes used vulgar, not so "pretty" language.

Mom was liked and accepted by the Beasleys but took a lot of razing from the boys.

My Uncle Robert Beasley's daughter, Lena, adored Mom as a teacher. Lena and Hallie remained very close friends for life. Uncle Tom's daughters, Audrey and Cleo, also had Mom for a teacher and thought she was about "it."

Don't know how Dad and his brothers avoided serving during World War I, but they didn't. After the war, with the cancellation of wartime contracts, unemployment was high, and this did, however, affect their chances of employment. Many American soldiers returning to the states from the war in Europe were also seeking work.

Americans settled back into a peaceful existence and did not wish to become involved in international affairs.

Edgar Beasley and Hallie Elizabeth Morris about 1919 in Sapulpa, OK

Dad, Edgar Beasley, and Mom, Hallie Elizabeth Morris, were married on May 21, 1919.

Dad attempted farming to support his new wife. I don't know if Mom continued to teach. It is possible with the bad economy that she did, at least until I was born.

CHAPTER THREE

For you created my inmost being;
you knit me together in my mother's womb . . .
All the days ordained for me were written
in your book before one of them came to be.
—Psalm 139:13, 16

Early Remembrances of a Sand Springs, Oklahoma, Lad

In 1920, after World War I, Warren Gamaliel Harding was elected as the twenty-ninth president of the United States. He kept the United States out of the League of Nations and supported Americans desire to remain isolated from world affairs, but his campaign promise for "normalcy . . . not heroics" was short-lived. He died of a heart attack and complications with pneumonia August 2, 1923. Vice President Calvin Coolidge became president.

Americans kept up with the political and social changes taking place in the United States by listening to the "new entertainment" radio. Will Rogers, Oklahoma's homegrown celebrity from Claremore, Oklahoma, was a favorite commentator. News reports fed: the "red scare"; reported restrictions placed on immigrants to weed out possible infiltration of communism; exclaimed the growing number of the Ku Klux Klan; told of Negroes migrating to the industrial centers of the north; sympathized with the WWII veterans left rootless and disillusioned; and praised and/ or preached the evils of the Roaring Twenties and the Jazz Age.

The Beasley and Morris clans were not unconcerned and unaffected by current events. They listened to the news and read the papers; but their first concerns were working their farms, working in the oil fields, supporting, and raising their families.

I, Gerald Austin Beasley, was born July 19, 1920, in Sapulpa, about fourteen months after Edgar and Hallie Beasley were married. I was to be an only child.

Mom apparently had a difficult time healthwise. I was told that during my infancy, Mom's appendix burst, causing major complications. Aunt Nancy Yokum, Dad's sister, had several children of her own, but she took care of me in her home on a farm on Euchee Creek until I was about six months old.

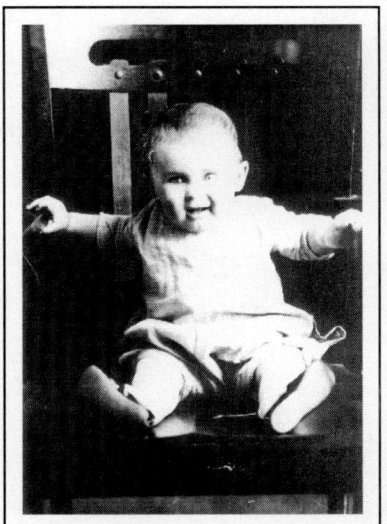

Gerald Austin Beasley about six months old, Sapulpa, OK, 1920

Dad then cared for me as best he could while Mom was still recuperating. He told me, "When you were still quite small, I took you out to the field where I was plowing and laid you on a pallet at the edge of the field."

Apparently, a pet collie dog became my "protector." Once while Dad was plowing behind his workhorses, a friendly neighbor approached the pallet where I lay. The dog snarled and would not allow the neighbor to come near me.

"Hey, it's okay, fella. I was just going to say 'hi' to the little guy," the neighbor said. Though the neighbor tried to talk reassuringly, the dog still resisted, growled, and showed his teeth; the man came no closer to me.

Dad had to get out of the harness, leave the horses in the field, and come over to calm the collie. "It's okay, fella! This is a friend! He doesn't mean any harm."

The collie still would not let the neighbor come near me.

I was told even as I grew and began walking at about the age of one, the collie would follow me, and if I toddled too far, it would gently take my little hand in its mouth and lead me back to the pallet. It was a smart dog, never jealous, never wanted to hurt me; it just protected its small ward.

Mom had always been an independent woman, so it was hard for her to be unable to assume the responsibility for my care. Her health did eventually improve, and she was able to get up and around.

For comfort's sake and practicality, Mom wore loose-fitting, culotteslike pants, not the normal female attire for the time, as she resumed her household tasks.

She had a mind of her own; I guess she was a woman's libber.

Gerald Austin Beasley, about age three Sapulpa, OK, 1923.

Mom and Dad often took me as a toddler to visit relatives who lived nearby.

Since Uncle Jim's family lived quite near, we visited them often. Uncle Jim's youngest boy, Gus, was crippled from polio. I played with Gus a lot. We got along real good as youngsters.

On numerous occasions we visited the Robert Beasley's large family. Harl, Grace, and Lena were grown by then; but Marvin, Alvin, and Jerome were still living at home.

I loved to play with them. Usually they willingly included me in their activities, but sometimes they preferred not to play with their younger nephew. They had learned to share, wore hand-me-down clothes, and received few toys. But as an only child, I guess I was pampered and often got my way.

One of my earliest memories was a visit to their home.

"Can I play? Can I have that? It's my turn," I would ask.

I didn't take kindly to, "No, you are too little!" Or "No, you can't have that!"

Often, I would cry and run to Momma and exclaim, "He won't play with me!" Or "He won't share." Mom would console and give me something to appease me.

Aunt Cordy looked directly at me and told me, "You are spoiled!"

Being called *spoiled* did not leave me with a good feeling. I had often watched mother as she spent hours and days canning lots of fruits and vegetables, and sometimes if the canning wasn't done right, the food would spoil. I had also been with her when she had opened and disposed of the smelly, spoiled contents. So when Aunt Cordy said, "You are spoiled," I connected that with spoiled canned goods. It did hurt my feelings!

But I remember Aunt Cordy as a fine religious lady.

When I was about four years old, my folks left the farm and moved into Sand Springs. Farming was difficult and just wasn't making enough to support the family. Dad went to work for the Pierce Oil Refinery in Sand Springs. We lived in a small house in a

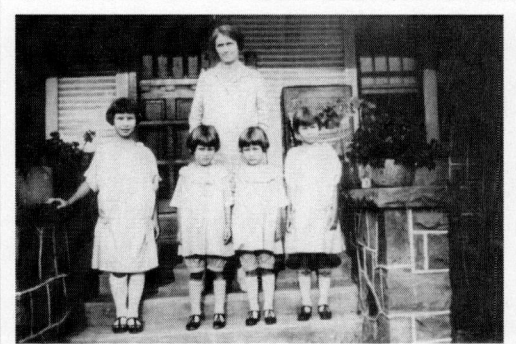

Georgia Floyd (Morris) Berry, daughters Louise, twins Madeline and Maurine, and Marjorie. 1930, Sand Springs

nice little neighborhood with other houses nearby, and I was delighted to have other children to play with.

I probably knew E. H. and Aunt Floyd Berry's family better than any of my other cousins on mother's side because they lived in Sand Springs. The girls and I went through the schools in Sand Springs together. (The two older Berry girls, Maurine and Louise, later married local boys in Sand Springs.) The twins, Marjorie and Madeline, were just a year older than me. (As an adult, one lived down in El Campo south of Houston. The other twin lived in Louisiana.)

Very soon after the move, I was in the front yard when a not-so-nice bully came up and demanded, "Give me your sucker!"

"Do what now?" I asked, somewhat confused. Surely I didn't have to give him my sucker.

"Give me your sucker, or I'll beat you up!" Ted threatened.

I gave him my sucker!

Intimidated and unsure of just how to react, I allowed Ted Shoefelt to take advantage of me. However, on other occasions, I did play with not-so-nice Teddy, but I was really kind of afraid of him.

CHAPTER FOUR

Leave your country, your people and
your father's household and
go to the land I will show you.
—Genesis 12:1

Southwest Oklahoma Homesteads

In the southwest corner of Oklahoma where the white sands blew and shifted in the hot wind, some two hundred miles away from Sand Springs, seemingly unrelated events had taken place.

In about 1902, the territory of southwest Oklahoma was opened for homesteading and/or purchase of cheap land. Of the many who came to the area, two such pioneering couples took advantage of this opportunity: (1) William and Rosa Smith and (2) Edmond Pinkney and Willie Herring.

William (of Cherokee Indian blood) and Rosa Smith had moved from the Panhandle of Texas, where they had ranched cattle on land close to Quitaque, Texas, to Old Greer County in southwest Oklahoma. The Smiths moved with their four Texas-born children. Four more children were later born to them in Oklahoma.

William and Rosa Smith eventually settled at Mountain Park, Oklahoma, near the North Fork of the Red River where they farmed. It was in this area that their eight children grew up and attended school.

John Earl Smith, their third child, was only about four years old at the time of the move. As he grew, he worked, played, and courted in southwest Oklahoma.

Edmond Pinkney and Willie Herrings were of Dutch origin. They had traveled in a covered wagon throughout farming areas in Louisiana, Arkansas, and Oklahoma, probably as migrant workers. They had two children, Myrtle Lavonia, and Maggie Lillian; both were born in Sailes, Louisiana.

With the promise of land of their own, the Herrings finally settled at Elkview, Oklahoma, in 1920.

Lavonia and Maggie had probably received a sporadic education while the family traveled as migrant workers, but Maggie graduated from the eighth grade from the Old Elkview School near Warren, Oklahoma, while living on a farm in Cold Springs, Oklahoma.

Parties, dances, and basket dinners were planned and advertised by word of mouth, which brought the scattered settlers of southwest Oklahoma together.

John Earl Smith, son of William and Rosa, was tall and handsome and quite the ladies man. He attended these affairs where he met and dated several young ladies. Bertha Malone was one of the young ladies he dated, and it was rumored that they would probably marry.

However, short and petite Maggie Herring had other ideas. Right after her family settled in Cold Springs, she had noticed twenty-two-year-old John; she was only fourteen but jealous when she saw him with or heard that he had been with other females. Maggie was madly in love with him and pursued him. Five-foot Maggie was determined that the handsome five-foot ten-inch John Smith would be hers.

So it was in the farmlands in Kiowa and Jackson counties in southwest Oklahoma, in the vicinity of the North Fork Red River, where John Smith met and courted Maggie Herring.

Twenty-four-year-old John married sixteen-year-old Maggie on July 26, 1922, in Mangum, Oklahoma.

Mr. and Mrs. John Smith moved by wagon to Frederick, Oklahoma, in 1923, where J. C. Smith was stillborn on January 21, 1923. J. C. was buried at the Frederick City Cemetery, Lot 59, grave #3, SE ¼ of block E.

In 1924, John and Maggie moved back to Warren, Oklahoma, traveling again by wagon, leading a cow.

Chapter Five

He who works his land will have abundant food,
but he who chases fantasies lacks judgment.
—Proverbs 12:11

Early Remembrances of an Ignorant Bend, Sand Hill, Elkview Lass

I, Clara Pauline Smith, was born March 15, 1924, to twenty-six-year-old John Earl Smith and eighteen-year-old Maggie Lillian (Herring) Smith at the Edmond Herrings' (Maggie's parents) house near Cold Springs (now under Tom Sneed Lake) in Kiowa County. I weighed 7 lbs and 12 oz.

According to my parents' old records, in 1926, Dad purchased the farmhouse at Route One, Blair, Oklahoma, from his father, William Riley Smith, for $100. William Smith had purchased the farmhouse and land on December 6, 1915. It had changed hands

Back room of Smith farmhouse, built on or before 1902. The house was torn down in 1966 because it was unsafe.

nine times since in 1902. (This information was recorded by Pauline Smith Beasley.)

The North Fork Red River was two miles east and down from the farm. The Wichita Mountains could be seen to the east.

Life in southwest Oklahoma was hot, dry, and difficult. My parents' busy days were filled with hard labor as they rose early and went to bed late. They worked hard, but they were self-sufficient.

With the use of the Almanac, Mom and Dad kept up with the seasonal tasks of plowing, planting, and harvesting. Because they had no motorized machines to ease the tedious work, plowing was done with mules or horses harnessed to a heavy tiller. Dad followed the plow as he held its handles trying to guide the tiller in even rows. Planting was done by hand. Weeding was done with a handheld hoe. Tall grasses were cut with a chisel. Mom and Dad worked beside hired migrant workers harvesting in their fields.

Cotton was their main crop, but they sometimes grew other crops in the shifting, white, sandy Oklahoma soil to the south of their modest house.

The orchard—started from apple, peach, pear, and apricot seedlings—was northeast of the house. Until they were deeply rooted, Dad would haul water in a large tank from the pond or the well to the orchard and then dip out buckets of water for the fruit tree seedlings. The orchard was fertilized, pruned, and

Old barn west of
John and Maggie Smith's farmhouse

harvested, and then the produce was marketed.

To the west up a slight hill beyond the barn, Mom had a vegetable garden for growing food for our personal consumption.

This garden was watered from a well. Mom was busy canning throughout the growing season.

Because the southwest plains of Oklahoma received light rainfall per annum, the cotton fields had to thrive as best they could.

The horses and cows were kept in the barn at night, but by day, the livestock watered and fed in the west and north fields around the small pond, which was just northwest of the house. Hay had to be spread in the barn during winter weather. Milking was done early and late each day.

Chickens roosted and eggs were collected from all around the farmhouse, barn, garage, and smokehouse, all clustered under the meager shade of some oak trees.

Pigs rooted within the fence by the barn. Turkeys wandered freely, roosting where they chose.

The entry to the farm was to the south of the land. To reach the farmhouse from the county road, vehicles had to drive north around the cotton field, past the barn, then east to the house. As the deepening ruts in this route became impassable because of the shifting sandy soil, a new route was made directly through the cotton field. While one path was used, the other would be left unused, so plant growth and packing of the ruts would again make it passable. These paths were alternated over time.

The rustic wooden farmhouse had no electricity or running water. On the north side of the house was a kitchen with a wood-burning stove and oven for cooking as well as a metal sink with a pipe drain that deposited used and dirty well water to the ground just outside the north wall. To the right of the kitchen sink and on a

Maggie Smith hauling water from the well

shelf at a higher level, we kept a water bucket with a dipper. We would quench our thirst, leave any leftover water in the dipper, and return it to the bucket. Today that practice would be seen as unsanitary, but we used water conservatively since it had to be hauled from a well some distance away.

With no running water in the house, water had to be carried from the well to the house in buckets. This well was hand dug to a depth of about twenty feet. There was a pulley and a rope to draw water up in a long cylindrical bucket with a collapsible bottom. Some of the water would seep through the bottom, so water was quickly poured into handled buckets to be carried to the house. Eventually, this well went dry. Dad tried to dig it deeper, but the sides of the well caved in. So that well was filled in. The spot was left marked, but another well was drilled nearer the house from which big slices of finely grained gyp (gypsum) came up.

Water was used very conservatively!

The front porch of the house was supported with four-by-fours at the corners and two in the middle. The front door opened into the living room area which was south of the kitchen. It was heated by a cast-iron wood-burning stove. There was a bedroom east of and behind the living room area. More rooms were added on later beyond this bedroom.

Since there were no indoor bathroom facilities, the "necessary" had to be done outside in the tall grasses where the snakes, bugs, and other critters observed uncaringly or, when startled, hastened away. In adverse weather, a potty bucket was used indoors and later emptied outside.

When I was a baby, Mom would carry me to the west garden and laid me in the shade of some oak trees near the garden while she turned the soil, planted, watered, hoed, and harvested her vegetables. As I became older, these trees seemed huge to me! When I began to toddle around, I joined Mother in the rows and tried to help drop seeds (cantaloupe, onion, corn, bean, cucumber, okra, peas, and tomatoes) into the holes that Mother made with a hoe handle. She taught me to push the dirt with my hand to cover the seeds. I probably hindered more than helped.

In the evening after a long day, I would crawl into Dad's lap, and he sometimes told stories of his boyhood.

One story he told was when he and several other young men went to the North Fork Red River to fish and swim. At this particular time of the year, the river was up from heavy rains. The young men got caught up in a "suck hole" while swimming. Several were pulled out or managed to swim out of the swift circular sucking movement of the water, but others were pulled out after knots were tied in a rope and thrown to the remaining swimmers. Apparently, Dad was one of the last to be rescued.

Years later, Dad attended the funeral of Willy Enkerbarker, the last young man to be pulled out. Dad stated, "Willy almost gave his life so that my life would be saved."

CHAPTER SIX

Be happy, young man, while you are young, and let
your heart give you joy in the days of your youth.

—Ecclesiastes 11:9a

Early Remembrances of a Sand Springs, Oklahoma, Lad—1925

Dad, Mom, and I frequently visited my Great-Uncle George and Aunt Mary Beasley's on their farm northwest of Sapulpa. On one occasion, we arrived to find nobody was home, but the house was open. So we went inside. I was hungry, and when I saw some cornbread on the kitchen table, I wanted some.

"Can I have some cornbread? I'm hungry!" I asked.

Mom asked Dad, "Edgar, do you think it would be okay if Gerald had some cornbread?"

"Sure. They won't mind," he answered.

Guess it was bad manners to help yourself to somebody else's food, especially when they weren't there. Anyhow, I was "spoiled," so I got some.

Many of the Beasley relatives lived close enough that we could pop in for a snack, but many of Mom's relatives lived in Missouri. I recall several trips Mom and I made to visit her relatives out of state.

When I was about five, Mom and I went by train from Sand Springs to West Plains, Missouri. It was an exciting trip as we clanked across Oklahoma, Arkansas, and into Missouri. In West Plains, we visited the family of Uncle Sid Morris, Mom's brother.

I really liked Uncle Sid! He had once been a barber, and at one time, he had been the Howell County Treasurer.

Sid and his wife had two sons. (The oldest son, Howard, later ended up in Las Vegas, Nevada, in the casino business.)

On another trip by train, we went to St. Louis, Missouri, to visit Aunt Florence, Mom's sister. She was married to Uncle Mustion who worked at a big dairy near St. Louis called the Peavley Dairy. (As far as I know, this dairy still exists.) Uncle Mustion took me to see the dairy and the cows.

The Mustions had two boys. (The younger one ended up in New York City building skyscrapers.)

Dad loved to play dominoes and billiards. Don't think my mom approved since gambling was likely involved. Reputable women just did not go into such places, so when I was only about five [was it reputable for a child?], Mom would send me down the outside steps and into the side entrance of the basement of the Rexall Drug Store in Sand Springs where the men had a dominoes and billiard parlor.

Inside I would present myself at the table where Dad was playing dominoes. Since all the men there smoked, there was always a haze of smoke, which I didn't like. It would usually take a while for Dad to finish up his game. Then as we got up to leave, Dad would buy me a candy bar. Of course, that kind of encouraged me to want to go down to get him.

Dad smoked heavily all the time. That finally got to him, of course, since he eventually died from emphysema.

Quite often, Dad would park in front of the confectionary on the main street in Sand Springs. It was my job to run in and get packs of Chesterfields. I must have done that hundreds of times.

Now, Mom was opposed to Dad's smoking. She did not let him smoke in the house. It would have been easy for me to follow his example, but I never did get into the habit. It must have been Mom's influence.

In the spring of 1926, Dad aspired to go out to Borger in the Texas Panhandle to the oil boom. He was restless and thought he could make more money there than at the oil refinery. I listened and observed Mom and Dad discussing the possibility of such a venture.

Mom was skeptical. "We're doing okay here. It's comfortable, and we are near our families. What about housing? What about Gerald? Is it the kind of place to take a five-year-old boy?"

"They have places to live there. It will be an adventure for him. He will be fine. And if it doesn't work out, we can always come back," was Dad's argument.

Even with all her doubts, we loaded up the 1925 Chevrolet touring car with cooking utensils, clothing, food, and bedding. Quilts were piled high in the backseat, and I sat or lay on the quilts as we made the journey out to the Borger oil fields.

Traveling southwest across Oklahoma we had to ford the Canadian River; people with a big raft pulled by mules and horses charged a fee to carry the car across. As we continued across western Oklahoma, I watched the open fields for prairie dogs and marveled at the abundance of the small creatures.

Many families as well as many single men had made their way to Borger with the dream of making their fortune. Because housing had become scarce, we ended up living in a crude tent with boarded-up sides just south of Borger.

The terrain was rough. It was dry and desertlike with tall grasses, cactus, prairie dog holes, ravines, and lots of snakes. Most were harmless. However, there were rattlesnakes! Any snake had little appeal to mother or boy!

Water had to be hauled. With no refrigeration, milk was impossible to keep fresh. I remember eating Post Bran with sugar and water.

Mom used kerosene to cook on a stove in the tent.

Dad had a pleasant-enough job driving a new 1925 oil field truck. But life was not very comfortable for Mom and son in the prairies near Borger.

Traipsing around in the plains south of Borger wasn't a whole lot of fun or pleasant. There weren't many other children to play with. So in the heat of the summer, I played by myself while dodging cactus and snakes. There was little protection from creepy crawling critters! The smell of gasoline and oil was in the air all the time! And summer in the Texas Panhandle was hot!

The living and social situation in Borger was not conducive to family living. Single and even family men often got pretty wild. All the activity involving work, play, and "recreation" encouraged a lot of gambling, drinking, fighting, and partying. The police had to become involved quite frequently. Since the jails were full a great deal of the time—and to keep the drunken men, and probably some women, under control—the police would often back guys up to telephone poles and manacle their hands behind them. Usually these fellows were left fastened to the telephone poles for hours.

Mom and I saw the drinking and fighting going on all around when we would go into town to do laundry and get supplies. I asked Mom, "Why are those men tied to the poles like that?"

Well, Mom had heard and seen enough. She was not at all happy with the situation in Borger. So she spoke quite assertively to Dad as she listed her objections. "This is no place to raise a child! I do not want Gerald to see and hear the things that go on around here! What is he learning as he watches and hears all the profanity and ugliness that goes on? It isn't safe for him to play in the fields where there are poisonous snakes. I don't like it here! Besides, here in Texas a child can't go to school until they are seven years of age. Since he turned six in July, I want to get back to Oklahoma so he can start to school. Can we please go back to Sand Springs?"

Anyhow, after being in Borger for a few months, the family loaded up again and headed back to Sand Springs.

Dad went back to work for Pierce Refinery, which was later bought by Sinclair, a much bigger and prestigious company.

The family eventually built and moved into a house at 425 Grant Street in Sand Springs. Mom was a good money manager as well as a hard worker. She made it possible for the folks to have the house built, and they were also able to buy two small rent houses nearby. Dad had some deficiencies when it came to money. If it hadn't been for Mom, it's likely they would never have owned the three houses in Sand Springs.

Mom became good friends with a neighbor, Mrs. Brown. Mom called her Nettie. Nettie's husband, John Brown, had a drinking problem. He had been injured, gassed in World War I. That was not an excuse, but it explained some things. They had two children. Carl was six, like me. Erlene was a year older. Anyhow, Momma and Nettie visited together quite often while we played.

For some reason Nettie and others called me Sonny Man. Nettie would get after Carl because his ears were dirty, "Look how clean Sonny Man's ears are!" Guess Mom kept me clean.

In the fall of 1926, I started first grade at Central Grade School in Sand Springs. Mom walked with me on the first day of school as I nervously but excitedly carried my supply bag over my shoulder.

Carl Brown was one of my classmates. All the first graders were seated at big old wooden desks with a shelf built in under the top for books, papers, and pencils. On the first day, the teacher wrote each child's first name with chalk in big letters on the top of his or her desk. Each child was then given little round-colored pieces of wood to place on top of the letters of his or her name. So I placed those on GERALD on my desk.

I liked my first-grade teacher.

Mom did not go back to teaching after I was born, but she took care to teach and train me. I learned reasonably good study habits and worked hard at school.

Central School first grade, 1926. Gerald on first row, third from left.
Carl Brown on second row, first from left.
Ross Courtwright on third row, fourth from right.

I started my entertainment career quite early performing in several school operettas while at Central grade School. Operettas written mostly in the 1800s and early 1900s were very popular, and many schools gave public performances. One was *Pandora's Box*;[*] and I played a page boy in another operetta about King

_____

[*] *Pandora's Box* was a comic operetta based on the Greek Myth. The German Weimar Cinema (1919-1933) filmed a version of *Pandora's Box* in 1929.

Go Rumpus (can't remember the name of this operetta).* I
remember the words to one of the songs sung by the chorus:

> King Go Rumpus, the mighty King Go Rumpus.
> He liked to raise a ruckus and pass dull hours away.

This King Go Rumpus, played by Ross Courtwright, liked to
brag on himself as he sang:

> There are kings of all dimensions short and
> lean and fat and tall.
> There are kings that think that they are great
> who are not great at all.
> But I state with all sedateness and delightful modesty.
> That for self-inflicted greatness,
> there was never a king like me.

Ha! And it goes on. Funny how words and melodies can be
recalled years later!

I was a compliant child and did not require much discipline
at home or at school. I probably whispered and talked and things
like that in school, but I didn't get in much trouble.

---

* This was likely a comic operetta based on the classic tale by Hans
Christian Anderson, *The Emperor's New Clothes*, published in 1837
by C. A. Reitzel in Copenhagen. My research was inclusive. It is
public domain.

Central School, Sand Springs, OK, 1929.
Gerald Austin Beasley at age nine. Fourth row back, fourth from left.

There were a few occasions when Mom had to prune the peach tree in the backyard for a twig. She would use the limb to thrash my legs, mostly for not coming when she called.

However, there was one time when I got into a fight on the playground with the notorious bully Freddie. A bunch of us boys were playing kick-ball when Freddie came over and demanded, "Give me the ball!"

The group looked at him and said, "Do what now? No way!"

Freddie got real mad and said, "Give it here or else!"

No one was sure why, but he decided to pick on and came after me. I was not a weakling, but I preferred not to fight. Well, it turned out that I got the upper hand, got on top of Freddie, and proved to be stronger. It surprised the defender about as much as it surprised the offender. A teacher came along and broke up the fight.

Anyhow, I don't remember getting into much trouble. I was basically a goody-two-shoes.

Mom and Dad did not attend church on a regular basis. However, Mom would sometimes take me to the Church of God's Christmas Pageant a block away. The church would give the children trinkets and things to eat. Mom and Dad would take me to special activities like this; they would do anything for their son!

Hallie's parents, George and Francis Morris, had been members of the church of Christ in Missouri. So when my aging grandparents came to live with us at 425 Grant Street in Sand Springs, they might have taken me to church some.

Grandpa Morris passed away in about 1927 at the house. Since Grandma Morris was alone, she stayed on.

CHAPTER SEVEN

Remember your Creator in the days of your youth,
before the days of trouble come.

—Ecclesiastes 12:1a

Early Remembrances of an Ignorant Bend, Sand Hill, Elkview Lass

When I was little, Mom and Dad preferred to call me Clara. But as I got older, many friends would call me by my middle name, Pauline. If my parents called me Clara Pauline, I knew I was in trouble.

I was too young to be much help on the Smith farm, but I liked to go with my parents as they went about their work. I especially loved to be with Dad.

Often after Daddy had listed the field, he would head out to see if the soil was ready for sowing, and I would beg to go with him. "Can I go with you, Daddy? Please! I'll be good! I won't cause any trouble!"

He would say, "Okay." I would take hold of Daddy's large work-roughened index finger with my little hand, and happily skip with him as he set out to check the field. He could step from one furrow to another easily, but my short three-year-old legs had to go down into a furrow, up on the ridge, and then back down into the next furrow as I rushed to keep up with him.

There were neighboring farmers with children, but I lead a solitary childhood and spent much time with imaginary friends, traveling to imaginary places.

I played by myself most of the time, but I did have a few occasions to play with other children. Sometimes I would go to Grandpa William and Grandma Rosa Smith's house which was a few miles west of our farm and play with my older cousin, Frankie, who was eight years older than me. But I mostly played by myself with my few toys.

Of my few toys, my favorite was a little red chair where I would rock my one baby doll. I was so upset one time when Daddy left in the car without me. I followed on foot carrying my beloved chair. Mom had to run about a mile to catch me. I was a very persistent, stubborn little girl. Mom gave me a good thrashing for running off.

William and Rosa May Smith living west of John's Smiths'

A sand pile in the front of the house (actually, there was sand everywhere around the house, if one could stand the stickers and cockleburs that grew everywhere) was my favorite place to play with the few toy cars that I had.

Being very imaginative, I liked to pretend that a little black metal clothes iron that Mother had given me was a car. Somewhere under the sand that iron was buried and lost.

Dad purchased a little wheelbarrow for me. I must have hauled tons of sand here and there. I especially liked when it rained; then I could mix up a sandy concoction and make molded stand-up shapes on the ground.

Occasionally after a purchase, a discarded cardboard box would become an imaginary house, a car, or a boat. They were a lot of fun to play in.

Daddy once brought a big balloon home and blew it up. We bounced it back and forth until it hit a wooden splinter in the house boards and burst. I was heartbroken and cried and cried. I have always loved balloons!

The folks acquired a beautiful Maltese-colored male kitten, which Daddy neutered in the right moon, of course. In the winter, the cat would sleep on Mom's treadle sewing machine, which stood in front of the south window of the living room. In the summer and fall, young men, hired hands to help with tilling and harvesting, would come to the house to eat the meals that Mom cooked. They would tease and pester my cat so that he would fight back.

I loved my cat. He lived to be over thirteen years old.

The John Smiths always raised chickens that the wild creatures were always getting at and killing. As long as the coops were near the house, we could hear the chickens cackling, and Dad would use the shotgun to kill the predators; but because the chicken droppings caused chicken diseases, the coops were made small, so they could be easily and frequently moved to different disease-free places away from the house and in the north pasture.

Polecats, snakes, possums, skunks, and civet cats, a foxlike carnivore, went after the fowl. Polecats and civet cats would cut the necks of the chickens with their claws and suck the blood.

Snakes mostly went after the small chicks.

The skunks around the farm were a small breed that killed by grabbing the necks of chickens with their teeth and sucking the blood, leaving the dead carcasses.

Many nights during the summer, the squawking of chickens would wake us.

One summer morning, we woke up to find twenty dead chickens! The skunks had gotten to them. The sight of the dead chickens was awful and made me feel sick!

Another night when the coops were located a distance from the house, a civet cat killed twenty-five chickens. Guess we counted them.

Another morning as the sun was just coming up and the family sat eating breakfast, we looked out the door to see a coyote sling a big buff light yellow Orpington hen over its shoulder and run away with it. It became necessary to keep the chickens in their pen and turn them out later in the morning.

Eventually a roosting house was built for the laying hens, but we still had to watch out for predators.

Mom also raised turkeys to sell and to have for our Thanksgiving and Christmas dinners. Many of the turkeys roamed free and roosted in the trees around the acreage. Some of the turkeys had a habit of nesting a quarter-mile away from the house. It kept Mom busy trying to find the nests.

One day while hunting for nests, she found one with several eggs, but there were two huge bull snakes trying to swallow the big turkey eggs. Using a fence post, she beat the snakes to death. Now, Mom was not quite five feet tall, but she came back to the house with both of those snakes draped on that fence post. Each of them was longer that she was tall.

Some of the turkey hens, however, would sit and hatch their little turkeys in pens. Mother would sprinkle cracked grain on top of cottage cheese made from our cows' milk to feed these turkeys and chicks. As I grew older, I was given the job of taking the cottage cheese out to the turkeys. Now, I loved cottage cheese, but Mom never let me eat any. So I would secretly eat some of the turkey's food that wasn't covered with grain.

Baby turkeys, poults, were very delicate, and it seemed if I just touched one, it would die. I grew to hate turkeys. Baby chicks I could pet, but not turkeys.

Because I loved and admired my daddy, I wanted to be just like him. Dad started to smoke many different times. He would smoke for a short time, discover it hurt him, so he would stop for a while; but he would try it again at a later date. On those occasions when Dad would get out a smoke, I would crawl into his lap and beg for a puff, which he eventually let me have.

He also chewed tobacco occasionally. One cold day in November when he got out the Prince Albert can, I begged for a chew. "Can I have some? Please!" I begged.

He said, "Help yourself!"

So I did. I really stuffed my mouth full, chewed, and spit into the coal bucket feeling big just like Dad. But in a short time I began to wilt and hurriedly spit the cud into the bucket. I found myself outside in the cold vomiting on to the snow-covered ground. Dad laughed. I didn't think it was funny! That incident ended any desire I had for tobacco. After that even the smell of tobacco made me sick.

Saturdays were special as that was the day country folk went into town to buy staples (flour, sugar, baking powder, salt) at the grocery store. Saturday, June 16, 1928, Mom and I headed to Blair in our touring car. As we left town after finishing our shopping, Mom kept watching over her right shoulder as a dark cloud came up from the southwest.

Arriving back at the farm, Mom and I both hurried to gather the little wandering chicks to get them into the hen house. But it rained before all of them were rescued. So I got to bring the wet cheeping chicks into our house where I placed them on a blanket on the floor near the heat of the cast-iron stove so they could dry and stay warm. As a four-year-old, I loved to play with the noisy little chicks and act as their protector.

"Come here, little chick. Oh, stay over here. Stay near the fire. You don't want to get cold! Get back on the blanket! You can't go over there." I shooed and gathered the chicks until the storm was over.

The next day, the *Oklahoma Overland* reported that Blair, Oklahoma, had been blown away by a tornado. A few days later, the family drove into Blair to see the terrible wreckage of crumbled brick buildings, splintered trees, tossed rubble, and damaged houses.

Another Saturday, during the Christmas season, the folks went into Blair to buy the weekly groceries. As Mom and Dad walked through the store, I happened by the produce where I saw and took the biggest most beautiful red apple I had ever seen and started eating it right there in the store. Since Daddy always bought the biggest apples and oranges for Christmas, it just seemed like the thing to do.

Well, as the folks came around a corner and saw me eating it, my eyes met their eyes—the joy left me! I wished I had never ever seen any apple! They gave me a long tongue-lashing before the checkout counter, so everyone there would know that my parents did not approve of what I had done. All the way home I was scolded and berated as the point was made quite clear that they had to pay for that red apple. That was an incident that I would never forget.

As farmers, we Smiths were basically self-sufficient. There was always meat available for eating even if there was little real cash. All we had to do was slaughter a cow, pig, chicken, or a turkey. The garden produced fresh vegetables, and the orchard provided fruit for canning, so there were always canned goods stored in the back room of the house or in the underground dirt cellar just outside the front of the house to the southwest of the porch. Milk was available daily from the milking cows. Butter was made from the fresh cream.

With all the homemade goods available, we never went hungry. But the waste-not-want-not principle was always taught and enforced.

As a small child, I had a habit of putting more food on my plate than I could eat. On one such occasion, I mashed and mixed a lot of syrup with butter on my plate to put on my biscuits. Usually, Daddy would eat the excess. Mother refused to eat it. One particular day, Daddy decided he was tired of this habit.

So he told Mother, "Put the excess up in the cabinet for her to eat later. She is not to eat anything else until she has eaten all of it."

Picture of Maggie and Clara Pauline Smith (four years old) outside at the Smith farm in winter of 1928 by a traveling photographer.

I protested, but Dad said, "You will not get anything else until you eat all of it."

It wasn't so good the next meal! After that, I was more careful to put less food on my plate.

In the winter of 1928, Mom heard that a traveling photographer was coming to Blair. We cleaned up and dressed to go into town. But instead, the photographer came to the farm. We dressed in coats and hats to keep warm so the photographer could take the picture outside for better light.

CHAPTER EIGHT

As fish are caught in a cruel net, or birds are taken
in a snare, so men are trapped by evil times that fall
unexpectedly upon them.
—Ecclesiastes 9:12

Early Remembrances of a Sand Springs, Oklahoma, Lad— the Depression

Dad's job and income from the oil refinery were pretty stable, and the rent from the two smaller houses covered their payments. But the stable times were not to last.

In March of 1929 when Hoover took office as president of the United States, the economy was thriving, except for agriculture. High production had lowered farm prices, so the Agricultural Marketing Act was passed in June to provide relief for farmers. The Federal Farm Board loaned farmers money to organize cooperatives, and the government began buying up surplus crops. However, these measures did not stop the stock market crash of October, the beginning of economic collapse.

A program of public works was initiated by Hoover in 1930 to construct highways, river, and harbor improvements and to build Hoover Dam at the Boulder Canyon Project.

The United States discontinued its loans to Germany, which had been paying reparations to the Allies, who in turn had been repaying war debts to the United States. In 1931, Hoover proposed a one-year moratorium on all war debts, but it was too late to stop the failing economy.

Dad was laid off at the oil refinery in 1929 as the demand for oil and gas products waned. We moved north to a little dairy farm with rolling hills just outside of Sand Springs. (This land is now the Canyons at Blackjack Ridge Golf course, located 1801 N. McKinley Ave., in Sand Springs.) We did not own the land. It was cash rented.

It was fortunate that we had this little dairy farm to fall back on. We began milking our cows and bottling milk to sell and deliver to customers in Sand Springs. It was just plain raw milk. The government at this time did not require the purification of milk.

Anyhow, this dairy farm supported the family. Grandma Morris was still living with us then. Her and my job was to wash the milk bottles. Grandma Morris would fuss at me because I would sometimes push the do-ma-flicky, the plastic lid, down into the bottles. She also fussed at me because the little rim on the bottles would catch milk that would sour; I was not getting them clean.

I helped deliver milk to many doors in Sand Springs. As either Mom or Dad drove the '29 Chevy, I would hold on to the car while standing on the running board so I could jump off with the filled milk bottles to deliver them to the customers porch or designated place.

Now, the folks didn't have a billing or collection service, so they kept a record of milk delivered to each customer, then went to each customer's house at the end of each month, or on payday, to collect.

One particularly cold and icy day, Mom and I stopped off to collect at a residence above a garage. The man had only a $20 bill. He let Mom take the bill with the understanding that she would get it broken into smaller bills and bring him back the proper change. As we arrived at the streetcar confectionary, Mom reached into her coat pocket. Finding no bill, she frantically looked around on the floor, on the sidewalk, then in the car; but she didn't find it. Mom started crying. I felt helpless! Twenty dollars was a lot of money then! Not only were we losing the pay for the milk, but we would also have to cover for the change.

She said a quick prayer. We got in the car and backtracked the way we had come. As we came to the intersection where we had turned onto McKinley Street, we saw the wet $20 bill in the middle of the intersection. I jumped out of the car and quickly retrieved the bill. It had not been found or picked up, probably because the cold and icy conditions had kept everybody inside.

There was great rejoicing, thanksgiving, and relief in our car.

Like so many others, we had financial concerns. I remember making a trip with Mom to Tulsa to the Home Owners Loan Association (Corporation) to get a low-interest loan. Without it, my parents could not have kept the three houses that they were renting in Sand Springs while they worked the dairy farm.

After grade school, my friends and I went to school at Garfield School which housed grades four, five, and six. Since the dairy farm was just outside of the city, I walked into town to school with other farm children.

The teachers would sit us alphabetically. So starting at the left, the As would be in front. I usually sat three or four seats from the front on the left. Melvene Borgwald often sat behind me. (I saw Melvene in 1996 in Sand Springs at the funeral for Johnny Armstrong's wife. Johnny was Aunt Grace's son. After the services, I heard the undertaker call out, "Melvene," to a lady passing by, so I approached her. Sure enough it was her. Of course, her last name was different. But it was the Melvene Borgwald I had gone to school with. We had a nice little visit).

While I was a student at Garfield, Mom bought a secondhand Albert System clarinet, so I began to play clarinet and I was pretty good at it. Mr. Wallingford was the music teacher at Garfield. He later advanced to band director at the high school.

At Garfield the boys played marbles and/or tops before school, during recess, and after school. Marbles and tops became very competitive. In the game of keeps, if one of the guys shot somebody's marble out of the ring, he got to keep it.

The boys also played keeps with their tops. Each competing boy would wind the string on his top and throw it down into a ring. If one's top knocked someone else's top out of the ring, the person knocking the top out got to keep the top he knocked out. Often friends would take sides and cheer as they gathered around to watch two "foes" challenge each other.

Jack Wiseman was especially good at marbles and tops. The other boys kind of resented him.

Nelson Hoss and I were pretty good friends at Garfield. When the children chose up sides to play ball, should Hoss be captain, he would choose me first. And of course, if I were captain, I would choose Hoss first. Hoss was left-handed and a pretty good-sized boy, bigger than me. He was a good batter and a good athlete.

One cold winter day, my school chums were daring each other, "Why don't you put your tongue on the pole and see what happens?"

I asked, "Do what now?" As we continued to chide each other, I foolishly took the dare and touched my tongue to a pole of the swing. It froze on to the pole! It really shook me up! Ha! Guess I finally got it loose. If there was any injury, it didn't keep me from talking.

All boys, especially on a farm, should have a dog. So some friends brought a pup out to the little farm on the edge of Sand Springs. I named my dog Fididdledy. Ha! I loved that dog!

I had always liked animals. I had an Indian pony, a riding pony, given to me when I was around nine, but Dad had to sell the mare sometime later.

We also had a big workhorse we called Old Joe. On several occasions he had to be treated for a fistula, a big boil on his shoulder caused when the collar rubbed on the horse in a bad way.

Despite the ratification of the Eighteenth Amendment in December 1917, which forbade the manufacture and sale of alcoholic beverages, many citizens made home brew or "moonshine."

Dad had been making home brew for "medicinal" purposes but not for sale for many years. Malt, hops, maybe a berry, and, of course, sugar was involved in making the fermented beverage. Obviously, I didn't pay much attention to how he made it.

Of course, it was illegal to sell the alcoholic beverage, but the law was not really enforced. It is possible that Dad could have gotten into trouble had he been caught with the beverage. However, there were a lot of people making home brew who were never arrested.

Dad and Mom drank a little, but very little, and they let me taste some of the awful tasting stuff!

When I was about nine, I did see Dad drunk. It made me feel really uncomfortable and ill at ease and gave me a kind of sinking feeling inside to see Dad wobbling and stumbling around, slurring his words as he spoke. Mom had seen him drunk before. But it wasn't habitual with him. He most likely got drunk on stuff he had made.

Quite often Dad, Mom, and I would visit Dad's cousin, Wince Beasley, and his wife in their little apartment. They had a record player and a record called "Three Black Crows."* The singers were three black men who bantered back and forth. I liked to

_____

* I was unable to find any information about this group of singers.

visit there where I would lay back with my hands behind my head listening to that group sing.

During the Roaring Twenties, my parents attended dances with Wince and his wife. They usually drug me around with them. One time when they went to a dance, probably sponsored by Wince, all of them got drunk. In their inebriated state, they became careless and slammed my hand in the car door. Mom and Dad felt very sorry and vowed to be more careful.

Americans enjoyed the more relaxed entertainments of dancing and jazz, and imbibed in liquor.

They preferred to remain isolated from world politics.

As the world depression struck Germany, the Nazi party was emerging in Germany, and the party's representation in the Reichstag (lower house of parliament) soared. Hitler gained support for his ideas: (1) the repudiation of the Versailles Treaty, (2) discontinuance of war reparations, and (3) the restoration of German territory.

The Nazis began to receive support from German military officers and industrialists, and party workers and storm troopers (Hitler's private army) formed a state within a state.

American remained unconcerned.

CHAPTER NINE

What does the worker gain from his toil?
I have seen the burden God has laid on men . . .
That everyone may eat and drink, and find
satisfaction in all his toil—this is the gift of God.
—Ecclesiastes 3:9, 10, and 13

Early Remembrances of an Ignorant Bend, Sand Hill, Elkview Lass—the Depression—1930

From an early age, I had an imaginary playhouse by the old smokehouse just north of the farmhouse. Mom insisted that I play where she could see me. I spent many hours there sweeping and caring meticulously for my furniture made of rocks, plow blades, old wooden crates, and anything that looked functional. Hours were spent playing with my baby doll; but mostly I talked to, loved, and cared for my imaginary children. I even had a switch for disciplining them. Using the gypsum from the well, I mixed pretend gravy, cake batter, cookie dough, applesauce, and other goodies.

To keep track of me, Mom would step out of the backdoor at the kitchen and call out, "Clara!"

I would answer back, "Yes, Mom?"

"Just checking to see if you are there," Mom would reply. Then she would go back to her work, and I would return to my play. If I had not answered, she would have come over to check on me. Mom wanted to make sure I stayed away from the nearby pond.

During the depression, and especially during the dust bowl, many poor, disheartened people were left homeless and hapless. Infamous bank robbers, often viewed as heroes, were taking what wasn't theirs, and gangsters were making themselves rich selling liquor to speakeasies. But my family survived through hard labor as we continued to work the land, doing what had to be done to make an honest living.

As if Dad didn't already have enough to do on the farm in the latter 1920s and early 1930s, he would take a team of mules or horses and a slip or fresno to work the county roads. He did this scraping and smoothing for the upkeep of the roads in lieu of paying county taxes.

In the spring of 1930 after the ground had been listed, I could now follow Dad into the fields as he determined when to plant the cotton. If I stretched, my six-year-old legs could step over the plowed ridges. I was now big enough to work beside my parents in the fields, milking the cows, gathering eggs, and other less strenuous and menial jobs around the farm.

When the cotton was ready to pick, Mom, Dad, and I worked beside migrant workers to pick the bolls of cotton. I would work two rows beside Dad; he always insisted that I stay near him since a lot of the migrant workers were men and we knew little about them. His bag always weighed many more pounds than mine. I worked slowly and carefully using my thumb and index finger to get hold of and pull the cotton out of its pod; the hard prickly cotton pods would tear and poke my fingers causing them to bleed. It hurt!

As different vegetables ripened, I would pick and haul them to the house. I especially liked the huge tomatoes the fertile soil in the large vegetable garden produced. When the cantaloupes were ready for picking, I would load a sack full of the delicious fruit, throw it over my shoulder, and tow it to the house.

The folks planted a watermelon patch some distance from the house but close to the county road west of the farm. We tilled the soil, fertilized with barnyard manure, planted, weeded, and waited all summer for the watermelons to ripen. Then one summer night, a group of teenagers invaded the patch, broke a bunch of the melons open, but ate only the juicy seedless hearts of the melons. We were so very angry! What a waste! Though reduced in quantity, we were able to haul a crop to the market.

I was required from an early age to help hand-wash the laundry. The dirty clothes were put into a tub in the garage. We applied lye soap on to the fabric as Mom and I rubbed up and down over the bumpy ridges of a rub board. Two other tubs were used for rinsing. It took all day to haul water from the well, scrub, hang the clothes to dry, and fold them. I liked to wash the towels and washcloths but hated to rub the overalls. The thicker less pliable fabric made it difficult to keep hold of and work the fabric over the rub board; it was also hard to twist and squeeze the excess water out.

One of our neighbors, the Powells, had a washing machine run by gasoline. The whole countryside always knew washday at their house; with its one-cylinder motor, it could be heard for miles.

The farmers' wives in the area eventually progressed to fifty-gallon barrels for doing laundry. So Momma got one. Notches were welded in the walls of the barrels where a paddle was inserted. One of us had to get hold of the handle connected to the paddle and pushed it back and forth to agitate the clothes in the barrel. The barrel was set on a rack where a fire was built underneath to boil the water. The folks used that for several years.

Finally, when laundry facilities with motorized machines were built in Blair, Mom drove into town to do the wash. The machines washed the clothes faster and better, and dryers were much more efficient. I was so glad we didn't have to manually wash anymore.

In the fall of 1930, I attended school at the new Elkview Country School (Mom had attended the old Elkview school), affectionately called Ignorant Bend Hill, which was about one mile north and half-a-mile west of the farm. School days were long; I had to rise very early, take care of chores, and then walk or ride a horse to the one-room school where one teacher taught grades first thru sixth; and there were still chores waiting for me when I got home.

Having spent so much time alone on the farm without children to play with, I found school exciting but a bit scary. I eventually graduated from high school with farm kids from all around the area that I met at this school.

Elkview country school, 1931. Grade 1 thru 6.
Front from left is Pauline Smith.
Others are Allene McElory, Aleta Hardy, Charles Zinn, Juanita Hardy, Cecil McElory, Warren Winters, Guy Wingrove, Harley Winters, Myrtle McElory, Opal McElory.
Back from left: J. D. McElory, Kay Jackson, Viola Perry, Ruth Snider, Murl Kirby, Drusela Kingsly, Elan Winters, Willie Wingrove, Otis Perry, Mr. Fancher (teacher).

After I learned to read and count, Daddy would play dominoes with me. I had a craving, almost an obsession, to play the game all the time; but Daddy grew tired of playing. I would beg and beg him to play; then he would play some more.

My parents got me a kitten for companionship which I named Ned, like in the First Reader at school. I loved Ned! He was so cute! My parents insisted that he always be put outside at night. On Christmas Eve, the family told Ned "good night" and put him out. He usually slept in an old shoe just outside the back door. The next morning we couldn't find him. I was so sad! A tomcat or a coyote probably killed him.

The winter of '30-31 was a cold one; ice remained on the ground for a long time. So one day I dressed warm and went outside to skate down the good slope of the cellar. But as I climbed to the top on all fours and attempted to stand, I wasn't able to keep my balance for very long before I found myself sitting on the ground with a bruised and tingling bottom. I decided ice skating wasn't for me.

The next summer, Mom and Dad left me, seven-year-old Clara, for a week with Grandma Rosa and Grandpa Riley Smith, who had moved to the eighty acres just west of our place. Their youngest child, fifteen-year-old Aunt Frankie and I spent time together.

At Frankie's suggestion we found, cracked open, and ate the pits of a bunch of peach seeds. We both got very sick and vomited. I had eaten a lot of the pits, so I got especially sick! I was so gullible! We didn't know it when we ate them but later learned that the pit of the peach seed is poisonous! Guess we were both lucky to survive!

Since Grandpa Riley and Grandma Rosa lived only about one mile west, they would often pick up Mom and Dad's mail from the mailbox by the county road. They liked to read our newspaper.

One day, Dad was plowing the south field with our team of young mules, Kate and Rip. These nervous mules were very prone to run, so Dad did not want to chance taking them near the road. Dad told me, "Go to Granny's and get the mail but return quickly. I'll be waiting here."

I went as I was told, but when I got to their house, Aunt Frankie insisted, "Wait until I finish washing my hair, then I'll walk back with you."

"No, I better get back to Dad. He told me to hurry," I stated.

"Don't worry, it will be okay. I won't be long," she replied. So I listened to her and waited.

Well, Daddy waited and waited; his anger was building at my disobedience. Finally, he left the team in a huff and came to get me. Frankie and I tried to explain the delay, but he would not listen. He pulled off his belt and really used it on me. I ran all the way home crying, went east of the house, and cried for a long time because I felt unjustly spanked. After all, I had tried to tell Aunt Frankie that I needed to return quickly. I'm sure Aunt Frankie felt bad that I got in trouble. Daddy never did apologize for the harsh spanking, and I held it against him.

I often felt that I could never do anything right in Mom and Dad's eyes.

Another time, Daddy took me with him when he went into Blair to talk to an insurance man about life insurance. When asked his age, Dad said he was younger than he really was.

In front of the insurance man, I stated, "Dad that's not your age. You gave the wrong age."

Dad's face turned red as his lips formed a firm line. He was quiet in the office, but on the way home, I got a strong tongue-lashing for the deed. But Dad had done wrong.

It seemed to me that I got a lot of criticism growing up—maybe to the point of mental abuse.

CHAPTER TEN

Two are better than one,
because they have a good return for their work.
If one falls down, his friend can help him up.
But pity the man who falls and
has no one to help him up!
A cord of three strands is not quickly broken.
—Ecclesiastes 4:10, 12b

Early Remembrances of a Sand Springs, Oklahoma, Lad—1930

The members of the Beasley clan helped each other get through difficult times. Relatives shared their various crops and/or products with each other.

My immediate family worked together during the depression.

In 1930, we moved to a farm out on Euchee Creek about twelve miles northwest of Sand Springs. There we had a dairy farm with more pasture.

It wasn't too long after we moved when I was almost eleven that Grandma Morris passed away on that farm. Guess I ended up washing all the bottles after that.

Another job I had was to go out after the cows at the end of the day to bring them in. There were several bell cows—in other words, cows that wore bells around their necks. Of course, in hot weather, when the cows would be standing very still in the shade of a tree, the bells wouldn't ring, making it hard to find them. It was very frustrating! Now, if the bells were ringing, I could follow the sound. I didn't really enjoy this responsibility and fretted over it. In fact, I had nightmares about looking for those cows!

Anyhow, the cows used a particular lane to go from the house to the main pasture. At the gated entrance into the pasture, there was a great big oak tree with low-hanging limbs. On one of those limbs hung a huge wasp nest! Now, I knew it was there and always avoided it, but one time, one of the cows must have swooshed its tail up and raked that wasp nest. Guess the wasps didn't know what had disturbed their nest because they took their anger out on me. I received fourteen stings on the face, neck, and chest! We counted them. I ran home screaming.

Mom treated the stings with vinegar and soda. Now, in 1930, home remedies were used; you didn't go to the doctor unless you were very sick. However, if I had had a violent reaction to the wasp stings, the folks would have rushed me to the doctor. Guess I healed just fine!

The Ledbetters were a large farming family who lived near the Beasley farm on Euchee Creek. Mr. Ledbetter's brother-in-law, who lived with them, wasn't real smart intellectually; but he could handle a team, plow, and things like that. As he plowed the field across the fence from our house, this fellow would get mad at his mules and want to cuss them, but he knew Mom was in the house or nearby. So instead, he would kind of mutter, "Now, I don't want to cuss you because Mrs. Beasley might hear, but you better get to doing what you're supposed to do, or I'm going to get real mad." Mom could hear him talking to the animals as he refrained from cussing. It amused her.

I spent a lot of time with their two youngest boys. Loyd was at least a grade behind me, and Jackie was probably two or three grades behind him. We were always fishing, hunting, swimming, playing horseshoes, and otherwise getting into trouble together.

Loyd, Jackie, and I tried smoking "rabbit tobacco" and possum grape vines; and sometimes the brothers would steal some tobacco from their older brothers, real tobacco, to roll our own cigarettes. The boys didn't take from their brothers very often because they knew they would get blistered if they got caught. But we did try smoking. Guess it made us feel big and tough even if we didn't really like it.

The Ledbetters had a fat, roly-poly riding horse, a roan. One day our trio decided to ride her without a saddle, but with her fat belly, our legs would not wrap around her. Something must have spooked her because she took off running real fast. Scared that we would fall off and be trampled under the horse's hoofs, we held tightly to each other as we bounced up and down, our bottoms spanked with the jarring slaps against horses' flesh. Somehow, we stayed on its back, and the roan finally stopped. We survived to ride again.

One Easter, the three of us sauntered down to Euchee creek to swim. The weather was quite chilly, and the water was cold. When Loyd and Jackie got home, and Mr. Ledbetter found out that we had been swimming in the creek, he whipped his boys mercilessly. Of course, he didn't whip me, but I felt really bad, thinking, "It's my fault! If I hadn't come over to their house to see if they could play, they wouldn't have gotten in trouble."

I felt ashamed as I went home, but I didn't tell the folks about the incident. My conscience did bother me though. In fact, I think I hurt worse than Loyd and Jackie. Of course, I didn't force the two younger boys to go swimming. As a matter of fact, it was probably their idea to go. I was somewhat of a chicken and wasn't real crazy about the idea; but being the oldest, about eleven, I knew it wasn't wise to go swimming when it was so cold.

Our threesome swam together on many other occasions. One time we went skinny-dipping north of the Beasley farm on Euchee Creek. A big ole black cloud came up, and all of a sudden, it started to rain and hail.

"Get your clothes on! We need to find shelter and get out of this hailstorm," I yelled. We real quicklike put on our clothes and ran up to the nearest house.

Banging on the door, we yelled. "Hello, is anybody home?" But nobody answered, and the door was locked.

Yelling over the roar of the falling rain, I hollered, "Run to that barn over there." So we went into a tin barnlike building nearby that was open. The hail beat on that tin roof making such a pounding racket that the noise about scared us half to death.

It kept raining and pouring terribly. Euchee Creek got up and overflowed its banks. In fact, the water backed up from all directions into the side streams that ran into the creek.

Finally, as the rain let up, we tried to go home because we knew the folks would be worried. Loyd, the taller of the two brothers, carried the younger Jackie on his shoulders. The water was plum up to Loyd's chin! Since I was slightly taller, the water was just up to my chest. We were holding on to each other's hands, wading through some of those backed-up streams, pushing against the flow of the current, and fighting to maintain our balance.

Meanwhile, the Ledbetter folks, my folks, and other folks had gathered up a search party to look for us. We were presumed drowned. As we got close to my house, we ran into the search party. Our parents might have wanted to beat us for running off, but they were so glad that we hadn't drowned their anger was forgotten in their joy and relief!

Of course, Mr. Ledbetter was pretty good about spanking. He'd had a lot of practice with his large family. It was surprising that he did not let his boys have it.

The Ledbetter boys and I made what were called bean flips. Some people called them nigger shooters. We would get a two-forked branch and attach a strip of rubber (often from an inner tube) to each wooden prong, as I recall, with a little leather pocket in the middle attached between their other ends. Our fearless trio was pretty good at shooting with our slingshots. We were always looking for just the right-sized rocks to shoot from the little pocket of leather. Sometimes we were lucky enough to find cast iron that we would break into small pieces. In fact, we preferred cast iron because it was more deadly. We were a deadly bunch! Ha!

The Ledbetter boys were good companions and playmates.

One time when I was alone in the pasture with my so-called bean flip, I shot what I thought was a squirrel across the creek. It fell over! When I got to it, I realized it was not a squirrel. I took it home. Dad said it was a mink. Skinned, stretched, and dried, it brought a fair price.

Sometimes with my friends, sometimes by myself, I trapped for muskrats on the creek.

I got an occasional possum. Dad would skin them, stretch the hides on a special board, and let them dry; then, of course, they were saleable. Probably didn't get much for them, but every little bit helped since money was tight during the depression.

When I was about twelve, Uncle Tom gave me an old .22-rifle. It was my first gun, and though it had some mechanical problems, I was proud of it. I shot squirrels and other critters.

Sometimes I'd take Fididdledy hunting with me. He wasn't much of a hunting dog, but I enjoyed the companionship. At night, I carried a kerosene lantern with a glass globe on my head which left my hands free to aim the gun as the light shined up into the tree illuminating the possum.

I was especially fond of my pet dog. A couple of years later when I was fourteen, Fididdledy disappeared. He probably knew he was dying and crawled off somewhere to be by himself. I looked everywhere and waited for my dog to come home. Fididdledy had been a good friend and a good companion. I cried when he didn't return.

I was given a chance to be an entrepreneur in the spring of '32. Dad let me use a large plot of land near the creek to plant cantaloupes. I planted, weeded, and watched the sprouts break ground. As the little green fruit balls began to show on the lush green vines, I dreamed of the money I was going to make selling my produce; but the dream fizzled and faded when an epidemic of terrapins and lice infested and devoured my beautiful patch. I was so disappointed!

Because we lived on a farm, we were not always well-informed about national and international events. While in town we would sometimes hear of a few things, and occasionally a salesman would drop by and trade a magazine or a newspaper for a chicken. So we were able to keep up with some of the news.

However, the folks were aware of (1) the national economic depression and the effect it had on country folk. They were especially interested when Franklin D. Roosevelt stated in his democratic presidential nomination acceptance speech, "I pledge you. I pledge myself, to a new deal for the American people." (2) The reports that the Nazi party had become Germany's largest party by 1932 was interesting but still a remote concern. (3) They were interested when Charles Lindberg married Anne Spencer Morris in 1929 and sympathetic in 1932 when their twenty-month-old son was kidnapped and murdered.

In 1932 while still living on the farm on Euchee Creek, at twelve years of age, I entered junior high school which included seventh, eighth, and ninth grades. The junior high and high school were housed in the same building, so I later attended the senior high school there.

The Ledbetter boys and I would walk to school in the morning along with several other kids who also lived out near Euchee Creek. The group would shortcut back home across the mountain. Of course, it was not really a mountain, just a hill.

While in junior high, I continued to play the clarinet, but I played with the high school band. By then Mr. Wallingford had advanced to be the high school band director. He was a very likable fellow and a very gifted musician. He knew music.

(Many years later in the 1970s, while living on Forty-Seventh Street in Wichita during the time I was a salesman for Goals Incorporated, I went over to El Dorado, Kansas, to sell material there. While there I went to the school district and learned that a retired music teacher by the name of Mr. Wallingford lived in El Dorado. From what I had been told, I was certain it must be the same Mr. Wallingford. So I looked him up in the telephone directory. It was my former band director! Of course, he was quite elderly then, but I had an interesting visit with him.)

Hitler had become chancellor of Germany's coalition government on January 30, 1933. When the Reichstag building burned on February 27, the Communists in the German government were blamed and expelled. Hitler was then given absolute emergency powers. He then (1) forced the non-Nazis from the government, (2) banned all political parties, (3) suppressed the trade unions, (4) abolished freedom of speech and press, and (5) began a violent crusade against the Jews.

With his growing power, Hitler (1) withdraw from the League of Nations and (2) demanded the return of Germany's 1914 colonies while proclaiming his desire to keep world peace.

When President Paul von Hindenburg died in 1934, Hitler was approved by the people and took the title of Fuhrer. He proclaimed his regime as the New Order and the German state as the Third Reich.

In violation of the Versailles Treaty, Germany began rearming.

On March 3, 1933, Franklin Delano Roosevelt had become the thirty-second president of the United States. He was America's leader through the Great Depression keeping his promise of "a new deal," and he was later to become commander in chief as America opposed Hitler's regime.

At the time of his inauguration, the economy was so bad that the public was in a panic. Roosevelt spoke on the radio and told his frightened listeners, "The only thing we have to fear is fear itself . . ." He filled the nation with new confidence. His first act was to close all banks; four days later, sound banks resumed business. He called a special session of Congress which met for ninety-nine days.

His New Deal attempted to (1) provide relief to the unemployed, (2) promote recovery from the economic depression, and (3) carry out a program of political, economic, and social reforms. These goals greatly expanded the functions of the federal government.

Among the many acts passed, the Agricultural Adjustment Act was established to provide subsidy payment to farmers who agreed to limit production.

The National Industrial Recovery Act was passed to (1) relieve the serious depression, (2) relieve unemployment, (3) regulate trade and competition, (4) regulate wages and hours, and (5) guarantee collective bargaining.

The Tennessee Valley Authority was a government-owned and—operated corporation set up to develop resources of the Tennessee River Basin.

During the drought from 1933 to 1937, the Dust Bowl raged in parts of Colorado, Kansas, New Mexico, Oklahoma, and Texas. Farmhouses, fences, crops, and equipment were buried during dust storms. Many disheartened farmers left their homes.

So in 1935, the United States Department of Agriculture began buying areas for reclamation. Conservation methods were taught and used to reestablish good farmland. "Day farming" and "stock raising" were started. Strips of trees were planted for windbreaks. Contour plowing was used in hilly areas.

In 1934 in Sand Springs, Oklahoma, Major Doetzel became the high school music teacher and band director. He had been injured and lost his leg in WWI fighting in Africa, so he had a wooden leg. Major Doetzel took over the band that Mr. Wallingford had built up.

The Major decided to take the band to the National Band Contest in Evanstan, Illinois. I rode Dolly, a blaze-faced sorrel, into town for band practices in the evenings when the band was preparing for the contest. Mr. Ledbetter loaned me a saddle.

The Parents Organization raised money to send the band to this big deal, which was quite a thing for Sand Springs. It was difficult for many families to come up with any money. As an only child, my folks would have done anything for me. All they could come up with was $10. They put that in.

When the time came, several busloads of band members made the trip and were gone for several days. I was only fourteen, the youngest in the band.

The checkered-rowed cornfields I saw on the drive thru Illinois were fascinating to me; they were so different from the haphazardly placed fields in Oklahoma.

The band did not do very well at the contest though they did get some kind of an award.

Gerald Beasley in his high school band uniform, Sand Springs 1934.

One lady chaperon died from food poisoning during the trip.

When I was fourteen, I had a very scary experience—a run-in with a big fat Osage Indian, Jody Lane. He lived north of our farm in the Osage Hills where the land was quite hilly with lots of post oak trees. Jody and one of his friends showed up at our house on Euchee Creek. Jody said he would pay me to drive them to Tulsa to a relative's home. He explained that his car would not start, and he wanted to get away. Dad was gone, and

Mom and I were at the house alone. I sensed there was more to their story, and I wanted to remove them from the premises so Mom would be out of harm's way.

So somewhat fearful, I drove our '29 Chevy Coupe with the three of us crowded on the one seat in the vehicle. I did not know the real reason why they wanted to get away when I agreed to drive them, but I silently listened as they talked. Apparently Jody had just shot his neighbor who lived on a ranch just north of his home. During the trip, the two Indians discussed and rehearsed how they would state the shooting took place.

Starring ahead, scared but listening, I tried not to show any reaction, but my mind was whirling and churning with no definite plan.

I drove to the front of Jody's relative's house, and as the men got out, I did not wait to see if Jody would keep his promise to pay. I just floored the gas pedal, spit rocks and dirt, and hightailed out of there.

We did not have a radio, and we did not get the newspaper, but we did hear that Jody was caught, tried, and sentenced to prison. He died while in prison.

The neighbor who was shot in the stomach survived. Apparently, his large metal belt buckle was instrumental in saving his life.

Nobody asked, and I did not tell anybody what I had heard while transporting them, so I was never called to be a witness.

CHAPTER ELEVEN

Six days do your work, but on the seventh day do not
work, so that your ox and donkey may rest . . .
Be refreshed.

—Exodus 23:12

Remembrances of an Ignorant
Bend, Sand Hill, Elkview Lass

As the drought continued, many farmers in the Dust Bowl region had begun to pack up and pull out after the dust storms destroyed their crops and made living conditions intolerable. However, the John Smiths had no plans to give up the land and home we had built up from nothing. We continued to work from morning to night.

Occasionally on Sundays, Mom and I would attend services at the church of Christ in Blair. Dad never went with us. He had no desire to go. Dad did rest some on Sundays, but the cows still needed to be milked, and the animals still needed to be fed.

As I grew older, more was expected of me. By 1934 at the age of ten, I helped more around the house, in the fields, and on the farm doing the less cumbersome jobs.

Once or twice a year, Mom would say, "Clara, get out the saved rendered lard and the lye."

Mom would get out the large iron wash pot to make lye soap. I helped her. First, we would build a fire around the wash pot, put the required lard and water into the pot, and heat the contents until it boiled. A can of lye was added and stirred very rapidly to keep it from boiling over. After a certain length of time, the burning wood from the fire was removed from around the pot, and the pot's contents were poured into a large flat pan and left to cool. When cooled and hardened, Mom and I would then cut the lye soap into cakes or squares. It was hard, hot work which could not be left unattended until the process was completed.

I was also put to work when butchering time came around. The folks waited until the weather was cold to butcher the hogs. First, Daddy would sharpen all of our knives and then build a big fire under big barrels filled with water. Dad would stick the hogs in the heart, lift each hog by a pulley, and hoist them to bleed well. After the bleeding, the animals were lowered and placed in the boiling water to scald. The hair and outer skin were then scraped off. The pulley was used again to raise the animals to make it easier to cut the insides out. The liver and heart were carefully removed and shared with the neighbors. Each animal was cut in half. The folks were very careful to remove the tenderloin—what is now known as pork chops. Mom would put some of the pork chops into fruit jars and pressure-cook them. These pork chops would be a delightful tender feast on a cold winter day.

Each side of pork was cut into three parts: ham, bacon, and shoulder. The fat trimmed off each cut was rendered over heat in the iron wash pot to make lard and then it was saved. Sugar cure was rubbed into the six pieces of cut meat to cure in the smokehouse for future eating.

My primary task was to grind the lean trimmings into sausage meat. After the seasoning was mixed in well, Mom stuffed the mixture into small bags that she had made out of old sheets. These were hung in the smokehouse to cure for future breakfasts.

Nothing was wasted, so the heads were boiled after the brains were removed.

Some lean meat was used for making mincemeat. Mom and I would grind raisins, apples, and spices into the meat; cook the mixture; and then seal the mixture in fruit jars.

All this work had to be done in a timely fashion with few breaks. I did not appreciate the long, difficult, and time-consuming process until later in life.

Even though meat was cured, in a mild winter, meat was sometimes lost to "warms"; so Mom packed a lot of the meat into jars, pressured the jars to seal the lids, and preserve the meat. I especially liked the sausage; it made a great breakfast with scrambled eggs!

The cracklings from the rendered lard were saved to be used for the next batch of lye soap.

Occasionally, as I got older, Mom and Dad would leave me at the house alone. I was left with specific instructions to be careful about fires and told to stay out of things.

One such time during the summer, for some reason, I had the urge to help Mother. So while Mom and Dad were chopping cotton with the chopping crew, I decided to wash the floors. Now, I knew Mom usually poured water on the pine boards to settle the loose dirt and sand that accumulated; then she would use a broom to sweep the floor clean. Well, I wanted to do a good thing, so I took the vanilla from the white cabinet, put some in water, and swept the floor with it. The room really did smell great! But when they arrived back home, I received a severe lecture and a paddling for using the vanilla.

One other time when they went into town and left me at home alone, I got into Mother's makeup. It was all over my face, and I must have looked horrible! Don't know why I didn't have the sense to wash it off before they got home. So guess what? I got into trouble! After that I had to go to the neighbors if they did not take me with them.

In about 1934, Dad had the foresight to increase the acreage of the farm. He acquired forty acres of bottomland on the North

Fork Red River. He homesteaded this land under still-existing Homestead Laws. It might have been land abandoned by desperate Dust Bowl refugees. Dad built a shanty and slept there for approximately five years to satisfy the requirements. Though Mom and I helped some at the homestead, it was a hard time for wife and daughter; we didn't see much of him. When the five-years were completed, Dad lived again at the house.

In the spring and summer Dad would hitch the horses to the wagon and take them to the bottomland to work the soil. Rip, a stubborn old orange-colored mule was tied to the back of the wagon and walked along. Rip was needed to help work the fields.

Sometimes Dad would ride Rip to run an errand, but one time, the mule did not want to go because it was feeding time. That stubborn mule tried to rub Dad off against a fence which made Dad really angry. Dad hollered at, pushed, and cussed that mule, but finally gave up and let the mule eat.

The cotton planted on the south place had to be cultivated in the summer. Though I worked in the fields some, I didn't help much. I spent a lot of time daydreaming under the huge cottonwood trees as I watched the beautiful white fluffy clouds drift across the blue sky changing into different shapes and images—the face of a man, a rabbit, an elephant, or other objects.

These cottonwood trees had sprouts that grew near the bases of the trees. For some reason, the leaves of these low-growing sprouts were much larger than the ones on the branches of the trees. I would pick these large leaves, take dried twigs, and pin them together. Just like in the story of Adam and Eve making clothes to cover their naked bodies, should I ever be found without clothes, I knew these leaves could be used to make a covering.

One summer as the family was in the "bottoms" cultivating cotton, a big black cloud came up from the northwest. We jumped into the wagon, headed northwest toward home as Dad forced the mules to run to try to beat the storm. But the rain came down hard, beating into the mules' faces. The mules wanted to turn around so the rain would fall on their backs instead of on their faces, but of course, Dad wouldn't permit it. Everybody got soaked as the heavy rain blew very hard against our faces.

We still hauled well water for use in the house and garden, but sometimes we got better tasting water at the river. There was a spring at a drop along the river on the section line south of the home place. A pipe was stuck into the spring allowing the water to drop down into the river. This water was cold and tasted good. We hauled empty gallon vinegar jars and half-gallon canning jars, filled them with this good water, wrapped the jars in cloth or newspapers to keep the water cool, and brought it back to the house.

I went to the Elkview School from first thru sixth grades. Then I attended school in Warren with many of the same students from the Elkview School.

The Warren School, Warren, OK.

My parents bought me practical clothes for school but nothing fancy. So when Aunt Frankie would bring over a box of clothes she had outgrown, I would rummage through the box looking for the ones with lace and frills. I wore these till they were threadbare.

By the time I was twelve or thirteen, I was in 4-H and began making my own clothes.

Seventh grade class of 1935-36. Warren, OK.
First row: Juanita Hardy, Pauline Smith, Geraldine Curtis, Thelma Godsby, Dorsalea Allen, Theda Pollard and Katherline Glispie. Second row: Jack Fancher, Mona Lea, Myrtle McElory, Jewel Young, Wanda Marble, Elfreta Ishman, Ella Jo Brazell, Moneta Bush, J. E. Taylor, and Owen Murphy. Third row: Harley Winters, Lawrence Le Vick, Marvin Blackafe, Franklin McDaniel, Leland McElory, J. C. Calhooun, Guy Erbie Wingrove, William Heath, Kenneth Cupp, Franklin Powell, W. C. Edson, Wilborn McDaniel, and Mr. E. M. Biddy.

I wasn't sure just how I felt when Mom announced that she was expecting another child. Nevertheless, Royce Zane Smith was born December 18, 1935, on the farm. He weighed 7lbs. and 8 oz. I was ten years old and jealous of the attention Royce got, especially from Dad.

As Royce grew older, he was allowed to do things like fish in the pond that I was never allowed to do. I just didn't understand that!

Though I was jealous, I really did love the little guy.

My jealousy was placated some when Aunt Frankie married J. T. Shockley, and they left an old broken-down car parked east of the house as a present just for me. Frankie had always had a soft spot for me. I drove that car billions of imaginary miles. The car provided many pleasant memories and helped pass many solitary hours.

Relatives came to visit on a number of occasions, especially around Thanksgiving and Christmas. Sometimes they showed up in the summer to get a load of free melons. On such visits, Mom always fixed a huge dinner with a great variety of good food.

There usually wasn't enough table space or plates to seat the entire bunch at one time. It was tradition for the men to eat first while the women served and washed dishes. Then, the children and women got to eat what was left after the men had finished. I would get so weak waiting my turn. It seemed to me, the men tried to see just how long they could stay at the table. It didn't seem fair!

The Moss family came to visit once. Their little girl was very spoiled and very hyper. Everyone else had already washed up in the wash pan that was usually left in the enamel sink. Well, this little girl insisted that the wash pan be put on the floor so she could wash her hands. Well, as the families were waiting to eat breakfast, she had a temper tantrum, unintentionally tripped over, and sat down in the pan of water. She cooled off quickly. The John Smiths pursed our lips, tried to keep straight faces, and tried not to laugh.

Aunt Lavonia and Jubie Hartzog, Maggie and Pauline Smith

One unusually snowy November, Dad killed a huge twenty-five-pound gobbler turkey for Thanksgiving dinner. Aunt Lavonia, Maggie's sister, her husband, and their son, Jubbie, came for dinner. The turkey was so fat; it made all of us sick.

Often, the various Smith families would get together in Mountain Park or Centerville, Oklahoma, for a reunion. It was always potluck. Usually, there would be a quarrel among the Smith brothers. Dad would vow that he would never go again, but to honor his folks, he did.

William Carson Smith, Bennie Leon Smith, Walter Riley Smith, John Earl Smith, Buddy "Big Boy" Rogers, and Robert Roy Smith

Dad had a volatile temper. One time, he wanted to change the milking pen from the west barn and bring it nearer to the house. He tried to drive the Jersey cow to the new location, but the cow refused to be driven. Dad lost his temper and beat that stubborn cow. I'm not sure who was more stubborn, the man or the cow! Dad finally gave up and turned that building into a chicken house.

John Earl Smith, Royce Zane Smith, Maggie Lillian Herring Smith, and Clara Pauline Smith, taken about 1938 at a family reunion in Centerville, OK.

I was disgusted that he didn't just lead the cow instead of beat it.

On more than one occasion, Mom tried to stop him from beating the horses and mules.

One time Dad had given me instructions to stay near the house as he drove the mules and horses, but I ventured out just as the animals came from the east, and I got caught in the middle of them. Though I was in the midst of the beasts, I was not touched. However, I did receive a severe scolding for my disobedience, but I could have been trampled to death!

Mom and I were both relieved when Dad bought a tractor in 1939; he didn't have to rely on the mules and horses for plowing anymore.

Mother wanted to let old Rip loose in the pasture to die of old age, but Dad got angry and didn't see any reason to keep a useless old mule, so he traded him.

CHAPTER TWELVE

Is any one of you sick? He should call the
Elders of the church to pray over him and anoint him
with oil in the name of the Lord.

—James 5:14

Remembrances of a Sand Springs, Oklahoma, Lad—Tuberculosis

In 1935, when I was in ninth grade, we moved to a farm on Delaware Creek in Osage County north of Sand Springs. A good-sized house with L-shaped front and back porches was set in the middle of the pasture. There was also a garage where the '29 Chevrolet Coupe was kept.

We had a big pet mare named Roxey, and a big workhorse named Queen. Roxey was quite a character. The horses could come right up to the house and the garage. One day Roxey went into the garage and decided she would enjoy the upholstery in the Chevy Coupe. She really chewed it up.

Another time Roxey got up on the back porch and broke through some of the porch floorboards. She was quite a character!

Anyhow, Dad would harness the horses to work the farm implements. Queen was very steady and very plodding, but Roxey was very flighty. It would have been difficult to work with Roxey without matching her to Queen. Two like Roxey would have been a mess.

We also had two work mules, Kate and Jude. Jude was real smart. Around the main barn was a barbed wire fence with a wire gate. This gate was fastened from the gatepost to the fence

82

post with a wire loop. Jude would go to the gate, get her lip working under the wire loop, and work it off the fence post to open the gate. Anyhow, she mostly wanted to get out, but I guess she could have gotten in as well had she wanted to. However, she probably never tried to get in once she was out.

Speaking of in and out, I remember a story I often told about two skunks:

A mother skunk had two baby skunks. They all lived in a fallen hollow log. Because one of the baby skunks liked to stick its head out of the hollow log to look at the world outside, it was named Out. The other little skunk liked to stay inside the hollow log close to its mother, and it was named In. When the little skunks became bigger, they would venture out of the hollow log together. One day In and Out asked their mother, "Can we go out into the forest and play?"

Their mother said, "Yes, In and Out, you may go out into the forest and play, but don't be gone too long. I want you to come in before it gets dark."

So In and Out went out into the forest to play. After playing out in the forest for a short while, Out became tired and returned from being out in the forest. In was not ready to return home and wanted to stay out in the forest to play some more. When Out got home, his mother asked him, "Out, where is In?"

Out replied, "In is still out in the forest, Mom. In didn't want to come in."

His mother told him, "Well, Out, I want you to go back out into the forest, find In, and bring In in."

So Out went back out into the forest to find In. In a very short time, Out returned home with In.

His mother asked him, "Out, how did you find In so quickly?"

Out replied, "In stinked!" ☺

Anyhow, at the age of fifteen, I did a lot of heavy work around the farm. Sometimes it got the better of me. To provide water for the livestock, I would load three or four empty fifty-five gallon metal oil drums in the mule-drawn wooden wagon. Finding a shallow spot on Delaware creek, I would drive the wagon into the creek, dip water into the barrels until they were full; then I would drive back to the house and tip the full barrels to fill the old tubs to water the cows. Once as I was tilting a barrel off the wagon, it slipped and landed on my toe. It hurt! I probably broke some bones, but I didn't go to the doctor. I hobbled around for a long time!

During harvest, the family would shuck dried corn for the livestock and throw the corn into the wagon with a bang board on one side to stop the corn from being thrown over the wagon; then, the whole ears of corn were taken to a mill to be ground and bagged into burlap sacks. We would haul and load these sacks to store them in the barn; then the cribs for feeding were filled as needed.

I liked animals, and since Fididdledy was gone, Mom and Dad got me another dog that I named Browny. Browny was alive when I went off to school at Oklahoma A&M, was still living when I graduated, and even when I went into military service.

Boots, our pet momma cat, kept having bunches of litters. We kept a cream separator near the kitchen door. As whole milk was poured in, the cream fat separated and left skim milk. In warm weather when the kitchen door was left open to let in some breeze, those kittens would smell the milk and be hanging all over the screen door mewing up a ruckus trying to get to the milk. Of course, the kittens always got some of the skim milk. Boots eventually disappeared and probably died somewhere in Osage County.

There were cows, chickens, and usually ducks roaming around the property.

We tried to raise turkeys but found the job too difficult. Our friends, the John Browns, who lived maybe a mile from us, raised turkeys successfully.

The Ledbetters had moved to another farm across the Arkansas River out west of Sand Springs. Loyd, Jackie, and I still attended the Sand Springs Jr. High School together, but because we were in different grades, we didn't have much opportunity to do things together. So after their move, we did not see each other much and kind of lost touch. I did visit them on occasion.

Tuberculosis can be spread when a noninfected person inhales the tubercle bacillus released into the air when an infected person coughs, spits, or sneezes. A person can also contract tuberculosis by drinking unpasteurized milk from cows that have the disease. Most healthy people can fight off the disease, but the bacillus might settle in an unhealthy person and spread in the lungs. In 1935, there were no drugs produced that would stop the germs from multiplying, so the natural defenses of the body had to effectively fight the spread of the disease.

Gerald Austin Beasley
Sapulpa, OK, Sand Springs
High School, 1935

In 1935 when I was fifteen and in tenth grade at Sand Springs High School, Mom started to cough an awful lot. After examination she was diagnosed with tuberculosis, sometimes called phthisis or consumption. And she had it pretty bad! (Since the Beasleys drank unpurified milk, she might have gotten it that way.) Mom had to go to the TB sanatorium at Talihina in southeast Oklahoma. She was there for several years.

In the early 1900s, there was no cure for TB. The treatment in 1935 was pretty drastic. Dr. Baker took care of and did surgery on her. The medical staff pinched her phrenic nerve, took out her rib, and did pneumothorax; that is, they forced air into the pleural cavity to induce the lung to collapse, hopefully, to make it inactive so it would heal. They even removed infected portions of her lungs.

It was difficult for Dad and me while Mom was ill and away. But we helped each other as we "bached" together. Dad became a pretty good cook. He made real good biscuits.

We worked together a lot on the farm, often clearing trees using a long crosscut saw with a handle on both ends. Since two people had to operate it, Dad had to instruct me on how to lean on it correctly.

Not all was work. Dad and I played softball together on a team out on Delaware Creek.

Father and son would drive south as often as possible to visit Mom at the sanatorium in Talihina. We were unable to go very often because of the farm and dairy work, because of my schooling, and because of the expense.

One time while heading to Talihina in our '37 Chevy pickup, we hit a swarm of bees that splattered the windshield with bee remains. Some of the bees even got into the cab of the pickup. The occupants were pretty frantic until we opened the doors and got them out.

Talihina was a pretty area with lots of pine trees and hills. When we traveled, we slept in the bed of the pickup under the stars with the bedding we had brought along.

Another time, E. H. Berry and Aunt Floyd, Mom's sister, went with us. Or I guess, we went with them. Since the Berrys had a new four-door Plymouth, we drove in it. Coming back rather late at night, Uncle E. H. got sleepy and asked me to drive. I had started driving by myself when I was fourteen, so while the others slept, I put my foot in the carburetor! That Plymouth engine ran well! I got that car up to 80mph! Ha! That was pretty fast!

While she was at the sanatorium, the preacher of the church of Christ from Talihina came out to the grounds to speak. Mom would go to hear him since she had a church of Christ background. Her faith increased during her illness though her health declined.

CHAPTER THIRTEEN

There is a time for everything,
And a season for every activity under heaven:
. . . a time for war and a time for peace.
—Ecclesiastes 3:1, 8b

Politics and Impending War

In 1935 during President Roosevelt's first term as president, two legislations were adopted: the Social Security Act and the National Labor Relations Act.

Roosevelt's foreign policy promoted his "good neighbor" policy by making nonaggression treaties with six Latin American countries. The United States Neutrality Act of 1935 restricted America from making commercial sales to European countries at war.

By 1935 Germany had a formidable air force and had drafted many young men into military service.

In 1936 Roosevelt was nominated and reelected for a second term as president. His Agricultural Adjustment Act and his National Industrial Recovery Act had been declared unconstitutional. However, the attitude of some justices changed as they began accepting Roosevelt's New Deal legislation.

The president began to turn his attention to international affairs. The Spanish Civil War had erupted in 1936, and it began to look like a European war was inevitable. In a speech he warned against the "epidemic of world lawlessness" and proposed that nations responsible for "international anarchy" be quarantined. Some Americans called him a warmonger.

In 1936 Germany and Italy signed foreign policy and commercial agreements. Each nation had its own agenda, but they became allies. Germany supported Italy's move to conquer Ethiopia.

In March of 1936 with well-armed forces, Hitler marched into the area west of the Rhine River and reoccupied the demilitarized Rhineland zone. France opposed this action but made no move to stop the advance. Hitler then began steps to reacquire Germany's old 1914 territories.

From 1936-40, while the nation was still in financial crisis, President Roosevelt was the most talked of personality on the radio. He was seconded by an undersized crooked-legged muddy-colored horse—Seabiscuit—who became one of America's heroes winning races against thoroughbred horses, creating attendance records, pocketing winnings for his owner, and giving renewed hope to the poor and indigent in America.

CHAPTER FOURTEEN

Follow the ways of your heart and whatever your eyes
see, but know that for all these things
God will bring you to judgment.
—Ecclesiastes 11:9b

Remembrances of a Sand Springs, Oklahoma, Lad—Dangling Over Hell

In eleventh grade, Don Boydston, one of my buddies, persuaded me to take a journalism course though I had no idea what journalism was. Of course, I then found out. The Sand Springs High School had a very good journalism teacher, O. C. Husted, and the school had its own linotype and printing press. The school was probably one of very few high schools in the 1930s that had that kind of equipment. It was an extra special thing.

I was involved in the publishing of and became the editor of the *Sandtonian*, the high school paper. My senior year I was the managing editor. I really enjoyed the experience and was glad I was talked into taking journalism.

While in high school, I attended the Landmark Baptist Church at the old stone schoolhouse near Delaware creek. Landmark implied "getting back to the original" church and so forth. All of the Sand Springs school board members were Baptist deacons. My motivation for attending might have been less than spiritual because that's where the young people met together, and that's where the country basketball, softball and football teams were formed.

I played everything the church team played. Our teams even beat the high school team on occasion. It was not really a church team; it was just a community team, but nearly all the guys went to this Landmark Baptist Church.

The Landmark Baptist youth were a pretty decent group. Most did not drink and get wild. Well, the Combs Boys! They drank and got a little wild sometimes, and their language would sometimes get pretty rough; but it was a good group, and we had a lot of fun together.

If the winters were real cold and Delaware creek froze over, the young people would go down on the ice and play ice hockey with sticks or clubs.

Farther down on the creek from the baptismal place was a swimming hole in a horseshoe bend. A pretty nice swimming hole. Somebody had put a big rope up in a tree that would swing out over the water. Swimmers could hold on to the rope, swing out, let go, and drop into the water. On warm Sunday afternoons there would be quite a bunch of young people swimming. Mixed bathing! Ha! Now they did wear bathing suits or clothes or whatever. There was no skinny-dipping in mixed gender situations.

While in high school, I dated Betty Lea Kennett who I met at the Landmark Baptist Church. Actually, she was Freewill Baptist, and once in a while, her family would go into Sand Springs to the Freewill Baptist Church. I would go with them. But most of the time, they attended this Landmark Baptist Church because it was closer to their home. The Kennetts thought their old "freewill" preacher was about the best preacher in the world.

Anyhow, the Landmark Baptist's building had hard wooden benches that would dig into my bones, but the discomfort didn't keep me from going to sleep. Even though I would tell myself to not go to sleep, next thing I knew I was waking up. Guess I didn't get much spiritual guidance.

The Landmark Baptist had a resident preacher in his eighties, but they also had different visiting preachers who would come and present lessons to the congregation. The visiting preachers probably received some compensation from the collection.

One young preacher was a barber in Sand Springs who drove eight to ten miles to preach. He would get pretty emotional and dangle the young people out over hell pretty good. It probably didn't hurt us any. He was younger than the other visiting preacher.

The other traveling preacher brought his good-sized family. His girls kind of appealed to the boys. He was also a barber but an older fellow. One time he got up before the audience, ran his finger under his collar, squirmed, and finally, in effect, said, "The Holy Spirit is not giving me anything." He dismissed the startled assembly. They didn't quite know what to do! They sat there for a spell and then got up to leave.

Well, by their doctrine at the Landmark Baptist Church, a person would get saved as he or she thought about it and felt called by God; then, maybe later on in spring or summer, the members would vote whether to receive that person into the congregation. The congregation would then go down to Delaware Creek and baptize the believer.

It was a beautiful spot on the creek where the baptisms took place with the wind rattling the leaves of the big cottonwood trees. The a cappella singing was always very impressive as the congregation sang, "Shall we gather at the river."

There in the building, of course, they had a piano. Fifteen-year-old Geraldine Bowman and her mother were the pianists.

CHAPTER FIFTEEN

Whoever believes and is baptized will be saved, but
whoever does not believe will be condemned.

—Mark 16:16

Remembrances of an Ignorant Bend, Sand Hill, Elkview Lass—Baptized

By the time I was about thirteen in 1937, I was very active in 4-H. I raised cows, pigs, and chickens; canned; sewed using Mom's treadle sewing machine; and cooked. I received many ribbons for my entries in the Jackson County Fair. I sewed, entered, and modeled dresses for the 4-H style shows.

While attending junior high and high school in Warren, Oklahoma, I was quite athletic. I was active and quite good on the girls' softball and basketball teams.

I received numerous Perfect Attendance certificates as well as Perfect Spelling awards.

Clara Pauline Smith age 13,
Royce Smith age 2; taken
December 20, 1937

93

As I grew older, I did a lot of work on the farm helping the folks—anything from milking the cows, planting and harvesting, tossing hay to feed the animals, gathering eggs, slaughtering chickens, even moving fence posts. I also helped take care of Royce.

I heard a high school buddy once say, "Clara Pauline works like a horse!"

Mom, Royce, and I had been attending the church of Christ in Warren, Oklahoma. In August of '38 when I was fourteen, Claude Guild baptized me in a farm pond just east of the Warren cemetery.

In 1937 the Germans continued their demands for the return of their 1914 holdings in Europe.

On September 21, 1938, President Roosevelt called Congress into special session to revise the Neutrality Act which was preventing the United States from furnishing arms to Britain and France.

Clara Pauline Smith age 15, at Warren High School, 1939.

In an attempt to maintain world peace, Great Britain's Prime Minister, Neville Chamberlain, met with Hitler. To appease the dictator, Chamberlain allowed him to annex his native Austria. Not satisfied with Austria, in the Munich Agreement of September 29, 1938, Great Britain and France agreed to the demands of Hitler to annex Sudetenland and border areas of Czechoslovakia.

The British and French leaders thought they were guaranteeing "peace for our time" as Hitler reassured them he did not want to start a war.

CHAPTER SIXTEEN

Let the wise listen and add to their learning, and let
the discerning get guidance.

—Proverbs 1:5

College Remembrances of a Sand Springs, Oklahoma, Lad— Oklahoma A&M—1938-39

I, Gerald Austin Beasley, graduated salutatorian of my graduating class of 128 students from Sand Springs High School in May of 1938. Mom was not well enough to be there for the graduation.

In the fall of 1938, I started college at Oklahoma A&M at Stillwater. Pop Boyd, superintendent of Schools in Sand Springs, had advised me. "You are a farm boy, and you should study agriculture." His probably wasn't very wise counsel because I doubted that that was my aptitude. But that's what I studied.

Before I left for A&M, Dad cautioned me, "Don't gamble with the boys out there. You'll have some guys who will want you to gamble." That was his man-to-man talk. "Just don't gamble." Of course, Dad gambled some, not heavily, but I knew that he did. Guess Dad knew the dangers of such a practice and wanted to pass on his wisdom.

My first roommate at A&M was Monty Montgomery who was quite a bit older than me. Monty was an odd one. In fact, he was married; at least, that's what he said. His wife was somewhere working but not in Stillwater. We didn't do much together.

Monty worshiped with and played the piano for a religious group there in Stillwater. According to him, piano playing just came naturally to him. Since I never heard him play, I had to assume Monty was telling the truth.

My freshman year, I played clarinet for the A&M symphonic band for a while but had to discontinue because I could no longer make the 7:00 a. m. practices when I got a job at the college dairy farm.

I had to get up at 3:30 a.m. to be at the dairy by 4:30 a.m. My very first day at work, as I was taking off my clothes to put on the provided white coveralls, the other male student workers grabbed me in my birthday suit, took me outside, and threw me into a big water-filled concrete vat. I skated on the thin layer of ice briefly before I broke through to the ice-cold water. That was my initiation! Guess all new employees got initiated.

I started out hand milking, but my hands hurt so much afterward, I couldn't write. So I was given a different job. I was sent to the room where the milk was received and poured over coolers then into ten-gallon cans. Then I had to lift the filled cans and put them into large vats filled with ice water.

I was first chair clarinetist in the ROTC band both my freshman and sophomore years. I stayed in the ROTC band because I liked playing and because the ROTC provided a uniform that could be worn whenever I chose. Ha! It was one more article of clothing to round out my limited wardrobe! Anyhow, I often wore overalls on campus as did many others.

With my studies and work, I didn't have time to sing in the college chorus. But I sang bass in church.

I had occasionally attended the Tenth and Rockford church of Christ in Tulsa with my Uncle E. H. Berry's family; we would drive over from Sand Springs. I met Forest Sweet there. He and I became best friends.

At that time Forest was working at a bank in the Tulsa area. Forest was not really from a well-to-do family, but they were probably better off than the Edgar Beasleys. (Forest's uncle owned the Sweet Publishing Company.)

Forest and I had a lot of fun together. Once we went to the skating rink where we tried to skate. But neither of us knew how, so we got kind of wild and crazy as we were falling and thrashing about. One of the guys working at the rink came up and told us, "You guys need to stop showing off."

We tried to explain, "We aren't showing off. We aren't falling on purpose. We're just trying to learn how to skate." Don't think the guy believed us.

I brought Forest to Osage County to show him the farm. We went down to Delaware Creek and skinny-dipped in an isolated part of the creek.

Don't remember all the details; but Forest met, fell in love with, and eventually married a Ruth. We remained friends, but Forest's attentions were divided.

Gerald and Forest Sweet swimming in Delaware Creek, July 4, 1940

Another of my friends, Lawrence, dated and proposed to Edith Wooten. But she refused to accept the ring with the oversized diamond. I didn't want to ruin a good friendship, but I then dated her some. She promptly went back to Lawrence. Guess I didn't make the right impression. By comparison, she must have decided that Lawrence was a good catch, after all. Glad I could help. Edith and Lawrence later married.

Sometime in 1938 Mom was finally well enough and able to come home. Mom and Dad still had the two-bedroom house at Grant Street, so they spent some time there. They still had the two smaller rent houses as well.

Mom had been away at the Sanitarium for several years. She had lost a lot of weight and was very frail. There were certain positions she could not get into; otherwise she could not breathe. She had to bend down on her knees, lean to the side, and reach down to scrub the floor because she could not lean forward.

I would go home to visit Mom as often as I could. She and I would attend a little anti-class church of Christ over at section line about four or five blocks from the house.

She had been studying the Bible, and she would argue with our neighbor, Bill Bowman, one of the deacons at the Baptist church. There were some matters of Baptist doctrine that she did not agree with.

In 1939, Samuel Porter Beasley, Edgar's widower dad, came to live with Dad and Mom. Mom would become exasperated because he was hard of hearing.

"Dad, it is almost supper time. You need to go wash up," Mom would say.

"Do what now? What did you say?" Grandpa Samuel would ask.

Hollering, Mom would repeat, "Clean up, supper is almost ready."

Mom could not go anywhere or do anything without Grandpa asking, "Where are you going?" Or "What are you doing?" He was very nosey and asked lots of questions.

Mom got frustrated with him, but she really did like him.

Grandpa had a mustache and a beard that looked scraggly and smelled bad. As he ate and drank, food and liquid would get in the hair. I thought he was messy.

Grandpa Samuel was a good Bible student. When I was a youngster, he often read the Bible to me and told me Bible stories. He was always telling everybody that I was going to be a preacher.

Apparently, during his last years, Grandpa had lived with different sons and daughters, but he was living with Mom and Dad at 425 Grant Street when he died on February 21, 1939.

CHAPTER SEVENTEEN

Why do the nations conspire and
the peoples plot in vain?

—Psalms 2:1

Conflict in Europe—1939-40

*H*itler continued to deceive the world as he moved troops into and annexed more of Czechoslovakia, border areas of Poland and Hungary, and an area of Lithuania by March 22, 1939. All without any opposition or fighting!

Italy then invaded and annexed Albania on April 4, 1939.

Germany had been preparing for war for a number of years. They had been manufacturing tanks and airplanes for a new kind of warfare, the blitzkrieg, the use of tanks for mobility and airplanes for surprise.

In fact, Charles Lindberg had been invited by the Germans to visit Germany in 1936, 1937, and 1938. He reported to government and military officials on his return that the Germans had a large air force with better planes and well-trained pilots.

Hitler also had the Siegfried Line, a series of concrete fortifications extending from the Swiss border along the French, Belgian, and Dutch borders built in 1938-39 along the West Germany border to delay any Allied offensive that might interfere with his conquest of Poland.

As early as 1939, German submarines had been torpedoing and sinking merchant ships, placing magnetic mines in British ports, seizing ships, and taking their supplies.

Neither Great Britain nor France was well prepared for war. Each country had some new airplanes but still relied primarily on the use of their WWI defenses. France was certain her Maginot Line along its eastern borders would stop a German offensive.

The whole world was startled in August 1939 when Germany and Russia made a trade agreement and a ten-year nonaggression pact.

Both nations were being deceptive since each had its own agenda. Germany wanted to assure a one-front war against Britain and France until it was ready to take on Russia. Russia wanted more time to prepare for war against Germany.

Great Britain and France, finally alarmed, began to increase production of armaments and conscript armies to support Poland and other small states against a German takeover.

Most Americans sympathized with the Allies, but they did not want to get involved in the European conflict. President Roosevelt was interested in defeating Hitler from the beginning, but Congress would not approve.

The United States did not join the war in 1939, but the Neutrality Act was amended to (1) permit the sale of munitions on a "cash and carry" basis, (2) ban United States ships from combat zones, and (3) forbid the arming of merchant ships on the sea.

After the German-Soviet Pact was signed on August 24, 1939, Hitler invaded Poland on September 1, 1939. Poland's air force and its bases were destroyed from the air and quickly eliminated the Polish army. Russia, now an ally of Germany, invaded Poland from the east on September 17. Poland fell on October 5 and was then divided between Russia and Germany.

Two days after German armies crossed into Danzig, Poland, Great Britain and France declared war on Germany on September 3, 1939. German troops on the Siegfried Line stopped the French at the Maginot Line from crossing over to assist the already-defeated Poland.

Hitler had fooled many statesmen with the impression that he wanted only peace and freedom from treaty restrictions. He foresaw that the other powers would not unite against him. World War II began only when Britain and France recognized that Hitler was not going to stop his attempts to seize all of Europe.

From September of '39 until May of '40, minor fighting occurred between the French at the Maginot Line and the Germans at the Siegfried Line. This nine-month stalemated fighting became known as the Phony War. Hitler used this time to prepare for further invasion plans.

German invasion of Poland—August 1939

CHAPTER EIGHTEEN

For attaining wisdom and discipline;
For understanding words of insight;
For acquiring a disciplined and prudent life,
Doing what is right and just and fair.
—Proverbs 1:2 and 3

College Remembrances of a Sand Springs, Oklahoma, Lad— European War, 1939-40

I resumed my studies at Oklahoma A&M in the fall of 1939 just prior to Germany's invasion of Poland. The students were aware of, but not overly concerned about, this far-removed conflict.

Floyd Hixon, an orphan from Holdenville, Oklahoma, was my second college roommate. Floyd was a strong Baptist. (I was not a baptized Christian yet.) Floyd was a real nice guy. Very poor. Struggling. Very determined. Floyd made some money delivering newspapers, and he would work at whatever job he could get.

Floyd Hixon, one of Gerald's A&M roommates, 1939-40

I didn't have much money either, but I could bring baskets of eggs from the folks' farm. Ha! I actually fed Floyd for a few semesters. We also ate lots of beans and cornbread.

We rented and shared an inexpensive one-room light-housekeeping place where we shared one-hallway bathroom with at least eight to ten other male renters in an old two-story house. All the guys did their washing in the bathtub—clothes, towels, sheets, everything. Grandma Wagonner was our grouchy old landlady.

The war in Europe was brewing. The college students, especially the male students, were well aware that many U.S. government officials were certain that America would eventually get into the fight and that preparations had begun for such an eventuality; but America continued to sit back and watch, allowing the Allies to do the fighting and dying.

In 1940, the United States began (1) a first peacetime conscription, (2) a two-ocean navy expansion program, and (3) the production of sixty-nine thousand airplanes.

While pretending alliance with Germany, Russia invaded Finland to gain its own territories for preparation to invade Germany. Ironically, Germany and the Allies both gave some aid to Finland. The Finns fought through a winter battle but accepted terms of surrender on March 3, 1940. Russia then annexed Estonia, Latvia, and Lithuania, which sealed the falling-out between Russia and Germany.

Germany wanted to seize control of Norway for several reasons: (1) before Russia did; (2) so Allied forces could not interfere with much needed iron-ore shipments across the Baltic Sea; (3) because the Norway coast provided Germany with a protected route to the Atlantic for German submarines and ships; and (4) so Germany could attack the British Isles from Norwegian air bases.

On April 9, 1940, Germany began its attack on Norway. (1) They shipped troops concealed in commercial ships, (2) landed airplanes full of troops at all Norway's airports, and (3) the German navy struck in full force from the sea.

The Norwegians resisted with aid from the British Allies until the British Allied forces were forced to withdraw after a strong German advance.

By the time the French plan to send help was arranged, it was too late.

On the same day, Denmark was attacked by German forces and surrendered without a fight.

Germany's next plan was to invade France by using the Netherlands as a trap for the Allied forces. So on May 10, 1940, they dropped four thousand paratroopers behind Dutch lines to seize airports and bridges and to disrupt Allied communications. Rotterdam was bombed. Additional airborne German troops isolated the Dutch army. The Dutch army surrendered on May 13.

Also, on May 10, 1940, Reich marshal Hermann Goring began Germany's First Phase against Great Britain with the Luftwaffe, raids by air, to destroy England's ships, docks, and ports.

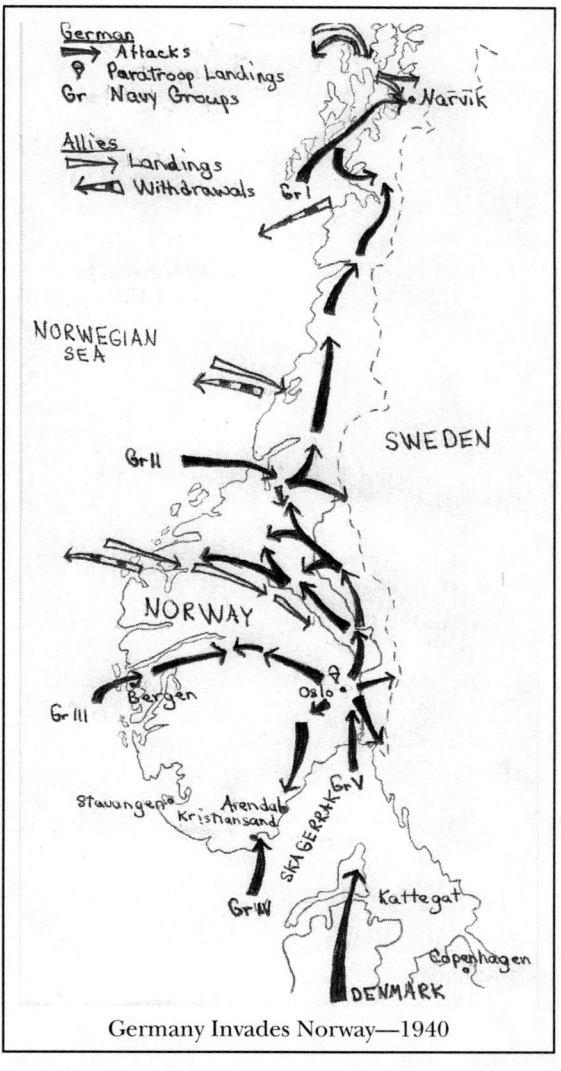

Germany Invades Norway—1940

The French believed the Ardennes Forest too difficult to pass through. So they had placed only *one division along the forest but had troops ready to aid in Belgium. But the Germans came thru the Ardennes forest with tank divisions and went between the French and Belgian forces.*

The isolated Belgium army surrendered.

The British retreated to Dunkirk.

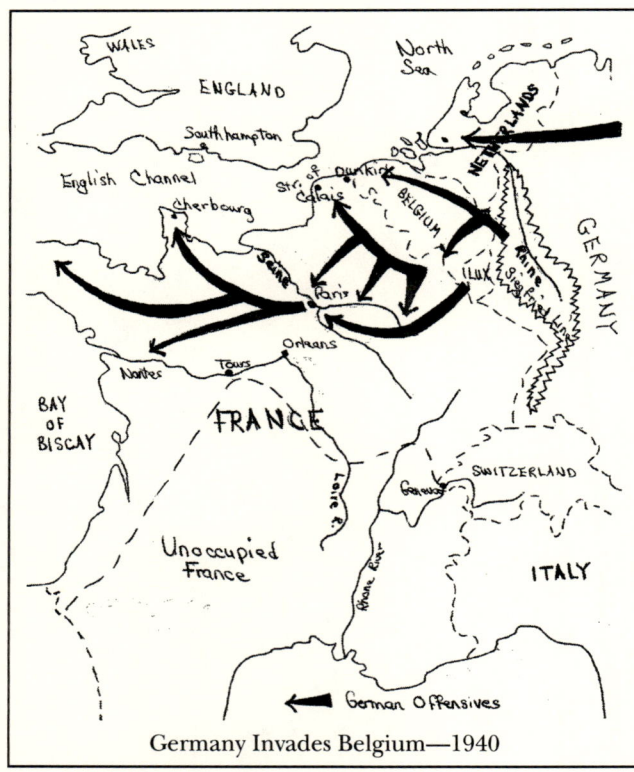

Germany Invades Belgium—1940

The French forces fell back.

The Germans swept across France toward Paris with only minor French opposition. No attempt was made to defend Paris. France signed an armistice with Germany on June 2, 1940. The French government officials and the French army had retreated from Paris to Tours, France, on June 10, 1940.

Italy declared war on France and Great Britain and attacked across southern France. France eventually signed an armistice with Italy on June 24, 1940.

Germany occupied north France while Italy occupied south France. About half of central France remained unoccupied under a Vichy government.

While Germany continued bombing Great Britain, Mussolini's Italian forces began the war in the Mediterranean on June 10, 1940. Hitler moved into the Balkans not so much to aid Italy as to protect his flank from an invasion by Russia which had seized northern parts of Rumania.

Starting in the summer of 1940, while Germany was occupying northern France, and later during the summer of 1941, I worked with the Agricultural Adjustment Agency, the reorganized version of the 1935 Agricultural Adjustment Administration.

These government programs were established to assist farmers in building terraces and to teach the farmers to plant wisely to assure the most productivity. This agency would take aerial photos of all the farms. There were restrictions on how much the farmers could plant of certain crops. They could plant only so much cotton, for example.

Anyhow, my job was to go out to these farms with the aerial photos, measure the areas where the crops were planted with surveyor chains, and draw my findings on the maps.

The farmers didn't especially like to see me, or any man from the government, come around. In fact, a neighbor who was visiting at one of the farms where I was measuring and who lived up on the top of the hill said, "You're not coming to my place!"

I could tell by the way the fellow made his statement that a man from the government would not be received warmly. In fact, he might be greeted with a shotgun. I reported this information to headquarters in Tulsa. Never knew what happened with that information, but I didn't go up the hill! The government employees had been told not to press their luck and go where folks were obnoxious or where threats were made. Some of the farmers did not like the government programs, not one little bit.

As I worked my assigned area, I drove my secondhand '35 Chevy. Now, my Chevy wasn't normally very fast, but heading back to Stillwater I would coast down a long hill near Yale, Oklahoma, at eighty miles per hour. ☺

At another time in that same area, I went to a place called Coyote Trail where quite a few black families lived. At one little farm, a forlorn-looking young black man came out of his shabby shack. His wife had just died. There were several sad little kids standing around. I was very touched by the scene and the situation. After considering the evidence, I came to the conclusion that this poor black fellow must have simply buried his dead wife without reporting her death.

(Later in the 1960s, the Keystone Dam was built on the Arkansas River near Sand Springs as part of the construction of an inland waterway system to provide barge transportation from Tulsa to the Gulf of Mexico. While working with the Agricultural Adjustment Agency, I had walked all over what became the bottom of Keystone Lake. The lake later became a popular recreation area.

In fact, one of my roommates during my senior year, Sequoyah Lee Cook, who had also worked for the AAA in that area, later moved back to his hometown of Cleveland, Oklahoma, right by Keystone Lake. Lee got into the insurance and real estate businesses and did very well for himself selling land and houses built all around the lake.)

CHAPTER NINETEEN

The fear of the Lord is the beginning of knowledge,
But fools despise wisdom and discipline.

—Proverbs 1:7

Remembrances of a Sand Springs, Oklahoma, Lad—College—1940-41

My third year at Oklahoma A&M, I had a new roommate, Johnny Morley, an orphan from Tipton, Oklahoma (but not from the Tipton Children's Home). We shared an apartment for a year starting in the fall of 1940. He was the first friend to call me Gerry; others then picked up the nickname.

Sand Springs was about sixty miles away from Stillwater, so I visited home as often as I could. Mom and I would attend church together. Up to that point, I had had religious encounters with the Landmark Baptist, Freewill Baptist, and Southern Baptist, and some exposure in Tulsa with the churches of Christ. After studying the Bible together, Mom and I were both baptized in 1940. I was twenty years of age.

Sometime in 1940, Dad bought a service station along the so-called Sand Springs Line, a streetcar line that ran from Sand Springs to Tulsa. There were several gas stations along this line. His was closest to Sand Springs near Lake Station where streetcar passengers were picked up and let off.

Glass cylinders on the gas pumps showed the gas as it was pumped up by hand. Gages would tell how many gallons of gas were being put into the car. I worked with Dad on weekends and during the week when I could. Sometimes we would go for hours without any customers; then, all of a sudden, everyone would be lined up all at one time wanting gasoline and service. I pumped gas, fixed flat tires, and did oil changes.

Dad didn't have this station very long; it didn't do well and was not very profitable.

CHAPTER TWENTY

Rachel was lovely in form, and beautiful.

—Genesis 29:17b

Remembrances of an Ignorant Bend, Sand Hill, Elkview Lass—1939-40

Sophomore class, Warren, OK, 1938-39
Front row: Dorselea Allen, Jaunita Hardy, Moneta Bush, Pauline Smith, Geraldine Curtis, Coleen Allen. Second row: Harley Winters, Wilborn McDaniel, Mona Cearley, Guy Erbie Wingrove, J. L. Pinner, Kenneth Cupp, Lawrence Le Vick. Third row: Mr. Whitten, J. C. Calhoun, Willis Savage, Franklin Powell, Jack McNeely.

I attended the Warren High School with many of the same students I had known since grade school. My friends began to call me Pauline.

In 1940, at age sixteen, I was a senior at Warren High School.

Senior Basketball Team, Warren High School,
1938-39
Front: Pauline Smith, Annie Ruth Robertson,
Coleen Allen, Mildred Spencer, Lucilla Allen. Back:
Mr. McNeely, Moneta Bush, Mona Lea Cearley, Jewel
Young, Wilma Savage, Elsie King, Mrs. Gladys Evans

I continued to play center for the girls' basketball team. The team went to the Cotton Belt Conference, where we won the warm-up game against Elmer, 43-19, our sixth win of the season. But we did not do well during the rest of the conference.

Some said I was a beautiful, likable young lady. I don't know about that, but I did date several guys. I spent some time with Charles Highsmith who I met at a district 4-H meeting. He was an amateur photographer and took numerous pictures of me. We were good friends.

I also dated Charles Abernathy. We attended the County Fair at Altus on September 17, 1940, where we had our picture taken together.

Located in a rural area, many of the Warren High School students also participated in 4-H activities.

I continued to be active in 4-H and won several prizes for my projects. My home economics teacher at Warren High School, Ms. Blackwell, was my mentor. She encouraged my participation in many 4-H activities.

In the spring of 1940, the following write-up and picture appeared in the Altus paper:

Toward the end of her senior year in high school, Pauline Smith was selected as the winner of the annual Times-Democrat 4-H club member's contest. She and Morris Caves won a trip to Chicago where they met with 2000 other boys and girls from all over the nation. Railway fare was paid by the Times-Democrat, and accompanied by 4-H leaders and supervisors from Oklahoma A&M College at Stillwater.

Pauline Smith, age sixteen, Warren High School

Sixteen-year-old Pauline, a club member for five years and a senior at Warren High School, was winner in the county "appropriate dress project" in Jackson County for 1940. In 1940 she had three local, ten county, and four state exhibits. She won a trip in 1938 to the American Royal livestock show and was in the blue ribbon class at the county fair in 1939. She won 16 firsts, 17 seconds, one third, and one seventh at local, county and state fairs.

In 1940 Miss Smith raised 50 chickens, had one acre of garden, raised a calf, canned 213 quarts of fruit, vegetables and meat, and tried 563 recipes. In addition, she had 11 articles of home improvement, made 34 articles of clothing and raised a pig.

The total value of her projects is $218, including prize money she has won.

> The trip to Chicago was December 5, 1940. She
> stayed at the Congress Hotel. Her roommates were
> Joan Ward, Newtha Krebs, and Josephine Long.

While in Chicago, I toured Washington Park, saw the carving of From Life to Death, the Rockefeller Cathedral, and the International 4-H Exhibits.

I met Joe Davidson from Dumas, Texas, at the farewell party, and we corresponded some.

I also met Billy Flowers from Ehrhardt, South Carolina. We corresponded while he attended college in Georgia where he was studying medicine.

On August 15, 1940, the German air force attempted its Second Phase to destroy the Royal Air Force (RAF) in northern England. The Germans caused heavy damage but did not succeed. In its third phase, the Nazis bombed London to destroy industry and demoralize the nation. The German bombers took heavy losses by the RAF who were aided by radar. Hitler postponed the Fourth Phase, Operation Sea Lion, of the proposed invasion of England.

The blitz in London and other industrial centers continued through May of 1941, with heavy civilian casualties. The RAF retaliated by bombing German industry.

Mussolini's forces advanced from Libya in September of 1940 crossing into Egypt. The English came from their bases on Crete, pushed the Italians back to Benghazi, Libya. The Italians fell February 7, 1941.

Hungary had seized Transylvania in September 1940.

On October 28, 1940, Italy attacked Greece through Albania.

Hungary joined the Axis on November 20, 1940, and was occupied by German troops. Fascist General Lon Antonescu became dictator of Rumania, and German troops moved in.

Bulgaria formally joined the Axis on November 23, 1940.

By the end of 1940, Europe was coming under Nazi rule.

The Congress of the United States voted vast sums for the armed forces. Military training of a million men was begun. And aid was given to the European democracies.

Roosevelt was reelected for a third term in 1940.

CHAPTER TWENTY-ONE

As no one is discharged in time of war,
So wickedness will not release those who practice it.
—Ecclesiastes 8:8b

European Conflict— World War II—1941

After bitter debate, Congress passed the Lend-Lease Act on March 11, 1941. Though the United States was still officially neutral, the act authorized the president to "sell, transfer title to, exchange, lease, lend, or otherwise dispose of . . . any defense article" to any country whose defense was deemed vital to the defense of the United States.

The German General Erwin Rommel organized the Afrika Korps, tank forces, at Tripoli, Libya. In March of 1941, he began pushing the English east along the coast of Tobruk. The German drive became inactive from April until November.

When it became apparent in March that Germany was going to aid Italy in an attack on Greece, British forces began moving into Greece. The Greeks, with British air and naval forces, broke through the Italian lines and held through April, struggled long enough for the British forces to evacuate, then surrendered on April 21, 1941. The British had to leave valuable equipment behind.

In April of 1941, Denmark agreed to let the United States establish bases on Greenland.

In the Middle East, the British met resistance from Raschid Ali Bey Gailani who seized control of the Iraq government April 4, 1941; but an armistice was signed on May 31. British and Free French troops then invaded Syria from Palestine, Trans-Jordan, and Iraq, to prevent the Germans from using the airfields in Iraq. British and Russian (now an Ally) troops stopped the Axis penetration of Iran on August 25, 1941. An agreement on joint occupation was made with the Shah on September 16, 1941.

Yugoslavia surrendered on April 18, 1941, after a blitzkrieg attack from Germany.

On the African front, the English then advanced into and forced Italian troops out of Sudan, Kenya, and Italian Somaliland. Ethiopian forces aided the English and Ethiopia was liberated from Italian control. On May 19, 1941, the Italians surrendered at the mountains of Amba-Alagi.

Germany's air invasion of Crete on May 20, 1941, caused the British to evacuate by May 31.

Germany continued to use submarines to destroy and sink the shipping of supplies to Great Britain. Magnetic mines were strewn across the entrances to British ports. Air power was greatly increased to destroy industry. The German battleship the Bismarck *raided and sank the British battle cruiser* Hood *and damaged the new battleship* Prince of Wales *on May 24, 1941, in Denmark Strait. Allied carrier planes and naval vessels then crippled and sank the German* Bismarck *on May 26 and 27.*

After eighty-five British destroyers were put out of service, the United States provided fifty destroyers to Great Britain in exchange for ninety-nine-year leases for naval and air bases on British islands. Aid was rushed to Great Britain and soon granted to China, which had been at war with Japan for several years.

Hitler began his attack on Russia June 22, 1941, with three major forces: (1) from the north, (2) from the center, and (3) from the south. Hitler's first objective was to hit and push the occupying Russian forces out of eastern Poland and Rumania using his blitzkrieg methods, which included use of air cover while tank divisions rapidly moved forward. After Hitler's successful invasion of France and the Low Countries by using tank warfare, he felt justified and ignored the advice of his generals who had advised him not to invade with tanks. General Bock encircled the Russian forces at Bialystok, Poland, and Minsk, USSR, on July 5. Some of the Russian forces escaped. The German victory in Smolensk was indecisive.

In July of 1941, United States forces replaced British forces on Iceland.

President Roosevelt and Prime Minister Churchill met August 14, 1941, aboard a naval vessel at Placentia Bay, Newfoundland, where they discussed and signed the Atlantic Charter, which outlined their nations' desire for peace after the war: (1) the right of self-determination for peoples and of self-government for nations, (2) worldwide economic cooperation, (3) safety from aggression, and (4) abandonment of the use of force.

Like many other young males, I made a decided effort to read about and listen to the war news. I knew there was a good possibility that American young men would soon be called into duty. I would grab an abandoned newspaper and/or listen in as I passed any radio that was playing. It truly was a world war. It seemed only America was not involved in the fighting.

During the summer of 1941, my dad bought a little place in the woods north of Sand Springs with about eighty acres. Mom and Dad lived there for a while.

There was a lot of sandstone in the woods north of Sand Springs. I helped Dad quarry great big solid slabs of sandstone on this place. These slabs were real difficult to handle, but there were people who would pay a good price for them.

Dad also hauled and used some of this native sandstone to cover the front porch of the house at 425 Grant Street which they rented out in Sand Springs.

PART TWO

Lad and Lass Meet

CHAPTER TWENTY-TWO

He went out to the field one evening to meditate, and
as he looked up, he saw camels approaching.
Rebekah also looked up and saw Isaac.
—Genesis 24:63 and 64

Remembrances—Love versus War—Oklahoma A&M—1941-42

I, Clara Pauline Smith, graduated from Warren High School in May, 1941, as salutatorian of my small graduating class of fifteen. I was seventeen years old when I attended Oklahoma A&M in Stillwater the fall of 1941.

Before I headed off for college, Dad advised me, "Dress modestly, keep yourself pure, and act like a lady."

My first roommate in Murray Hall at Oklahoma A&M was Elizabeth Griebel.

I, Gerald Austin Beasley, returned as a senior to Oklahoma A&M in the fall of 1941.

Graduating class of May 1941,
Warren High School, Warren, OK
Front: Wilma Savage, Geraldine Curtis, Moneta Bush, Mona
Lea Cearley, Collen Allen, Jaunita Hardy, and Pauline Smith.
Back: Ms. Bessie Lee Blackwell, Guy Erbie Wingrove, J. L.
Pinner, Franklin Powell, Kenneth Cupp, J. C. Calhoun,
Lawrence Le Vick, Willis Savage, and Wilborn McDaniel

I had previously visited at the Tenth and Rockford church of Christ that met downtown in Tulsa, Oklahoma; but since my baptism, I had been attending the church of Christ in Stillwater.

Tenth and Rockford Church of
Christ Young's People's Class
Gerald is in the middle.

The first Sunday of the 1941 fall semester at Oklahoma A&M, all the young guys at church eyed the new young females in attendance. I spotted Pauline Smith as she sat on the right side of the auditorium in a pew about halfway back from the front. I knew that she was new and I said to myself, "Who is that beautiful girl? I've got to meet her!"

She was about 130 pounds, 5 foot 5 inches tall, with dark brown shoulder-length page-boy hair; she made a pretty picture. She caught the eye of many single young males.

I hung around after dismissal on the front steps of the church building

Church friends from left: ??, Muriel Smith, Dale Brooks, Evelyn Brooks, Bill Best, Theodore Haire, Gerald Beasley far right; the two in the back unknown

waiting to be introduced to this pretty new face. However, I was not the only guy who had noticed her, and I had to wait my turn.

Pauline dated quite a few guys while at Oklahoma A&M. She dated Forest Talkington and Jack Nausbaum. (She should have stayed with Jack because he became a millionaire. As an architect, he designed some of the buildings on the Oklahoma Christian University campus. Jack died February 23, 2003.) She also dated Theodore Haire and Cecil White, as well as other guys, before I got up the nerve to ask her out. Most of these guys were a part of the good-sized bunch of college students that attended the Stillwater church of Christ.

Stillwater Church of Christ friends
Front: Olin Walcher, Pauline Smith, Eva Dunn, Sue Kates, and Lydia Mae Best
Back: Aubrey McNally, T.J Finley, Kelsa King

This group of college students had a lot of fun at the church social functions.

Among the group of young church friends were Bill and Rachel Best, Lydia Mae Best, Dale Brooks, Verna Coffee, Doris and Thomas Cunningham, Brother Dixon, Geraldine & Eva Dunn, Elton and Eleanor Dilbeck, T. J. Finley, Theodore Haire, Jim Tom and Ira Hill, Wilburn Hill, Vinita Jenkins, Sue Kates, Kelsa King, Aubrey McNally, John Meek, Ruby Lee Morris, Jack Nausbaum, Denver Patterson, Lena Pearl, Avis Redman, Erma Muriel Smith, Mildred Tinius, Victor Tomaso, Erma Deanne Tucker, Olin Walcher, Irlene Williams, Maxine Williams, and Joe White.

I did eventually asked Pauline out for a date. On our first date, Pauline and I went bicycling at the park on rented bicycles. Ha! I lost track of time, and we kept the bikes longer than I thought.

When we got back, I didn't have enough money to pay for the extra time, but she happened to have some money with her. Guess I didn't make a very good first impression. (Don't remember if I ever paid her back.) However, she did go out with me again!

I was close enough during our very first encounter to noticed that her hair smelled really good!

On another date I rented a boat at Yost Lake north of Stillwater.

Pauline Smith in rowboat on Yost Lake. Gerald is rowing.

I made sure I brought plenty of money that time. I tried to serenade her with my harmonica. Ha! She went out with me again so I must have made an impression!

Another time we went to an agricultural club picnic at a lake northeast of Stillwater where there was a recreation area.

There was a softball lying on the ground, so I picked it up and said, "Let's play catch!" She had no problem handling the ball. She could catch and throw as well as I could. She was quite good. I was surprised.

We were both novices, but on another date, we went to the skating rink in Stillwater and had to work hard to stay upright on the roller skates.

Don't know if Pauline was taken with me from the beginning. She did date a lot of other guys. Well, there were too many other guys wanting to date her.

I sure liked what I saw.

While the group of college students at the church of Christ in Stillwater were enjoying many pleasant times and experiences, the war in Europe continued to rage.

As early as 1931 Japan had invaded Manchuria and had set it up as a puppet state (Manchukuo). There had been minor clashes along the Chinese border in 1937 near Peiping, and by 1940 Japan held key positions in eastern China.

Britain had closed the Burma Road, China's only access to the outside world.

The United States had always opposed Japanese aggression and did not renew a commercial treaty with Japan on January 26, 1940. Japan was dependent on goods imported from the United States, so in September of 1940 when the U.S. declared an embargo on the shipment of scrap iron and steel, Japan was on the defensive.

After Japan became one of the Axis powers by signing the Berlin Pact on September 27, 1940, Britain reopened the Burma Road in October. The United States then made loans to Chiang Kai-shek's Chinese government under Lend Lease.

In Europe, German armored forces moved south where Rundstedt's group captured Kiev. German troops entered the Crimea in October '41 and reached Rostov in November '41.

In November '41 the United States Neutrality Act was amended to allow the arming of merchant ships and sending of United States arms to England.

Russia, acting on its own interest, had signed a neutrality pact with Japan in April 1941.

After gaining military control of French Indochina in June of 1941, Japan showed an interest in the Netherlands East Indies.

Under false pretenses, a Japanese diplomat was sent to Washington in November '41. The United States demanded that Japan stop all aggression in China and withdraw from Indochina.

During the fall 1941, World War II was really brewing. The United States was "unofficially" involved through the Lend Lease Program. Congress still had not taken steps to send troops to fight in Europe, but U.S. bases had been established at several strategic locations.

At that time there were four guys batching together in an upstairs apartment.

My roommates and I were well aware of the possibility of the war bringing young men into active duty.

The landlady, a Christian Scientist, was an interesting lady. She called me Doc. She would say, "Doc, I don't sin." Of course, Christian Scientists believe there is no such thing as sin. In 1941, I had traded in my Model-A Ford and purchased a 1935 Chevy standard four-door for $185. My jolly landlady gave it a Shakespearean name, True Love, because "it does not run smooth."

Anyhow, the four of us guys were all in the landlady's apartment listening to her radio December 7, 1941, when the Japanese attack on Pearl Harbor was broadcast on the radio. We were startled and unbelieving as we leaned forward listening intently.

Now, all of us knew for sure that the draft would be after us.

We four guys had worked out a schedule for sharing the responsibility for the preparation of lunch and supper based on each roommate's class schedule. Since I had no class the following Monday, the guys said, "Doc, why don't you go find us a used radio so we can keep up with the war news. We'll pay you back for our part."

So I went and found a used radio for a couple of bucks. Don't remember if the guys ever did pay me back.

Anyhow, we got a radio to keep up with the war news.

Japan's reply to the United States' demands of November was handed in a note to Secretary of State Cordell Hull after the attack on Pearl Harbor. Japan's claim was that the Japanese diplomat did not have a Japanese typist who could type fast enough, so the type-written reply, which was to have been delivered before the attack, was not completed until after the attack.

On December 8, 1941, my roommates and I listened to Roosevelts' speech to the Congress of the United States as it was broadcast on the radio:

> Yesterday, December 7, 1941—a date which will live in infamy—the United States of America was suddenly and deliberately attacked by naval and air forces of the Empire of Japan . . . As commander in chief of the Army and navy, I have directed that all measures be taken for our defense . . . I assert that we will not only defend ourselves to the uttermost, but will make very certain that this form of treachery shall never endanger us again . . . we will gain the inevitable triumph—so help us God . . . I ask that the Congress declare that since the unprovoked and dastardly attack by Japan on Sunday, December 7, a state of war existed between the United States and the Japanese empire . . . *

Congress declared war on Japan on December 8, 1941.

On December 11, Germany and Italy declared war on the United States, and Congress declared war on Germany and Italy on December 11, 1941.

---

* **en.wikipedia.org**/wiki/Infamy_**Speech**

Japan's surprise attack on Pearl Harbor disabled the United States Pacific fleet, but most of the ships were refloated and repaired. Japan's action united the Americans behind the war effort. Under Roosevelt, the United States had more complete national unity than in any previous war.

While Pearl Harbor was under attack, Japan had also led a series of simultaneous attacks on numerous island strongholds throughout the Pacific: (1) Guam was taken December 10, (2) Wake Island was taken December 23, (3) the Philippines were invaded December 10 but held only until May 6, 1942, (4) the British surrendered Hong Kong, December 25.

With various land forces, the Japanese crossed into Burma, December 11, where the American Flying Tigers did heavy damage to the invaders, but they and the British were repulsed. The Japanese occupied Sarawak in the East Indies on December 16.

Just after the attack on Pearl Harbor, the German General Bock surrounded Vyasma. The Russians, under Marshal Georgi K. Zhukov, launched a strong counteroffensive from Moscow, driving the Germans back. Hitler retired to winter quarters after ordering the ill-equipped, cold, and hungry German troops to hold their ground in Russian territory at all cost.

Because Hitler dispersed his armies and ordered the armies not to retreat, instead of concentrating his troops on a main objective, this action became a turning point in the war.

Songwriters began producing a number of propaganda and war songs that we heard played on the radio I had purchased. "Angels of Mercy" was dedicated to the American Red Cross nurses; "Cowards over Pearl Harbor" was meant to make the listener feel anger at the Japanese, sympathy and sorrow for American losses, and to boost the American spirit; "I've Been Drafted, Now I'm Drafting You" dealt with the pains of separation and the dreams of reunion; and "Ma! I Miss Your Apple Pie" expressed the soldiers desire to get back home to the America they were fighting for.

Feeling the call to patriotism, many young men enlisted for military service. I was among those who were influenced by the patriotic frenzy but with mixed feelings. I waited to see if my number would come up.

CHAPTER TWENTY-THREE

"O house of Israel," declares the Lord,
"I am bringing a distant nation against you—an
ancient and enduring nation.
A people whose language you do not know, whose
speech you do not understand."
—Jeremiah 5:15

America in a Two-front War

From the outset of aggression, Japan wanted to (1) extend its empire, (2) protect its empire by controlling bases on the islands of the Pacific, (3) defend its territory until the United States and Britain were war weary, and (4) then negotiate a peace.

The Japanese began attacking various strongholds in the Pacific. They attacked Borneo and Celebes from Sarawak in January 1942. Despite damage by air attacks from United States destroyers, the Japanese landed on the islands of New Britain and New Ireland. Singapore was then attacked by planes and fell February 15, 1942.

In only about five months, Japan's offensive had seized numerous strongholds in the Pacific.

America was now involved in a two-front world war. The Allied plan was to (1) fight a holding war against Japan, (2) keep its main effort against Germany, and (3) turn against Japan after Germany surrendered.

American Admiral Nimitz conducted raids in February and March of '42: (1) Marshalls Island on February 1, (2) Wake Island on February 24, and (3) Marcus Island on March 4.

February 27-28, 1942, British, Dutch, American, and Australian naval forces fought together in the Battle of the Java Sea and lost five cruisers and fourteen ships; but the Japanese took Java on March 9.

On April 18, 1942, in retaliation for Pearl Harbor, Colonel James Doolittle led sixteen B-25 bombers on an air raid from the carrier Hornet to Tokyo. This raid did no great damage but raised American morale.

Japan vs. Allies was a draw but a strategic Allied victory in the Battle of the Coral Sea, the first major sea battle with carriers on May 4-8, 1942, off NE Australia, three months after the Java Sea loss, 1,800 miles to the west.

After the Coral Sea setback, the Japanese headed to Midway June 4, 1942, but the United States Navy had broken the Japanese code and was waiting for them. At Midway, a major turning point of World War II, Japan lost four carriers, one cruiser and a major part of its air force. The United States lost the carrier Yorktown (re-floated and crudely repaired at Pearl Harbor), and one destroyer. Midway was defended and the Japanese withdrew.

A United States major offensive, the Battle of Guadalcanal in the Solomon Islands, northeast of Australia, began August 7, 1942, and secured the islands in the area by February 9, 1943.

Both sides lost hundreds of men, several cruisers, carriers, and battleships.

On the European front, the ill-equipped German army remained stranded in Russian Territory during the winter of 1941. The Russians continued a winter offensive and retook some ground. But in May 1942, the Germans went through the Crimea into the Caucasus to capture the oil resources. Moving along the Don River into Stalingrad, the Germans thrust full air power at the unyielding Russian defenses.

In North Africa, from November 1941 until July 1942, the control of North Libya seesawed back and forth between the Germans led by Rommel and the British led by General Auchinleck.

Manhattan Engineer District was established in 1942 as a unit of the U.S. Army Corps of Engineers and was in charge of secret operations for producing the atomic bomb.

CHAPTER TWENTY-FOUR

He has taken me to the banquet hall,
and his banner over me is love.

—Song of Songs 2:4

Gerald's Remembrances—
True Love—1942

America was heavily into the war as I continued my studies at Oklahoma A&M. I knew this conflict was likely to affect my future. The draft would be after me, and as a Christian, I preferred not to carry arms against my fellow man regardless of nationality.

Pauline and I were dating seriously by then; I did not want to leave her.

During my senior year, I traveled southwest and did practice teaching in Tipton, Oklahoma; I taught agriculture at the high school.

I stayed with the Whitaker family, members of the church of Christ. I spent a lot of time at their house with their two boys playing Carom, a board game (smaller, but similar to pool) where a puck was snapped with the middle finger to impact against other pucks in succession to knock them into corner pockets. (Years later, in 1989, Mike and Carmen Lewis, Pauline's and my fourth daughter, moved to Houston where Mike preached for the Bammel Road church of Christ. Wayne Whitaker, who was one of the boys I had played carom with, was an elder there. It's a small world!)

I also did some preaching. In the spring of 1942, during the rainy season, I took Pauline with me to Ripley, Oklahoma, where I had my first paid preaching experience. I was covering for Elton Dilbeck, an Oklahoma A&M student who usually preached there on Sundays.

The surrounding farm area had flooded from heavy rains, so all the farmers were out chasing and tending to the cows, horses, and livestock in the floodwaters. So I was the only male in attendance at the services and had to do everything: lead singing, pass communion, pass the collection plate, say the prayers, teach the Bible class, and preach. It was quite an initiation!

After batching all four years at Oklahoma A&M, I graduated May 1942 with a BA in agriculture and a minor in dairying. I had lived simply and cheaply in four different apartments in Stillwater as I worked to pay my way through school. Floyd Hixon and I did not room together all four years while at A&M, but we both graduated together in '42.

After graduation I corresponded some with Floyd. Floyd had stayed in the ROTC for four years, but I got out of ROTC after the required minimum of two years. When Floyd got out of ROTC, he went directly into the service as a second lieutenant and went to the Pacific.

Every so often I would get an unexpected check from Floyd. He was repaying me for feeding him eggs, beans, and cornbread for

Gerald Beasley—1942 at Stillwater

several semesters at school. I had not expected him to repay me.

I stayed on the Oklahoma A&M campus the summer of '42 because Pauline was attending classes. I wished to stay near her.

During that summer I lived in a bedroom at a boarding house across the street from the campus. I cooked family-style breakfasts for the whole bunch of boarders to get my meals free. I actually took a summer course in sheet metal work, a skill used in building airplanes and such, hoping to get employment, but nobody would hire me because they knew I was draft bait.

So how long did I date Pauline before I knew she was the one? That's hard to say! I liked what I saw from the beginning. When I graduated, I'd known her about nine months. By then we were pretty involved and going places in True Love.

Pauline Smith and Gerald Beasley
standing in front of True Love, Gerald's car

Pauline had determined that she would date only Christians. She knew I had a desire to serve the Lord. I knew I saw the heart of good woman.

We had a lot in common; both had grown up on farms working with our folks; both knew what it was like to work hard; both knew what it was like to have little; both believed in God and desired to do his will.

By then, I knew she was the one for me!

CHAPTER TWENTY-FIVE

When you go to war against your enemies . . .
Do not be afraid of them,
because the Lord your God . . . will be with you.

—Deut. 20:1

Operation Torch

In July of 1942 the British had been pushed back to El Alamein in Egypt where the line held. After receiving a new shipment of supplies, on October 23, 1942, the British Eighth Army commanded by General Sir Bernard L. Montgomery barraged the poorly supplied, retreating Germans with artillery.

The Battle of El Alamein was a turning point in the war in North Africa.

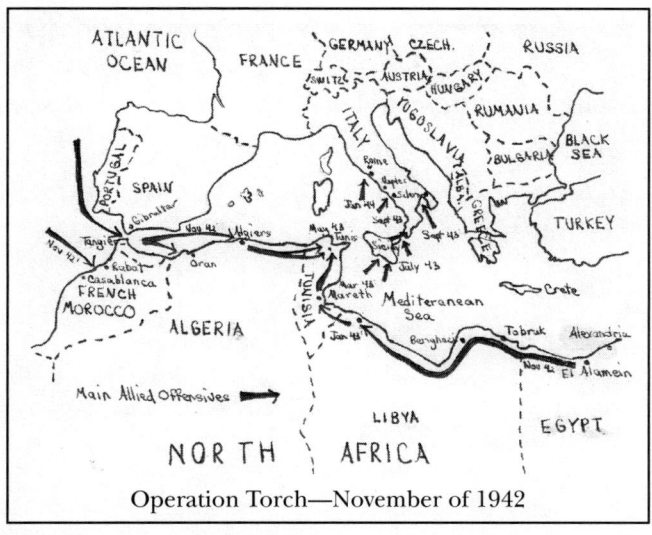

Operation Torch—November of 1942

The first major offensive in North Africa, Operation Torch, the joint operation of pro-Allied French, British, and the Americans, began on November 8, 1942, as the combined forces landed in North Africa. It required complicated technical planning of the army, navy, and air forces of two nations sailing in separate expeditions: one group, British and American forces under General Dwight D. Eisenhower, sailed from England to Algeria at Oran and Algiers; and a second group sailed from the United States to Casablanca, Morocco. It was timed to coincide with Montgomery's offensive at El Alamein, Egypt.

Many Allied ships and troops were torpedoed by German subs and lost in transport at sea.

The Allies secured Casablanca and Algeria on November 11, 1942.

Rumors of the mistreatment of the European Jews by the Nazis had leaked to government officials of several countries through messages discreetly handed to Red Cross personnel, pictures, word of mouth from escaped Jews, and the Zionist movement. At first the stories were not believed, but the evidence was compelling. Finally, December 15, 1942, several representatives met at a Bermuda Conference to prepare a joint statement for the League of Nations about the German atrocities against the Jews.

Secretary Breckenridge Long, who was in charge of emergency war matters and the refugee problems, knew that many countries were refusing asylum to the fleeing Jews. Long and the others in attendance concluded that a public statement about the Jewish atrocities might cause the Germans to hasten extermination and destruction of any evidence. So other than acknowledge the truth of the rumors, nothing was done.

CHAPTER TWENTY-SIX

All of them trained and skilled in music.
——I Chronicles 25:7

Gerald's Remembrances——
Military Band at
Camp Hulen, Texas——
Fall of 1942

In 1942 all young American men starting at the age of eighteen were required to file with the selective service. When I knew that I might be drafted, I drove Pauline in True Love to Sand Springs to meet my folks. They really liked her!

Once America was in the war, the government commissioned propaganda songs and recruiting efforts. Many war songs were written and aired on the radio. The America Calling posters and songs made a statement of American beliefs and inspirations that boosted the morale of the country and encouraged many men to enlist in the armed services.

I'm sure I was influenced by the popularity and spirit of patriotism, but I did not enlist. Actually, I hoped to avoid being drafted. I was, however, notified by the draft board to show up for an interview in the summer of '42; and was drafted into the army in October of '42. I was stationed very briefly at Fort Sill, Oklahoma, near Lawton.

During the interview process with the draft board, I revealed that I had played the clarinet in grade school, junior high, high school, and some in college. So one of my so-called military occupational specialties was musician, clarinetist.

At that time the military was building up military bands on many posts throughout the country. So all of a sudden, I was on my way from Fort Sill to Camp Hulen, Texas, an AAATC training camp down by Palacios on Matagorda Bay approximately ninety miles southwest of Houston.

Private Gerald Beasley, Camp Hulen, Palacios, TX, 11-11-42.

The commanding officer, Major Betts, was crazy about military bands. He put together a good band. A military band was usually composed of twenty-eight pieces, but the Hulen band had fifty-six pieces, plus attached personnel. The major tried to direct it, but he was not really a musician, so Sergeant Johnson directed for a time. Two warrant officers, trained musicians, also took turns directing.

Shortly after arriving at Camp Hulen, as the troops were standing at attention for inspection, Major Betts walked past all the men but stopped in front of me. He said, "Private, why is one of your shoulders lower than the other?"

I answered, "I don't know, sir!" That was the first time I was made aware of my irregularity.

Pauline remained at Oklahoma A&M. We corresponded. Being apart was not easy! I had left True Love with my folks. Dad drove it some. I left my heart at Oklahoma A&M!

I visited Pauline at Oklahoma A&M on furlough in November '42. The weather was nice so we walked to the park. Guess I was a little nervous as I tried to help Pauline study her Organic Chemistry at a picnic table. I was not thinking of chemistry, at least not that kind, but rather of the

Pauline Smith and Gerald Beasley, Camp Hulen visit

simple engagement ring in my pocket. We had previously talked about marriage, but I couldn't help but wonder if she would really accept my proposal.

"Um, Pauline!" I spoke softly, and gently took her hand.

"Yes!" she answered tentatively as she looked up. She probably knew what was on my mind.

"Would you marry me?" I asked as I held my breath.

"Yes! You know I will." She whispered as she squeezed my hand.

I slipped the sweat-warmed simple golden band on her finger. Forgetting the open book on the picnic table, our lips met in a gentle kiss.

So there in the park with chemistry on our minds, I proposed to Pauline.

After returning to Camp Hulen, I contemplated our future and wrote the following poem about Pauline:

My Gal Sal by Private (Grandpa) Beasley

"I'm in the army now"
Is just a trite expression.
Such simple words, I vow,
Were coined with no discretion.
Five small words can't begin
To designate the fate
Of us who've entered in
This war of greed and hate.
My thoughts are flitting and varied,
Like birds that fly above,
But, always, even when harried,
I'm quickened by memories of—My Gal Sal.

I try to be an optimist,
To see the dark clouds through,
To face, defy, resist
Those things that make me blue.
I realize that I'm just common—
A cornbread country hick.
And I've no right to "put-on"
And fuss, and rave, and kick.
But I'm justified to debate
About something not a myth:
Just who on earth could rate
A maiden to compare with—My Gal Sal?

I'm too dumb to be dramatic,
And why is there the need?
Why should I be fanatic
About what I hear and read.
I'm just a plain buck private,
And I'm not the only one

Who left the old home climate
With all its friends and fun.
I'm not the only khaki-clad
Who eats spuds at every meal,
But I claim to be a lad
Who knows an angel that is real—My Gal Sal.

When my hair's a silvery maze
And my chest is thin and sunk
I'll remember those past days
When I lay in an army bunk.
I'll remember the thoughts I had,
The plans and pledges I made,
And like any true Granddad[*]
I'll proudly raise my head,
For any old man would thrill,
With thoughts of the past unfurled,
To know that his thoughts were still
Of the sweetest girl in the world—My Gal Sal.

It's time for taps right now—That means a "blanket drill,"
But first I want to bow
And pray that God's love fill—My Gal Sal.[**]

We ended up being engaged for almost two years.

---

[*] As of 2012, Gerald had seventeen grandchildren and sixteen great-grandchildren.

[**] *My Gal Sal* was a Twentieth Century-Fox movie made in 1942, based on the biography of songwriter Paul Dresser. Sally (Sal) Elliot, played by Rita Hayworth, was Paul's love interest. Paul, played by Victor Mature, wrote the song "My Gal Sal" and won her heart after a lover's conflict.

While the war was raging in North Africa, Russia, and the Pacific, I was first-chair clarinetist in the military band at Camp Hulen. It wasn't that I didn't appreciate the easygoing life in the band, but I approached Major Betts and explained, "I want to serve in the medical corps."

The major did not want me to leave the band though I kept trying for a transfer. Major Betts raised my rank to corporal to try to appease me, which increased my pay. In other words, he bribed me.

CHAPTER TWENTY-SEVEN

Which I reserve for times of trouble
for days of war and battle.

—Job 38:23

Allied Offensives—1943

The Allies met at the Casablanca Conference January '43 where their previous objectives were changed to (1) prevent further Japanese expansion, (2) provide sufficient forces for an offensive in the Pacific, (3) have General MacArthur's forces seize the northern coast of New Guinea and end the Japanese threat to Australia, and (4) get within striking distance of the Philippines.

In the Central Pacific, the American Admiral Nimitz was to (1) seize Japanese naval and air bases on various islands, (2) draw closer to the Philippines and Japan, (3) avoid direct attacks on large Japanese bases, and (4) gain control of and cut off supply routes to these large Japanese bases.

Nimitz seized New Guinea by January 22, 1943.

Admiral Halsey began to seize the Solomon Islands one by one beginning on February 21, 1943, closing in around the Japanese base at Rabaul, New Britain.

Allied planes spotted a Japanese convoy of twelve troop transports and ten warships moving toward Lea in the Bismarck Sea on March 1, 1943, and destroyed them in three days.

Australian and American Forces seized northern New Guinea by October '43. The island of Bougainville was attacked and an Allied base was established by November 1, 1943, after the Japanese naval force was driven off. No attempt was made to complete conquest of the island.

Then, in December '43 the Allies attacked New Britain Island.

General Krueger advanced toward Japan through the Central Pacific securing Gilbert Island in November '43.

As Operation Torch in North Africa continued into 1943, the British and Americans in Morocco and Algeria pushed east to Tunisia where the Germans were being reinforced by air at Tunis.

Montgomery's forces pushed from Egypt, and Rommel's German forces retreated west through Tripolitania along the northern coast of Libya. Rommel stopped behind the Mareth Line south of Tunis, cut off from General Jurgen von Arnim's German forces. General Omar N. Bradley directed the American forces north and attacked Bizerte.

With Allied forces pushing on all sides, the Germans and Italian troops in Tunisia surrendered on May 12, 1943.

Montgomery's Eighth Army then crossed the Mediterranean and took Catania, Sicily, while General George S. Patton's Seventh United States Army took Palermo. The American and British converged on Messina on August 17, 1943. German forces then retreated to the mainland of Italy.

After the overthrow of Mussolini on July 15, 1943, the new Italian leader Marshal Pietro Badoglio accepted terms of surrender. The Allies drove the German forces back to the Volturno River. Italy then joined the Allies on October 13, 1943.

The Germans continued fighting in Italy until the end of the war.

While the Americans and the British were securing Casablanca and Algeria, the Russians launched a two-pronged drive in November 1942, broke through behind the German lines before Stalingrad, and besieged the Germans.

By February 2, 1943, Field Marshal General von Paulus surrendered the German Sixth Army.

General Field Marshal von Kleist retreated from the Caucasus to Rostov. The Russians made several offensive moves and recaptured Kursk, Rostov, and Kharkov.

The Germans then made a last major offensive on July 5, retaking Kharkov, but were halted July 16 by a Russian counteroffensive that took Orel and Kharkov on August 23. The Russians continued to push and recapture various German holdings along the Dnieper River by September 25. By November, the Germans were pushed back across the river. Russia recaptured Kiev, Ukraine, in November '43.

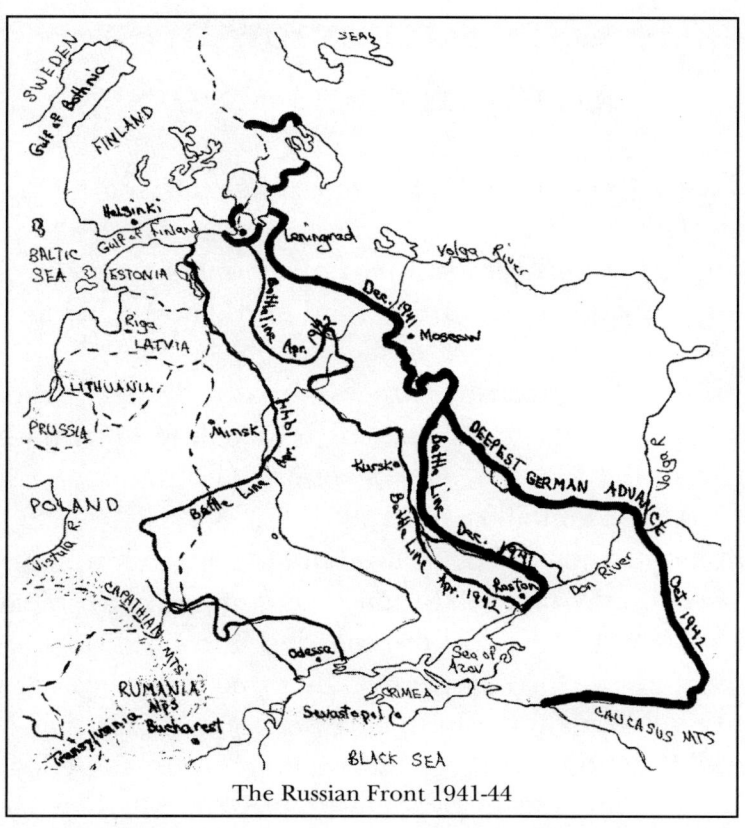

The Russian Front 1941-44

CHAPTER TWENTY-EIGHT

All who were skilled in playing musical instruments.
—2 Chronicles 34:12b

Gerald's Remembrances— Camp Hulen—1943

I knew I had it good at Camp Hulen playing in the Anti Aircraft Artillery Training Center (AAATC) band although I kept requesting to become a part of the medical corps. In the meantime, I kept busy, worked hard and enjoyed being in the band.

During the recruiting process, many draftees who had musical talents and experience were sent to different army bands throughout the U.S. The Camp Hulen band was comprised of musicians from all walks of life.

At Camp Hulen the band lived in little green hutments with three sets of bunks in each hutment. For most of the time, three of the guys in my group were married and lived off the base with their wives. So there were only three guys staying in our cabin. Otherwise, there would have been six. At one time, Mario Camomilli was one of the band members who shared one of those little green huts by the sea with me. He called me Gerry.

For two years the war was getting hotter, but the band was "living the life of Riley." Well, living a life of professional musicians and entertainers. Our hutments were distinctive from all the other hutments. We even had our own dayroom.

The following is an explanation of the expression "living the life of Riley":

The Reilly Coat of Arms with a severed hand originated in 1300s Ireland from the legend that the father of the Reillys told his sons that the one who touched Irish land first got first choice of the countryside. The sons raced their boats toward the shore, but as one of the lads fell behind, he hacked off his own hand, threw it ahead onto the beach and won by a bloodied fist.*

The County Cavan Rileys established their clan and minted their own money. These "O'Reillys" were accepted in England as legal tender, and became synonymous with a "gentlemen freely spending his cash," or "living the life of Reilly."

Then, in the 1880s, Pat Rooney's routine and the song "The Best in the House is none too Good for Reilly" helped epitomize the expression "living the life of Reilly" to depict the lives of barefoot boys loafing and living a life of ease.

The "Life of Riley" was also the title of a radio show in 1943 with Jackie Gleason in the title role, and later, a TV show with William Bendix portraying Riley.**

Two of the former band members, Robert Habercorn and Van Kirkpatrick, made it their project after the war to correspond with the former Hulen band members. They have corresponded with many of them for over fifty years.

Many of the musicians had gone on to become professional musicians in big symphonies, jazz bands, one played with the

---

* www.phrases.org.uk/bulletin_board/17/messages/400.html
** The Life of Riley from Wikipedia, the Free Encyclopedia

New York Philharmonic, one worked on TV writing songs for a children's program, one was a music teacher, and other professions.

Anyhow, in the fall of 2002, Carmen Lewis, my daughter, sent letters to the living AAATC band members asking them to contribute their remembrances. Excerpts from their written responses are included in the telling of the Camp Hulen band experiences.

> Gerald was a good friend and I remember him very well. We did live the "life of Riley" while we were in the band at Camp Hulen, only we didn't realize it at the time. When the bands were broken up and four of us ended up in the 20th Armored Division as medics, we found out just how great those times had been at Hulen.
>
> Speaking of the expression, "living the life of Riley" . . . The outfit next to us used to razz us a lot for the easy life we had, but it did not bother us. Musicians are different.
>
> However, I wondered what they thought when the news came out that our band had out-shot every outfit in Camp Hulen on the Rifle Range.
>
> There was an event that affected all the members of the band. The band always played for retreat each afternoon. Some "higher up" in headquarters came up with the idea of firing a cannon and then playing the National Anthem. Everything went well until the cannon went off. They had put too much powder in it! The result . . . the blast rendered the band "stone deaf"! There we were, trying to play and the band could not hear a thing. I'm sure those listening could hear us grasping for a sound that we couldn't hear. After that, the corrected amount of powder was used. It bothered us no more. (Van E. Kirkpatrick)

Many were the mornings that "old Sergeant Fish" kicked the bedposts so that we could "fall out" to play for the troops marching drill. And that was before breakfast! There were rehearsals, retreats, and, of course, there were also formal concerts, parades and war bond drives. The band played concerts in Houston, Wharton, El Campo, Bay City, and Corpus Christi. We marched in many parades. Many of the band members also had dance band jobs at night at the various USOs. (Mario Camomilli)

It was decided that skits would add another entertaining element to the band programs, so different band members helped write skits for the concerts and shows in Houston and in many surrounding cities. Bob Dorough and I participated by writing

The truck the band rode in on trips

and performing in various skits, and I'm sure there were other writers as well.

I remember several of the skits some of the band members performed as part of the program while the army band traveled about. I, known for being a nondrinker, quiet and reserved, dressed up like a woman, performed "Pistol Packing Momma," and sang about "Drinking beer in a cabaret and dancing with a blond . . . I'll by your reg'lar Daddy . . . Pistol packing Momma, lay that pistol down."*

---

* Lyrics written and composed by Al Dexter, performed by Al Dexter and his Troopers, recorded by Okeh.

Another skit I wrote mimicked Longfellow's "Hiawatha" poem, "By the waters of . . . ," about the legendary Indian leader. I changed the warrior's name to Athleeta Feets and wrote a comical version. I can't recall specifically what I wrote. Tommy Seal narrated while others pantomimed the actions on stage.

Tommy was a trombone player with a good sense of humor. I enjoyed working with him. Once I went to visit him while he was in the hospital. As the nurse entered the room, he asked her, "Friend or enema?"

Christianson and I acting screwy in front of hut at Camp Hulen, 1942-43

I can't remember if the following story was one written for the shows, or if it was a wartime story that circulated around Camp Hulen. I might have written it, but I don't really recall, but over the years, I have often retold the following tale:

> In a remote area some explorers came upon a rather large egg. Though they did not know what was inside, they packed it very carefully, returned home with it and decided to incubate it.
>
> Sure enough, a most unusual creature hatched from the egg. It was a cuddly, lizard-like creature. Quite rare! The finders and the nearby community became quite attached to the gentle creature. Not knowing what it was and not wanting to call it "creature," they named it "Rary" since it was so rare.
>
> Rary had a ravenous appetite and grew rapidly! In fact, it became very, very large! The bigger it became, the more it ate. It became HUGE!

The people began to realize that, though they were much attached to the lovable creature, they did not have the room, or the money, to keep providing food for its insatiable appetite, and they could find no one who would assume responsibility for Rary.

Sorrowfully, they made the decision to get rid of it. Holding back tears, the participants loaded Rary onto a monstrous dump truck, and drove to the Grand Canyon. As the back of the dump truck began to rise and Rary slid over the canyon's edge to its death, one lamenting gentleman spoke through his tears, "It's a long, long way to tip a Rary!"

Of course, the above story is a takeoff from the popular song, "It's a Long Way to Tipperary," which was used as a marching song during World War I, and bands and soldiers also marched to it during World War II.

Refrain:
It's a long way to Tipperary,
It's a long way to go.
It's a long way to Tipperary
To the sweetest girl I know.
Good-bye Piccadilly,
Farewell Leicester Square,
It's a long, long way to Tipperary,
But my heart lies there . . .

1. Up to mighty London came
An Irish lad one day,
All the streets were paved with gold,
So everyone was gay!
Singing songs of Piccadilly,
Strand, and Leicester Square,
'Til Paddy got excited and

He shouted to them there:
Refrain:

2. Paddy wrote a letter
To his Irish Molly O',
Saying, "Should you not receive it
Write and let me know!
If I make mistakes in Spelling,
Molly dear," said he,
"Remember it's the pen, that's bad,
Don't lay the blame on me.
Refrain:

3. Molly wrote a neat reply
To Irish Paddy O',
Saying, "Mike Maloney wants
To marry me, and so
Leave the Strand and Piccadilly,
Or you'll be to blame,
For love has fairly drove me silly,
Hoping you're the same!
Refrain:[*]

Various famous celebrities joined the AAATC band at some
of our rallies and parades.

Gale Storm, who was a leading lady in many 1940
movies and also had a successful singing career, was
with us at one of our rallies and parades. (Howard A.
Olsen)

---

[*]   Lyrics by Jack Judge, Harry Williams, British Music Hall by Florrie
Forde in 1913. public domain.

Some of the members of the band also formed a men's chorus and sang at the band concerts. We were quite good, so we decided to do something special for the president of the United States. We sang and made a recording of Fred Waring's song, "This Is My Country,"* to send to President Roosevelt. Since I was the only bass, they moved me forward to a microphone. But on the first recording, my voice dominated, so the song had to be rerecorded. Anyhow, this time I was moved back a bit. The second recording was sent to the president.

> We did make a recording for the President. One of the fellows, Private Carleton Scales had a good recording outfit. Scales owned a bar and apparently he made pretty good money, which is why he had expensive recording equipment and an expensive cadillac just like the base commander's. Every time Scales entered Camp Hulen, the MP's (mistakenly) saluted him. He never really marched with the band as he was quite heavy and was excused from marching. I think he was excused from a lot of things. (Bob Habercorn)

There was often free time between practices, performances, and parades. A lot of the guys played volleyball to pass time.

> Various guys passed time playing different sports. Berny Sheppard and Gerald played a lot of volleyball together. (Bob Habercorn)

> I remember the volleyball games, as well as, Sergeant Fish and his lackadaisical attitude toward

---

* Lyrics by Don Raye, music by Al Jacobs, performed by the Fred Waring Band, Decca Records in 1940.

"working." It was a wonderful and talented band we were part of. (Berny Shepard)

Camp Hulen periodically published a newsletter. (Clyde Duquette, one of the band members, had saved some of the old clippings and he mailed them to Carmen.) I

AAATC band members playing volleyball
at Camp Hulen

was mentioned several times for various things. The following are excerpts from several of the newsletters:

> Corporal Beasley, one of our clarinetists, is versatile along other lines! Sunday, he presented the exhortation in one of the Palacios churches. His topic: "Theory and Practice." Nice going!

> The other day at the first aid lecture, someone was twisting Stutz's arm so that Beasley, the instructor, would have a "victim" to practice on. Stutz, luckily, got away, so Charles Gibson went "on his face" so that Beasley could give artificial respiration. "Goose Crick" Seale assisted in the demonstration.

I got along real well with the other guys in the band though I was viewed as a serious, conservative, religious person. They respected me, I think. I had a reputation with the other servicemen as a churchgoing, morally upright, tee totaling guy. But they did like to try to trip me up.

There is an incident as clear in my mind today as if it had happened yesterday. It is as follows:

My parents had wired a fair sum of money so that I could return home on leave. The following afternoon I went to shower, got all spruced up and was ready to leave camp, when Gerry entered the hut and handed my wallet to me. Needless to say, I had dropped my wallet in the shower dressing room. It was my good fortune that Gerry found it. Otherwise, I probably could have kissed that money (and my leave) good-bye.

I can truly say this. Gerald was a man of high moral standards, a good Christian and a Good Samaritan; and, obviously a good father! (Mario Camomilli)

In today's ratings, Gerald was a scholar and a gentleman! As a soldier, ideal! Bob Habercorn has told me of things that took place that I was not aware of. As an old married man of 21, I did not sleep in camp very often. But I do recall a flag-lowering ceremony when Gerald saved the band considerable embarrassment.

We had played the National Anthem many times and many places, but once we were in a small town for an evening concert and the Mayor asked the band to play "Retreat" at 5:00 p.m., prior to our 8:00 p.m. concert.

During our short concert, we were asked to lower the flag. The military then and now were to fold the flag in a special manner. As First Sergeant, I was to be in charge. I was afraid we might goof up the folding, so I asked the band if anyone had ever done this. Gerald had. He did his usual great job and I was greatly relieved!

He was a real good clarinet player!

I feel lucky to have known him. (Harlan, HC, Bud Turk)

The most outstanding characteristic about Gerald was his conduct with his fellow soldiers. He always conducted himself on a very high plane as he went about his duties. He was truly a minister of the Gospel. I always enjoyed talking to him. (E. W. Brockman)

Palacios, Texas Church of Christ—1942-44.

While stationed at Camp Hulen, I attended services at the church of Christ in Palacios where I met the preacher, G. L. Mann. G. L. asked me, "Would you like to go out with me to a little town in the hills where I sometimes preach?"

So I went. As we drove, I observed that orange trees had been planted in the area and had somehow survived for a time, but it was apparent that it was not orange-growing country.

At this little town there was a small church that met in an old dilapidated, abandoned, denominational building which had an old wood-burning stove right in the middle of the old auditorium. Some of the windows had been knocked out. It was winter, and it was cold!

As the few members arrived, I especially noticed one particular family as they drove up in an old truck. There were a bunch of kids sitting around the edge of the flat bed truck, obviously a very poor family! They were all barefoot and didn't have on warm clothes! And I was chilly in my winter military garb!

Anyhow, as they came into the building, the dad started a fire in the stove. He kind of got the fire going, but it wasn't going very good. So he just picked up a can of kerosene, opened the door of the stove, and emptied the container. I was ready to take out of the building. The fire did kind of "whoosh," but the stove didn't explode.

The Dad then proceeded to have a children's Bible drill with his kids.

There were others present at the service, but my focus was on this large family. There were so many kids on the edge of that flat bed truck!

When Brother G. L. Mann left Palacios, I volunteered to help the congregation. So I did some preaching while there. Well, I practiced preaching on the brethren.

Tommy and Edith Reed

Tommy Reed, a drummer in the military band was also a member of the church. He spoke some as well. Tommy was a nervous, skinny type of guy. One Sunday morning he got up to preach, or tried to, he all of a sudden took out the side door and had to vomit. It was just nerves.

I believe your dad was very friendly with another preacher, Thomas A. Reed. They did chum around with each other. I did locate Thomas in La Jolla, California, years ago, where he was working as a custodian. He was also a Harvard Grad. He gave up his calling, was disgusted with the religion he had accepted, and was going into some modern, metaphysics or something like that. I believe he had six children. However, I lost track of him. He said he was quitting his job and going elsewhere in California. (Bob Habercorn)

Since Pauline and I didn't get to visit each other very often during the Hulen experience, I wrote often to my Gal Sal.

Anyhow, I was sitting on my bunk one day writing to Pauline when Danny Scott, a little Jewish guy from Perth Amboy, New Jersey (he also played clarinet) came in. With a coke in his hand, he grabbed his stomach, and said, "I just don't feel good."

He set the coke on top of an unheated stove in the middle of the room, got on his bunk groaning and moaning, and said,

Pauline Smith and Gerald Beasley, taken in Palacios, Texas

"Beasley, you better drink that coke! I can't! No point it going to waste! Go ahead and drink it!"

Grateful for the freebee, I picked it up, turned it up for a swallow, and quickly realized that it was heavily spiked with alcohol of some kind. Danny took out the door and ran down the path in front of all the cabins yelling, "Beasley took a drink! Beasley took a drink!" ☺

Danny and I had a lot of fun. Danny was a liberal Jew from a pretty well-to-do family who owned a big dairy. (He told me his brother was a brain surgeon.)

Danny Scott moved to Florida a few years ago and we lost tract of him. There were several Danny Scotts listed in Nat Tel Service living in Florida. (Bob Habercorn)

I knew several Jews in the band. Philip Meyers, a trumpet player, was an Orthodox Jew. He was a real nice guy. I played ping-pong a lot with Phillip and Danny.

I never talked with Phillip and Danny about Jewish persecution. The stories of the atrocities to the Jews in Europe had not yet come to the attention of the general public, or—if stories had been told—Americans simply did not believe them. However, Jews were certainly willing and ready to fight the Germans!

While she was still attending Oklahoma A&M, Pauline came to visit me at Camp Hulen. She met some of my comrades. While in Palacios, she stayed at the home of a couple from the church, George and Lydia Hunter. I would go to their home to be with Pauline.

One evening, I must have stayed quite late because the Hunters had gone to bed. Mr. Hunter came back out later a little upset and invited me to leave.

Mr. and Mrs. George L. Hunter,
Palacios, Texas

I was embarrassed. I should have been more thoughtful, but I just wanted to spend as much time with Pauline as I could.

CHAPTER TWENTY-NINE

Young and old alike, teacher as well as student,
cast lots for their duties.

—1 Chronicles 25:8

Pauline—Novice Teacher in Plainview, Oklahoma

After attending the summer school session of '43 at Oklahoma A&M, I accepted a teaching job with the Mangum Consolidated School District. Clyde L. Suffridge, my former principal from Warren, had become superintendent over the Mangum District. He had contacted me and asked if I would come teach for him in the Brinkman,

Plainview school—1943

Plainview, Willow, Granite, and Mangum area. He remembered me as a good student, and I guess he thought I would be a reliable person.

Plainview teachers—1943-44. From left: Mrs. Nora Paxton, Ms. Pauline Smith, Mrs. Hassie Taylor, Mrs. Dorothy Chambers, and Mrs. Suffridge

Schools in America must have been hard up to find teachers with the men off to fight the war. I did not have a finished a college degree, and I had no teaching experience. I was only nineteen and was a bit nervous and uncertain about my abilities, but Mr. Suffridge assured me that I would do fine and there would be support and help available to me.

I'm sure the war effort influenced my decision to accept the job. Money was an issue, and though Gerald and I were engaged, we didn't know when he might be deployed; so we hadn't set a wedding date. So it was good that I had gainful employment.

I was concerned about finishing my degree, so my plan was to take some correspondence courses during the teaching terms and attend summer classes at Oklahoma A&M.

In Plainview, I taught fifth, sixth, seventh, and eighth grade classes as well as home economics during the '43 and '44 school year.

The school was located in isolated farming country one mile north and then one-and-a-half miles east of the town of Plainview and about twelve miles northwest of Mangum. The ride from Mangum was through farmland and then over rough rocky land with ravines.

Farm children were bussed in from the surrounding area.

My folks' farm near Blair was about twenty-five miles southeast of the Plainview School, certainly too far to walk. So without a car, I was not able to visit the folks much.

I was able to work with Ms. Blackwell, my former home economics teacher from Warren, who had become the Home Demonstration Agent for 4-H. I enjoyed working with her.

The school in Plainview provided a teacherage next to the school building with crude utilities. I cooked on a kerosene-heated stove, stored nonperishables in a pantry, carried water from an outside pump

Plainview teacherage, 1943-44

for baths, dishwashing and cleaning, used the outhouse, had to get a ride to do my wash in town, hung the clothes outside to dry if the weather permitted, and pressed my clothes with irons.

I spent a lot of time preparing for my classes but still felt incompetent, ill-prepared, and incapable as a teacher.

However, I enjoyed getting to know and work with some of the high school girls from Plainview; after all, I was not much older than them. Mabel Ruth Johnson, whose family lived in the area, became a close friend.

Seventh and eighth graders at Plainview, OK, 1943-44
First row left to right: Calvin Rainey, Jimmie Rogers, Hazel Burris, Faye Griffin, Trevey Smith, Donnie Rains, Corral Treadway, ?, ?, Stonewell Second row: Doris Gibbs, Coralie Rains, Lilla Fay Harkins, Winona Fay Hill, Wanda Callen, Jean Taylor, Freddie Barton, ?, ? (unknown) Back row: Harold Sears, Jean Nippert, Jimmie Eastham

It was very lonely out in the boonies when school was not in session and the students were not at the school. The other teachers had families and homes to go to, so I was left alone out in the country at the teacherage. I had the coyotes and wolves to serenade me at night.

The weekends were especially difficult with too much idle time to think about Gerald and feel sorry for myself.

When I wasn't planning and preparing for classes, I spent a lot of time sewing, crocheting, embroidering, reading, listening to the hit songs on the radio, and writing letters to Gerald, friends, and family.

I enjoyed receiving mail from friends and family.

I lived for letters from Gerald.

High School of Plainview, OK, 1943-44
First row, left to right: Georgie Lee Catlett, Helen Rogers, Betty Hamilton
Second row: Sue Culwell, Patricia Johnson, June Hamilton, Ruby Bea
Bradley, Faye Scroggins, Anita Culwell, Crita Faye Snow, Bonnie Eller
Third row: Mabel Ruth Johnson, Joyce Taylor, Delbert Durham, Eugene
Snow, Billy Nippert, Alfred Rogers
Tall guy in back: Joe Dale Hart

CHAPTER THIRTY

The army was going out to its
battle positions shouting the war cry.
—1 Samuel 17:20

European and Pacific Fronts—1944

On January 22, 1944, an Allied landing made up of several nationalities was made at Anzio Italy. Initially, they gained little offensively, but a heavy attack May 11 broke through the German lines. Rome was taken on June 4.

The Germans began retreating, then in the summer of 1944 halted at the Gothic Line, a defense system 150 miles north of Rome. After three months of fighting, the Allies broke the German line.

Mountain fighting against a German line covering Bologna continued through the winter until in the spring, allied forces broke through and spread out over northern Italy. However, the German armies in Italy did not surrender.

On January 15, 1944, the Russians launched a major offensive along the northern front, and by March 3, the German armies had retreated to within Estonia and Latvia.

On March 4, 1944, a Russian offensive in the Ukraine had pushed to the Rumanian frontier before continuing to the border of Czechoslovakia and into the Crimea May 9. The Germans had little hope of holding in Russian territory.

On the Pacific Front, General Krueger (Allies) secured the Marshall Islands in January 1944, putting Truk, one of the Japanese's strongest bases, within bombing range.

By the end of February '44, the Australian and American forces had secured the Green Islands in the northern Solomons and the Admiralty Islands. MacArthur moved along the north coast of New Guinea closer to the Philippines. Rabaul was encircled, sealed off, and out of the war.

Chapter Thirty-One

The elders are gone from the city gate;
the young men have stopped their music.
— Lamentations 5:14

Gerald's Remembrances— Camp Hulen—1944

While the war was raging in Russia, Italy, and the Pacific, the AAATC band at Camp Hulen continued to have an easy life. The army musicians hardly knew that there was a war going on. But that couldn't last forever. Finally, a new commanding officer, a Jewish psychiatrist, addressed the soldiers in the band and said, "Fellows, you don't understand what's going on! You've got to understand more about the military!"

So the band members, who had never even gone through basic training, began pulling guard duty and going through the so-called infiltration course, a frightening experience while crawling on our bellies with real bullets flying over our heads.

Years later through written correspondence, a buddy from the band, Rainer DeIntinis, said that I saved his life while on maneuvers. Apparently, he was standing or his head was up as the bullets were flying. Anyhow, he stated that I pulled him down and prevented him from being shot. I don't remember the incident. I assume he knew what he was talking about.

Van Kirkpatrick and I have kept a good record over the years of the whereabouts of the band boys. DeIntinis says that Gerry saved his life. (Bob Habercorn)

I vaguely remember an incident on the infiltration course when the soldiers were firing the machine gun tracer bullets in our direction. But as to whether Gerry saved DeIntinis's life, I could not say. I would trust DeIntinis to know. DeIntinis and I were very good friends and after the Camp Hulen Band was dissolved, he and I were together in the Band Training Unit at Camp Lee in Petersburg, Virginia.

After the war was over, I visited him in New York where he was playing in the New York Philharmonic. He and his family lived in New Jersey. (E. W. Brockman, Jr.)

Even with the increased training maneuvers, the band members still had time for fun, but sometimes I had a difficult time understanding their humor. It seemed fishy to me. The men had a lot of fun razzing Sergeant Fish as they kept up with his exploits.

Mervin Fish, our drum major, loved to play tricks on Tom Johnson, our director. At one of our band parties, Mervin presented Tom with a nicely-wrapped gift. It contained a large raw soup bone. It was rather embarrassing! (Howard A Olsen)

There was a fellow in the band, Mervin Fish, who had joined an army band in D.C. at the end of the WWI and had been in an army band since. He was in his forties and we called him 'Pop' or 'Dad.' He had a lot of stories to tell and we thought he was very interesting. He could lead the band in marching, or he could stand up in front and use the baton. I know he could play the drums, the peck horn and the saxophone. And he told me he could play any instrument in the band.

I asked him one time how he met his wife and he said he looked in the New York phone book, found a Fish and made the call. Just happened to be a woman! They became acquainted and got married. (Dick Selander)

Sergeant Mervin Fish told the story of a blind date he had with a girl who was supposed to meet him at a certain corner. Well, Merv was on time and waited and waited; but no one showed. What he did not know was that the young lady, Miss Fish, who worked on the base, was checking him out across the street. They did get together later. Fish meets Fish. (Bob Habercorn)

Sergeant Fish visited the church of Christ at Palacios one time. He was a nice guy but ignorant of the scripture. He stated to me, "No one could possibly be as good as you say Jesus was!" He did at least take the time to visit the church. Perhaps, a seed was planted—God would give the increase.

The men made a presentation to Sergeant Fish when it became known that he was going to be a dad. An announcement appeared in the base newsletter. Fish and Fish were going to have a minnow!

T/Sgt. Mervin Fish, who has spent 24 1/2 years of his life in the army, was recently the recipient of a gift by the boys, the occasion being Father's Day. A dedicatory poem, composed for the occasion by Corporal Gerald Beasley, was read preceding the presentation.

DAD FISH

E'en though you're weak in flesh and bone,
And on the flute you got no tone,
E'en though the proverbial fuse you've blown,
We reverence thee, O ancient one!

In your every action and deed,
In every law that you've decreed,
You've taught us your obedient seed
To lie on our bunks and sleep and sleep.

To us you've been the faithful chum.
You've been patient with all—even Lum.
In saddest time—when things are glum
You smile and show each toothless gum.

Often you receive treatment that is wanton.
You're abused and often called Sergeant Johnson,
But dauntless you stand without a weapon
And defy even the bully Rickman.

Oh, venerable one, our aged Dad,
'Tis on this day our hearts are glad
That we see fit to leave the pad
To honor thee, a Sack not sad.*

---

* *Sad Sack* was a carton created by Sgt. George Baker and debuted in the May 1942 issue of *Yank Magazine,* the U.S. Army weekly. The draftee was popular among servicemen and the public. The strip also appeared in the Sunday comics of civilian papers, and was later published as a comic book. Mel Blanc starred as Sad Sack in a short-lived radio show during World War II. Jerry Lewis starred in the movie *The Sad Sack* in 1957.

> We'll ne'er forget the times you've led
> Our ranks through drill and back to bed.
> To thee and Maw, the lass you wed,
> We wish much luck, old hammerhead.

We occasionally had some pretty rough weather that came in from the gulf. In 1943, while the band was still at the Naval Base in Corpus Christi, a hurricane came ashore.

> I was a part of the fifty-six piece military band at Camp Hulen for over two years . . .
>
> My hometown was Corpus Christi, so when the band performed anywhere near Corpus, I stayed at home with my wife. The band marched and performed on the street most of the time. The huts where the band lived were located near the water front in Matagorda Bay.
>
> Once when a hurricane was in the Gulf and as it came ashore, the men stored all their personal belongings at a storehouse near headquarters. The hurricane was not as bad as was expected. (Robert N. Dietz)

> We were stuck in the USO in Corpus Christi for three days sleeping on the floor due to a hurricane. (Howard A. Olsen)

Eventually, the band was busted up and began to disperse. We were "scattered to the four winds"!

> Camp Hulen was practically adjacent to endless marshy rice fields. Due to the location, the soldiers were subjected to extremely hot and mosquito-infested summers. It was, therefore, necessary to sleep under mosquito nets, and we would find ourselves swatting

those nasty insects even during the daylight hours. The summers were so hot that the tropical custom of "siesta time" was adopted at the camp and we would enjoy two to three hours off duty at noontime.

I joined the band at a much later date than the other fellows . . . Not too long after I came on board, half of the members, many of whom had been there from the beginning, had been transferred to other outfits and, looking back, I have a feeling that Gerald may have been one of them . . .

Altogether, there were about sixty musicians in the band before the transfer.

Among my fondest memories of those days was 1) memorizing our music for the parades up Main Street in Houston so that we could concentrate on marching in perfectly straight lines and, thereby, "show up" the popular Ellington Air Force Band, a first rate military band based near Houston and a favorite among local parade-goers; 2) learning the intricacies of music arrangement by studying the arrangements of our very own fellow bandsman, and the very talented Lee Meredith, and, very importantly; 3) having my first exposure to Mexican food, which I have savored ever since.

The expression, "living the life of Riley" hit the nail on the head.

What remained of the band was de-activated and I was transferred to the 13th Armored Division Band. The division was leaving immediately for the war in Europe; we became soldiers first and bandsmen second. I then really appreciated what a carefree experience we had enjoyed at Camp Hulen. (Grant Whisler)

Toward the end, the band members did finally go through basic training before most of them were transferred to Camp

Lee in Virginia, the "collection" place for military musicians. From there, the individual players were sent out to other posts where their skills on an instrument were needed.

> Before my orders were sent out, I stayed at Camp Lee for a while. Thinking I might be sent overseas, I called my wife who came up from Corpus. She stayed for several days. But I got lucky! My orders were to report to Fort Sam Houston in San Antonio, Texas, where I replaced the 1st Sergeant. I lived in Company housing. (Robert N. Dietz)

> After Hulen, several band members were assigned to outfits that were sent to Europe and saw action. Several were captured by the Germans, but none were killed or wounded. Several were affected by the cold weather, were frost bitten, or just plain frozen, which affected their legs. (Bob Habercorn)

At the beginning of the summer of '44, since I was Corporal Beasley, I was put in charge of other soldiers from Camp Hulen as they were being transferred to other bases. As the train traveled through Texas, into Louisiana and New Orleans, and then headed to Mississippi, I corralled and checked to make sure the men got off the train at their assigned posts.

I was transferred to Camp Shelby at Hattiesburg, Mississippi, where I eventually became a part of a medical detachment.

I had been with the AAATC band at Camp Hulen from the fall of '42 until the summer of '44, almost two years. During that time various popular war songs were aired. Among them were "Cleanin' My Rifle—and Dreaming of You" which is about a soldier who misses his girl and cannot wait to see her again; "Hello, Mom" was heard on the home front to help ease a parent's worries about a son who was away at war and to promote the purchase of war bonds; "I Wish That I Could Hide Inside This Letter" was about two lovers separated by war; "On the Old Assembly Line" spoke to the Americans who worked in boring, tedious jobs that helped in the war effort; and "Wonder When My Baby's Coming Home" portrays a girl gazing out of a window dreaming of her loves safe return from war. And many others.

Epilogue to Camp Hulen

Don't rush down to Palacios to see old Camp Hulen! It doesn't exist anymore.

I was band director at Palacios High School from 1965-1974. Word is that the sheet music that was used by the Camp Band ended up at the Palacios High School.

The first thing I did after I settled in was to go out and visit the old camp. What I found was nothing! All the buildings were either sold or destroyed, the streets were overgrown with grass and weeds and nothing remained of the fishing pier that used to be near our mess hall. Time and several hurricanes had cleaned off the entire area, and there was nothing to see.

Palacios today is a thriving city that is the home of the South Texas Nuclear Power Plant, and the homeport for numerous shrimp boats. The schools are good and the people very friendly, but most of them never heard of Camp Hulen, or the fine AAATC band that was stationed there during WWII.

Time passes on . . . (Van E. Kirkpatrick)

CHAPTER THIRTY-TWO

Nevertheless, I will bring health and healing . . .
I will heal my people . . .
—Jeremiah 33:6

Gerald's Remembrances— Camp Shelby—1944

In the early summer of '44, when I first arrived at Camp Shelby, I was put into the infantry. I went to the commanding officer of the company, Captain Austin, and told him, "I registered at the draft board as a conscientious objector, and I requested the medical corps. I've been trying to get into the medical corps all along. I'm not supposed to be in the infantry."

The captain, though sincere, was pretty crude and haughty with his reply. "I'll give you noncombatant duty!"

So he put me on KP duty in the kitchen mopping and washing dishes. I did what I was told. However, the captain's first sergeant had been listening in on the conversation and told me, "He can't do that to you! You can have the captain court-martialed."

Though the captain was a bit rude, he must have thought I was a chicken and a coward. Believe me, later when in the middle of battle in Europe, I was scared plenty of times. However, my conscience would not allow me to agree to bear arms, but I was willing to serve my country. I just wanted to get my assignment corrected and be a medic; my preference was to help wounded soldiers and save lives, not kill my fellowman. I didn't want to cause any trouble or get anybody court-martialed. I did not bring charges against the captain. I just kept submitting my request.

This incident prompted me to write the following poem shortly after arriving at Camp Shelby:

The Dreaded Day

Oftentimes during the quiet of night
I search my mind with a probing light,
And deep in that abyss of thoughts and dreams
I hold a dread of the future it seems.

We privates house this horrible thought
Because we've not been better taught.
We shudder and quake at the dreaded time
When fate deems we must stand in line.

That such as this could come to pass
We'd never realized, but now alas,
We're in this thing, and come what may
We must face that awful day.

What mortal doesn't dread the nearing
Of that day . . . so conscience searing . . .
When he, midst sweat and heat does plea
That the cooks give him a light KP.

(Corporal Gerald Beasley)

Meanwhile, through correspondence, my request for a medical status was straightened out, and I was transferred into the medical detachment.

Captain Austin later became the commander of Company A and was killed in combat.

The commanding officer in the medical detachment was Major Leo Litter, a Jewish obstetrician from Boston. When he said, bottle, he said "baw-l." While studying medicine in Germany, he had experienced the Germans hatred and contempt, and he hated the Germans!

I appreciated Major Litter at Camp Shelby. He would not allow ugly language in the dispensary where the GIs were examined, received medicine, and where records were kept.

While stationed in Hattiesburg, I attended the church of Christ where I met Kyle and Carmen Woods who invited me to Sunday lunch on more than one occasion.

One particularly memorable Sunday, another GI and I were invited to the Woods for lunch. Carmen was busy serving the three men quite a lavish meal that started off with a shrimp cocktail. She was putting on the Ritz!

The topic of discussion somehow turned to focus on black people. All of a sudden there was this big crash from the kitchen as dishes were smashed onto the floor. Carmen had slammed them down in anger. Kyle knew immediately what had happened. In his easygoing deep-south manner, he left the table to talk to her. The guests could hear him speaking calmly, "Honey, you need to go to the bedroom and cool off!"

He returned to explain, "Her family had a plantation and slaves. I think she is trying to accept that the black people have souls, but she has a hard time changing her attitude."

It was an embarrassing situation. She had a temper! Perhaps, Kyle should have cautioned his guests in their conversation, but he didn't. He probably thought it needed to be said. It was clear that he believed that the black folks had souls and were people deserving consideration.

The Woods were nice people! Kyle had a responsible position with the telephone company. He was a graduate of Alabama University where he had played football.

(In 1994, Hoyt, my son, and I went to the Lubbock Christian University Lectureships. One of the speakers was from the Deep South. I visited with him and found out that he knew Carmen Woods. Kyle had died, but Carmen was still living in Hattiesburg. I doubt that she is still living now. She would have to be over one hundred years old.)

I never intended to make fun of anybody on purpose, but after church one Sunday, I rode back to the base in a camp bus with a fella from Kentucky. He was obviously very "country." As we got out of the bus, he turned to shake my hand and said, "Well, I guess this is probably the last time I'll see you."

I took his outstretched hand and asked. "Why is that?"

He stated rather seriously, "Well, I'm being transferred to a 'constipation' camp."

I had to work hard to contain my smile as I didn't want to insult the guy. ☺

Since the Hattiesburg church did not have a preacher at that time, I preached for a while. I would leave the base, come into the church office on Saturday to study, and prepare a sermon to preach on Sunday morning. Saturday nights I slept on a folding canvas cot that I had purchased (bet I still have it stored away somewhere; my philosophy has always been "if it works, don't throw it away") and set up in the study of the little church building. Early Sunday morning I would go to the USO just a couple blocks away to shave and clean up.

The church did eventually hire a preacher so they didn't need me to preach anymore.

As training maneuvers continued and increased, I knew my stay on American soil would soon end. Only a miracle, the ending of the war, would prevent me from being shipped out, and there was no sign that the end of the war was near. The news reported major Allied offensives, and rumors spread that masses of American soldiers were to be sent to the European and Pacific Fronts. I hoped that I would be sent to Europe because I heard that the Japanese had little regard for American lives.

The medical training I received was very limited. I felt ill-prepared, but prayed that God would protect me and enable me to be of assistance on the battlefield to injured comrades when the time came.

Operation Overlord was an historic combination of American and British sea, land, and air forces commanded by General Eisenhower and Air Chief Marshal Tedder of the RAF, deputy commander.

The massive amphibious operation of four thousand ships moved the Allied troops across the English Channel to beaches of Normandy on D-Day, June 6, 1944. Eight hundred guns on eighty warships showered the landings with fire, while eleven thousand planes were in action. Three parachute divisions landed behind the coast to disrupt German defenses. Extensive fighting caused heavy casualties on the Omaha and Utah beaches.

CHAPTER THIRTY-THREE

For this reason a man will leave his father
and mother, and be united to his wife.
And the two will become one flesh.

—Ephesians 5:31

Two Become One—June 1944

Pauline and I had corresponded and discussed getting married before I was to be shipped overseas. So in the first week of June '44 after the spring school session ended, Pauline left Oklahoma by bus and headed to Hattiesburg, Mississippi. The plan was to find a preacher who would marry us, but the plans got messed up!

Probably as a result of what had just happened on the Normandy Beaches, my unit was called up and sent into the Desoto National Forest in Mississippi on maneuvers. Pauline was already on her way, and there was no way of contacting or stopping her. I couldn't even let her know that I would not be there to meet her. So Kyle and Carmen Woods picked her up at the bus station and kept her at their house until the unit returned to the base.

And that was that. The unit had been gone for a little more than a week when it returned Saturday the tenth. I then went into town to get her. We went to a nice park near the church building to discuss plans. We decided to go ahead and get married.

We made arrangements to rent an apartment from a widow. There were apartments everywhere in Hattiesburg, but most were already rented out. People tried to cash in because many

GIs were getting married before shipping out. Chicken coops were even being converted into makeshift apartments. We were lucky to get a decent apartment.

Well, we found out that the church of Christ preacher in Hattiesburg, who was in the process of moving, was out of town. He was probably somewhere looking for another preaching job. Strike one!

Pauline and I wanted to get married the next day, Sunday, so the next morning we impetuously caught a bus to Laurel, Mississippi, a small community not too far away. Early Sunday morning, we found the church building. A neighbor who saw us prowling around the building came over and said, "If you're looking for the preacher, he's gone!" Strike two!

Since it was almost time for morning church to start, we stayed for services and Bible class. An elder of the church invited us grateful young sweethearts over for dinner. (He had a fish market in Laurel, Mississippi, but his wife served chicken.) He said, "If you go to Meridian, you can get the preacher there to marry you."

So we left for Meridian. In Meridian, the church of Christ met in an old southern three-story colonial mansion. Services were conducted downstairs in the dining and living areas where chairs were set up. The preacher's study was on the same level. The preacher and his wife lived upstairs. But nobody was there! Strike three!

It seemed we were out of options. But the game was not over. Since the building was wide open, we went into the study. Looking around in the desk drawer, I found a file box with the members' names. As I thumbed

Mr. and Mrs. Gerald Beasley

through the cards, I pulled one out

and told Pauline, "This will be an older woman who knows everything about everybody." And sure enough, it was!

I called her number, and the lady who answered informed us, "He is in the country preaching. He will be back at six o'clock."

So we played another inning and waited. Sure enough, C. R. Franks and his wife returned just before 6:00 p.m. C. R. tied the knot with a simple ceremony; his wife was a witness.

After a wild goose chase, Pauline and I became husband and wife shortly before 6:00 p.m. on June 18, 1944. We stayed for the six o'clock evening services. Meanwhile, I had phoned the bus station and had found out that a bus to Hattiesburg would leave Meridian before the services were to end at seven o'clock. I told the preacher, "Now, we will have to leave before services are over. It's not because of your preaching. We just have to catch the bus."

Rather than let us sneak out, the preacher paused in the middle of his lesson, looked at his watch, and announced to the congregation, "I have just tied the knot for this nice young couple and they have to leave now to catch a bus back to Hattiesburg." The congregation chorused their congratulations.

A taxi picked us up at the building and took us to the bus station. So after much ado, we returned to Hattiesburg a married couple.

Had we just waited we could have saved ourselves a lot of trouble. The Hattiesburg preacher returned the next day. Ha! Oh well, guess we got to see a little Mississippi countryside.

Besides, I had to be back on the base early the next morning, so it's just as well that we were hitched the day before.

As Mr. and Mrs. Gerald Beasley, we had our picture taken in Hattiesburg shortly after the wedding day. Pauline wore the special wedding outfit that

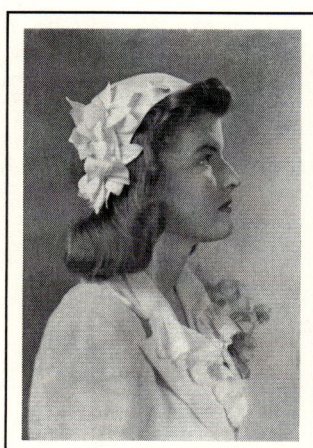

Clara Pauline
Smith Beasley
Picture displayed in
photographer's window

she had made. After the photographer had taken pictures of us together, he requested permission to take some of just Pauline. The photographer didn't request that of me. He enlarged one profile shot of Pauline and displayed it in his window on the street. He didn't display my picture.

Fifteen days after our marriage, I wrote a letter to John, Maggie, and Royce Smith, my in-laws. Maggie kept the letter and years later gave it to Pauline:

> Monday night, July 3
> Dear Folks,
>
> I guess that's kind of a queer greeting, especially from a person you've never seen. I'm sorry that I haven't written you sooner. I know you would like to know me better. I'm hoping we'll soon have the opportunity to meet, and you can see what a worthless husband Pauline has chosen.
>
> Of course, she has talked for hours about Royce, and I'm anxious to know him, too. In fact, I really mean for this letter to be addressed to him, too.
>
> Right now it's kinda warm down here in Mississippi. I'm perspiring as if I were working hard. Pauline and I have just come from town where we found some ice-cold watermelon. Pauline tried to eat the rind, but I took it away from her.
>
> As we were walking down the street, a soldier suddenly pounced on my back. He was an old acquaintance from Camp Hulen. He had met Pauline there, too. He was very talkative, and we must have listened to him for half an hour.
>
> I hear the landlady cuddling her dog. She cares for it like it was a baby.
>
> Every day I'm becoming more convinced that I have the sweetest wife in the world. I want to thank you for rearing such a wonderful girl. We're just as happy as two dead pigs in the sunshine. Of course, we both

realize that we'll have to face some problems together, but I believe, with God's help, we'll continue being happy in spite of hardships.

Mrs. Smith, don't ever stop working! When I was on the farm I used to do a little work, but since I've been in school and in the army, I've almost forgotten what hard work is.

Your cow, Blackie, sounds like one we used to have. I called her "Wild Cow." She always hated me and used to get both hind feet in the bucket every time I tried to milk her.

It hardly seems possible that harvest is nearly over. The summer is getting by in a hurry. I'd like to be feeding a thresher instead of pounding a typewriter.

I spoke last night at the church. I think Pauline was the only one who stayed awake. In fact, she was nearly the only one there.

It looks as if I'll get to be with Pauline all the time she is here because our field problems have been put off until the last part of August and September.

Transportation means are very crowded here. We rode the city bus back from town, and we almost had to use a can-opener to get in and out of the bus. I hitch-hiked from Camp to town this evening and had very good luck. I'll have to try it more often because it is faster than riding a bus.

Well, it's getting late and 4:30 is going to come too soon in the morning. I've given Pauline the job of turning off the alarm because I can't find the thing. I nearly tore the room up trying to turn it off one morning. I'll be glad when I'll have the opportunity of talking with all of you. Running out of space, so . . .

Sincerely,
Gerald

Camp Shelby was a huge camp with thousands of GIs. The GIs had to get up as early as three-thirty in the morning to ride what the GIs called cattle trucks to camp since there were no buses. A truck was hooked to and pulled these trailers with windows and seats out to Camp Shelby.

During the summer of '44, the first couple months of our marriage, the European and Pacific offensives continued. Pauline and I knew it was just a matter of time before I and many others at Camp Shelby would be shipped out.

CHAPTER THIRTY-FOUR

The army was going out
to its battle positions shouting the war cry.
—I Samuel 17:20

European and Pacific Fronts—Summer 1944

The Allied offensive, Operation Overlord, continued as (1) Bradley's American First Army captured the port of Cherbourg on June 27, 1944; (2) Montgomery's British forces took Caen July 9; (3) Patton's Third Army copied the German blitzkrieg through a German gap and cut off four German divisions on the Brittany peninsula; (4) at the same time, General Hodges's First Army and the British Second Army stopped a German attempt to cut off the thrust at Avranches; (5) Patton swung eastward; (6) the British drove toward Falaise capturing one hundred thousand German troops, but many German soldiers escaped toward the Seine; (7) Patton then swung his armored divisions south of Paris taking Mantes along the Seine on August 19; (8) and General Patch's United States Seventh Army invaded from south France near Cannes on August 15, moved up the Rhone Valley, and reached Lyon on September 3.

The Nineteenth German Army was cut off.

The German forces retreated to the Siegfried Line within German borders where their defense was strong.

Flooding, bad weather, and difficulty getting supplies slowed the Allied advance. The First Army took Aachen on October 21, and the

Third Army took Metz on November 20. The Ninth Army broke through the line between the two armies.

The Russians under the command of Marchal Zhukov had opened a counter attack on June 23, 1944, on the German Central Front. The Russians captured Vitebsk, regained Minsk on July 3, and moved near Warsaw by August 1.

During this time 158,000 German troops were captured.

Russian Generals Yseremenko and Maslennikov captured Pskov and Kaunas in the north by August 2.

Toward the end of the war, high-ranking German officers knew the war was going to be lost. They planned and tried to kill Hitler with a time bomb on July 20 but failed. When Hitler found out about the plan, he had thousands of German soldiers killed, many of them innocent.

Germans still occupied Latvia and Estonia.

In August, Russia launched an offensive in Rumania. Rumania signed an armistice on August 23 and then declared war on Germany.

Russia declared war on Bulgaria, so Bulgaria declared war on Germany and signed an armistice with Russia on September 9.

On the Pacific Front, two American movements crossed the Pacific and converged on Japan. Japan's cities were bombed in air attacks that continued throughout the rest of the war. Lieutenant General Smith's Fifth Amphibious Corps attacked Saipan in June, and captured the island by July 9.

Commanded by Admiral Raymond Spruance, the Fifth Fleet won a "turkey shoot" against the Japanese fleet.

Islands steps were made toward the Philippines till July 31.

The Third Amphibious Corps secured Guam in early August.

On August 26, under Halsey's command, carrier planes made strikes against the Philippines, Yap, and the Palau Islands. Before Peleliu was taken, there were many casualties.

The entire Japanese fleet, commanded by Admiral Toyada, was divided into three divisions. Two of the divisions were to converge on Leyte Gulf and oppose the landing of MacArthur's two divisions on Leyte.

Admiral Kinkaid's Seventh Fleet destroyed Vice Admiral Nishimura's Japanese fleet. Vice Admiral Kurita's Japanese force was punished so severely that he withdrew.

Under Vice Admiral Ozawa, the third division with four carriers was used as a decoy. Not realizing that these Japanese carriers were without planes and troops, Admiral Halsey's Third Fleet pursued Ozawa to the north and sank three of their carriers.

The Battle of Leyte Gulf on October 23-26, 1944, decided the outcome of the war with Japan.

Some minor fighting on the China mainland kept the Burma Road closed. These conflicts kept some Japanese troops out of the Pacific fighting. An airline of supplies got to Chinese divisions who were able to extend the Ledo Road so supplies could get into China.

British forces drove the Japanese from India in August 1944.

Using new methods of jungle-fighting and airborne forces, Brigadier General Frank D. Merrill pushed the Japanese forces out of Burma in early 1945.

In late 1944 Franklin Roosevelt was reelected for a fourth term as president of the United States, with Harry S. Truman as his vice president.

PART THREE

Apart From One Another

CHAPTER THIRTY-FIVE

My lover had left; he was gone,
my heart sank at his departure
. . . Tell him I am faint with love.
—Song of Songs 5:6 & 8b

Pauline's Remembrances
Apart from One Another

Gerald and I were able to spend a little more than two months together as a married couple in Hattiesburg, Mississippi, before I had to return, very reluctantly, to Oklahoma in late August to resume teaching for the Mangum School District.

Eastview teacherage in Brinkman, 1944-45

During the 1944-45 school year, I was assigned to teach seventh and eighth grades at the Brinkman School some days; other days, I coached girl's basketball and baseball, and I sponsored the 4-H club at the Eastview School several miles south and west of Brinkman. I was again able to work with Ms. Blackwell, the Home Demonstration Agent for the 4-H in the Mangum District.

This time, I lived in an apartment above the Suffridges at the teacherage in Brinkman.

Mr. Clyde Suffridge was still the superintendent of the schools in the Mangum School District. I had taught with his wife, Burnice, at the Plainview School the previous year.

It was a lonely time for both Gerald and me.

In September, Gerald had a furlough and hitchhiked from Hattiesburg, Mississippi, to Oklahoma to visit me. At Vicksburg, Mississippi, right on the Mississippi River, he caught a ride with two other GIs heading to California and shared gas expenses with them. He rode with them as far as Wichita Falls, Texas. From there he made his way north to Oklahoma for a short visit before returning to Camp Shelby.

In early October when it became apparent that his company was going overseas, I left my teaching job (probably put the school in a bind) and took a bus to Mississippi. Since Gerald had moved back into the barracks, we had to get a different apartment in Hattiesburg.

The words of *"Ten Days with Baby"* heard on the radio epitomized our feelings, and the feelings of thousands of other couples who were to be separated because of the war: "I wouldn't trade my ten days for any amount . . . I'm gonna get ten days of loving!*

I wasn't in Hattiesburg very long when in late October of '44, Gerald's unit was sent by troop train to Camp Kilmer in New Jersey. I remained in Hattiesburg briefly with Kyle and Carmen Woods.

In Madison Square in New York City, the Pepsi Cola Company had a building fitted with telephone booths for GIs to use free of charge for a few minutes. So Gerald called me, and

---

*   *Ten Days with Baby was* composed by James V. Monaco and Mack Gordan, performed by the Merry Macs Orchestra, recorded by Decca Records in 1944, from the film *Sweet and Low Down.*

we discussed my coming up from Mississippi to New Jersey; but decided it wouldn't be smart for me to pay the expense knowing he wouldn't be there very long. And of course, he wasn't. In about two weeks, his unit boarded ship November 15, 1944, and convoyed across to England.

I went back to Brinkman to the same teaching job. I was very forlorn, and I know he felt alone and empty too. We were both fearful that we might not see each other again. It had been a lonely courtship as we had been apart during most of our two-year engagement. Now, Gerald would be overseas for a long stay. Lord willing, he would come back!

Many marriages had taken place as the men were waiting to be sent to fight in the war. Many husbands would not return! Many marriages would not survive! But I knew that Gerald would be faithful. I would be faithful and wait. I prayed that God would keep both of us safe and return him to his family and wife.

CHAPTER THIRTY-SIX

May the Lord keep watch between you and me
when we are away from each other.
—Genesis 31:49

Gerald's Remembrances— Somewhere on the Atlantic

President Roosevelt had been sending conveys of supplies to the Allies for sometime; many American troops had already been shipped over and had been engaged in the various battles. But on November 15, 1944, I was among the troops that left New York City on the SS Leif Ericson, a pleasure boat that had been turned into a troop ship. For twelve days the convoy of supplies, troops, and battleships zigzagged across the Atlantic to avoid enemy submarines.

I don't remember if Pauline and I had agreed by design or whether it was a coincidence; but after our separation, Pauline started a diary, and I began a journal. Pauline wrote brief statements about her daily life—what she did and how she felt. In my journal, I philosophized about various things as I made observations of my comrades and viewed the war situations I found myself in. Thoughts from my journal and excerpts from her diary are included in italics.

From: Property of T/S Gerald Beasley 38319244, U.S. Army
An un-dated diary of my thoughts from time to time—begun
somewhere on the Atlantic:
Thoughts

> *For no definite length of time have I thought of penning*
> *my occasional thoughts which, I trust, are guided by the Word*
> *of God. Perhaps, God willing, there shall come a day when*
> *I, pursuing the noblest profession, shall profit by reading my*
> *past musings. Admittedly an unwilling military soldier, I*
> *am prone to pass much time daydreaming—thinking joyfully*
> *of the time when I can whole-heartedly engage in teaching*
> *man something which his very nature demands, but which he*
> *himself rejects. I'm acutely aware now of my inability and lack*
> *of preparedness to thoroughly and capably instruct wayward*
> *men in the business of saving souls; and I'm sure, at the same*
> *time, that the way of salvation is fantastically simple.*
>
> *It is difficult to approach men concerning their eternal*
> *destiny. This statement I make hesitantly lest it seem my excuse*
> *for my lack of usefulness in God's Kingdom. Many, many*
> *questions of life do I ponder! The answers seem vague until*
> *answered in a Gospel light. Then the Word of God must take*
> *precedence! Its truths are final and supreme! No doubting*
> *and reasoning of men can bear any significance in the light of*
> *Christ's teachings. His teachings are not philosophical. Their*
> *substance is, "Yea, yea!" and "nay, nay!"*

While on board the SS *Leif Ericson* ship, I had some regimented
activities and duties but very few. There was a lot of idol time, so
I wrote brief descriptive statements about my surroundings and
events:

> *The men ate chow at the dining room at a scheduled*
> *time. They could purchase soda, cookies, snacks, etc., near the*
> *empty swimming pool. Lots of men got seasick. Once after I*

came back from buying a cookie, I could not eat it. I just could
not stomach it.

The men slept in hammocks that were close together. The
weight of the man in the hammock above would sag down
pretty close to the belly of the man in the hammock below.

There was too much idle time! The men thought about
Mom's apple pie, the girl(s) back home and the pleasures left
behind; as well as the unknown future that held only fear,
anxiety and uncertainty. Because of the boredom, the men
indulged in gambling and other sundry busyness.

Observing my compatriots, I knew that the circumstance
of war that the men found themselves in contributed to their
base behaviors, but I could not condone many of the actions or
the language of many of the soldiers. Many seemed to decide
to indulge in satisfying their basic fleshly cravings since they
assumed they would be dying soon anyway. Perhaps, I was too
judgmental.

Man has thought for centuries that war justifies and/or
explains base and immoral behaviors during war. I can't agree
with that. I'm sure that many would have considered me to be
self-righteous had I spoken freely then about how I felt. I know
I was naïve, idealistic, serious, and conservative; but it was still
hard for me to accept that others did not hold to my sense of
rightness. I really did not wish to pass judgment, but I did see
the condition of the lost souls all around me. Since I wanted
someday to become a minister in God's Kingdom, I could not
bend or ignore the truths taught in the Bible.

I should be ashamed to try to excuse the evil that proceeds
from the mouths of my companions. No reasoning can modify
the awfulness of their sin! Their adulterous tongues cannot
sing the praises of God acceptably! It is that from within which
defiles the man. Is man too reliant on God's mercy?

It seems obvious in the light of God's Word that false teachings have entered into preachers who figuratively make broad their phylacteries. Intelligent men, prospective preachers, surely must ignore Gospel truths in helping man advance headlong into the abyss while taking his proffered contributions.

Military soldiers are saying that there is a set time for them to die, anyhow—a statement conceivably born of their desires to claim every evil indulgence before their earthly stay is done.

I tried to spend my free-time constructively by writing to "My Gal Sal," writing in my journal, reading the Bible and praying. I spent a lot of time reading the Bible!

I missed his wife, family and the easygoing fun of a war-free environment.

I tried to forget where I was headed, what could happen to me and what kind of horribleness I might become a part of.

Sometimes I felt terribly alone that no other compatriot felt the way I did!

God was my companion!

How refreshing it is to ponder a deed or thought which is clarified and substantiated by plain Bible teaching! For a while it seems that no one is on your side—then, there is God! What accomplishment there is in re-reading many times those precious truths and gleaning new valuables each time!

At times I am pretty proud of myself. Those times are when I evidently better my mind and become intellectually more capable of understanding men and how to approach them. It is fascinating to read even profane history and realize the bloodshed there has been over religion. I am sad because I didn't see fit years ago to avail myself of the most important information in the world and become informed in

*things spiritual (not supernatural). I must not fret, though,
because I am still young. I almost hesitate to see opportunity
at every turn, but it must be there! "The fields are white for
the harvest!" Even now I write carefully on a swaying sea
vessel amid an environment that is abnormal and revolting.
The consolation is that endurance and faithfulness to God
will surely bring reward. It must be profitable, too, to have a
thorough understanding of human nature. That I'm gaining,
I believe.*

When I wasn't tuned to the Word of God for consolation, I
observed my comrades dealing with their fear and uncertainty
by indulging in worldly pleasures while forsaking their better
nature. I often questioned what I should do and how I should
feel.

*Penning vivid descriptions and examples of the evil that
man knows and practices would defile the cheap paper on
which this is written. My personal opinion is that many men,
so cleverly wicked, would be, indeed, talented workers in God's
Kingdom if they could only see the light.*

*Historical facts indicate that religious freedom and the
open Bible are now gloriously abundant, but in our nation, the
Saturday night and weekend complexes have encroached upon
the Lords' Day and worship services. Our men, presuming
themselves free, are selling themselves by the installment plan
to the evil one. The open Bible that first inspired men to seek
freedom has been forgotten. How carelessly and foolishly men
mimic ministers and quote Holy writ in disgusting jest. Surely
my indignation against these evil tongues is justified.*

*Sometimes, when my indignation is not aroused, I think
that perhaps my opinion of the men is a little too severe and
accusing. But what would Christ say? Would not he upbraid
and ridicule?*

The men are living unnatural lives and they are under constant tension, but I can't apologize for them; nor can anyone else. The demands of God's Word are not flexible. Whether in a troopship or in his front parlor, the man's tongue drips that which springs from the heart.

The farther I got from home and the closer I got to the battles of war, the more sure and confident I was that I was going to dedicate my life to teaching God's Word and following God's will for my life, even if it should lead to death. I prayed for strength, self-control, and a steadfast will to obey God's commands.

These times are abnormal for me and wonderful is the consolation I get from meditating upon and studying God's Word! I pray through God, our Savior, that I shall ever love and cherish God's Word even when my earthly joys are fullest—and there have already been many times when I've thought my happiness unequaled! I thank God for those glorious times! Always when I pray I seem to first think to ask God's blessings upon my loving wife. God has heard my repeated thanks for her. If it be God's will that I return to her and to my other loved ones, I am seriously convinced that no other man on earth will be happier than I. I believe seriously that no other man has greater motive for living than I. Nevertheless, I pray that I may be prepared to meet my God at all times. I want to know an increasing anticipation of Heaven, which holds joys so unspeakable; man is left endlessly imagining possible glories of the New Jerusalem.

I had never really wanted to be a soldier. When I was drafted, I had signed on as a conscientious objector obeying the laws of the land, willing to serve my country as a medic helping men, but unwilling to bear arms. "Thou shalt not kill!" was to me a literal command, and my conscience would not allow me to place myself in a situation where the use of a gun against any man might be required. I found myself in a place I did not wish to be, heading for a war I did not start, and really did not wish to be a part of.

I believe I can truthfully say that I have talents and abilities which suit me for ministering in God's vineyard. How contrasting and wonderful is that work compared to my present occupation.

Certainly very few of my present associates enjoy their present duties, but none of the dissatisfied majority can know the revolt that is constantly in my heart.

Even if I were of the same mind as my associates, I would naturally prefer my home life. Am I unfair in believing that I have greater motive for forsaking military life?—Not that I anticipate AWOL. As a student and follower of God's Word, I am sure I cannot be mentally and socially militarized. It seems to me I have no ambition to advance my position in the army. I prefer to remain passive. However, I believe I perform most of my duties efficiently. I abhor regimentation, but realize the necessity in running an army. Army efficiency is famous, but its faults are multitudinous. Nothing more can be expected of an organization that is entirely human.

Wondrous are many of the works of man, but how could this vessel float without an ocean? Who created the men who accomplish wonders?

If I were to orally explain my attitude to many of my present associates, my discourse would be considered "bleeding"' and I would probably be offered a towel on which to "dry my tears." I'm not persecuted, I think, nor am I a so-called psycho-neurotic, but I'm dissatisfied. I positively cannot adjust myself because it would be necessary to forsake some of the principles of Christ to become a true military soldier. I'm convinced no Christian should enter into military service. This attitude has provoked many lengthy arguments, but the Kingdom of Christ must perform its own functions. Its members must regard its noble purposes. Christians are a peculiar people! As long as they are diligently pursuing God's work they will not be ostracized. On second thought, that could be untrue. Even so, being merely ostracized cannot compare with indescribable persecutions suffered by martyrs of ages past. Happy indeed, is my estate when I think of the situation of the compassionate Stephen—praying, and facing the biting, killing stones! And what of Christ? Yes, how thankful I can be!

My comrades, though likable, were in need of the salvation that God offers; but did they want it? What would they have said and done if I had tried to talk to them? Perhaps, I should have spoken boldly. Mostly, I prayed that I would live my life and they would see Christ in me. If they asked about why and how I could refrain from temptations, I would try my best to explain.

Many of these boys are kindhearted and good-natured. They even suspect that they are regarded as "good guys." Can they lack something? Pathetically, they do lack something. Even Cornelius lacked something. It is not my idea that man should obey God's precepts.

I am convinced, though, that God is a jealous God. A fact that too many will realize too late. Is that my opinion too? What kind of appeal must be made to man? I just heard a soldier say that he threw his conscience away when he came into the army. "God is not willing that any should perish." The soldier threw his conscience away; God didn't.

Unwillingly, I hear raucous, false voices bragging, consenting, cursing, and conversing in a horribly unholy manner. To speak to them Words of Wisdom is akin to "casting pearls before swine." That's not my idea. It is not mine to formulate such expressions—so universally applicable. It is childish to say, "I told you so." But surely many, agonizing in the depths of hell, will sense that, perhaps, someone is saying, "I told you so." The rich man did a lot of thinking, didn't he? And that was only a small part of his discomfort. "Discomfort" is a gentle word.

As the convoy drew closer to England, enemy submarines were detected. Ashcans with explosives were dumped off the ships into the water where they sank and exploded, hopefully, damaging or eliminating the enemy submarines. The men on board were tense and alert, fearful that the ship might be torpedoed. Many quiet prayers were spoken during this time, and not just by me, I am sure.

Guiltily, I resume my writing; several days have passed since last I penned a paragraph hereon. If I thought an excuse justifiable, I might say I have been too busy. But does it take long to write a few lines? At present I am tired physically and mentally. I'm sure of that! My state is such that I might go to sleep while praying if I didn't constantly remind myself that I'm talking to God. Would I go to sleep talking to my commanding officer? Many Christians will ashamedly acknowledge that they go to sleep while praying to God at night.

After twelve days at sea the convoy arrived safely at Southampton, England, on November 26, 1944. It was humid and chilly as the troops debarked and then traveled northeast by train and/or truck to Winchester.

CHAPTER THIRTY-SEVEN

A prudent man keeps his knowledge to himself,
but the heart of fools blurts out folly.
—Proverbs 12:23

Gerald's Remembrances—
Winchester, England—
December 1944

My company was stationed at Winchester, England, the ancient and historic capitol of England. The rubble of an ancient wall could still be seen around the city. Winchester Cathedral was located there. Legend says that King Arthur's roundtable was once located in Winchester.

While in Winchester, my company stayed for a while at an old all-boy's school; the building where we were housed was a two-story building. Other soldiers had occupied these barracks before us, but as they shipped out and the barracks were vacated, the newly arrived soldiers settled in. Somehow while bunked there, this building caught on fire, but it was put out quickly before there was much damage.

Anyhow, we stayed in the ancient army barracks heated by great big ancient fireplaces. The beds were crude with straw-filled mattresses. The USO was a few blocks away where off duty soldiers could go, especially in the evenings, to play ping-pong, to drink cokes, and to find some entertain.

As the troops set foot on English soil, with nothing constructive to occupy their time, their behavior didn't get any better. Civilization offered them pleasures of the flesh that hadn't been available on the ship. I wrote:

> *This finds me in England. In the street outside, inebriated soldiers are noisily singing and silly women are "being led captive." I grit my teeth and clinch my fist and shake my head—not like a sageful presbyter, but like any Christian who studies God's Word and learns therein the answer to every human need.*
>
> *I pray that my wife and I may never desire salaries and worldly gain. We want a home, not a place to sleep after a round of indulgences in the dens of evil. My room at present is shabby and crude. My mattress is straw. My Lord had no place to stay! Who am I to expect every comfort?*

The usual hope and cheer and goodness of the impending Christmas holiday were contrasted by the fear and anticipation of the fighting just across the English Channel. Many tried to assuage their fears by participating in fleshly evils, but quietly and alone, I continued to write down my thoughts:

> *Another day and it seems my associates are no more righteous. Several minutes ago I heard a soldier give a bitter, loathing denunciation of prohibitionists. So sincere was he in assailing dry citizens, it seemed Satan himself must surely have schooled him in word usage and phrasing. This individual, however, has not received exclusive schooling. His vocabulary is shared by thousands of others. I cannot quote just now, but I do recall that George Washington denounced profanity and his famous statement is publicly posted in*

many military buildings. Am I just acting, or do I sincerely abhor my environmental language so much that I shudder and become tense when I think of it?*

"Sometimes I try to examine myself to see if I am thoroughly sincere in my agonizing convictions. I do know that those convictions are convictions about which I should be sincere.*

I hear distorted strains of "Silent Night" coming from drunken lips. What can the heavenly host think of that?

There had been no church services offered on the ship that I knew about, and I did not know where to go in England. I really missed meeting with other Christians of like-mindedness. I needed the encouragement! However, in my backpack I always carried my Bible, a hymnal that my mother had sent me, and my own "bread and fruit of the vine" for communion. I carried these even as I traipsed across Europe into Germany. Most of the time, I had my own silent devotional and communion services. Occasional I was able to meet and commune with other Christians.

I remember one such soldier who gave me hope of such fellowship.

Another Lord's Day has passed. I was angry this morning because I was suddenly put to work. At that moment I was anticipating a day of rest. May God forgive me for that spell of anger! It hurt my reputation and was surely unpleasant to God. I didn't partake of the Lord's Supper. I must avail myself of the opportunities and constituents.

---

* "The foolish and wicked practice of profane cursing and swearing is a vice so mean and low that every person of sense and character detests and despises it." Quote by *George Washington*, *http://www.brainyquote. com/quotes/quotes/g/georgewash146833.html#9MmTZm0lZeqIsOOS. 99*

I have been pleased to make the acquaintance of a soldier who is singularly conspicuous because of his good nature. Further revealing is the fact that his father is a Christian. Surely it is an opportunity to lead the soldier to Christ. He does study and think upon the subject and is prompted and instructed by an interested Christian uncle.

I do not do enough individual work (for God). I desire to become well-informed so I can better cope with Satan's arguments. I must not let that attitude interfere with my personal work though, because, realizing my own inabilities, I might never feel fully capable of approaching individuals concerning their soul's salvation. The Gospel story is simple. I should make a more valiant effort.

While in England, there was just too much idle time. There were only a few regimented duties and way too much time to think of home and loved ones. Idleness bred unsavory thoughts and discontent. I expressed my unhappiness in my journal:

Tonight I don't seem to find anything to write about. I can't flatter myself into believing that I can think of a subject and write extemporaneously upon it. To believe that would put me in the same class as men who rely upon their own intellect and whims and fancies in doping out philosophies which reek of ungodliness.

I think I find it hard to be meek and passive, and often I'm not sure about the proper time to speak up concerning my own rights and welfare. I'm sure I gossip too much and express too many opinions about other men. I have a lot to learn.

I actually believe my abilities aren't recognized, and oftentimes I think I'm not given a chance. Perhaps, too, I'm guilty of thinking that I am more intelligent and efficient than some of my military superiors. I must prevent myself assuming a persecuted attitude.

I heard a high-ranking army psychiatrist state that the beer-guzzling soldier was the most proficient in his profession. Probably that is true because the beer-guzzlers are so greatly in the majority and their thoughts and actions are kindred. The non-beer-guzzler has two strikes against him.

Military life offers little privacy. My every thought seems interrupted.

There was some free-time to walk around and visit historic places in Winchester. I went sightseeing when I could and used this time to think, walk, and relax; it helped to lift my gloomy outlook. So after some reflection, prayer, and Bible reading, I wrote:

Another day, the gift of God! I have rather enjoyed reading what I have previously written. Strangely enough, I agree with everything I've written. I can write confidently when I adhere to scriptural thoughts.

There wasn't much for me and others in our waiting unit to do while in Winchester; and sitting around got to be pretty boring. So some in the Medical Corp, including myself, volunteered to go to the hospitals and help. Many GIs gave blood, which was used to treat cases of shock to help build the blood pressure back up when a wounded GI had lost a lot of blood. A lot of lives were saved with our blood. The volunteers also mopped floors and helped to attend to the wounded.

Earlier in the war after France had been taken, Germany started a big rocket building campaign on the northwest coast of France and began shooting V-1, and later the more sophisticated V-2 rockets across the channel at England. Many of the rockets made it across. The Germans also dropped bombs from airplanes.

In early December while in London on a pass from Winchester, I was staying in a Red Cross building. When an explosion was heard from a distance, an English charwoman cringed and fearfully remarked, "Oh, those bombs! They keep getting closer! One of them is going to hit this building!"

Of course, it was not a bomb but a rocket. There was a lot of damage in London, but Winchester was far enough away to avoid getting bombed. However, Winchester was blacked out at night because of the bombings from the Germans off the French coast.

After returning to Winchester, once again I quietly observed my comrades occupy their time in empty pursuits. I remembered what my Dad had said about gambling and guarded against allowing myself to participate in their activities:

> *In my presence now dice games are being played. The game is typically GI. It is popular. Men are drawn into the game and the habit is quickly formed. In the eyes of the men the widespread popularity of the evil nullifies any objections raised.*
>
> *Just a few nights ago I wrote about an individual who was conspicuous because of his former Christian environment. Imagine my disappointment, disgust and pity when he came in late the same night—an inebriate. He had been encouraged to drink and his associates were hilarious in their accomplishment. He was ridiculed, tormented, laughed at, and it was suggested his wife should hear of it. His replies were those typical of an inebriate—disgustingly amusing. Finally the laughter subsided and a few boys consoled him, "That's all right, boy. You were just being sociable."*
>
> *I supposedly slept. Probably observing that I was not partaking of the hilarity, one soldier declared, "When I see Beasley coming in like that, I will have seen everything!"*
>
> *The intoxicated one said, in my defense, "No, he'll never do it! He has too much will power!"*
>
> *I have not myself to thank for what will power I may have.*

I am reminded of the following scripture: "A righteous man is cautious in friendship, but the way of the wicked leads them astray" (Proverbs 12:29).

Many soldiers did have altruistic concerns and filled their time with constructive activities as they waited for the inevitable—battles of war that they would soon be involved in.

My battle was also with spiritual matters. Often I felt alone and peculiarly different. I was even approached and a suggestion was made that I should lighten up; I should forget my resolve to remain Godly and enjoy life while I had it. It wasn't that I was never tempted, but I could not turn my back on God and His Word! If I was harsh in my judgments as a young man, it was because of concern for the souls of my comrades. I was confident I was better off than they were.

> *Have I mentioned that a soldier informed me that I had been part of the topic of conversation at a nightly "roundtable"? He mentioned that I was pretty well regarded, but that constructive criticism had been mentioned. I can easily imagine (Am I too presumptive?) their discussion and suggestions.*
>
> *Americans are traditionally freedom-loving and opposed to regimentation. My Gospel knowledge deepens my feeling in both instances, but the human error in the army has provoked my feeling to a loathing of the organization in general. It produces such gregarious lewdness! If only my associates were nobler and cleaner-minded! Better still, if only I could perform my duties and live separated from the masses of military personnel!*
>
> *I am a peculiar person after Peter's teaching. I'm not queer though. I possess gregarious instincts, but those instincts are defeated when the crowd is evil. I thank God when I can meet with Christian groups!*
>
> *When I was a civilian my landlord, detecting my "narrow-mindedness" (I acknowledge and defend it),*

approached me and quite voluntarily explained that he, too, had been religiously strict when a young man. He finally had military experience and thereby, learned "broad-mindedness." That is his story, briefly told.

I'm not stubborn in my position. I'm just sure of it! I don't say that with forced determination. Two plus two equals four. I'm sure of that. The parallel doesn't indicate that my Bible knowledge equals my mathematical knowledge. I will ever learn from God's Word!

I can look at each man in the room with me and know that each individual has a soul. It is even possible, I think, to detect character traits by individual appearance. One soldier is rolling the dice. His face is rather expressionless, a cigarette dangles from his lips and he mumbles incoherently to the dice. Very audibly he renders occasional expressions of delight and disgust. Both attitudes seem to warrant blasphemous remarks. The soldier is young, but his soul is surely seared. It is aged and sin-worn.

The days passed slowly. Sometimes I expostulated on things as they tangled in front of me. I have to admit that sometimes I grumbled about my circumstances.

A later date at midnight: Due to crowded quarters and disregard for common principles of courtesy, a pair of feet is hanging in my face. Feet are crude and ugly possessions, but their value is un-named. Christ and the early disciples traveled on their feet. They performed God's Work with all legitimate conveniences at their command. There are many conveniences now for propagating the Gospel, but have I even used my feet yet? It is late and I am tired.

The change in climate, the cold, and the crude heating in the old building had its effect as fatigue and illness began to wear on me. I caught a cold. Even then there was opportunity to glory in God and his creation.

A later date: If I wrote everything I thought I'd probably have writer's cramp. Sometimes, I think I think too much about my own disappointments, and I'm sure that at times my imaginings are absurd. I seem to be capable (asset or liability?) of thinking with movie reel rapidity on a variety of subjects.

Perhaps this description fits every man. Man is a wonderful being! Physically he is wonderful! At present I feel rather stale and tired because disease organisms are tampering with my physical body. Brilliant minds have proven the organisms exist. Medical men with whom I associate have an almost alarming knowledge of the anatomical and physiological intricacies of the human body. Physical beings are tangible and it is only proper that men with God-given intelligence and reasoning should vastly increase their knowledge of everything about them. Every time I learn a fact associated with my physical self and surroundings I want to realize that God can be thanked for providing the fact and the intelligence to understand the fact.

It is most gratifying to realize that God has left unrevealed, and tangible and recognizable evidences of a hereafter. Trusting in His promises brings the deepest consolation when earthly blessings are so beautiful and enjoyable. I anticipate returning to my loved ones and pursuing God's Work. I also anticipate Heaven and its wonders. Sometimes, I'm even guilty of wondering how heaven could be more wonderful than some earthly joys I have had and now anticipate.

Each day I pray that God will permit me to return to my beloved wife and other loved ones, that my wife and I may devote our every ability to his work. Some might think my attitude was, "Please God, spare my life and I'll repay you." But God knows my heart. I want so much to return! That indeed is a sentiment echoed by millions. May not a Christian cease praying acceptably? May not a single Christian forget to ask God, "Nevertheless, thy will, not mine, be done?" Even when we say this in our prayers, we may not actually be willing that God's will be done. We may be anticipating that God will do what we want him to do, and we won't be prepared for a seeming disappointment—something that was God's will! If Christians are truly willing that God's will be done, ultimately His will will bring us into an eternal home of bliss.

Was it Solomon who wrote, in substance, "A wise man changes his mind"? When I was younger, I thought I adhered to this saying, but there have been times when I have suddenly realized that I had been holding doggedly to a wrong opinion for years. Even now I am probably clinging to assumptions which will endure, then suddenly change in the light of God's Word. In many ways, I'll learn how to be more pleasing to God and more effectual among mankind. I want to realize my obligation to God and man, being ever concerned about every man's soul.

Too much boredom! Too much idleness! I wasn't any different from the other soldiers who preferred to be home in America. I could have claimed total conscientious objector status and been exempted from serving. Had I let the patriotic propaganda influence me? I'm sure I wasn't the only soldier who had second thoughts about involvement in military service.

I did know that my first concern was my duty in service to God.

A later date: I find I'm increasingly cynical and complaining. I'm convinced I have reason to complain, but I'm sure I don't express myself in a tactful, Christian manner.

Obviously, I have permitted myself to become a part of a huge human organization—an organization that produces customs, traditions, and habits, which make a popular appeal. Individuality is largely stymied and each soldier seems obligated to submit himself to that which he feels has been submitted to by millions of others.

Ignorantly, I believe I was once influenced by the popularity of the army. It is not popular to be an out-and-out conscientious objector. Was I afraid I'd be unpopular?

Even now I have a tendency to say to myself, "Aw, quit your bleeding and resolve to take things, uncomplainingly, as they are." If I did that it might indicate my approval of everything that takes place!

I recall the early disciples "turned the world upside down." Did they do it by "taking things as they are"? Yes, I am hampered to the point that I can hardly do my share of turning the world upside down. Perhaps, I've not taken advantage of all the opportunities I've had to be engaged completely in the Lord's work. In fact, I know that to be the case.

On December 16, 1944, the Battle of the Bulge began, just across the English Channel. The German General Rundstedt struck through the Ardennes Forest in Belgium making a fifty-mile advance through the Allied lines, threatening Allied supplies. The 101st Airborne Division was surrounded. When the German general asked the American Brigadier General Anthony McAuliffe if he wanted to surrender, McAuliffe replied, "Nuts!" Word of his response spread to soldiers in England and Europe. The American troops got a good laugh and morale boost as the story of General McAuliffe's reply was retold.

The Battle of the Bulge was a terrible battle with a lot of casualties. Many of the casualties and the injured were flown or shipped across the channel to England to the many military hospitals in the area. During the days that followed the battle, I and other medical personnel continued to volunteer as the wounded were brought across the channel to the military hospitals. I believe our efforts blessed those injured and dying soldiers and I am reminded of the following scripture: "A generous man will prosper; he who refreshes others will himself be refreshed" (Proverbs 11:25).

I saw all kinds of wounds, and I saw many GIs that looked like they weren't going to make it and probably didn't. Some of the amputees were very cheerful, and some were very down in the dumps. Many of the wounded were from the Battle of the Bulge, but there were wounded from other battles.

My observations and involvement at the hospitals gave me a different perspective.

> *Another day: In a gathering place I am observing soldiers and thinking of the sacrifices they are making. Don't all of them desire to be "home" where happiness and comfort are most exhilarating to their thoughts?*
>
> *Even as I think of the sacrifices the men are making, I permit a scandalous thought to enter my mind. Do our fighting men seek to sustain freedom of religion and worship, or do they want to preserve an America that boasts of sundry entertainments, which provide nightly fulfillment of fleshly lusts?*
>
> *I almost reprimand myself as I pen these accusing lines, but can I say they are untrue? May God forgive me and may I be readily corrected if my skepticism is unwarranted.*
>
> *Admirable, indeed, is the courage of young men who are giving their lives against the nation's enemy.*

It didn't seem much like Christmas! The sky was not lit by sparkling stars of hope but rather by rockets flying across from the enemies' shore and by explosions lighting up the land and ripping up homes and buildings! Some green trees were colorfully decorated, but red blood was being spilled and splattered! Men were being killed and deformed by other men! There was no sumptuous Christmas dinner! Food was scarce! Everything was rationed. Peace on earth and goodwill toward men? It was the Eve of Christmas 1944.

But in the spirit of Christmas, some of the soldiers sang Christmas carols and pooled together to do something special for some English children who would otherwise have had a meager Christmas. I gave a gift to a very shy small girl; she looked down as she accepted the gift.

The spirit of goodness did cast a splinter of hope through the curtains of gloom! Even the drunken singing of Christmas carolers reflected a remembrance of God.

> *Many times I've heard heartfelt remarks* (from fellow soldiers) *which proved the speaker to be truly envious of the civilian back home who could "go to the corner bar any time and pick up a broad at will."*
>
> *This is Christmas Eve and the beautiful strains of "Noel" can be heard. In light of the spirit of the occasion can I be so "hard-hearted" to my fellow man?*
>
> *Can the solemn soldier-caroler tonight be a drunken sot tomorrow night? If God presents another day, I meaningfully predict many carolers will prove themselves—shamefully prove themselves.*
>
> *To be pleasing to God, we must be "hot"! Even though Christmas is not Christ's actual birthday, my heart cries out against heathen Christians who will have their "good times" at this season.*
>
> *May I ever possess the zeal and concern that wells in my heart now against ungodliness! God knows me so well! He knows that I am small and trembling, and fearful, and variable. He knows my faults are innumerable, and he would have me be a devoted servant of his. He knows my doubting and coldness.*

There were moments when I was able to see the good in my fellow soldiers; but admittedly, the use of foul language, the taking of God's name in vain disturbed me greatly. War brought out the worst in them.

> *The name of God taken in vain; how rasping and horrible it sounds!*
>
> *War experience makes a person unmindful of even social courtesies. In conversation men have no respect for women, and women defy all principles of feminine decency by actually competing in masculine vulgarity. It is horrible to think that such language is being simplified and popularized . . . proclaiming as frankness, a polluted language.*
>
> *"Even so the tongue is a little member, and boast of great things. Behold, how great a matter a little fire will kindle?" How irreparable the damage wrought by a careless tongue!*
>
> *Wagging tongues gain momentum and ultimately find themselves hideous and undesirable.*
>
> *What an accomplishment to possess a tongue that will not offend. "If any man offend not in word, the same is a perfect man, and able also to bridle the whole body."*

The tongue of the righteous is choice silver,
but the heart of the wicked is of little value. (Proverbs10:20)

CHAPTER THIRTY-EIGHT

This is what the Lord says to you:
"Do not be afraid or discouraged
because of this vast army.
For the battle is not yours, but God's . . ."

—2 Chronicles 20:15b

Gerald's Remembrances—
Crossing Over—January 1945

To counter the German bulge into the Allied advance, Patton's Third Army came up from the south, Hodges's First Army and the British XXX Corps came from the north, and the Fourth Armored Division reached Bastogne on December 26, 1944. The Germans were pushed back and began to retreat from their fifty-mile advance, back into Germany.

My unit had been in England about a month when, shortly after Christmas, we boarded at South Hampton, England, and crossed the channel aboard the Llangibby Castle, a British ship. The ship was manned by British sailors.

The GIs had one night of sleep aboard ship, that is, if one could sleep in the hammocks. GIs were anxious as they wondered what their fate might be. Would they be brave in battle, or would they be cowards? Would they be maimed? Would they live, or would they die?

An unforgettable breakfast consisting of "tay" (tea) and boiled potatoes in the jackets was served that morning on board.

That was it! Ha! Of course, the English rations had been very limited, so we received a breakfast comparable to the daily meal that the English had been receiving.

The ship landed the next day on the French side at Le Havre. Most buildings and landmarks in Le Havre had been bombed, many by D-Day allied bombs. After crossing the channel, the unit was billeted in a French chateau near Le Harve, a sizeable two-story building in the country. There was lots of snow on the ground.

Some GIs had discovered a cafe in a nearby small village where they purchased some really good apple cider. They came back to the chateau and exclaimed to me, "We found a café that serves some really great apple cider! You should go there and give it a taste when you get a chance!"

So when I went into the village to the Regimental Headquarters to get medical supplies for my medical pouch, I decided to check it out. Using French money, I purchased and drank a great big glass of apple cider! It was really delicious! As I started the mile trek back to the chateau, I began to suspect my "buddies" intent. With wet and melting snow on the ground, I discovered that I was having difficulty staying in the rut of the road that had become two-rutted by the army jeeps! Ha! I realized then what had happened. The stuff I had enjoyed so much was hard cider! It was obviously alcoholic! So when I got back to the chateau, I found my way back to the barracks, kind of isolated myself, and managed to sleep it off. I knew the guys would razz me for my imbibitions. It remained a secret, until now! ☺

When I woke up, I worried whether anyone had seen me in my inebriated state and contemplated whether my example made any impression on any of them. I wrote a prayer in my journal:

I pray God, my righteous fervor, perhaps insignificant,
may grow and ever be a store of energy in my soul that will not

empty on any occasion, but consistently and effectually propel Christ's Gospel tidings to men whose natures are so complex and unpredictable. I pray through Christ that I may be able to face the most difficult of skeptics and impress him with God's Word—impress him to the point of belief and obedience.

How hard it is to say to my fellow men, "Your religious practice is not according to God's Word," but men must know that their souls are valuable enough to be insured by God's plan. I find it hard to make men understand that I, myself, am not condemning their practices; but the Word of God is refuting and correcting their beliefs.

It seems that a Godly example cannot help the fellows with whom I associate because they are totally unfamiliar with God's unalterable plan of salvation. If only they could learn the simple truths which demand a noble obedience. Then a Godly example would have greater effect. In any environment, I pray God; "May I be a righteous example before all" But more and more am I convinced that my good example, if good in God's sight, doesn't save the souls that might render obedience if impressed with Gospel truths. I want to be a useful vessel in God's Kingdom.

I'm reminded of the following scripture: "The fruit of the righteous is a tree of life, and he who wins souls is wise" (Proverb 11:30).

I always got along pretty good, how be it quietly and distantly, with the great majority of my comrades. I had a reputation as a good guy who was "religious" and morally upright.

Though I had no occasion to preach a sermon while overseas in Europe, many of my comrades called me Deacon. And of course, some would call me Doc. Some soldiers came to me with their problems, their feelings, their fears, and asked for advice about girlfriends and/or wife's back home. I didn't really know what to say, so I mostly listened, which is probably all they wanted anyway, a listening ear. I hope I was able to help. This was good practice since I wanted to become a minister.

> *Another night and I am made to think of the statement, "To err is human." How acutely man should realize his imperfections, placing his trust in a faultless God.*
>
> *I seem to have a justifiably smug satisfaction from having gleaned a great deal of spiritual good from God's Word, particularly Paul's writings.*
>
> *I picture myself as a future minister of a congregation and joyfully anticipate the time when, God willing, I will have opportunity to worship with congregations of my acquaintance. It is most pleasurable to anticipate a time when I shall be a respected minister—preaching, teaching, studying, and visiting.*
>
> *Actually, I accuse myself of those anticipations. Perhaps my ministry won't be so ideal. Perhaps the Lord wills that I perform a capable service in a field that is distant and difficult.*
>
> *I pray that my loving wife and I may ever love our God and the souls of men no matter where we are.*

Hodges's First Army was made up of many Divisions. General Reinhart was in charge of the Sixty-Ninth Division. There were three regiments within the Sixty-Ninth Division, the 271st, 272nd, and 273rd. Within each regiment were battalions. Each battalion had companies, and within each company there were platoons.

I was in the First Battalion attached to Company A, which was in the 271st Medical Detachment, which was a part of the 271st Regiment, which was a part of the Sixty-Ninth Division, which was part of Hodge's First Army. Within Company A there were three platoons, each with a medical aide to take care of the wounded for each platoon. However, within my company, one of the other medics got trench foot and had to leave. So by and by, I became the only medical aide with Company A.

I and other medics did not get much, if any, medical training. Perhaps, my delay in getting into the medical detachment prevented me from getting more training. Had I not revealed on the draft board questionnaire that I was a clarinetist, things might have moved along differently. Training came on the battlefield through experience. It was a hard way to learn. I didn't dress wounds while in the hospital in England, but of course, later in France and Germany, I worked crudely with wounds while out with the infantry. Mostly, I gave morphine as I deemed it was needed. I did some splinting, used bandages, and carried sulfa drugs to be used on the wounded on the battlefields. The doctors eventually ordered the medics to stop using the sulfa drugs because it took too long to clean the wounds before surgery could be performed. Later, penicillin was developed which killed bacteria much better; the use of sulfa drugs was discontinued.

CHAPTER THIRTY-NINE

Hope deferred makes the heart sick.
But a longing fulfilled is a tree of life.

—Proverbs 13:12

Pauline's Diary—Lonesome on the Home Front—January 1945

(The words in italics are quoted from Pauline's diary)

A new year began and I was alone. It was January 1, 1945, the first day of the spring '45 school session for the Mangum School District. I lethargically *turned over in bed and looked at the time displayed on the wind-up alarm clock. It said 8:45. I had slept late again. I did not feel motivated, but got up, cleaned up, and dressed. I* contemplated the past six months *as I hurriedly walked to catch the school bus* to get a ride to the Eastview School.

The last six months of 1944 had been very difficult for me. Like tempestuous rolling waves on the ocean, my emotions had vacillated from ecstasy to despair. After eloping on June 18, 1944, I had been able to stay with Gerald until the end of August, about two blissful months.

Gerald and I had discussed and decided that I should return in the fall to the teaching opportunity in Oklahoma since he would soon be sent overseas. So in late August as the fall school session began, I had reluctantly torn myself away from my husband to return to teach in the Mangum School District.

After moving back into the teacherage located in Brinkman above the Suffridges, I divided my days between the Brinkman School and the Eastview School which was about three miles west of Brinkman.

In September, Gerald had managed to hitchhike while on furlough to come be with me in Oklahoma for a very brief visit. My heart felt ripped out of my chest again as I watched Gerald ride away with *Ms. Blackwell* who *drove him to Mangum* where he hoped to catch a ride to *hitchhike back to Mississippi.* It had almost been harder to have him there briefly and then to have to tear away again; but I had been glad to spend some time with him.

After he had gone, I curled up in bed and cried, longing for his arms to be around me again; I was so sad and knew it could be months before I would see him again.

When it had become clear in early October that Gerald's unit was soon to be shipped to Europe, I left the teaching job in Oklahoma and rushed to Hattiesburg, Mississippi, to be with my beloved husband. Most of my friends and family understood that I wanted and needed to spend as much time as possible with Gerald; but there were some who thought it irresponsible of me to leave during the school semester. Nevertheless, I left.

In late October, Gerald's unit had been sent to Camp Kilmer in New Jersey. Once again we were torn apart. I remained briefly in Hattiesburg, Mississippi, where I stayed with Kyle and Carmen Woods. I hopefully and anxiously waited to hear from Gerald about possibly joining him in New Jersey.

I had last spoken to Gerald by phone in mid-November while at the Woods. We decided that since he would be shipped out very soon, I should not join him. Gerald was at Camp Kilmer only briefly.

Sad and lonely, I had returned to Brinkman by bus and was allowed to return to the same teaching position. Gerald then shipped out on November 15, 1944. I was like a butterfly with broken wings; my spirits floundered and I could not fly.

I really was grateful to have the job to come back to, but it had been difficult for me to stay focused and fulfill my duties. I missed Gerald so much and was easily distracted and depressed. From November through Christmas, I had *made a lot of mistakes* and was often unprepared for my classes which *others noticed and criticized.* I'm sure I felt sorry for myself, but I really had tried to think, plan, and do a good job.

Maggie, John, and Pauline Smith Beasley at the farm, fall 1944

Preparing lesson plans, writing demonstrations for 4-H, cutting borders for the school room, making up tests, working on the register (the farm children were allowed to be out of school to help during harvest so records had to be kept that showed the attendance, work completed and subjects passed by each student), *doing lunchroom reports, and writing up claims* had kept me pretty busy.

However, weekends had been hard as I tried not to focus on my loneliness and thoughts of Gerald.

While alone in my apartment, I had tried to keep myself *busy crocheting, embroidering, sewing, reading, writing many letters to family and friends, and writing to Gerald.*

Thankfully, just a couple weeks after returning to Brinkman, school had let out *for the winter holiday.* I was *glad for the chance to leave Brinkman*

Royce Zane Smith, fall 1944

and travel the short distance to my folks' farm near Blair to celebrate Christmas.

Being home had been *relaxing* and it had been *fun wrestling and playing with my ten-year-old brother, Royce.* (I didn't know it at the time, but while I was enjoying my stay on the farm, Gerald was getting ready to cross the English Channel into France.)

But now, on a *cool clear* January day, I was back in Brinkman *feeling inadequate* as a teacher, but determined to make a new start.

I also determined to keep a daily diary starting with January 1, 1945. My first entry was: *"Today is a new year with a clean slate. It was good to see the students again! They seemed to truly miss me. The day went well!"*

My days were pretty routine: I tried to be up between seven and seven-thirty most mornings; taught my classes and gave tests; after school I often went home and *rested* briefly; and *went to the store* and post office to *check for mail* (Brinkman had a post office, a couple of stores, cafes, barbershop, two large elevators and four cotton gins). The walk to town from the teacherage was the equivalent of several city blocks. Once home, I *finished up chores, worked on borders, prepared and planned for classes, made out tests, made out lunchroom reports, worked on the register, cooked, and ate.* In the evening, I *studied the Bible, wrote a letter to Gerald,* wrote in my diary, and—as I went to bed—*prayed for* the safety of *my sweet husband.*

Some days varied because of *4-H meetings with Ms. Blackwell and Mr. Beck.* On those days I did not have classes, and I would *let the students have an activity* while I *made out a lunchroom report.* I did not like doing it, but I occasionally had to give some *boys two licks each for fighting at recess.*

Part of my job was to coach girls' basketball, so since the basketball season had begun, I gave the *students an activity and spent that time coaching the juniors. They got so excited about the ball games.* Our first game was *between Eastview and Centralview. They won both games.* It was good to be involved and attend these exciting games.

A highlight for me each day was receiving a letter or package from Gerald. When I didn't get any letters from him, I would get depressed. Delivery of mail from overseas usually took anywhere from ten days to three weeks. Some days no letters came! Other days many letters would arrive! And they weren't always received in consecutive order according to the dates in which they were written.

Airmail letters from Europe usually took up to twelve days to be delivered, but were faster than mailed letters. By boat, letters could take up to six weeks.

V-mails were written on forms that could be purchased at a "Five and Ten" or the post office. These were short, cheerful, and frequently sent letters that were photographed, put on film, flown across the sea, and then reproduced at the mail center closest to the recipients' location. V-mails reduced the time it took for delivery, the compact size and weight left more space for military supplies on cargo transport, and they minimized the chances that the enemy would intercept the letters. The military were always concerned that any information in letters about location and numbers of Allied troops might be intercepted and provide useful information to the enemy.

Monday, January 1, 1945, there was no mail! I felt depressed! So *I went down the stairs to visit Burnice Suffridge,* my older, wise pregnant friend, who I knew would listen and speak words of encouragement. I spent a lot of time with the Suffridges. Sometimes I would even go *to town with them.* Eleven-year-old Tommy and inquisitive three-year-old Fred would often come up to visit me. *Delightful Fred* could always cheer me!

On this evening *I talked to Mrs. Suffridge for a long time. She was worried that Mr. Suffridge might be leaving* Brinkman. Apparently, he was checking into other educational/superintendent positions. I couldn't help but wonder what would happen to my teaching position if he left. Should they leave, would the new superintendent keep me on? I tried not to worry about it.

After returning upstairs I needed some noise to distract me from thoughts of Gerald and my loneliness, so I *turned the radio on to listen to music.* It ended up not being such a good thing! The song *"My Heart Tells Me"* was playing on the radio. This song was about a female separated from her lover by the war who questioned her partner's motives and true feelings. I was sure of Gerald's love for me and my love for him; but the following words *depressed* me and left me *feeling sad:* "My heart tells me I will cry again, lips that kiss like yours . . ." I was nostalgic and lonely. It didn't matter that the meaning of the song did not apply to Gerald and me. Those few words were all it took to set my emotions plummeting. That night *I cried* as I wrote in my diary*: "These holidays I miss Gerald so much. It has been two months ago since I have seen Gerald. I read until late. 1:00 a.m."*

The next day, I felt somewhat better because *I received four airmail and two v-mails from Gerald!* Sometimes I shared the less intimate stories and information from Gerald's letters. *He told of his trip to London; I read it to the class. They enjoyed it. I read it to the Suffridges. I felt fine.*

I had a tendency to stay up too late at night, so some mornings I was late and had to *rapidly walk* to the Brinkman School. On those days I did not *get to all of my classes;* I did not cover all the planned material. I was criticized, and after Friday's teachers' meeting, I was given a directive—*I have to get up early to get out to school early.* I determined to get to bed earlier. The next day I actually got *to school on time* and *got to all but one of the classes.*

Being criticized always made my emotions tailspin into depression. But this particular evening, my little friends from downstairs came up to visit me as I was *typing a letter to Gerald.*

While *listening to the radio, I put Tommy to work drawing. Fred came up and sat on the bed talking and writing in the arithmetic book.*

Later I was able to get out of the apartment to witness *Ms. Moss* (a co-teacher) *get married to Morris Griffith,* another teacher. It was a happy moment, but I could not help but think of Gerald and how I missed him.

To make up for days students missed because of harvest or bad weather, school would meet full days Monday through Friday and often on Saturdays till twelve-thirty. There was no school this particular Saturday; however, it didn't look like I would be able to go visit the folks. But after school let out at twelve-thirty, I walked the short distance *to town where I* met up with *Ms. Blackwell* who *offered to give me a ride home.*

The distance from Brinkman to Blair was about twenty miles. Without a car or a horse, it was certainly too far to walk. Ms. Blackwell was kind enough to provide me a ride when it was convenient for her. Actually, I think she went out of her way to accommodate me because she knew how hard it was for me to spend weekends alone. She was a very nice lady!

Arriving unexpectedly, I gave *Mother and Daddy a big surprise.* We *ate supper; then Royce wanted to make popcorn balls. We also roasted peanuts as we listened to Roosevelt's* State of the Union *speech on the radio.*

On January 6, 1945, all over the nation, families like ours were gathered around their radios leaning forward to hear his words:

> In considering the state of the Union, the war and the peace that is to follow are naturally uppermost in the minds of all of us. This war must be waged—it is being waged—with the greatest and most persistent intensity. Everything we are and have is at stake. Everything we

are and have will be given. American men, fighting far from home have already won victories which the world will never forget. We have no question of the ultimate victory. We have no question of the cost. Our losses will be heavy . . .

The wedge that the Germans attempted to drive in Western Europe was less dangerous in actual terms of winning the war than the wedges which they are continually attempting to drive between ourselves and our allies . . . We must resist this divisive propaganda . . .

It is appropriate at this time to review the basic strategy which has guided us through 3 years of war . . .

It was plain then that the defeat of either enemy would require the massing of overwhelming forces—ground, sea, and air—in positions from which we and our allies could strike directly against the enemy homelands and destroy the Nazi and Japanese war machines . . .

As a result of the combined effort of the Allied Forces, great military victories were achieved in 1944: The liberation of France, Belgium, Greece, and parts of the Netherlands, Norway, Poland, Yugoslavia and Czechoslovakia; the surrender of Rumania and Bulgaria; the invasion of Germany itself and Hungary; the steady march through the Pacific islands to the Philippines, Guam and Saipan; and the beginnings of the mighty air offensive against the Japanese islands . . .

The greatest victory of the last year was, of course, the successful breach on June 6, 1944, of the German "impregnable" sea wall of Europe and the victorious sweep of the Allied forces through France and Belgium and Luxemburg—almost to the Rhine itself.

The cross-channel invasion of the Allied armies was the greatest amphibious operation in the history of the world . . .

This cross-channel invasion was followed in August by a second great amphibious operation, landing troops in Southern France . . .

These two great operations were made possible by success in the Battle of the Atlantic. Without this success over German submarines, we could not have built up our invasion forces or air force . . .

The tremendous operations in Western Europe have overshadowed in the public mind the less spectacular but vitally important Italian front . . .

In the Pacific during the past year, we have conducted the fastest-moving offensive in the history of modern warfare. We have driven the enemy back more than 3000 miles across the Central Pacific . . .

The people of this Nation have a right to be proud of the courage and fighting ability of the men in the armed forces—on all fronts. They also have a right to be proud of American leadership which has guided their sons into battle . . .

Our overall strategy has not neglected the important task of rendering all possible aid to China . . .

The Burma campaigns have involved incredible hardship and have demanded exceptional fortitude and determination . . .

Although unprecedented production figures have made possible our victories, we shall have to increase our goals even more in certain items . . . One of the most urgent immediate requirements of the armed forces is more nurses . . . Since volunteering has not produced the number of nurses required, I urge that the Selective Service Act be amended to provide for the induction of nurses into the armed forces.

In the continuing progress of this war we have constant need for new types of weapons, for we cannot afford to fight the war of today or tomorrow with the weapons of yesterday . . . If we do not keep constantly ahead of our enemies in the development of new weapons, we pay for our backwardness with the life's blood of our sons . . .

Last year, after much consideration, I recommended that the Congress adopt a Nation Service Act as the most efficient and democratic way of insuring full production for our war requirements. This recommendation was not adopted. I now again call upon the Congress to enact this measure . . . That "to bring the conflict to a successful conclusion, all of the resources of the country are hereby pledged by the Congress of the United States." I recommend that the Congress immediately enact legislation which will be effective in using the services of the 4,000,000 men now classified as IV-F in whatever capacity is best for the war effort.

In the field of foreign policy, we propose to stand together with the United Nations not for the war alone but for the victory for which the war is fought . . . In August 1941 Prime Minister Churchill and I agreed to the principles of the Atlantic Charter . . . We must not this time lose the hope of establishing an international order which will be capable of maintaining peace and realizing through the years more perfect justice between nations . . . We and our allies have declared that it is our purpose to respect the right of all peoples to choose the form of government under which they will live and to see sovereign rights and self-government restored to those who have been forcibly deprived of them . . .

We support the greatest possible freedom of trade and commerce . . .

I am clear in my own mind that, as an essential factor in the maintenance of peace in the future, we must have universal military training after this war, and I shall send a special message to the Congress on this subject . . .

I say now, that these economic truths represent a second bill of rights under which a new basis of security and prosperity can be established for all—regardless of station, race or creed . . . the most fundamental . . . is the "right to a useful and remunerative job in the industries or shops or farms or mines of the Nation." After the war we must maintain full employment with Government performing its peacetime functions . . .

Most important of all—1945 can and must see the substantial beginning of the organization of world peace . . . It must be the justification of all the sacrifices that have been made—of all the dreadful misery that this world has endured.

We Americans of today, together with our allies, are making history—and I hope it will be better history than ever has been made before.

We pray that we may be worthy of the unlimited opportunities that God has given us.[*]

---

[*]   **en.wikipedia.org**/wiki/Franklin_D._**Roosevelt**

After listening to Roosevelt's lengthy and comprehensive comments regarding the war and the state of the union, I was left with a lot of things to think about.

I felt a strong need to reach out to God. So Sunday, January 7, Mom, Royce, and I were *up at nine, ate, but were ten minutes late for church,* probably because I had *polished shoes and hemmed pants for Royce to get him ready.* Dad did not go with us. He never did go to church.

That morning, *Bro. Errol taught a good lesson on Giving.* We went back to the farm and after dinner I *took a roll of films, sat around talking, and dried the dishes.* As I *got the irons ready to take* with me, *Royce* very thoughtfully *brought me a sack of peanuts.* Ms. Blackwell met me at the church building in Warren and dropped me at the apartment *at 9:30 p.m.*

Before retiring I *wrote a letter to Gerald . . . did a few odds and a bath.*

The visit to the folks was uplifting, and I was so glad I had the chance to go.

The second week in January started out positively. After several days without a letter from Gerald, Monday I was ecstatic because *I got five letters from Gerald! He* wrote that he was *sending me a package. I was so happy! I could hardly wait* to find out what he was sending*!* He also wrote that *he got a little girl on Christmas.* Apparently, some soldiers in England decided to give gifts to English children who would otherwise not be receiving any Christmas gifts. Gerald said s*he was bashful.*

Before retiring, I wrote in my diary, *studied the Bible, prayed, wrote a letter to Gerald, and went to bed.* I had a few laughs . . . *heard Bob Hope* on the radio.

Tuesday I *was busy all day. I had the students* help me *write the* their *tests on the board. Believe it or not, I got to every class. I was so lonesome for Gerald,* but the receipt of *three airmails and two V-mails from Gerald* made me feel some better.

It would have been nice to have the day off, but *school met Saturday until 12:30 p.m. I received three letters and a package from Gerald containing a shopping bag and a burlap recipe book. I was very proud of them.* I loved receiving things from Gerald! He said he *had received a box of cookies* that I had sent overseas to him. I was glad. But that night I *got so lonesome for him . . . I want to cry.*

The weather Sunday, January 14, *was windy; otherwise a beautiful day* as I got a ride and *went to church in Mangum.* With no school I needed to keep myself busy; but I felt so *lazy . . . I did straighten up the closet!* Later I *listened to the radio, wrote Brother Franks* (the preacher in Mississippi who married us), *and Gerald . . . did a bit of other work . . . crocheted until late.* I tried to be brave and strong; but ended the day *so lonesome* for Gerald *and cried, which I shouldn't have done.*

I felt better when Monday turned out to be *a beautiful day,* and I *received five letters from Gerald! He said he had received all my packages.* I was glad when *Tommy visited me . . . his parents were gone to town. We made a border* together! Thank God for small friends!

While alone in my upstairs apartment, it helped to have some noise versus silence. So I would listen to music and the various radio shows while I sewed, crocheted, and cleaned the apartment. My favorite hit songs were "Scatter Brains," "You Must Have Been a Beautiful Baby," "White Cliffs of Dover," "There Are Such Things," just to name a few.

The following words to "There Are Such Things" described how I felt about Gerald's and my relationship: "A heart that's true, there are such things . . . Someone to whisper, 'Darling, you're my star . . . ,'" and it goes on.*

---

* Words by Stanley Adams, Abel Bair, and George W. Meyer; sung by Frank Sinatra and the Pied Pipers with the Dorsey Band; recorded by Tommy Dorsey in 1942.

I was also able to keep up with the news and *listened to President Roosevelt speak* to the nation in his "Fireside Chats." Those were always enjoyable. Like so many others on the home front, I wanted to know how the war was going though sometimes the knowing caused me fear and anxiety. Was it better to remain ignorant of what was happening or to know my loved one might be in the middle of the reported battle? No matter, I was unable to turn the radio off, choosing instead to keep up with the news.

CHAPTER FORTY

The Lord your God, who is going before you,
will fight for you, as he did for you in Egypt,
before your very eyes . . .
—Deuteronomy 1:30

Gerald's Remembrances—Moving Across France—January 1945

The Sixty-Ninth Division of the First Army was preparing to move across France. My unit was not in Le Havre very long before piling into old-fashioned 40 and 8s, railroad cars that would hold forty men or eight horses.

Crossing France in early January, it was very, very cold! Then crossing over to eastern France toward Germany, the weather became extremely rainy and muddy. The mud was knee deep everywhere.

Going east toward Belgium and Luxemburg, the trains went in the general direction of Aachen, Germany. Somewhere in France, the army set up and camped in a tent city where the mud was knee deep in the cold of winter. It was so very frigid!

While sitting around in the mud and cold, my comrades and I were able to listen to the BBC broadcasts. We could really relate to the words of the song "Cleaning My Rifle and Dreaming of You"* (though I did not bear arms) which depicted a soldier

---

* Composed by Allie Wrubel, performed by Lawrence Welk and his Orchestra, recorded by Decca in 1943.

hanging around the camp and dreaming of his sweetheart: "Wondering what tomorrow'd bring . . . A little bit lonesome! A little bit blue . . . Cleaning my rifle and dreamin' of you!"

It was a lonesome time for all the soldiers. I was no exception. I longed for my wife and for encouragement from Christian companionship.

At this mud camp, I met up again with a Christian Church chaplain who had also been chaplain at Camp Shelby. As the troops had crossed France and Germany, he had acquired various religious books that had been left behind by Allied GI prisoners of war as they were released from German captivity. Apparently, the Red Cross had been allowed to visit the German prison camps to leave food, blankets, books, and other necessities. The chaplain gave me some of these religious books to read. (I still have them.) While in this tent city, the chaplain had a service in which communion was served. I participated in this very meaningful service! It was great to worship with other Christians!

Another time at First Battalion headquarters, I met up with several former Christian acquaintances from my Company. Matthew Beers had a great tenor voice. (He was from Arnett, Oklahoma, near Geary, Oklahoma, where I now live. He planned to return to Oklahoma, build a sod house, and raise horses. He loved horses!) Another gentlemen from Kentucky (I can't remember his name) sang the lead. We had previously held religious services and sung together, so at this time we stayed for a while at headquarters and sang several hymns. I sang bass as we sang "Jesus, Lover of My Soul" and other hymns.

> Jesus, lover of my soul,
> let me to thy bosom fly.
> While the nearer waters roll,
> while the tempest still is high,

Hide me. O my Savior, hide,
till the storm of life is past.
Safe into thy haven guide,
Oh, receive my soul at last.[*]

As we finished the singing and got up to leave to go back to our various units, a lieutenant was sent in by the colonel. He said, "The colonel would like you to keep singing!" The colonel ordered—no, he requested that we continue to sing. It refreshed our souls to know that our singing had touched and inspired others. As requested, we sang some more.

I also had the occasion to meet and sing with Ray Wright, a soldier from a different company who had attended church in Hattiesburg.

It was uplifting and a great encouragement to be able to worship and pray with fellow Christians. The study of God's word and prayer were my sword and shield during this difficult time:

A later date: How wonderful is God's Word! A great joy wells in my heart as I study the inspired writings of the Apostle Paul. Is it wrong that in the blessing of studying God's Word, I dwell upon the innate loveliness of mind of my life's companion? Would not God have me concerned about the one with whom I am made one flesh?

So simple and majestic are God's Words! I pray my Heavenly Father through his matchless Son that my zeal and knowledge in his blessed word will ever grow, and not be hampered, nor quelled by problems brought to bear from sources outside.

Why do I not more boldly proclaim God's Word? Why do I become zealous and full when His Word's are before my

---

[*] Words by Charles Wesley, music by Joseph Parry, from *Hymns and Sacred Poems*, 1740. Song is public domain.

eyes, then falter for words when expressing my views—God's view?

I pray God, that the desire within me is sincere and lasting, the desire to study diligently, lovingly, consistently God's Word, and to teach it to hungry men—men whose souls are emptied of godliness and filled with most illegitimate substitutes. I thank thee, Dear God, that I know of men who by virtue of age and experience have submitted their own intelligence and popularities of the world, have forgotten their old paths and youthful zeal, and are uneasily reminded that the wisdom of men is as God's foolishness. I pray that I may profit from those examples, that I may bask in thy knowledge always. Ever through Christ!

There wasn't much to do except sit around and shiver in the cold rain and mud in north France in January. I penned a few shaky words to get my mind off the uncomfortable climate and the fighting that was sure to come soon.

Always, I tried to focus on God's will.

In a material sense I have often had visions of grandeur in which I imagined myself accomplishing feats and producing results that brought recognition and material gain. I think that not an abnormal function of my mind, but I'm sure my visions can be more nearly and gloriously attained if I confine my imaginings to great accomplishments in the Lord's vineyard—not for human recognition, but for the glory of God.

CHAPTER FORTY-ONE

Not only so, but we also rejoice in our sufferings,
because we know that suffering produces perseverance;
perseverance, character; and character, hope.

—Romans 5:3 and 4

Pauline's Diary—Stormy Weather— January and February 1945

The weather in Oklahoma during the first couple weeks in January had been *very beautiful and warm* as I *hung the clothes out to dry*. But on the evening of Wednesday, January 17, 1945, the weather changed for the worse; *it began raining hard* and I figured *there would probably be no school* the following day. The country roads were not paved, and I knew it would be dangerous for the school bus and other vehicles to slip and slide around in the ice and mud.

I was right! Mr. Suffridge came up the stairs and announced, "Pauline, there will be *no school Thursday*."

The next morning I did not wish to stay cooped up alone, so I walked through the mud and rain to nearby Brinkman to mail my letters. While out, I *went by the store* and *found Retha Durham* (I had taught her in fifth grade at Plainview, 43-44) *playing the piano*; then I *sat with all the teachers at "Clydes" until 11:00 a.m.* Among the teachers were Mr. & Mrs. Griffith, just recently married, Ms. Blackwell, Mr. Beck, Ms. Burcham, Mr. Post, and Will G. Jones.

After returning home I wanted to keep busy, so I *cut out a dress and skirt from a* secondhand *evening dress* that I had acquired. The dress had plenty of fabric that was still in great condition. During the depression, my family had "recycled" used products, and because of war rationing, I conservatively reused what was at hand.

Little *Fred paid me a visit* while *I was sewing on the skirt.* I couldn't help but think, "*Fred is a mess* but such a delight!" While he jabbered constantly, I did some *crocheting.* He helped the evening go by quickly.

Cold, wet, gloomy days continued for five days with no school. Incarcerated during these days, I continued to *sew on the skirt and the dress, and cut out another dress, but* got frustrated because I *made so many mistakes.* Tired of taking out the stitches and correcting my mistakes, *I then crocheted while listening to the radio.*

Sunday brought no reprieve from the rain, mud, and cold; there was *no church.* But I *sang hymns and studied* the Bible *alone.*

On January 20, while alone in my apartment, I listened as *President Roosevelt took his fourth oath into office.*

> We Americans of today, together with our allies, are passing through a period of supreme test. It is a test of our courage—of our resolve—our wisdom—our essential democracy . . . As I stand here today, having taken the solemn oath of office in the presence of my fellow countrymen—in the presence of our God—I know that it is America's purpose that we shall not fail. In the days and in the years that are to come we shall work for a just and honorable peace . . .
>
> We can and will achieve such a peace . . . The Almighty God has blessed our land in many ways. He has given our people stout hearts and strong arms with which to strike mighty blows for freedom and truth. He has given to our country a faith, which has become the

hope of all peoples in an anguished world. So we pray
to Him now for the vision to see our way clearly—to
see the way that leads to a better life for ourselves and
for all our fellow men—to the achievement of His will
to peace on earth.[*]

I dressed and was ready for school, but again there was no
school Monday. I kept sewing while listening to the radio, and
by evening I had *finished the skirt and dresses.* I had also *used up a
ball of crochet twine.*

It was depressing being cooped up. I just couldn't keep
busy enough! Because of the stormy weather, I had too much
time alone; it made me realize just how lucky I was to have the
teaching job that gave me somewhere to go and something to
occupy my mind and time.

*Three endearing letters from Gerald dated January 8, 10, 11, three
v-mails from Gerald,* and a letter *from Mrs. Beasley* did lift my spirits
some; but I was frustrated and lonely as I wrote in the diary:
*"I love Gerald so much and I got very lonesome for him. I cried today.
I need to be working all the time. It is going to be a long time before I
get to see him. Only 1/8 of the time gone!"* Gerald ended up being
overseas for close to a year!

Monday ended *cold, but a beautiful day.*

Thank goodness there was school Tuesday, January 23! *It
was cold,* but I was glad to get back to school. It was *enjoyable to
have ball practice.* Since I would not be able to get to Mangum, I
planned to *send a check I received to the banker* in Mangum. *I typed
three letters to Gerald.*

The last Saturday in January, *it rained a slow rain most of the day*
as school met. *The buses certainly did slide* as they made their way
to school. That evening as I wrote to my *true love,* my emotions

---

[*]   **en.wikipedia.org**/…inauguration_of_Franklin_D._**Roosevelt**

clouded over. I cried as I listened to the following words of the song "I Wish That I Could Hide Inside this Letter":* "My heart's in this letter I'm sending . . . I'd pop right out and kiss you like you'd never been kissed before."

Sunday, January 28, *there were very few present at church, but they had services just the same.* After services, thankfully, I was invited to the Hoods for *a delicious dinner and a game of Bingo and Flinch* which were a nice distraction. Because of the muddy slippery roads, *I walked home* so they would not have to get out in their car. Writing *six-weeks tests* used up some of the evening; then I *crocheted* and *wrote Gerald.*

It was cold with a heavy frost covering the ground the next *morning.* I *stayed out at the schoolhouse to grade papers* which meant that I had a brisk walk to the teacherage in the late afternoon. It was so cold, but the exercise was invigorating! When I got home, I had to go *after and carry kerosene for heating.* I then *listened to the "Lux, Screen Guild Players"**** on the radio *while crocheting.*

Tuesday evening *was a beautiful moonlit night* as I *listened to the radio announced President Roosevelt's sixty-third birthday.*

Friends were always looking out for me. *Kathleen Davis and Irma Trout* (two of my students) *came to be with me for a while. I put on slacks, and we went to the school gym to play basketball. I had a big time; however, I was tired, and* the next day I *was very stiff and wobbly.*

---

* Composed by Nat Simon and Charlie Tobias, performed by Lawrence Welk and Orchestra, recorded by Decca Records in 1943.

** The screen Guild Theatre was a popular radio anthology series during the Golden Age of Radio, broadcast from 1939-1952, with leading Hollywood actors performing adaptations of popular motion pictures. The show lasted for fourteen seasons and 527 episodes. The actor's fees were usually donated to the Motion Picture Relief Fund.

Since they lived below me, *I visited with Mrs. Suffridge often.* Over the weekend, she invited me to lunch and *as we talked I finished a dress. I learned lots from her about babies.* I longed for children of my own and was reminded of when as a child I had nurtured my imaginary children.

Another evening while visiting with Burnice, I *hemmed a skirt, embroidered a cup towel, and did a lot of crocheting on a chair set.* Crocheting was addictive; *I could crochet for years.*

During the month of January, I also attended three wedding showers. Nadine Clark's was on the eleventh. Joe Meta had one the twenty-fourth. On the twenty-fifth while at the *shower for Era Thay Griffis,* I enjoyed *a long chat with Mrs. Durham.*

Surprise! I had crocheted my gifts!

Since basketball season had begun in early January, I *coached the girls' team during recess.* We didn't have great teams, but the basketball games for both girls and boys got me out of the apartment. (1) Tuesday the ninth, *there was a ball game here. Reed beat both of our teams . . . very badly.* (2) Thursday the twelfth, there were *ball games between Eastview and Ozark. Ozark won both of the games.* (3) Tuesday the sixteenth, while the students *had an activity, I spent time coaching the junior students. They were so excited about the ball games between Eastview and Centralview. They won both games!* (4) Friday, the twenty-sixth, after giving *tests most of the morning, my ball players ate early and we went to Plainview to play. They* (Plainview) *beat both of our teams. Both of our teams are very inexperienced, but they played well the last half.* (5) Tuesday the thirtieth, *Plainview came here* (Brinkman) *to play. Our boys won, but the girls lost only by five points. I was very satisfied with all the games. My girls played very hard.* (6) *I also went to the ball game at Reed. They were good games, but both teams lost.*

The basketball games that continued into February were good for my morale. (1) *We went to Willow. Both our teams won the games! I was proud of them! They played well!* (2) But Friday *my girls lost to Cityview. They had too much competition. Our poor junior boys had to play Mangum* who had a really good team, *but they* (Brinkman) *made eleven points. Our seniors lost too.*

I tried to keep busy and get out of the apartment to spend time with friends so I wouldn't worry about Gerald; but for a number of days as the weather was stormy, I was distressed and agitated.

I wrote to friends and relatives and looked forward to receiving letters back from them. I wrote *a card to Aunt Lavonia. I heard from Mrs. Beasley and Wilma Ogar* (an Oklahoma A&M friend).

Thursday, February 1, we *had classes until noon because of the funeral for Mr. Denny.* Not a fun thing, but it did get me out of the apartment.

Later that day, the news on the radio announced *fighting in Belgium,* and again there was no mail from him. *I was fearful that Gerald was in Belgium.* Was he injured and unable to write? Or worse! He just couldn't be dead! God forbid that I think such a thought!

I had received a letter from Lydia Mae stating that *Lloyd,* her husband *(friends from Oklahoma A&M) had been there* (Belgium) *since January 1.* But I hadn't *heard from Gerald since last Saturday.* I prayed, *"God keep Gerald from harm! I love him so much!"*

On Friday it was *cloudy all day* during school, and then in the

Pauline Beasley and
Lydia Mae Best.
Best friends at A&M.

evening it was misty and bad. All games and parties were called off. I did not like bad weather days! They were gloomy and depressing!

As the stormy weather persisted, there was no school Saturday either. I kept myself busy around the apartment while listening to the *radio programs, crocheted, ate, cleaned up the house, put up glass shelves, and sewed on dresses all afternoon. Tommy came up for a while.* Thank God for small favors! Then I *visited the Suffridges for a while . . . got water, kerosene, burned paper, carried out water, ate, listened to radio, looked at Life* (magazine), and *wrote a letter to Gerald.* I just couldn't keep busy enough!

When there was still *no letter . . .* I became more worried because I had heard news reports that the Sixty-Ninth was in Germany. I wrote: "*I know that he is in Germany by now! God protect him and all others there! I love him with all my heart!*" I slept, sandwiching my prayers between intermittent sleep.

After church February 4, *I did not do much of anything . . . listened to the radio most of the day* hoping for some good news!

A lot of people were getting sick! *I visited the Suffridges for a while. Mr. Suffridge was ill with the flu.* I decided that *I must doctor up some.*

Monday after school, *I went to town* (Mangum) *with Mr. Suffridge to get ball suits and stayed until the seventh graders came to the show "Till We Meet Again."** It was a decent show, but the movie made me sad; *it was about war. I cried my eyes out* as I thought about how Gerald was in the middle of the fighting.

I got a disturbing *letter from Lydia Mae* which caused me to worry. *Lloyd,* her husband, *had been wounded and was in England. I received no letter from him and was so afraid for Gerald! I* went down stairs and *talked with Mrs. Suffridge* who listened and tried to reassure me and told me to be strong and persevere. Before turning out the lights, I wrote in my diary: "*I am worried almost sick! I love him so much!*"

My worry continued the next day when still there was *no letter from my sweet!* Busy! I had to stay busy! *After school I played ball with the junior girls, typed a letter to Gerald, made out a lunch report, got water, went to the store, graded papers, washed my hair, and fixed it.*

---

*   A 1944 film directed by Frank Borzage and starred Ray Milland, Walter Slezak and Barbara Britton. It was about a nun who posed as a pilot's wife in an attempt to help him escape out of the country during war.

I prayed, "I can't stand it much longer! I love him so much! He can't get hurt or killed! God be with him!"

For eleven long agonizing days from January 29 through February 8, I had received no letter from Gerald. As each cold day passed, I became more anxious that he had been hurt and was unable to write. I kept myself almost *obsessively busy* as the weather continued to be *cloudy and misty. I continued to write Gerald* as I prayed for his safety.

Finally! I was overjoyed and relieved on Friday, February 9, when I *received a letter from Gerald!* His letter said *he was somewhere in France* and *there was a lot of snow on the ground. I wrote a letter to Gerald.*

I knew Gerald had been in France in the middle of January but did not know if he had been in any battles. Obviously, there was a delay with delivery of mail from the front; it had taken several weeks. Of course, by the time I received this letter, he was likely already in Germany. Even if he was okay when he wrote his letters, by the time I received them, his circumstances could have changed. Not a pleasant and reassuring thought! Still, it was good to hear from Gerald!

I was feeling better when my little friend *Tommy came up to listen to the radio.*

A shower of mail on Saturday eased my anxiety some; the storm within was calming down when *I received two letters from Gerald* from Europe! *He requested eats. I also received many letters from England!* I went downstairs to share the good news and *finished up a crocheted chair set* while visiting with *Mrs. Suffridge until 10:00 p.m.* That evening, *I felt fine since I heard from Gerald!* I also *got a letter from Aunt Lavonia; she sent pictures of her and Jubie. I rested soundly* that night.

I just lazily lounged around all day Sunday, February 11, a cold but *beautiful day.* My diary entry that night was: *"I love my sweet husband with all my heart."*

Being alone where I endured so much silence made me think, *"I will never complain when Gerald makes a noise . . . though noise is all around me."* (Years later with six children, I would eat my words.)

CHAPTER FORTY-TWO

I tell you the truth, whatever you did for one of the
least of these brothers of mine, you did for me.
—Matthew 25:40

Gerald's Remembrances—
in Germany—February 1945

GIs loved to receive letters and packages from a sweetheart, family members, or friends. It took a while for these to reach the addressees. For security reasons on the battlefront, I used a return address "somewhere in France or Germany" Corporal Gerald A. Beasley, APO Army Post Office # so-and-so. APO wouldn't tell the Germans anything about the location of the unit or the date of the letter. Letters were scrutinized by an officer, which the soldiers didn't really like, but that's the way it was. Sometimes incoming mail would not get delivered immediately to a soldier's position, so GIs would go for days without receiving any mail, sometimes longer; then a soldier might receive several at a time.

I received a lot of letters from Pauline and Mom, depending on my unit's circumstances.

Also, for security reasons, military personnel were told not to keep a diary. Should the enemy find a lost diary or information on the body of an American GI, the enemy might be privy to secure military locations, movements, and accessible weaponry. I wish I could have kept a diary.

While overseas, military personnel were encouraged to request food from loved ones who could then show the written request for food to the post master; then their package would be mailed.

On the front line I received several packages from Pauline and Mom. One package was crumbled cookies from Pauline. They were eaten! I requested canned black-eyed peas, canned apricots, and other foods. Ha! Since the jars had to be wrapped really good to prevent breakage, I did not get many packages like that, and they did take longer to get delivered. Of course, I shared my goodies with the other guys, and most of the other soldiers shared what they received.

I wrote less frequently and fewer words in the journal as the troops moved across France and into Germany, partly because of the cold, but also because of the unit's circumstances. I continued to write my thoughts about my weaknesses and prayed for God's answers for peace and joy:

> *A later date: It is most enjoyable to spend an evening meditating and studying about the complexities of life. Further, it is comforting to know that the reasons for the answers to these complexities are at my fingertips—in divine writ. The solution is so simple, yet men who'd rather define and exact their solutions for the complexities abhor this simplicity.*
>
> *I pray God that I may do my part in teaching my nation about the Prince of Peace. Only God's Word holds the answer to a lasting peace.*
>
> *In the light of man's pathetic weaknesses, God appears so mighty and all wise! Man's efforts to look after himself spiritually are as vain as his efforts to stop the wrath of storms that bespeak an awesome power. When will man with his meager mind cease trying to cope with his Creator?*
>
> *How simple is it for each person in this world to heed the gospel of Christ? The answer to this question, it seems*

to me, defines the difficulties of establishing a peace between nations—a lasting peace.

I am reminded of Isaiah 9:6: "For to us a child is born, to us a son is given, and the government will be on his shoulders. And he will be called Wonderful Counselor, Mighty God, Everlasting Father, Prince of Peace."

My unit wasn't at the tent city in France very long before pushing off again toward Germany. In early February, the Sixty-Ninth Division went in undercover of a snowstorm. The situation was ideal for replacing the Ninety-Ninth Division in the front lines because the Germans could not detect what was going on. The objective was to move fast and cut off the enemy supplies. The troops rode the trucks and tanks just like ticks on a dog's back.

Entering into the area where the Battle of the Bulge had been fought, we saw some very gruesome sights . . . Lots of destruction. We could see mass graves, and there were dead GIs still in their sleeping bags.

Moving fast thru Belgium into Germany in mid-February, we crossed over to the old Siegfried Line, the concrete bunkers and defense setups that the Germans had built. There had been fierce fighting in Belgium, so there were many wounded and dead all around and much destruction.

Somewhere along the Siegfried Line, I treated a wounded German soldier who had been shot through the head. He could actually walk, but there was stuff spilling out of the wound. I attended to him as best I could; then took him to an American medical unit for treatment. The doctors were busy with an American GI. My unit had continued to move forward as I transported the German, so I left pretty quickly to catch up with my unit. I never knew whether the German received help or not. He probably died.

I felt despair, and later I wrote a prayer:

> *Dear God, if it be thy will, may these murderous hostilities cease that the lives of our loved ones and the loved ones of other nations may be spared! May thy people everywhere gird themselves and spread thy mighty, peace-giving Word to every man!*
>
> *Dear God, may every mortal in thy creation be cognizant of thy mercy, love, jealousy and holiness! We are so weak and helpless and dependent on thee. Hear us as we pray through Christ, our redeemer! Amen!*

As a medic I could stop, eat here, and ride there. Soldiers could sometimes get a ride on a jeep or a tank as the troops moved across Germany. At least, that is what I did as I headed back to my unit. I finally caught up to my unit to find that one of our tanks had been rocketed. The rocket had gotten inside and just banged around and burned everything. The bedroll that I had left behind was peppered with shrapnel. Some of my buddies were wounded.

God had spared me!

The unit then moved rapidly across Germany toward Leipzig. I wrote in response to the "sights" that I had seen:

> *Am I becoming hardened to the evil that is about me? Formerly I was shocked at occurrences and events that now I accept as only commonplace. The unleashed minds of men, who vouch for their own intelligence as productive of thoughts and expressions, can aptly be described as horrible.*
>
> *If only men would study God's word and find all their sins unerringly denounced.*
>
> *How universal and personal is God's Word! What a store of God-glorifying knowledge for the diligent seeker.*

CHAPTER FORTY-THREE

A friend loves at all times,
and a brother is born for adversity.
—Proverbs 17:17

Pauline's Diary—Friends— Valentine's Day—1945

Monday, February 12, *was a beautiful day!* As Valentine's Day approached, the weather became *cool*, but the *sun shone.* My work continued as *I had a class of arithmetic all morning, met with the 4-H club,* made *out claims for Mr. Suffridge, had 4-H club meetings, coached and went to basketball games, graded papers,* and had *class meetings.*

After I got home, *I wrote letters to Gerald, Mother, Aunt Frankie,* and sent *pictures to Gerald and Mother. I got a letter from Gerald* reassuring me that *he was well.*

Tuesday, I received a *sweet Valentine's letter from Gerald* dated January 25. He expressed how much he loved me and longed to see me again. *I read it over and over!* He had sent it early in hopes that I would receive it by Valentine's Day. It had taken nineteen days to find its way from Europe to Oklahoma.

Then on Valentine's Day, *I spent all day teaching English and arithmetic, plus some spelling and reading.* Then, *I served the children "pops" and received a number of valentines* from them. But there was *no letter from Gerald* to complete the celebration, so I reread his Valentine's letter.

By the end of the week I was down in the dumps. I had *received a wedding present of three bath towels,* which was a good thing; but *wished I could share the joy with Gerald.* And I was again feeling inadequate as a teacher. I had tried to work *about forty problems in arithmetic,* but I did them incorrectly. I didn't know what I was doing! *The pupils were the teachers . . . Mary Ellen and Norma taught the classes.* I was concerned that *maybe I lost* the students' *respect.* It didn't help my mood that the weather began to turn cold and wet again and just kept getting worse; *it was cloudy,* and it *rained and hailed some.* But worst of all, I had received no mail from Gerald.

I really wanted and needed to get out of town, but *there were many things that needed to be done, so I doubted I would get to go home.* However, Saturday I *went to town . . . shopped and talked to Ms. Blackwell* at the store. I'm sure she could tell that I was depressed.

"Pauline, I'm headed to Blair. Would you like to go home? I could take you," Ms. Blackwell asked.

"Well, yeah, I would. But I would need to pack a few things." My spirits rose as I responded.

Ms. Blackwell stated, "Do it quickly. I'll be waiting here."

"Okay, I'll be back in a jiffy. And thanks so much." I hastened to say, then headed out, and was back in about fifteen minutes. It was great to have friends who were sympathetic and did kind things for me.

We *met the folks in Blair;* they *stopped at the store; I saw a few people* from town.

Going home to visit the folks helped to lift my spirits somewhat. However, Sunday, my mood was like the weather; *it was foggy and drizzled. I had a bad fight with Royce.*

"Hey, sis. Let's play checkers," Royce exclaimed as he carried the boxed game into the living room where I sat crocheting.

"Not now, Royce. I don't feel like playing right now." I tried to respond with patience.

Royce grumbled, "You haven't done anything with me since you got home. All you do is sit and crochet."

"I don't want to play anything right now. Just leave me alone," I angrily replied.

Royce angrily accused, "Why did you come home then. You could have crocheted in Brinkman."

"Royce, just leave me alone." All patience lost.

"Just be that way then," he glared at me and stomped out of the room.

I felt ashamed and guilty for not taking the time to play with him, but I just wanted to be left alone.

The rest of the day I just *sat while Mother cooked . . . I did wash dishes . . . made one bed, rested, and the remainder of the day crocheted while the folks did the work.* Mom gave me a quiet reproofing look, but otherwise, the family just tried to ignore me and leave me alone.

Sunday afternoon *Ms. Blackwell brought me home against my will . . .* I did not want to go back to Brinkman. To sweeten the departure, Mom insisted that I take some things with me. *I brought back apple pie, meat, soap, and pickles . . .*

Hoping fellowship would be an encouragement I *went to church at Mangum* that evening. When back at the apartment, I was still feeling sorry for myself as I *wrote a short letter to Gerald and went to bed.* My foggy attitude persisted as I wrote in the diary: *"I love Gerald so much. It has been eight months today of marriage,"* but only a little more than two months of the eight had been spent with my husband.

The groundhog must have predicted six more weeks of winter because all the next week the weather was *rainy and bad. It was rather cold!* The *students stayed inside most of the day.* Like the weather, my attitude remained dismal!

I felt better on the nineteenth when I *received a letter from Gerald dated February 2.* However, it turned out that I would not receive another until February 27.

The rest of the week *was cloudy; it rained and drizzled* and *it snowed some* on Wednesday. As the cold weather continued, my mood remained cloudy and despondent.

The radio announced that there were *horrible battles on Iwo Jima and the Western Front* which caused me to worry. I knew that Gerald had been in Germany for several weeks.

There was *no letter from Gerald, but I received my correspondence course. I almost hated it;* I didn't want to apply myself to some study. *I felt sorry for myself!*

Thank God for little friends! *Tommy came up to see me!* His visit cheered me, but still I lamented as I made a diary entry: *"No letter from my sweet husband. I love him so much. I miss him so much."*

When the *State Inspector came* on Thursday, *I wasn't prepared. I didn't have many things prepared for him. He was very nice* about it, but I was ashamed. *He asked for the register—the only teacher he asked.* I felt so humiliated and lamented, *"I am a failure as a teacher. I have no business teaching. I never do anything right."*

So I went down stairs and *talked to Mrs. Suffridge.*

"Hi, Pauline," Burnice said as she answered my knock on the door.

"Hi," was my brief sad reply.

My perceptive friend stated, "You okay?" She continued to wash dishes and patiently waited, knowing I would talk when I was ready.

After a brief silence, I spoke softly, "I messed up again. I'm just not cut out to be a teacher."

"So what did you mess up?" my wise mentor calmly asked.

I let out a big sigh and said, "The State Inspector came today, and I didn't have the register ready."

Burnice paused and then asked, "Was he upset? Did he get angry?"

"No. He was very nice, but I could tell he was disappointed."

"Did he say anything else to you?" Burnice asked.

"He just said to try to have it updated for his next visit." I sighed again.

"Well. It doesn't sound to me like he was too upset. All you can do now is get it caught up. We all mess up sometime. I'm sure everything will be okay," my sensitive friend replied.

"Yeah. Guess I need to work on the register," I responded. I already felt better. "Where are those boys? Think I'll go play with them for a while."

After visiting with my little friends, I went back to my apartment determined to work harder. *I fixed the register and wrote Gerald a letter.* I was still concerned for Gerald's safety and made an entry in my diary: *"I love Gerald so much! He must come back!"*

Friday, Mabel Ruth Johnson—a student, a 4-H member, and a friend—arranged for me to come to her house near Plainview for the weekend. I couldn't help but wonder if Ms. Blackwell, or maybe Burnice, had put her up to it. Nevertheless, I was glad she called.

Tommy came upstairs to get me. "You have a call."

Mabel Ruth Johnson, 1944

I was a little worried and prayed that it would not be about Gerald. "Do you know who it is?

"Some girl," he said and turned to leave.

I rushed down to the Suffridge's. It was Mable Ruth. She asked, "Hey. I've got it arranged for you to get to my house for the weekend?"

"That's great!" I responded.

Thank God for friends! She told me of the arrangements she had made. So I headed to Plainview: *I rode the bus to the corner; Gerald and Gladys Durham picked me up* there; *I rode to Durhams and ate supper with them. It was delicious; then Mabel came to the Durhams to get me to take me to the Johnsons.*

What a relaxing Saturday! The Johnsons made me *feel like one of the family. I crocheted . . . sewed on dresses. All the family sewed . . . Jim crocheted a rug. Mabel crocheted . . . The day passed just too rapidly. I had a big time* talking and laughing.

Sunday, February 25, the Johnsons *thought about going to church; but it was foggy, so they stayed at home . . . had dinner . . . talked . . . crocheted. All the students* (from Plainview) *gathered around the table to get their lessons.* It was good to see them again! *I helped them with literature and arithmetic. It was a lot of fun to be with a group to laugh. We went to bed early.*

Since I had my diary with me, I entered "*I wrote my husband a letter. I love him very much. My period began today.*" That explained my stormy emotions.

The next morning *the wind was blowing so rapidly and sleet covered the ground* as I *dressed, ate, and prepared to meet the bus. Elbert Johnson called the Suffridges to find out about school . . . there was none.* So at the Johnsons' we continued to *crochet and sew . . .* laughed and *had a big time . . . we went to bed early.*

Again on Tuesday I *dressed and prepared to meet the bus in case there was school, but there was none because of the falling snow.* The white blanket covering the ground *was beautiful* but treacherous. Since no vehicles were getting out, *after dinner Mabel Ruth and I prepared to ride horses to Brinkman . . . left at 3:00 p.m. We were very cold* by the time we got there; but I warmed up when I saw *many letters from Gerald. He was now in Germany* but *not in battle. The letters were dated from January 27 to February 12.* He said *it was so muddy there. My* (early) *birthday gift* from Gerald *was $30. I decided to get Fostoria and put the rest in the bank.*

Well, I was back in the apartment, but there was no school on Wednesday either. *It was a beautiful day, but still lots of snow on the ground. I dressed, ate, wrapped a package for Gerald; but missed the mailman* after traipsing into town through the mud, snow, and ice. My spirits were renewed and I stayed busy . . . *cleaned up . . . mopped and waxed all the floors and then washed the dishes. It took all day.* At the close of my busy day, there was *no mail; it all comes at once.* My little friend, *Fred, came up to see me, and we listened to the radio. I wrote a letter to Gerald, Mother, and Mrs. Beasley.*

I have $150 in bonds and $251.56 in the bank.*

The last day in February, I was *still unhappy about the gossip about me. I wished I could tell someone a few things.* There were backbiters who seemed to scrutinize and criticized everything I did and probably thought I was immature. They were probably right, but I really was trying! I felt I could do nothing right!

Without my friends to cheer me, it would have been difficult for me to keep my spirits up and keep trudging forward. Thank God for friends!

---

* May 1, 1941, the first Series E U.S. Savings Bond was sold to Franklin D. Roosevelt by secretary of the treasury, Henry Morgenthau. The War Finance Committees sold a total of $185.7 billion of securities to help finance the war. The war bond campaign was used to stir the consciences of Americans who had a financial and a moral stake in the war. Also, it showed a patriotic attitude and the spirit of sacrifice of Americans on the home front. By January 3, 1946, 85 million Americans had invested in War Bonds.

Chapter Forty-Four

All those gathered here will know that it is not by
sword or spear that the Lord saves; for the battle is
the Lord's, and he will give all of you into our hands.
— Samuel 17:47

Gerald's Remembrances—First Taste of Combat—March 1945

On February 23, as the news was reporting the *"horrible battles on the Western Front,"* my unit had already moved along the Siegfried Line. The medical personnel were billeted in a house in the German village of Lispenhausen along the Rhine. Most likely the house had been vacated by the fleeing Germans, or it is possible that the civilians had been told to leave.

Anyhow, the medical detachment stayed in German homes. The Germans could not possibly take all of their belongings so many valuables were left behind. As the medical detachment moved across Germany, the commanding officer, the Major, insisted to his superiors that he needed the finest home in each town for his unit to set up medical facilities.

Now, this is no exaggeration! He would go through the house(s) and pick out the things he wanted! PFC cook, called Cookie, a pretty good carpenter, would make wooden boxes for the major to use to send items such as grandfather clocks and ornate music boxes back to the states. Guess the major never got in trouble for doing that. He was a Jew who had studied medicine in Germany, and he hated the Germans. He probably saw it as payback.

Of course, the Germans went through homes and confiscated personal items, valuable paintings and other valuable items from the Jews as well as civilians throughout Europe as the refugees were forced out of their homes or fled. The spoils of war! Did that justify such pillage?

Lispenhausen was located in a mountainous area where there were ski slopes. The medical unit was billeted in a house that apparently belonged to a Catholic priest; one of the GIs had found priest vestments in one of the closets.

The Germans were shooting "screaming meemies," rockets that made a horrible noise as they flew in. Of course, the personnel had been told not to go outside without a helmet. However, there was a garden at this house, so I ventured out to get an onion, and I didn't have my helmet on. Here came a "screaming meemi"! I hit the ground as it sailed over and landed a distance away! It was frightening! I wasn't hurt, but that was the last time I went outside without a helmet! These "screaming meemies" could do a lot of damage if they hit close enough! And they were noisy!

There were also enemy riflemen situated at vantage points as well as artillery coming in and going out! Shells could be heard going over!

In late February, the unit was told to move out, to move forward. Well, fight! Looking at an area military map, our unit's objective was to take Hill 630. American artillery was supposed to come in ahead of the infantry to "soften" the place; then the artillery was supposed to stop so the infantry could move forward with their rifles. The timing must have gotten messed up because as the GIs neared the top of Hill 630, the American artillery started to come in, and I'm sure some of our men were injured and/or killed! It was sad, but many times during the war American artillery would drop in on its own men. They couldn't pinpoint exactly where the American troops were or where the artillery was dropping. A lot of Americans were killed by friendly fire!

Anyhow, the unit made it up near to the top of Hill 630 where some Germans were dug in firing machine guns. We were terrified as we lay face down with our noses buried in the dirt while the bullets from the German machine guns were shooting over our heads, clipping the branches of ceiling-high pine trees all around us! Branches were dropping on our helmets!

That was my unit's first real taste of combat! Well, the unit took the hill after the infantry engaged in "marching fire." The Germans were boxed up in foxholes with a bunch of GIs walking and shooting. The Germans didn't dare stick a head out! So the hill was taken.

Later I reflected on the bravery, fear of my comrades, and violence of war:

> *I think it logical to hold respect and admiration for the loyalty that many of my comrades have for their country where their loved ones live. Privations and dangers are endured for many reasons.*
>
> *It seems unlikely that any soldier fights solely because of love for his country. Ultimately pressure is brought from all sides and he finds himself face-to-face with a foe that probably is very startled, too. The business of killing begins! Hate and rage know no bounds! Love our enemies? Do good unto them that despitefully use us?*

Moving across Germany, Americans, along with their Allies, took thousands of German captives. Many captives were sent back to concentration camps, but of course, there were atrocities! There were atrocities on both sides! Both sides! I knew that then, and I know that now! In any war there are atrocities!

Anyhow, the unit took Hill 630 and dug in on top of the mountain where there was one German captive. He was sitting where the Americans told him to sit. Uh, just the one guy . . . In fact, I recall that he was eating something that he had pulled out of his garment. The captain gestured and told his First Sergeant to "take him to New York City!"

There was no particular discussion from the other soldiers protesting this action. Perhaps, they were too stunned or just didn't comprehend what was going on, or perhaps, they agreed with the decision. Without a doubt, a lot of atrocities took place on all sides . . . In the thick of battle, and particularly ground fighting, a soldier is not removed from what's happening around him. Fear, anger and emotion take charge. It's unlike the guy in the airplane who can drop a bomb and be removed from what is happening down below . . .

Anyhow, the First Sergeant took the German, and went out into the woods and did as he was told. Just went out somewhere in the woods, and uh . . .

Later I wrote briefly in my journal: *"One loses respect for the zealot who declares he is anxious and fit for battle. Surely such a person thinks it is a game."*

The captain was kind of bloodthirsty. I got along with him okay, but sometimes I would kind of tell him where to head up. As a medic attached to the unit I could make decisions about the medical condition of a soldier. This same First Sergeant later went down with battle fatigue; he obviously cracked up! Perhaps the related incident was preying on his conscience. He didn't last very long. I was the one who made the decision to send him back to the hospital. The captain resented me for that decision.

At another spot on Hill 630, I didn't see it but was told that there were Germans in foxholes ready to surrender. The captain told a young soldier whose brother had been killed earlier in the

war, "Go on up and take care of the Germans in the foxhole."
And the soldier did just that!

These events prompted me to write in my journal:

> *A much later afternoon: Procrastinations and negligence steal away time, which could be well spent.*
>
> *This finds me in a most undesirable place. I am seeing war and realizing more and more each day the awfulness, the expense, the utter folly of war. It seems that most of my immediate associates are cognizant of the awful absurdity of war, but their consciences, nevertheless, propel them in an abiding hate for the enemy. I find myself more oppressed and revolted by what I see and hear. Perhaps, there will come a time when I will very outwardly have to revolt. I'm even now praying to God that I won't be faced with a situation wherein I lose altogether my respect for my comrades who are actively and willingly engaged in fighting their enemies.*

As I think back, I realize that a person doesn't think things through in war like that. Emotions take over! Things happen! A human being doesn't decide, "Okay, I've got all the rules of war right here, and I'm going to follow them right down to a T. I'm not going to violate any of the war rules." Emotions take over! It is so true that "war is hell!"

However, I did not want to give the impression that I agreed with the violence and killing and wrote: *"It seems to me I must meticulously guard my actions and words, lest I leave the impression that I see no wrong in mortal combat."*

Occasionally, there were even incidents when an American soldier would threaten another American soldier, and I'm sure some of these threats were carried out. Back in Hattiesburg, Lieutenant Wroblewski, a medical administrative corp. officer, had been rough on his command.

One night after he'd been drinking, he came into the barracks in the middle of the night, woke everybody up, and made them get up and scrub the barracks down. Of course, it was just because he'd been drinking.

Well, for some reason, he really got after Tony Securo. Tony had grown up in Philadelphia where he had worked in a steel mill. He was brawny and rough talking, obviously a pretty tough guy. Lieutenant Wroblewski was on his case all the time.

Tony had told the lieutenant, "When we get into combat, I'll take care of you!"

Anyhow, overseas Lieutenant Wroblewski was a lot nicer guy. He got along with everybody. And Tony didn't kill him. But there were other threats like that from GIs, and some of the threats, I'm sure, were carried out.

The GIs were given C-rations, most of which were small-can-rations, such as beans and wieners, a kind of hash, Nescafe and little wafer cookies. A lot of these smaller cans could be easily carried in the backpack. The bigger packets of rations had more variety, food that tasted a little better, but these took up more room and were heavier.

Some of the guys scorned the C-rations, but I ate everything I could get my hands on. Maybe that's why I came home heavier. Many guys scorned the powdered lemonade that was mixed with water. I drank it because it had good Vitamin C content that I knew I needed. I was thankful for what I had.

A mobile "kitchen" went with the unit, but, of course, the supplies didn't always keep up with the needs at the front lines. Sometimes the cook would bring the prepared food right up close to the troops in large thermos containers.

While in the area of captured Hill 630, the kitchen came up the hill with the thermos containers full of so-called hot pancakes and syrup, but the pancakes were ice-cold and as leathery as a boot! The GIs were really hungry, so they just dipped them in the syrup and ate them as best they could. It was better than nothing. After waiting for a long time for the food to arrive, it was quite a disappointment.

My unit didn't have a very good cook, but as a medic, I could eat anywhere depending on the availability of another unit. I knew a heavy weapons company that had a really good cook who labored to please the guys. I would get over there every chance I had. There a soldier could get "hot" pancakes. Out of concern for my unit, I asked, "Can I bring some of my buddies over?"

The cook said, "Sure, bring them on over." There were big differences between mess sergeants.

After the area had been secured, the platoon sat around for days on top of snow-covered Hill 630. Artillery was coming in from the Germans. We could see some German civilians coming across the snow-covered open country toward the American lines walking through what was thought to be a German mine field. These mines were antipersonnel, antitank or antivehicle mines. Some antipersonnel mines when triggered would jump up high and throw out shrapnel. Others would just blow up from the bottom.

As we watched the civilians crossing, German artillery began to fall in on them. When the artillery hit the white snow-cover, it gouged a hole showing the brown dirt where it had hit. An older male civilian was hit and hurt. Impulsively, I jumped up and started out across the minefield picking my way gingerly, trying not to put any weight down. I managed to get out to the civilians without triggering a mine while leaving foot tracks in the snow. There were several women and children crouching, afraid to move. This older fellow had been hit by artillery in the leg. I quickly did what I could for him. I spoke in limited German to try to reassure him. (I had picked up some German from the booklets given to all the soldiers. On other occasions when the need arose to communicate with Germans, Lindy Lindquist of

Company A, who had studied German in high school, spoke and interpreted for the unit.)

Two other GIs cautiously followed in my foot tracks with a litter, got the injured man, and carried him out without any problem; then the other civilians followed my tracks. Nobody stepped on a mine.

Returning, aware of the possibility of mines, I carefully crossed the field back to my unit stepping in my tracks! Had I stopped to think first, I might not have dashed out like I did. I just didn't think!

I didn't know until later, but the enlisted men in the unit got together and recommended to the officers that I get a medal for bravery and my selfless gesture in regards to the wounded German civilian. At a much-later date, one of the captains presented the Bronze Star to me. The decoration came as a complete surprise! I had put the incident out of my mind!

On another cold night on Hill 630, the snow on the ground was frozen and crusted, and it would crunch loudly when stepped on. There was a rumor that there were several German patrols out in the area. It was dark. Very still! Very cold!

While crouched undercover, we heard a lot of crunching noises, became alert with guns poised, and saw several GIs coming toward us carrying two GIs. One was dead. The other was wounded pretty badly. These soldiers had hit antipersonnel mines. The wounded boy's legs were just peppered! A nice kid!

He asked, "How's my buddy?"

After checking his buddy, I told him, "I'm sorry, he didn't make it."

"No, check him again!" he exclaimed!

I bent over the body as if I was checking for life, and stated, "I'm sorry, son, he's dead."

"No, no! You don't understand! I just received a letter from his mom! She told me to watch out for her boy! He has to be okay! Check him again!"

Sadly, wishing I could make a different diagnosis, once again I leaned down to check for a pulse. "He's gone. I'm sorry!"

I had two GIs put the sobbing lad on a litter, and we headed out to carry him back to the headquarters of the medical detachment where the doctors, the MAC'S (Medical Administrative Corp), the officers, and the attached personnel were billeted in a ski resort some distance away in the mountains.

As we crunched along in the cold dark night, a verbal "Halt" from under cover was ordered. Since we didn't know whether English-speaking Germans or Americans were stopping us, I fearfully spoke the password and we were then allowed to pass. It was frightening! That night we heard the scary command to "Halt" a number of times as we proceeded.

Finally, after many cold hours of walking and carrying and brief stops to rest, we got to headquarters with this kid. When we knocked on the door, it got very quiet from inside! I said, "It's Beasley!"

It remained very still and quiet, but nobody responded. "It's Beasley," I repeated. The atmosphere was very tense for a few uncertain moments on both sides of the door.

I slowly opened the door and cautiously stepped inside. Lieutenant Wroblewski was standing there with a carbine aimed right at me. Only when he recognized me did he put the gun down! But the wounded boy was finally delivered.

The two infantrymen and I had not slept for several nights, so the Jewish doctor ordered us to lie down on the floor and sleep. He didn't get an argument. The traipsing trio was more than glad to do just that!

When we finally woke up, the wounded GI was sitting up in bed, smoking. That was the first time I had ever been glad to see somebody smoke! The rescue party was told that the extreme cold during the transport had probably saved the soldier's life. The injured boy was sent back to the hospital. I never knew how he got along.

Later I made a journal entry that expressed misgivings, questions, and a prayer:

> *How long can I perform my duties in helping the sick and wounded? Does my participation show approval of the awful business? What else is there to do? An escape question? What would Christ do? What would Paul do?*
>
> *Another day: I must ever express my great pleasure at a particularly gleanful study of God's Word. How perfectly God's Word anticipates, yea, actually knows, our every complaining thought. Indeed, these are troublesome times for God's children and me. I pray that all other Christians may be so diligently studying as to find the answers to their doubts and misgivings. "For whom the Lord loveth he chasteneth, and scourgeth every son whom he receiveth."*
>
> *Joyfully, I anticipate the time when, if it is God's will, I may stand before God's people and teach men the truth about their trials and tribulations. May this very writing be a reminder to me. May I recall memories that will aid in the presentation of a lesson of profitable clarity. May it all be done to the glory of God to whom I pray that I may have further and increased opportunity and zeal to do His will.*
>
> *Even now I can picture my expressions, mannerisms and illustrations, which will help to open the souls of men. I thank God for an increasing understanding of men and I pray for an exacting ability to fathom the penetrable aspects of every man's personality.*
>
> *"But to do good and to communicate, forget not, for with such sacrifices God is well-pleased." Can there be a definite capacity for doing good? Is it possible to do enough good that no more is expected? What restraint should a Christian use concerning his talents and abilities?*

The First French Army advanced from the south to the Rhine River from Strasbourg to the Swiss border by February 9. The Ninth Army reached the Rhine near Dusseldorf on March 2. The First Army took Cologne, and the Ninth Armored Division seized a bridge at Remagen on March 7. The First Army centered its action from this bridge. The Third Army reached the Rhine two days later. The First Army took Aachen on March 21.

Allied forces had established a barrier all along the Rhine River.

My unit had been stationed along the Rhine from the middle of February thru most of March.

CHAPTER FORTY-FIVE

There is a time for everything,
and a season for every activity under heaven . . .
A time to weep and a time to laugh.
A time to mourn and a time to dance.

—Ecclesiastes 3:1, 4

Pauline's Diary— a Touch of Spring—March 1945

There had been no school the last couple of days in February due to a cold front with high winds, sleet and snow. So when school resumed Thursday, March 1, *it felt strange to go to school;* but it was good to be busy and back to work! My routine had been interrupted, so *I had to make several trips* back to the apartment *before I had everything I needed.* It's a good thing that the teacherage was near the Brinkman School.

Friday *was foggy at 8:00 a.m., but it cleared off and a stiff, sandy wind* blew *from the north.* With the sandy, grinding wind it probably wasn't the best day *for dressing up,* but *I put a ribbon in my hair and wore a new dress.*

I did not feel like working *after school,* and I did not try to go to my folks, but I wanted to get away and laugh. So I called a taxi and *went to town* (Mangum) *to the show, "Costello and Lou."** They *were nutty!*

I really enjoyed the movie, but when I got home, there was *a note left by Mabel Ruth. She had come while I was gone.* I felt really bad and *was so unhappy; I was sorry I missed her. I know it hurt her;* she had gone to the trouble of stopping by.

In fact, *I was told not to do it*—to venture out alone; it was not proper for a young married woman whose husband was overseas to create any cause for gossip. I knew I would probably be scolded again. I just wished others could understand that sometimes I needed to get away?

There was no school Saturday, so *I listened to the radio most of the day* as I hung around the apartment, checked for mail, and prepared *several packages* of goodies *for Gerald. I had no mail from Gerald, but received a letter from Mother and Royce. His letter* was written *better than a lot of my seventh and eighth grade students'* could write.

While at the store I *played the piano some* though I could only play very simple arrangements. I always enjoyed playing the piano; it relaxed me.

After visiting the Suffridges I wrapped a package and wrote two letters to my sweet.

I was happy to be able to chaperone several school events; it provided a change of pace, got me out of the apartment, and it was fun to be with the students. So after school Monday, March 5, *I went with the seventh-grade girls to a show, "The Merry*

---

*   The "Costello and Lou" show as quoted from the diary had to have been one of the movies that Abbott and Costello made in 1945: (1) *Here Come the Co-Eds,* 2) *Abbott and Costello in Hollywood,* or (3) *The Naught Nineties.*

*Manahans."** It was a fair show with a cute ending.* I returned home that evening feeling pretty good and was ready for a good nights' sleep. However, that night I was awakened by a bright and loud percussion show of *lightning and thunder.*

Though the weather *was chilly with a clear sky* on Tuesday I *attended a carnival sponsored by the junior and senior classes. They took in over $100—almost clear! They had everything imaginable. It was quite enjoyable!*

After I got home *I had a call from Mabel Ruth Johnson.* Since I had no phone, Tommy came up to tell me I had a phone call. *It almost scared me to death!* I feared bad news. Maybe Gerald had been wounded, or worse, killed! I headed down the stairs fearful, but I felt relieved, then ashamed. It was Mabel Ruth.

"Pauline, I came by the other day and you were gone. Are you okay?" Mabel asked with sincere concern.

I sighed, hesitant to admit my folly, "I saw your note. Sorry, I missed you. I went out."

"I was worried about you. Where did you go? Did you go by yourself?" she inquired.

I ashamedly answered, "I called a taxi and went to see a show. I really needed to get out and laugh."

"Pauline, you know you shouldn't do that—that is, go out alone. I understand, but will you call me next time you want to get out? Anyway, I was calling about the party Friday. Would it be okay if I came and stayed with you after the party and stayed till Sunday?" Mabel asked.

"Oh, certainly! I'd love to have your company. It'll be fun!" I stated after her slight rebuke. "Mabel, I'm okay. Sorry, I worried

---

* The comedy, *The Merry Manahans,* was directed by Charles Lamont, and starred Ann Blyth, Rosemary De Camp, John Miljan, Donald O'Connor, and Jack Oakie. It was about a comic who meets his former sweetheart and partner, both with grown children.

you, and you're right, I shouldn't have gone off by myself. But hey! I'm looking forward to having you stay with me."

"Great! Pauline, I'll see you Friday then. Bye."

She had been concerned about me ever since she had missed me several days earlier. I was sorry I had worried her.

Though chilly, Wednesday was a sunny, *beautiful day. The children were noisy and restless* at school. Spring was trying to show its smiling face; the sun was out, the trees were beginning to bud and the grass showed signs of new green. The students would have preferred to be outside.

I would have preferred to be outside too. Before the day was over I had *played softball, and walked four miles with Ms. Burcham and Tommy to the Posts where we were fed. It was a delicious meal . . . I played their piano some,* then came home and *wrote a letter to Gerald.*

I received a letter from Gerald dated February 19, so my spirits remained high Friday as I attended *the freshman class party at the gym. I helped them make sandwiches . . . and became very tired. Mabel had called and came. We had a lot of fun at the party; we helped clean up and got to bed at twelve-thirty.* We were too tired to talk much.

Mabel Ruth stayed with me thru the eleventh (Friday to Sunday). It was nice to have a companion. Sunday, we went to church. Afterward I *fixed a lunch of carrots, potatoes, breaded steaks, and the trimmings. We ate so much . . . did some talking after lunch . . .* then *she left about five.*

I enjoyed a short walk at the end of *a beautiful warm day.*

March 1945 in Oklahoma was blessed with twenty-three beautifully *typical spring days.* The nice weather made it possible to participate in outdoor activities with friends and students; *I had a lot of fun playing softball* with the students; *I played first base; Ms. Blackwell invited me to supper. It was so very good. I helped wash dishes, then came home, and Ms. Burcham and I rode around a section on bikes. It was a beautiful scene with the wheat waving in the wind.*

Before retiring I *played softball with the small boys* (Tommy and Fred).

The pleasant weather persisted as my birthday approached. Monday, March 12, was *a beautiful but cloudy, warm day.* It seemed spring was here to stay. It was also time for *six weeks tests, so I had many papers to grade.*

Friends and family helped make my birthday special. *I received a letter, birthday card and a five-dollar bill from Mrs. Beasley.* She probably couldn't afford it, but I appreciated her thoughtfulness. Tuesday, *the seventh graders had a class meeting to decide on something for* my birthday, so I did not attend the meeting. I received an early present from Mother, *a beautiful dress.*

However, there was *no letter from Gerald!*

School let out at noon Wednesday because there was to be *a funeral at the gym.* I didn't go because I needed *to study on the correspondence course . . . didn't do much but did read some history. Later I went back to the schoolhouse to get some books and was caught by a big rain and hailstorm . . .* had to stay *there one-and-a-half-hours* until the storm passed. I didn't like being alone in the building with the hail beating on the roof; I was glad when the storm was over.

I had already received several early birthday gifts, including one from Gerald ($30); but on March 15, my twenty-first birthday, I received still more presents. *The seventh graders gave me a beautiful satin robe; the eighth graders presented a fruit shower; then* I went with the *seventh graders to the show at Granite . . . had a lot of fun at a cafe laughing. It was a wonderful day but not complete because of no letter from Gerald.*

Letters from Gerald kept me informed about how he was doing and where he was. March 5, *I received a sweet letter written February 14 . . . He was still in Germany.* On the sixth, the *letter received from Gerald said he is going to send me something from Germany!*

I was so proud; I could hardly wait to see what he was sending me! On the seventh, *I received four letters from Gerald written February 20 through 23. He sent a paper . . . about Germany. Gerald was still in the place where he last was* (along the Rhine).

But there was also a stretch of fourteen days from March 12 through March 23 in which I had no letters from Gerald. Those long intervals with no word from him caused me to worry about his safety. Each passing day I became more agitated, *lost patience all day,* and was *quite unhappy at the students for not getting their lessons.* I continued to write *v-mails to him* hoping he would receive encouragement from them. I made a desperate diary entry: *"I love him very much! He is such a wonderful person! No letter today! He must be very busy, and the mail is late in coming.* (I refused to contemplate that he might be injured or worse.) *I must have letters along the way!"*

It *was a beautiful typical March day as I let the students have an activity and gave out the report cards.* But there was still *no letter from Gerald, so after visiting the Suffridges, I went to the Posts to play the piano.*

The radio news of March 22 stated *"the Allies were at the Rhine River ready to cross."* I was so worried! He must be in the middle of the fighting. I wrote: *"I hope it ends soon. I had a good cry."*

When *Mrs. Hoffman received six letters from James* on the twenty-third, I was jealous and angry and disgusted with the mail service. Why had I not received any? Surely, Gerald had written! I had no ambition; but I had to go to work. *After school Mr. Suffridge and I had a good talk about the lunch program; it was to be stopped as it wasn't paying off very well. When I got home I did nothing but read a book. I wrote Gerald a letter and went to bed.*

I was overjoyed and recharged Saturday after *school turned out at noon.* I had received a letter from Gerald, the first in fourteen days! My diary entry reflected my mood: *"I was ambitious today . . . received a letter from Gerald. He is in the First Army. He said his face looked like a brush pile* (I guess he had been unable to shave?). *I know he must be working so hard. I also received a letter from Mrs. Beasley. She stated that he wrote her a letter dated March 4. I love him so much! I studied some in the afternoon, washed dishes, hair, and cleaned up. Studied and to bed."*

On Sunday, the shining sun warmed the earth as I went to church and prayed for Gerald's safety. *It was a beautiful day and beautiful night. I listened to the radio and wrote two 4-H demonstrations. The "Blondie and Baby Snooks"* radio show was especially good.*

The last week in March the weather allowed the students and me to *play some softball. The classes had two hours of activity.* Then I *went to wash* and was able to *hang the clothes outside to dry at the end of a beautiful day; I then brought them into the house in the beautiful moonlight . . . I was so very tired . . . fixed the lunch report . . . started my period.*

But Tuesday, my demeanor was like the weather; it *started out a beautiful day but ended very stormy. I couldn't seem to do a thing but wrong. I was becoming very cranky and crabby. After school I voted in the school board election. It was my first election . . . received a food chart and a lot of mail of no importance.* I was disappointed, *exhausted,* and worried! *I went to bed and folded clothes* as I listened to the radio; *the news was good* for the Allies. *The First Army advanced twenty-seven miles and is now fifty-eight miles east of the Rhine.* I just knew Gerald was in the middle of the conflict! I prayed, *"I love him so much. God be with Gerald and keep him safe!"*

Wednesday *was a beautiful day* as I went about my school business. I was overjoyed when I *received a letter from Gerald which*

---

* This radio situation comedy featured the Bumsteads. Each show began with Dagwood's howl, "Bloooonndie!" Dagwood, a bumbling architect at Dithers Construction Company, and their two children, Alexander and Cookie, and the dog Daisy created much chaos. But calm, in control Blondie would always set things right.

was written February 24. It had taken thirty-two days to arrive. *He had seen the Siegfried Line and had heard the jerries.*

Information received from Gerald was so outdated, and I knew he was no longer at the Siegfried Line; but I needed to hear from him every day. The radio news reported *"the First Army is still moving but has a blackout."* I knew for sure he was in the fighting zone in Germany.

The radio was playing the song "Wonder When My Baby's Coming Home"; it expressed my feelings. I was worried, sad and "haven't seen a sunny day ever since he went away . . . haven't slept a wink at night worrying if he's all right . . ."[*]

Next morning I had trouble waking up because I was having a pleasant dream; *I was certainly dreaming about Gerald when I had to get up . . . I felt fine until lunch, then, I began to feel drowsy. After school I had five letters from Gerald, and I read each* of them *dozens of times. They were written February 26, March 1, 4, 7 and 12. My* diary entry read: *"It is wonderful to hear from him! He is wonderful! I love him so much . . . God be with us so that this war may end soon. The news is good!"*

Good Friday, March 30, was *a windy, cool day;* but the school had an *egg hunt and program in the afternoon* anyway. But I was confused and upset again because *I made another mistake by telling the students to stay until six.* Guess some parents were upset when the kids got home late. Of course, I got scolded. I felt so down and wrote: *"It worries me . . . nobody gave me any instructions. I don't wonder he* (Gerald) *should want to bust up with me. I am making so many mistakes. No mail today,"*

I was not in the mood, but I made myself work *on the correspondence course.*

---

[*]   Composed by Kermit Goell and Arthur Kent, performed by Helen O'Connell with the Jimmy Dorsey and his orchestra, recorded by Decca Records in 1942.

Saturday, I was depressed and did not want to stay in Brinkman. I had to get away! *I was so hurt.* I went to town and *bought a few things;* then *Ms. Blackwell drove me all the way to the folks' farm.*

The folks were at home but not expecting me. *We went fishing on Elk Creek. Royce was a mess; he made a cute rod and reel.* We *caught three fish* and *had a feast. Royce and I went to sleep on the bank of the creek* as the sun was warming and coloring our faces. *It was a beautiful day as I thought, "The country is so beautiful. I love Gerald and wish he could have been with me."*

April 1, Easter Sunday, Royce and I *dressed and ate a lot of fish for breakfast . . . then went to church. I drove the car. I enjoyed the services very much; the church building looked very nice.* That afternoon *I ate a lot of supper. I slept and read a lot.*

The country was beautiful. The orchard was in full bloom. I had a great time at home and did not want to return to Brinkman. But *Mother* was firm and *took me to meet Ms. Blackwell. Ms. Blackwell brought me home much against my will. I went to church at Mangum . . . wrote a long letter* to Gerald after getting back. I prayed, *"I love Gerald so much! God protect him and bring him home! He is wonderful."*

CHAPTER FORTY-SIX

How the mighty have fallen!
The weapons of war have perished!
—2 Samuel 1:27

Gerald's Remembrances— in Germany—April 1945

Our unit got a new lieutenant, Lieutenant Jones, who was with the unit for the remainder of the war. He was with the First Battalion as we began to move across the Rhine into Germany toward Leipzig.

We experienced some wet, warmer weather as we moved through Bod Ems and Sevsizullich. By April 4 as the weather was warming, the First Army had moved further east through Giessen and April 12 to Marburg and on toward Fulda located on the river Fulda.

Fulda and the surrounding areas became where the U.S. Army stationed the Fourteenth and later the Eleventh Armored Cavalry Regiments as an invasion route against the Germans for the U.S. V Corps.

It was after midnight as the unit came into the blacked-out city of Fulda, a pretty good-sized town. Our unit thought we were unobserved, but we were not so lucky. All of a sudden there was a big explosion right in the midst of the troops! Everybody scattered! Adrenaline propelled us, and some of the men and I went into the basement of a nearby house. When a flashlight was turned on, the others discovered that I was bleeding. I had been hit with shrapnel in my left cheek. Well, the cheek by my nose. Ha! It was treated with sulfa. It wasn't a terribly bad wound, but my face did swell up mostly on the one side.

However, I wasn't sent back to the hospital because the doctors treated the wound. It healed up just fine. For this injury I received a purple heart and a scar that continues to scale over when the weather is cold.

At a later time, we were somewhere near a lake and the Germans were throwing artillery all around. A soldier near me hollered, "I've been hit!" (I can almost remember his name; the same name as some producer of some TV show. I'm sure he is not that producer, but I think about this incident every time I see the credits.) I ran to him.

"I've been hit! I've been hit," he repeated!

I asked him, "Can you stand up?"

He replied, "I think I can."

I asked him, "Can you walk?"

He grimaced, "I think I can."

So I asked, "Can you run?"

He responded, "I think I can." Meanwhile, as we finished our conversation, a shell hit right beside us in the mud, but it didn't explode. Nevertheless, we got out of there!

Though artillery shells were intended to explode as they hit the ground, many artillery shells were duds. Was divine providence a factor in saving my life? Did God still have a plan for me?

News of President Roosevelt's death on April 12, 1945, did not reach the troops immediately, but when it did, the soldiers had little time to mourn as they were on the move and engaged in battle.

By mid-April 1945, the Ninth Army attacked along the Ruhr where the German defense was concentrated. Hodges' First Army and Patton's

Third Army broke through into the heart of Germany. The Ninth joined with the First in cutting off the Ruhr. In eighteen days three hundred thousand German prisoners were taken as the armies drove deep into Germany. Montgomery's forces in the north crossed the Netherlands and drove toward Bremen and Hamburg. In the south, Dever's armies took Munich and swept into Austria.

After Latvia and Estonia had been cleared of German troops in September 1944, Russia invaded Prussia, German soil, on October 13. Russian troops took Warsaw, Poland, on January 17, 1945. Then Russian troops took Danzig, Poland, on March 30 and Vienna, Austria, on April 13.

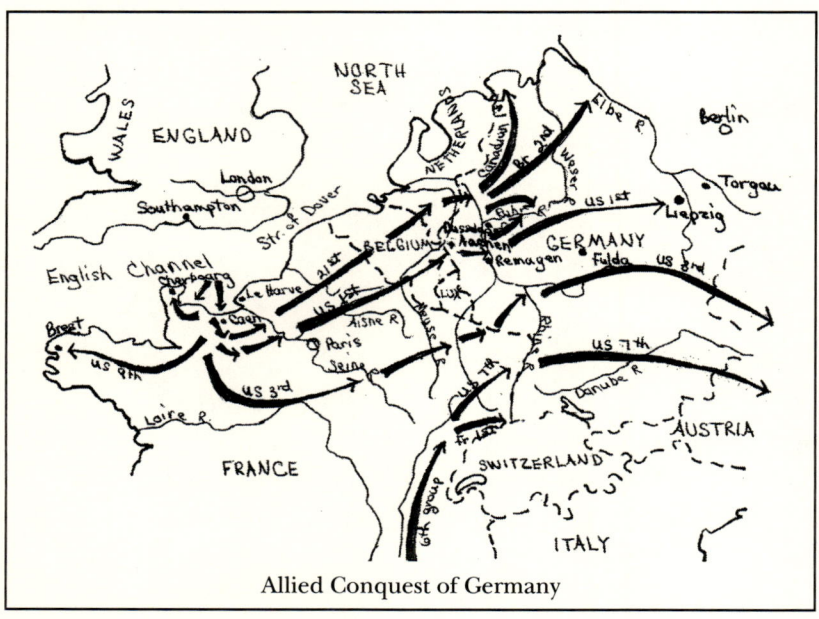

Allied Conquest of Germany

The Sixty-Ninth Division engaged in the battle of Leipzig on April 19, 1945.

The last fighting my unit did was in Eilenburg, just east of Leipzig. Allied artillery had just flooded into Eilenburg and had left a wake of fires and destruction everywhere. The Allies knew that the war was about over, and they just wanted to fire everything they could. We saw a lot of destruction, and we knew we were under fire from our own artillery. Many soldiers and civilians were injured.

It was very frightening with shells falling, artillery whizzing over head, guns firing, and injured civilians and soldiers crying out in pain. In Eilenburg there were "duds" everywhere. However, many shells did explode. Experts eventually had to be sent in to defuse these "duds" because if messed with they could explode.

I was in one spot where a German home had just been destroyed. As the German civilian family came out of their underground shelter, an old German gentlemen held his hands to his face and in despair kept repeating, "Meine haus! Meine haus!"

While street fighting continued in Eilenburg, a German civilian wearing a railroad uniform had been mistakenly shot for a soldier. I was delayed when I stopped to take care of this fellow who was hit in his legs. I took him inside the house to give him morphine and dress his wounds.

Afterward, I attempted to find my unit. I cautiously went into the front of this long row of two—and three-story apartment buildings and came to the back exit. Looking out to see if there were any GIs around, there at eye level in the glass window was a bullet hole. Looking down the stairs, I saw a recently killed GI collapsed on the floor. I checked for a pulse, found none, then left that position quickly!

Leaving the building and rounding a corner I bumped into a German officer. I was not sure where he had come from; he just seemed to show up. He startled me. There was a strange and awkward moment as we both just stood silently looking at each other. The German officer knew, of course, that the GIs were all around the area and that the end of the war was near. Yeah! He knew that.

I didn't really fear for my life since I was wearing a Red Cross insignia on my helmet and shoulders, but I did not know what his intentions were. The German officer spoke politely in English. "Could you please come with me to the underground hospital and get the belongings of a dead American officer? He was in our care, but he died." I agreed to do so.

On the way we passed a little-bitty church building made of very heavy stone; the building was very ancient. The German officer conversed freely, "Martin Luther preached here." I could speak only a little German, so the conversation had to be in English.

Anyhow, I went with him into the German underground hospital and picked up the belongings of the American officer who had died. It was strange to walk among the wounded enemy and their caregivers; their questioning, weary eyes staring into mine as I was allowed to leave. They all knew the war was about over.

I caught up with my unit and we moved to the southeast part of Eilenburg along some railroad tracks where there was street fighting.

American artillery started landing around the American GIs. I was by Lieutenant Jones when we both fell face down in the dirt. Shrapnel hit the lieutenant's helmet and ripped it to pieces. It didn't kill him or even hurt him, but he sure turned white.

CHAPTER FORTY-SEVEN

Yet the Lord longs to be gracious to you;
he rises to show you compassion.
For the Lord is a God of justice.
Blessed are all who wait for him!

—Isaiah 30:18

Pauline's Diary
Spring of Hope—April 1945

In March, spring had peeked out of the clouds giving hope of warmer weather in April; but April's weather and world events ended up being unpredictable.

There was also hope that the war would soon end. All week *the news was good.* The Pacific front was progressing in favor of the Allies as *the Island of Okinowa was invaded.* On the European front the Allies were advancing, taking German prisoners and pushing the German troops back. On the home front, there was an electric feeling of hope. Hope that the killing would stop and loved ones would soon be coming home!

I was restless. I wanted to pack up and head northeast to meet the soldiers coming home, but I knew I had to wait. The waiting was awful, waiting for warm weather, waiting for the war's end, waiting for Gerald to come home. Waiting, waiting, waiting!

After spending Easter Sunday with the folks, the first day back in the classroom went well. *I felt fine and got in most of the classes*. However, the students were restless, possibly due to the changing weather and the growing sense of hope. *I felt bad* when I had to puncture the balloon of optimism, but *I had to give some students Fs for not getting book reports in on time.*

Later in the week when the morning *was cloudy and rainy,* the children were restless again. *Edward stuck Luther with a pin,* and *he had to write fifty lines.*

Thank goodness by afternoon it was *clear again.*

The weather during the first week in April started out *clear but cold; then* a *cold freezing rain* threatened Oklahoma with a *chilling freeze.* Each day I *woke up freezing,* jumped out of bed, *dressed quickly* and warmly, and *hurried off to school.* I could *feel the chill* through my clothes *as I went out at eight-thirty.* By Friday, the *farmers feared their fruit was ruined.* I was concerned that Mom and Dad might lose their fruit crop, but later on *April 17, I received a letter from Mother; all the fruit wasn't killed* by the freeze. I was glad that their profits were not destroyed.

To make matters worse, the loose sands of southwest Oklahoma were vulnerable to the wind. Though it began to warm, it *was windy and sandy.* I was glad there was no school Saturday morning; even a brisk walk to school would have left my hair dirty, and my mouth and eyes grated by the gritty sandy air.

Lydia Mae Best and Avis Redman, Pauline's A&M friends

I continued to fulfill my responsibilities; *I filled out claims for Mr. Suffridge . . . made out a lunch report . . . planned for and taught classes . . . prepared 4-H demonstrations . . . coached softball and attended the evening board meeting.*

I received and wrote letters to family and friends. It was always great to receive letters from friends. However, some left me with concerns. In *a letter from Avis Redman* (an Oklahoma

A&M friend) *who was with Bob,* she stated that *they were going to nightclubs.* That worried me! She was a Christian! What was she doing going to nightclubs? I determined to write her.

I also *received letters from Mrs. Beasley and two government checks. I paid a big two-month grocery bill* since the store had let me make purchases on credit. *A letter from Lydia lifted my spirits; Lloyd was doing fine* in England and was recovering from his wounds. I enjoyed *a letter from Maxine Williams,* another church friend from Oklahoma A&M. She was also a teacher; *she had been busy teaching, grading papers, preparing, and teaching classes.* I also *received* several *letters from Mother.*

I was still concerned about Gerald. The news reports stated that the war should be over soon, but Gerald was still in the middle of the conflict in Germany. But all I could do was wait.

I planned to stay busy so time would pass more quickly.

I was confused as to what I should do in the upcoming summer. Would the war end before summer, and would Gerald be home? Should I return to Oklahoma A&M and take more college courses? Should I go stay with my folks where I could wait to see how the war developed? Should I keep myself free for travel to the northeast to meet Gerald should he come home? Again, I knew I had to wait and see how things developed.

It helped to pass the time with others and get out of the apartment. I spent a lot of time with *Mrs. Suffridge.* She was a great friend. *I talked with her a lot!* She showed me *some of her baby things.* They were so small! I longed to have babies of my own, but I knew that would have to wait. *I also took care of Fred for a while, and* I was invited to go *to Reed with Mrs. Suffridge* where *Tommy and Fred had their pictures made.* One time while with the Suffridges, we *ate supper with the Carpenters.* Dinner *was delicious!*

Sunday, April 8, I was glad when Mrs. Suffridge asked me *to go to Granite with them to visit Grandma Suffridge. I went but with the fear my folks might come* to visit me in Brinkman. They had spoken about coming some time but had no phone to let me know when they might come. We went to Granite and *had a wonderful time . . . had a delicious dinner of fried chicken and all the trimmings. It was late when we returned.* Thank goodness, my folks had not come to visit while I was gone. I would have felt really bad.

As I headed to school for *a meeting of the 4-H club* the second week of April, *the wind and sand were bad. All* Tuesday *morning* we had another *4-H meeting* to get ready for an upcoming 4-H show, and then I *had spelling and history in the afternoon.* After school we headed to the 4-H show, and *it came a big rain at Mangum.* The rain was welcomed because it settled the sand, at least for a while.

Finally, *Wednesday, the day was beautiful; calm and clear . . . had school all day without many interruptions. I wasn't very tired* after I returned to the apartment; *I let Tommy put me to work digging up the front yard to plant flowers and vegetables . . . got a nice big blister in the palm of my hand.*

The government had promoted the planting of Victory Gardens during the war because of shortages of vegetables and problems with transporting goods. The importance of these gardens was talked about in schools, and colorful flower and vegetable gardens were being planted everywhere across the country. Tommy was determined that we should have one.

I had determined to *work on the correspondence course to finish it by the time school was out* in May, but my blister was a good excuse not to work on it this fine evening. It had been a good day, but I got *no mail.*

The weather took a turn for the worse again. While at Eastview School, *there was a tornado alert,* and all the students had to file down to the narrow basement and wait until an all clear was given. The experience was a bit unnerving for both teachers and students. Thankfully, a tornado did not set down in our area. However, the news reported that a *tornado hit Oklahoma City, Antlers and Muskogee.*

And storms kept coming! While listening to the radio on April 12, the nation and I were hushed into silence. After reporting to Congress on his conference with Churchill and Stalin at Yalta, and meetings with King Saud of Saudi Arabia, King Farouk of Egypt, and Emperor Haile Selassie of Ethiopia; President Roosevelt went to Warm Springs for a rest. On April 12, 1945, while signing numerous documents, he slumped in his chair saying, "I have a terrible headache." He died at 3:55 p.m. of a massive cerebral hemorrhage.

I wrote in my diary: *"President Franklin D. Roosevelt died suddenly this p.m. FDR was 63 and had been president for 13 years. It was a great loss and a shock. Harry S. Truman took the oath of office as Thirty-third president. Victory for the Allies in World War II was close."*

The following day Oklahomans enjoyed *a beautiful day* weather-wise*, but the nation was in mourning as President FDR was moved to Washington.* For several days, *the country mourned quietly as the funeral train brought Roosevelt's body to Washington where memorial services were broadcast on the radio.*

Despite, or maybe because of the tragic news, I busied myself *planting flowers* and vegetables *in the afternoon . . . then washing and setting my hair to serve as door keeper at the senior play.*

I spent the evening of April 14 listening *to the memorial service for FDR at the White House. The service was very simple and lasted only twenty-five minutes.*

Then, Sunday, April 15, a rainy and chilly day in Oklahoma, the radio broadcast the funeral. *Pres. Franklin D. Roosevelt was laid to rest at 10:00 a.m. It was a very simple ceremony.*

I listened to Harry S. Truman's radio statement before Congress, April 16, 1945:

> It is with a heavy heart that I stand before you, my friends and colleagues . . . Our departed leader never looked backward. He looked forward and moved forward . . . That is what America will do . . .

Today, the entire world is looking to America for enlightened leadership to peace and progress . . . It can be provided only by a united nation deeply devoted to the highest ideals.

With great humility I call upon all Americans to help me keep our nation united in defense of those ideals . . . I will support and defend those ideals with all my strength and all my heart. That is my duty and I shall not shirk it.

So that there can be no possible misunderstanding, both Germany and Japan can be certain, beyond any shadow of doubt, that America will continue the fight for freedom until no vestige of resistance remains . . .

The responsibility for making of the peace . . . must rest with the defenders of the peace . . . But the laws of God and of man have been violated and the guilty must not go unpunished . . . Lasting peace can never be secured if we permit our dangerous opponents to plot future wars with impunity at any mountain retreat . . .

We shall never cease our struggle to preserve and maintain our American way of life . . . America, along with her brave Allies, is paying again a heavy price for the defense of our freedom . . .

The grand strategy of the United Nations' war has been determined—due in no small measure to the vision of our departed Commander in Chief. We are now carrying out our part of that strategy . . .

Our debt to the heroic men and valiant women in the service of our country can never be repaid . . . In the memory of those who have made the supreme sacrifice—in the memory of our fallen President—we shall not fail!

It is not enough to yearn for peace. We must work, and if necessary, fight for it . . . Hope has become the secret weapon of the forces of liberation . . . Nothing is more essential to the future peace of the world than continued cooperation of the nations . . . I appeal to every American, regardless of party, race, creed, or color, to support our efforts to build a strong and lasting United Nations Organization . . .

Today, America has become one of the most powerful forces for good on earth. We must keep it so. We have achieved a world leadership which does not depend solely upon our military and naval might . . . We must now learn to live with other nations for our mutual good . . .

At this moment, I have in my heart a prayer. As I have assumed my heavy duties, I humbly pray Almighty God, in the words of King Solomon: "Give therefore thy servant an understanding heart to judge thy people, that I may discern between good and bad; for who is able to judge this thy so great a people."

I ask only to be a good and faithful servant of the Lord and my people.*

Less shocking but nevertheless tragic, Wednesday, April 18, a cloudy and cold day, a newscast reported that *"Ernie Pyle, a well-known war correspondent, was killed on Te Island today. He was shot by a Jap."*

That evening I made a special written notation that as of April 18, Gerald and I had been *married ten months today*. My worries were renewed when *I heard over the radio that Gerald's division was in the battle of Leipzig*. I prayed: *"God protect him!" I wrote Gerald a four-page letter*.

I visited the Suffridges; then went to Mrs. Clark's to take some sewing . . . had a very nice chat. The walk back was a pleasant diversion. I was lazy, so there was *no studying done on the course . . . wrote Gerald a letter and made out six weeks test in arithmetic.*

---

* www.**famousquotes**.me.uk/**speeches**/presidential-**speeches**/

I had finally resolved to take classes at Oklahoma A&M during the summer. The settling of summer plans created a welcome anticipation of the future. So Saturday with the weather *cold and rainy*, I began to make preparations. I *wrote a letter to Mother* to let her know of my plans*, cleaned up the house, cleaned out the closet, and removed all the* (Gerald's) *letters from envelopes*; then put them in chronological order. *It took a long time to do it. I* then *worked very diligently on the correspondence course.*

A letter from Mabel Ruth excited me; *she was going with me to take summer courses at A&M!* This would be her first college experience, and she would be my summer roommate.

After recovering from weather, restlessness, confusion and grief, life went on.

The third week in April was time for six-week tests. The weather was pleasant, so I allowed *the students to have an activity and we played a game of croquet and softball.*

Monday after school I *graded some papers, worked on a border, and talked to Ms. Burcham while she ironed. I made and boxed cookies to send to Gerald; then wrote a long letter to Gerald* telling him *how much I loved him, and talked about our future,* where we would go and what we would do when he came home. I let him know that I intended to go to summer school at Oklahoma A&M, so he should send mail to me at the church in Stillwater. I let him know how much I anticipated his return.

Friday, April 20, was hot, almost like *a very July day* as softball and baseball games started up. There were *ballgames during school with Centralview . . . we won!*

After I *graded papers,* I *dressed for the junior play,* Mama, Baby Boy. *It was very a good show.*

Exciting, happy things were about to happen! Monday, April 16, *Mrs. Suffridge had come up to see me to tell me they might have to go to the hospital.* She was having contractions and *asked if I might stay with Tommy and Fred* which I was more than happy to do. But it was *a false alarm.* Next day she must have felt pretty certain that the baby would not come because *I went with the Suffridges to fish. They didn't catch anything.*

However, on Saturday, April 21, Mrs. Suffridge did go into *labor sometime early in the morning. In the afternoon a 9 lb. 8 oz. girl was born.*

I was kept busy taking care of the Suffridges' chores and was pleasantly surprised when *Mabel Ruth came to visit* and helped me . . . *I enjoyed her visit. We washed* dishes and clothes, *cared for the cow, milked, took care of the milk, made ice cream, and washed dishes.*

After Mabel left, *I took a bath and wrote Gerald part of a letter.* I was worried again because the news stated that the First Army was in Leipzig and I wrote: *"No mail today . . . I just know he is in Leipzig, or near there."*

Doing chores for the Suffridges and teaching kept me very busy. Sunday *was a beautiful morning* as I *milked the cow, cleaned the dishes, ate, and got ready for church.* I accepted one of *several invitations for dinner . . . slept and listened to the radio . . . wrote letters to Mother, Mrs. Beasley, and Gerald. I didn't have to milk that evening* since Mr. Suffridge was home, *but I stayed with Tommy for a while* when Mr. Suffridge headed back to the hospital.

Before going to bed I wrote: *"I love Gerald so much! I wish I could be with him. He is the most wonderful husband on this earth."*

Mrs. Suffridge and Mona Carolyn came home Monday, April 23. *It looked rainy but only sprinkled.* Every day after school I went to see the baby and *helped for a long time.* I longed for a baby of my own. *Mona was so sweet and good and cute. "My kingdom for a baby! I want our babies to come soon."*

The next day *was a pretty, but chilly day* as I *cared for Mona and Mrs. Suffridge. The baby was so sweet and good . . . just eats and sleeps* and . . .

"With the good, a little rain must fall" seemed a fitting saying for April; the weather turned cold and wet. I had received no letter from Gerald since April 18. It had been seven days. Since letters from Gerald were intermittent, I listened to the radio a lot. I hoped to hear some encouraging news but also feared to hear of the battles in Germany. Even with my fears, I did want to know what was going on in Europe. It was a contradiction. I did not want to hear bad news but could not stop listening to the radio. Tuesday evening I prayed, *"Dear God, I love Gerald so much. I know he is in Leipzig or near. I wish I could be with him. He is the most wonderful husband on this earth. Keep him safe."*

On Wednesday, *a chilly day with wind from the north,* my feelings of incompetence resurfaced, I think more from worry over Gerald and lack of sleep, but I became impatient and intolerant. I wrote: *"I feel that I should never have set foot in a schoolhouse! I am not capable of teaching!"* As I *hung clothes* to dry *and gathered them up,* I sighed from frustration, *listened to the radio . . . then to bed."*

Thursday, dawned with *pretty weather* as I *dressed and went to school.* I was *tired, nervous, and hateful with the students.* To lift my spirits after receiving *no mail from Gerald, I went to see the baby and Burnice.* I felt better.

In late April, spring finally left its hiding place from behind the clouds. By then, with one month of school left, I had plenty to do to keep me busy. The 4-H students were finishing up their dresses and other projects for a dress review. So after school Friday as *it rained and drizzled, I prepared to take the students to town to the dress review,* and to set up the displays of their finished projects.

That evening, I *wrote a letter to Gerald. I was so tired . . .* and desperately needed a letter from Gerald. I recorded my feelings: *"I feel that I can't go any longer! I love Gerald so much! He is wonderful! May God bring him safely home and soon!"*

Saturday I *dressed and called a taxi to take Jessie Faye, June, and the Dickinson child to the dress review. They got three blue ribbons, seven red ribbons, one white ribbon, and a grand champion! I was very pleased with the girls'* accomplishments.

That afternoon I was so glad that I was able to get a ride *home with Ms. Blackwell!* Shortly after I got home, *the folks went fishing at the river. It was a beautiful night. The moon was shining* and reflecting *on the water.* I lay back and relaxed by the river and let my thoughts meander. I had been thinking for some time that I needed a change, so while in Blair, I had my *hair cut.* I just hoped that Gerald would like my hair shorter.

Sunday, April 29, *I cleaned up the* (folks') *house, ate hot cakes for breakfast. Royce and I dressed and drove to church.* I was saddened to find out that *Brother Curry had died the past week. We came home, ate fish for dinner . . . I slept for a long time.* Mother then took me to *meet Ms. Blackwell.* Ms. Blackwell *came in to see the baby.*

At the end of the day I had *cleaned up, written a letter to Gerald, and gone to bed.* I prayed, *"God be with Gerald!"*

Monday *it was a very nice, pretty day. I gave the students an activity.* After school I *was so tired and slept.* I stayed in the apartment and *then read . . . wrote a letter to Gerald and Mrs. Beasley and a card to Mother and Sis Straughn.* Sis Straughn had agreed to let Mable and I rent their apartment in Stillwater for the summer, so I let her know when we would be arriving.

Finally, after eleven days of receiving no letter from him, I rejoiced when I *received three letters from Gerald.* My written prayer that evening was *"I love him so much. He is wonderful. May God bring us together soon, but God's will as he desires."*

The information in letters received from Gerald had been somewhat confusing because I did not receive them in chronological order as they were written. So when I read his letters in order by date, they confirmed and corresponded with earlier news reports of the First Army's movements. I was able to get an idea of where Gerald had been and when he had been there.

Gerald's letters indicated (1) he was in England in December; (2) in late December, he crossed the English Channel into La

Havre France; (3) in January, he crossed France into Belgium through the area of the Battle of the Bulge; (4) he was along the Rhine in Germany from middle February through most of March in the area of Lispenhausen; (5) Gerald's *airmail written March 8* stated . . . *he was near the front lines. He saw a bomb fall and the crew bailed out behind German lines;* (6) *two v-mails written March 13 and 15, Gerald* wrote he *was on the Rhine;* (7) a letter dated March 14 indicated *he was still resting but was hungry all the time.* Apparently, he had been sick but was recovering. (8) Mail dated *March 16* revealed *he wasn't feeling so well; (*9) a *letter from Gerald written March 17 . . . he was well and fine. I received money from Gerald.* He had been sending me some of his pay from the army to put in the bank; (10*) March 18, 24, and 25 . . . he was well and fine. He was still on the Rhine;* (11*) March 27 . . . he was still on the Rhine . . . He had "visited" Blankenheim;* (12) His *letter of March 26* stated that . . . *he was doing very little . . . Gerald was fine, still on the Rhine;* (13) *March 29 and 31 . . . Gerald was moving around in Germany. He* had *"visited" Bod Ems, and Sevsizullich;* (14) news reported the First Army had moved fifty-eight miles east of the Rhine in late March and April; (15) *April 4 . . . he had visited Giessen;* (16) *three letters written April 6, 12, and 15 . . . he had visited Marburg;* (17) It was sometime around April 19 during the Battle of Leipzig that Gerald received a shrapnel injury to his cheek. But of course, I had received information of his recovery before I received word of his injury. I was eventually able to put the story together and was grateful that it was only a minor wound. I knew Gerald had been in Germany in the middle of the battles with the First Army Division.

I studied German geography to follow Gerald's movements.

CHAPTER FORTY-EIGHT

The fear of the Lord adds length to life;
but the years of the wicked are cut short.

—Proverbs 10:27

Gerald's Remembrances— the War Is Over—April 1945

By the end of April '45 near Eilenburg, Germany, spring had arrived, grasses had turned green, and trees had budded and blossomed. Walking along a road through the countryside with my unit, we passed an orchard and picked some eatable cherries. It was pretty country. At that moment, we were marching forward, but no blood was being shed, no killing. It seemed peaceful.

As the Russians invaded from the east, unarmed German civilian refugees in East Germany were pushed toward the American lines to the west. You just wouldn't believe the number of civilians that were coming toward the Americans: old people, some men, women, babies and children. Many were pulling horse-drawn and human-drawn wagons loaded down with salvaged personal belongings. Others just carried what they could over their shoulders. The German civilians were especially afraid of the Russians and wanted to get back behind the American lines to get away from them. But the Americans wouldn't permit that. German civilians were retreating from the advancing Russians all up and down Germany. But nowhere along the front were they allowed to penetrate the American lines.

The sun was shining and warming the earth on April 25, 1945, when the First Army first met the Russian advance at Torgau, a small village on the Elbe River east of Eilenburg.

My unit had moved several kilometers downstream to where two rivers met. The waters were high on the banks from spring thaws. Birds were flitting and singing while busily building their nest, insects were buzzing about and hope was in the air.

The American troops were told to clean up, spruce up and look good. They were also instructed not to fire their weapons and guns into the air when we met up with the Russians. I was with American troops as we waited on the bridge where the two rivers came together when we saw the Russians coming over the hill.

They were a motley crew. Their clothes were dirty and torn, and it turned out they were pretty hungry. Talk about lend—lease! Among the American equipment that the Russians had was a Studebaker lend-lease truck. Some of their weapons were German. As they had cut across Europe, they had scoured and taken what they wanted or needed. They even had women medics with the unit.

Now, remember, the GIs were told not to fire their weapons at all . . . and they didn't . . . but the Russians were holding their weapons up in the air and shooting them wildly. They were jubilant! Liberated Russian captives from the German villages approached the advancing Russian soldiers; they embraced each other and kissed each other full on the lips. The Americans were standing on the bridge gawking at the goings-on. Shortly, a Russian soldier began playing a concertina, and the Russian men began dancing and jumping around.

Facing south along the riverbank was a dense forest. I saw a waving white flag come out from among the trees. I told the sergeant, "Sergeant, looky there!" He took over and with gun-bearing GIs, he rounded up surrendering German soldiers who knew the war was over. In the closing days of the war, thousands of German prisoners were taken all along the lines north and south as the Americans met the Russians. German soldiers by the hundreds were lined up along the river; they must have been somewhat fearful, uncertain as to what their fate would be.

The Russian unit continued to freely fire their weapons in the air. They set up their camp by the river, and the amazed American soldiers beheld the Russians tossing grenades into the river, exploding them to kill fish. The dead fish floated to the top and the Russians waded into the cool waters to retrieve the best meal they had had in a while. Apparently, Russian food supply lines had not been bringing in much food.

My unit returned to Eilenburg.

The big-shot military men and dignitaries came from other locations to where the Russians were. It's likely that General Rinehart, the Sixty-Ninth Division Commander, showed up. News media flocked there to record history.

After that, the war in Europe wound down quickly!

Mussolini was captured by Italian partisans and put to death on April 28, 1945.

Hitler and his new wife committed suicide on April 30, 1945. (The Russians were the first to push into the area where Hitler's bunkers were located. Rumors persisted for years that Hitler had actually escaped until in 1968 when Russia finally published an autopsy report of their remains showing they had died of cyanide poisoning.)

I'm reminded of the scripture: "When a wicked man dies, his hope perishes; all he expected from his power comes to nothing" (Proverbs 11:7)

The German armies in Italy surrendered on May 2.

The Russian armies of Zhukov and Konev attacked Berlin until May 2, when the city surrendered.

British forces in the north made contact with the Russians on May 2, and all German forces in northwest Germany, the Netherlands, and Denmark were surrendered on May 4. On May 6 German forces in Austria surrendered.

May 7, 1945, Col. Gen. Alfred Jodl and Gen. Adm. Hans Georg von Friedeburg met in General Eisenhower's headquarters in Reims and signed the final surrender document, effective May 8. On May 9 Friedeburg, Field Marshal Gen. Wilhelm Keitel, and Gen. Hans Jurgen Stumpff signed a similar document in Marshal Zhukov's headquarters in Berlin.

On May 8, 1945, shortly after the initial meeting with the Russians, VE-Day was announced. The European war was over.

My unit went to and remained in Querfurt, Germany, where I made the following entry in my journal:

14 May 1945   Querfurt, Germany

VE-day has come! I wonder if I thanked God enough! Have I lost any ability to give God credit for all good things? I've seen God's will being done in this Earth and I'm stunned to think of the rebuilding of souls, personalities, bodies and buildings that must take place. It is God's will, though.

How impatient I become when I think of return to my loved ones and work in the church. There are times when there wells up within me a fervent confidence in my innate ability to perform capably the duties of a minister of the Gospel. There are other times when my mind submits to blankness that almost emits pessimism. Many times have I thought and known that I could profit from sitting down and recording my thoughts, but a weakness overcame me. How miserable it is to submit to weaknesses. I always think, "There will come a more suitable time." Another victory for Satan!

I have much to accomplish toward "putting on the Lord Jesus Christ." I have undesirable personality traits that I must shackle lest they harm the name of Christ. The importance of this can never be magnified too much.

After the war the world became aware of the extermination of six million Jews. Heinrich Himmler, an early follower of Hitler, had risen in rank from leader of the SS in 1929 to Minister of the Interior by 1944. He was responsible for the deaths of numerous Jews in gas chambers.

Many Jews had escaped to the United States, Canada, Latin America, and the Zionist movement made it possible for many to find refuge in Israel, land of their ancestors.

CHAPTER FORTY-NINE

With God we will gain the victory,
and he will trample down our enemies.
—Psalm 60:12

Pauline's Diary—VE-Day— May 1945

Tuesday, May 1, 1945, trees were budding, flowers were blooming and thirsty bees were sucking sweet nectar. America was buzzing with rumors *"that Hitler is dead!"* After the initial meeting of the Americans and the Russians on the Elbe River, the news reported that minor fighting continued in Germany. Throughout the states, Americans were exhilarated as newscasts announced that the war was nearly over.

May Day in Oklahoma showed itself as *such a beautiful day, but a little windy* as I went about my day high on hope even though there was *no mail from Gerald.* The electrifying, contagious optimism renewed my energy, and my *blood boiled to be moving places. I felt fine except to get sleepy in the afternoon . . . after school did some typing, read and dressed for the Educational films* that were showing at the theater. *They were about Pan-America and the Alaska Highway.* Very interesting! My day ended pleasantly as I wrote *a letter to Gerald, studied, and went to bed.* I slept wonderfully that night!

The next day blossomed into *a beautiful day* in more ways than one. Wednesday's news reported *"Italy surrendered and Berlin fell!"* Radio reports verified that *"Hitler is dead!"* Surely this is the end of hostilities! But as I went about my daily routine, I realized that there was still *a long way to go yet* before my soldier could come home and we could be together again.

I visited the Suffridges and worked on the lunch report. There was *no letter from Gerald,* but I did not let it get me down. I wrote: *"I feel fine today, but became so sleepy in class this afternoon. I love him and miss him so much."*

For the rest of the week, though tired, all the excitement left me more determined than ever to be productive. *I taught all the classes . . . paid the bill at the store and listened to the radio.* I was motivated to finish the correspondence course and busied myself with it. *I cleaned house, rearranged furniture, washed dishes, and starched some clothes.* I wrote: *"I love Gerald so much. Words cannot express my love for him. As each day goes by, he is dearer to me."* After writing *a letter to Gerald, I slept. It came up a* thunder-*cloud, but I didn't know much about it as I was so tired* and fast asleep.

Sunday, May 6, was warm as *I dressed in white* for church. *I went home with Mr. and Mrs. Gilbreath . . . had a fine meal, especially the custard pie . . . returned at six, admired Mona, and ironed. Did the chores and read a story stretched out on the floor . . . wrote a letter to Gerald.*

Perhaps, it was the change of weather on Monday, a *clear and cold day,* or the contagious excitement of the recent announcements of victory that caused the unruly behavior, but I *gave nine boys a board of five times each for throwing paper wads.* That afternoon *the baseball team had a ball game,* providing a much-needed release for vented-up emotions. After supervising a restless *study hall, working with 4-H club members, making out claims, I visited at the store and played the piano.* My day was complete with *a letter from Gerald written April 16. The news said the war in Europe is about over.* I was thrilled and wondered, *"Can it be possible! I love Gerald very much."* That evening after listening to the news, sleep came easy.

As I was getting ready for school on Tuesday, May 8, 1945, the radio was *"proclaiming VE-Day in Europe and all fighting is about over."* *Tears of joy fell* silently as I listened to President Truman's broadcast to the American people:

> This is a solemn, but a glorious hour. I only wish that Franklin D. Roosevelt had lived to witness this day . . . The flags of freedom fly over all Europe.
>
> For this victory, we join in offering our thanks to the Providence which has guided and sustained us through the dark days of adversity.
>
> Our rejoicing is sobered and subdued by a supreme consciousness of the terrible price we have paid to rid the world of Hitler and his evil band. Let us not forget, my fellow Americans, the sorrow and the heartache which today abide in the homes of so many of our neighbors whose most priceless possession has been rendered as a sacrifice to redeem our liberty . . .
>
> We must work to finish the war. Our victory is but half-won . . . For the triumph of spirit and of arms, which we have won, and for its promise to the peoples everywhere who join us in the love of freedom, it is fitting that we, as a nation, give thanks to Almighty God, who has strengthened us and given us the victory.
>
> Now, therefore, I, Harry S. Truman, President of the United States of America, do hereby appoint Sunday, May 13, 1945, to be a day of prayer.
>
> I call upon the people of the United States, whatever their faith, to unite in offering joyful thanks to God for the victory we have won, and to pray that He will support us to the end of our present struggle and guide us into the ways of peace.
>
> I also call upon my countrymen to dedicate this day of prayer to the memory of those who have given their lives to make possible our victory.

In Witness Whereof, I have hereunto set my hand
and caused the seal of the United States of America to
be affixed.*

Excitement was everywhere! It was the *most beautiful of days!*
The students were loudly running, laughing, and leaping! We
weren't going to get much done! It was just as well that the
school *had an assembly to celebrate our country and to sing patriotic
songs.* I did have *the last 4-H club meeting for a while.* Full of hope,
I *brought out clothes* to dry on the line, *went to the store, visited
Burnice and Mona, and worked on the correspondence course. I got a
letter from Gerald written April 27,* which made the day complete.
I thought, *"I am so happy, yet I can't celebrate yet. Not until Gerald is
in my arms."*
     The fervor continued on Wednesday as a change in weather,
a hard rain, seemed to affect the behavior of the students. *It
was a storm indeed! Mr. Suffridge gave fifteen spankings. I gave one
and Ms. Burcham gave seven.* It was frustrating for the teachers
and superintendent, but there was just too much to be excited
about. Thank goodness *Plainview came to play softball,* allowing
the students to let off some steam. *They won,* which made it even
better*!*
     I went to town after the hard rain to get a new radio to replace the
old one that was kaput. I was not going to miss any of the good
news! I saw *Ms. Blackwell and enjoyed talking to her . . . wrote a letter
to Gerald.* Didn't have a letter from Gerald, but *I received a letter
from Vic* (an Oklahoma A&M friend) *in Hawaii. He doesn't like it
there.* I couldn't imagine not liking Hawaii!

     For the next couple of days, radio broadcasts were *explaining
the point system that would determine which servicemen would get to
come home first.* While I was certain that *Gerald didn't have a chance*

---

*   www.**famousquotes.me.uk**/**speeches**/presidential-**speeches**/

with the point system, I learned that *a lot of the boys were* already *on their way home to stay. It would have been wonderful if he were one* of the soldiers already headed home. I read *the letter from Gerald written April 25* (the day the Allies met the Russians). What an interesting day that must have been for him.

The weekend of May 12, I was able to get a ride *home with Ms. Blackwell. Royce and I had a round or two of boxing. I won, but he gave me some blue spots on the left arm.*

Saturday *the folks were making preparations to go to Craterville for the family reunion.* I helped them *fix chicken, pies, and a bit of everything good to eat.* Dad really didn't like going to these affairs, but he went for his parents' sake; he and his brothers usually got into an argument. But my dad's family reunion on Sunday was enjoyable. I saw so *many of those I hadn't seen in a long time. They were much larger than I. There were so many children! How they had grown!*

We had dinner, skated, and rode the Ferris wheel. It was so hot! I became so tired. We returned to the farm rather late, and I had to get up early in the morning to head back to Brinkman.

It was already warm Monday morning as I got up early. *I dressed and went to the corner* by the county road *to meet Ms. Blackwell. We arrived at school just as the bell was ringing. It was a hot day!*

With only a couple of weeks left until the end of school, I had two busy weeks ahead of me. To prepare for the upcoming 4-H show, *I helped Ms. Blackwell even Erma's dress hem and worked on a demonstration.*

I received *a long letter from Gerald written April 26.* It was written after they had met the Russians and knew the war was very close to being declared over! His optimism was very apparent! He was very positive and happy! I prayed that he would get home soon!

After holding *Mona for a while, I read and went to bed early.* A babe in arms! There was no better way to end a most beautiful day!

Tuesday started out as *a beautiful day, but before the day was over, it was raining. After school I went to town* (Mangum) *to do some shopping, bought shoes, and got ready to attend the Junior/Senior banquet at Franklin Hotel* in Mangum. *It was very cold* that evening, and *it came a rain.*

Since it was late and I had ridden with her, *I spent the night with Ms. Blackwell.* The next morning, as Ms. Blackwell and I *went to town to eat breakfast at Wade's, it was cold.* I went *to the district office to wait for Will G. Jones* (another Eastview teacher) to take me *to the schoolhouse. I felt fine in spite of little sleep.* There were *no letters from Gerald,* but I was fine.

I heard that *Joe and Waunita were to marry May 29.* It was a good thing I had lots of crocheted gifts!

Thursday was *a beautiful day,* dampened only by *complaints about something Mrs. Griffis did* the day before. I felt sorry for her; I know how she must have felt. I had a *very busy day. I gave tests most of the day,* and *Ms. Blackwell came out in the afternoon to practice on the 4-H demonstrations.* After reading *four letters from Gerald written April 30, May 2, 3, and 4,* I wrote *a letter to Gerald.* I was sure *he was still in Leipzig.* I hoped there was no fighting there! I don't think there was.

Friday was *a clear and windy day* as I *gave tests all day in arithmetic.* The long days and late nights finally had their toll on me. *I was dead after it all . . . rested some and did some running around* to get ready *for the banquet . . . a military affair. The banquet was very nice . . . wrote a long letter to Gerald. No letter today.*

Since there was no school on Saturday, *it was wonderful to lie in bed until all hours. I arose at nine . . . did very little. Erma and Mabel Ruth came to practice on their 4-H demonstrations.* It gave me great pleasure to read *a letter from Gerald written May 7, the day of surrender. He was* safe and *very happy.*

Mrs. Suffridge came up, and while I was working on *her hair,* the news reported *a bloody battle on Okinawa.* I was so glad that Gerald was not in the Pacific. I prayed that that part of the war would soon be over. I *wrote a long letter to Gerald.*

Sunday, May 21, *it rained some and hailed. It was still wet and windy when I attended church. I heard a good sermon about Hiding Sins by Brother Willbright. I ate an enormous dinner with Darene Hoffman and Jimmie.* She brought me to the Baccalaureate, but she went back home. The program *was good. Brother Mark McEthaney gave a good inspirational talk. The white gowns were very pretty.* The graduation ceremony *reminded me of my graduation* from high school *about four years earlier.*

That evening I wrote a prayer in the diary as though I was speaking directly with my beloved husband: *"My Darling Gerald, this day finds me well, yet very lonesome for you and your love. It seems years since I was in your arms. I wrote a six-page letter to you. May God send a speedy return of you to me. I love you with all my heart. You are wonderful. I will study and pray as if with you, though you are so many miles away. God protect every Christian in this war wherever they may be. Goodnight and sweet dreams. Amen."*

The last week of school was winding down. *The high school went to Hobart* for an end of the year party. *Mr. Suffridge and I went as chaperones. I enjoyed skating very much,* and *then we went to the park. We almost froze returning in the back of a truck though we had quilts to cover with. I was very tired at the end of the day* but still felt pretty good; *I had four letters from Gerald!*

Then the radio announced *"the First Army is going to the Pacific by way of the U.S."* I thought, "Please, God! It would be wonderful to see Gerald if he came through the U.S., *but it can't be true* that Gerald might be sent to the battle in the Pacific!" I just didn't think that I could endure that!

Tuesday, May 22, after I *finished giving tests and grading some papers . . . the eighth-graders practiced,* then later I nervously *marched in with the eighth graders and presented them their diplomas . . . The exercises were very nice. Mr. Shuman gave a long speech.*

Wednesday, I *graded papers, cleaned up the classroom and let the students have some fun.* After school I *rested and dressed to go to the Plainview commencement exercises. I enjoyed the exercises so much because some of the graduates were 4-H students—Anita Culwell, Mabel Ruth Johnson, and June Hamilton. It was a very beautiful night, but chilly.*

After reading *a letter from Gerald written May 12, my hope of seeing him soon was gone.* Gerald was assigned to remain in Germany. But at least that was better than going to the Pacific! And the fighting was over in Europe!

After *working all day Thursday grading papers . . . fixing report cards,* I was *very tired.*

The last day of school, Friday, May 25, 1945, teachers *gave out the report cards.* It was bittersweet watching the student empty their lockers and leave the building. In the quiet afternoon I *worked on the register . . . worked on lunchroom reports.*

The school year was over. I had completed the year sane!

It was a very hot day and a beautiful night as I sighed a somewhat anticlimactic sigh; once home I *hung out clothes and visited the Suffridges.*

I had concluded, I *doubt Gerald gets to come home for a while.*

CHAPTER FIFTY

Perseverance must finish its work so that you may be
mature and complete, not lacking anything.

—James 1:4

Pauline's Diary—
Return to Oklahoma A&M—
Summer 1945

Mabel Ruth Johnson
graduation.

I was excited to be returning to my Alma Mater, Oklahoma A&M, to attend the summer session. Mabel Ruth Johnson was also to attend for the first time after graduating from Plainview High School. But I had several tasks that needed to be finished before leaving Brinkman. Erma Dean Tucker and Mabel Ruth were to participate in a 4-H show on the Oklahoma A&M campus before the summer session was to begin, so I helped them prepare their projects and practice demonstrations. I also *packed, washed dishes, and did a bit of everything* around the apartment.

It was a very warm day Saturday, May 26, as I *dressed* to meet with *Ms. Blackwell; she* had invited me to visit her. *Mr. Post* was heading to Mangum and was more than willing to give me a ride *to town with him.* Ms. *Blackwell* and I had

Maxine Williams and Erma Deanne Tucker

plans to *do a few things;* we *saw the parade and went to the mock battle, which was nice,* but I had conflicting emotions about it. *I could have cried several times because I know that Gerald must have seen such things.* While watching I silently prayed, *"I pray to God that he will bring Gerald back to me."* After an enjoyable day, I met up with Mr. Post for a ride back to Brinkman.

After attending church on Sunday, I *worked on the register, cleaned up the house, packed* what I would need for the summer, *and slept while I waited for Erma and Mabel Ruth. They arrived in town about five and practiced their demonstrations.* Then, *we took baths, dressed for dinner, and went to* evening *church.* We were very tired, but *Mabel Ruth was so excited as we cleaned for bed.* We had trouble sleeping because it *was a very warm day and night.* Before turning out the lights, I *wrote a letter to Gerald.*

Our trio was *up* Monday *at 6:00 a.m.* and ready, when Ms. Blackwell drove up in her car to chaperone us to Stillwater. I was *very sleepy* as we *packed all the things in the car . . . left at 7:10 a.m. We ate breakfast in Hobart* on the way north. Because of *some trouble with the car, we arrived in Stillwater about 4:30 p.m.* I needed a place to stay during the 4-H show; I had not made arrangements ahead of time, but *was fortunate to get to stay in the dorm.*

After *a picnic lunch on the lawn* on the A&M grounds, *we* walked to and *visited the Straughns; we enjoyed talking to them . . . found out so much news* about church friends.

I had arranged for my mail to be forwarded to the church building in Stillwater, so after walking the nine blocks to the building, I was thrilled when I *received a letter from Gerald.*

We were up at 5:45 a.m. Tuesday to get ready and make it to the 4-H assembly and demonstrations. Afterward, we *went on a campus tour . . . took a bath and cleaned up for supper. I walked to the Straughns to unpack some things* at the apartment; *then I went to church.* It was wonderful to be back with my friends. *I certainly did enjoy the singing. Afterward, the young college students made plans for their summer Bible study. I talked to the Thomases for a long time . . . Wrote a letter to Gerald and received one written May 12.*

The next morning our threesome was *up at 6:45 a.m. I did some running around on campus. After lunch* during free time, *we went to the recreational clinic and played games.*

When the 4-H judging was completed, *Erma was fourth from the top.* I was proud of her!

After supper I went to vesper services. It was very nice with such good singing. Being with my church friends was such an encouragement. I had *no letter* but *wrote a letter to Gerald . . . then to bed.*

We were up at 6:00 a.m. the next morning *and attended short courses . . . enjoyed them very much.* I called *Brother Scott* (the minister who lived by the church building) and was told I *had a letter, so I walked to their house to get it. Brother Scott was going to the 4-H club meeting,* so I rode back with him.

I retired after a good dress review, wrote Gerald, and to bed.

CHAPTER FIFTY-ONE

I wait for the Lord, my soul waits,
and in his word I put my hope.
My soul waits for the Lord more than
watchmen wait for the morning.
—Psalm 130:5 and 6

Gerald's Remembrances— Occupation in Germany—May 1945

I did not become directly involved in the actual European conflict until January '45. Since the war ended in early May of '45, I participated in only the last four months of the fighting; but it had seemed like an eternity in hell!

Allied Occupation of Germany

I was never in a situation where I had to defend my life. Never was! I always believed that the Germans respected the Red Cross medic insignia that was worn on the helmet and the clothing. I also believed that I was probably in the sights of German snipers who did not pull the trigger because of the insignia. I was glad that I was in the European theater instead of the South Pacific where the Japanese had no respect for the Red Cross. I also believe that God had a hand in my safety and survival.

In May, after being in Leipzig briefly, I was moved to Querfurt, another small town in Germany. At Querfurt, the medical detachment stayed in a nice German home with a sunporch which became my office where the guys would come to get doctored.

Well, once again, my comrades and I were living the "life of Riley" as we luxuriated in this nice German home. The wounded had been removed to hospitals for better treatment, so there were only mundane illnesses and minor wounds to be treated. And thank God, there was peace!

Willy Pate was an old Texas cowboy from Houston who had been in many rodeos, including in Madison Square Garden. He came into my sunporch office one day with a boil. After I lanced it and put an ointment on it, Willy exclaimed, "Doc, I think you're a quack."

I replied with a tight-mouthed smile, "I resemble that!" Willy gave me a crooked smile.

Willy was a real nice guy.

In peacetime, I had a chance to visit and enjoy different places in Europe. In late May, while on leave I visited in Brussels, Belgium. While there as I was playing volleyball with some other soldiers, I dove for a ball, skidded and skinned my chin on the cobblestone street. It messed up my chin!

In my off-time, I thought about the future and about what I wanted to do after returning to America.

I thank God for this hour of relaxation when I can meditate. During such a time I'm inspired, and my desire to serve my Lord abundantly is intensified. I must learn to better apply myself, and my time. I must learn how to get the most benefit out of each twenty-four hours—all for the glory of God.

It might become easy to cater to the whims and compliments of fellow men. I must better learn to examine and know myself. I fancy I know myself now, because I'm cognizant of many of my faults, but I'm sure I can say with certainty that I have much to learn about myself.

While the allies remained in Germany during a military occupation, my buddies and I were moved about. We billeted briefly in a small town called Givford, then, for about a month in another town called Mucheln. While at Mucheln, I impatiently waited to be sent home. I entered and dated several journal entries.

1 June 1945   Mucheln, Germany

This is another day which taxes the patience of any young man who has the instinctive desire to return to those whom he loves. Joyous anticipation is harried by uncertainty. The soldier's mind is a receptacle for many rumors, which he retains simply for the telling. He learns to take everything with "a grain of salt."

I have, I believe, kept alive my every ambition to serve my Lord more abundantly despite the awful experiences that have been mine during the past months.

God has spared me in very dangerous situations. I had prayed frantically to God when the destructive devices of men were reaping their toll all about. Even in those pleading petitions, I tried to remember to ask that God's will be done, and I groped for visions of Heaven, assuring myself that Earth is only the "staging area." Unpleasant were the expectations that any minute a shell might tear into my mortal body. Combat experiences taught me the more proper precautions, but I learned the value of prayer. Prayer was my greatest precaution.

My comrades have often unashamedly confessed that they have prayed to God. Formerly they would shun God. Even now it seems to me, God is largely forgotten by them. How distressing it must be to a most wonderful and personal God to be forgotten so often and remembered so little!

For most of June, I was not very busy. I and many other soldiers were impatiently waiting to be sent home. I neglected to make more journal entries until the following:

24 June 1945　　　　　Mucheln, Germany

I feel caught in the unthinking group of a government of a nation that is a contestant, a winner, even though losses are fantastic. I'm part of the so-called winning team, but I want to be solely on God's team. I want to work solely for God. If only my controlling officials could recognize and heed my pulsating, deep-rooted desire to be freed to devote my every talent and ability to God's work.

I must never become discouraged. I must pray without ceasing.

CHAPTER FIFTY-TWO

Wait for the Lord; be strong and
take heart and wait for the Lord.

—Psalm 27:14

Pauline's Diary—Oklahoma A&M— Summer 1945

Earlier in May before leaving Brinkman, I had written Edgar and Hallie Beasley, my in-laws, to inform them that I would be in Stillwater for the summer. Since Mabel Ruth was to be my summer roommate, the Beasleys had invited both of us to visit.

So when the 4-H show was over Friday, June 1, Ms. Blackwell drove from Stillwater to Sand Springs to drop Mabel and me off at the Beasleys. We *were up at 6:00 a.m. to pack up at the dorm, moved everything to the Straughns' apartment, unpacked there; then repacked a few things to go to Sand Springs. We left* Stillwater *at 4:00 p.m. and arrived at Sand Springs about 6:00 p.m.* Mrs. Blackwell and Erma then headed on to Brinkman.

Hallie *had a good supper* prepared for Mabel Ruth and me. We *talked* with the older folks for several hours; then all *went to bed.* Before retiring I *wrote a letter to Gerald.*

We were very tired and glad to be able to sleep until 8:00 a.m. the following morning. *We washed and ironed for most of the day; then* for adventure and exercise, we *rode the trolley to the end of the line* (to Tulsa) *and walked several miles back* to the Beasleys'

317

home. We were quite tired when we got back, but it had been a pleasant excursion!

Hallie and Edgar really seemed to enjoy having us there. *I enjoyed being there so much. They were so sweet to me.* Before retiring, Mabel and I *wrote letters and then to bed.*

After attending Sunday church with Hallie, we hurriedly ate dinner, dressed, washed dishes; but *had to catch the bus at 2:17 p.m.* to return to Stillwater. It was first come, first served, but we *managed to get a seat on the bus.*

Back at A&M, we leisurely *wrote letters and dressed for evening church.* That evening we *had such a good young people's meeting and lesson* and *did a lot of singing after church; then* Mabel and I *walked home.* I had *no mail but wrote a letter to Gerald.*

Monday, June 4, 1945 (while Gerald was in Mulcheln, Germany), Mabel Ruth and I were enrolling in summer classes. It was almost like prewar years back on campus with familiar friends and places, except Gerald was not there. It was also the beginning of a very busy summer school session; but that's what I wanted; I wanted to be so busy that the time would fly and I would not have time to think about or miss Gerald. So I got up early, headed to the campus, and *enrolled for eight college credits . . . sewing and upholstery, history, and physical education classes.* Looking back, eight credits were probably more than I should have signed up for.

After enrolling, Mabel and I *went to town* (there were businesses about six or seven blocks from the campus) *to get a few things. I bought some Fostoria* using my birthday money, *then* after *returning, we hurriedly ate and rushed to church* for the evening devotional. Later back at the apartment Mabel Ruth and I *talked to Sis Straughn* while sitting in chairs *on the lawn.* It was so very relaxing!

The time for relaxation was soon over since classes were to begin the next morning. I was *up at 6:30 a.m., dressed, ate, and headed to class.* When the *classes were over at 3:00 p.m.*, I *went to the infirmary for shots; then I went to town to buy wool* material to make a coat *and to look for a worn-out chair* for my upholstery class. *I walked so much,* but did not find a chair. I had to eat *supper* quickly to get *ready for church.*

I had determined to attend as many of the evening young peoples' Bible classes at the Stillwater church of Christ as I could. *Mabel Ruth went with me* most of the time. Her family did not attend the churches of Christ, but she was willing to attend services with me. At the worship service, I learned that *Lydia Mae Best was in the hospital.* I don't remember what she was in the hospital for, but I do remember that her husband had not yet returned to the states. She was staying with her mother until her husband got back. I determined to pay her a visit the first chance I had.

Squeezed into my days for the next couple of months, I spend time *studying history, sewing, participating in various PE classes,* churning ice cream, playing on the piano when I could, attending evening services, and *studying the Bible.* I also participated in other extracurricular activities.

Since I had not found one the day before, I *went to town again to look at chairs.* Found one and hauled it back to the campus. Don't remember just how I got the chair back to campus to the upholstery classroom. Perhaps I borrowed somebody's car. I certainly couldn't have carried it on my back!

Then I stayed at the library to study, went to the gym for PE class, and *walked to church for Bible class* and to see if I had a letter. I swelled with pride as I read *Gerald's letter of May 28; he had received the Bronze Star for Heroes Deeds as a medical aide.*

My diary entries continued with brief statements about events in my day, how I loved and missed Gerald as well as brief prayers for his return. Each evening before falling asleep I whispered, *"I love him so much!"*

Sending and receiving letters were still important to me! I answered letters received from friends and family. Right away, I *wrote to Mrs. Beasley* to thank her for her hospitality.

As busy as I was, I still felt very *lonesome and wrote letters to Gerald* almost every day. There were a few occasions when I was too tired and other times when I was frustrated at not receiving correspondence from him and stubbornly refused to write.

The first week in June, I received two letters *written May 25 and 27; Gerald said he had four stitches in his chin* from a volleyball mishap where his chin became acquainted with the Brussels' cobblestones. Later, I received a picture showing his scrapped chin.

That first week in June *was hot, humid, and cloudy* as I headed to the classes each morning. I *worked some on the chair.* I had to first take the old fabric off the chair, so I could use the old covering as a pattern for the new upholstery fabric. Taking that chair apart was harder than I thought it would be, even with the special upholstery tools I was required to purchase. I scrapped up my hands and broke my nails taking tacks and staples out.

As classes continued, *I went to the physical education class* that started out with *table tennis. Enjoyed it!* Later in the week, we started bowling; I was not at all pleased with my first score *in bowling . . . bowled only 76 . . . A very poor score . . . must do much better.*

I went to the library almost every day *and studied in the document room.* On more than one occasion, I *almost went to sleep.*

I started work laying out the fabric *on my coat,* then *sewed on the coat at class* and *went to the rest of my classes and enjoyed them very much.* After returning to the apartment, I *read my history assignment.*

Outside of classes, Mabel and I would *churn and eat ice cream* back at the apartment; *then went to church to class.* I would visit and *play piano* at *Sis Billingsley and Straughns' living room* when I had time. *I* also *went to the doctor for a checkup. He took an x-ray* (don't remember what for).

Pencil sketch of Gerald done in Brussels, Belgium, June 1945

At the end of the week *came a very hard rain and wind.* The rain helped decrease the discomfort of the high humidity but made for a wet trip to the church to get my mail. I got *a letter from Gerald written May 29.*

By Saturday the rain had stopped, and it turned out to be *a warm day.* Mabel and I slept till *nine and then went to town to buy a few things. It was late when we returned* all hot and sweaty. *We dressed to go to Sis Billingsley to play the piano;* we *enjoyed it so much. No letters today.*

Brother Dawson, an elder at the church, had passed away earlier in the week, so Sunday, June 10, after church I helped *serve dinner at Sis Dawson's.* After the dinner I *went to Brother Dawson's funeral and to the cemetery. It rained all the while.* After returning, the rhythmic patter of rain relaxed me and *I slept.*

I dressed and *then went to the young people's class and services* where I was assigned to *the refreshment committee.*

It continued to rain as I *wrote a letter to Gerald and Kyle.*

The second week of classes, I was up early to *exercise, eat, dress and get to school in the rain.* Though it was difficult to stay dry, I was glad; the rain had cooled the temperature! *I enjoyed the classes so much; especially the furniture class . . . bowled 93 and 99 on the two lines today* which was some better but still needs to improve.

I was late for history class and felt uncomfortable as I entered the classroom. Everybody, including the teacher, turned their eyes to look at me. I determined not to be late again!

Later I studied at home and churned ice cream; then ate and went to church.

I received two *letters from Gerald written May 31 and June 1. I got a letter from Mrs. Beasley. I wrote letters to Gerald, Mother, and Mrs. Beasley.*

The rest of the week was busy as I rushed around. Tuesday I slept till 7:00 a.m. and had to *rush to school. Then I went to the church class for a business meeting about the building.*

Wednesday, I *did not get much done. Had my teeth cleaned—fun! I went to see Lydia Mae at the hospital.* Enjoyed visiting with her.

Had a letter from Gerald written June 6 at Leipzig; he had remained there as a medical aide briefly after meeting up with the Russians. *He was going to go to Brussels again on a pass.*

Thursday, I *was very sleepy at school . . . did very little . . . had to go to town after class* for more items for my sewing and upholstery class . . . *walked very rapidly. I was very tired but attended the Bible class.*

I wrote in the diary: "*I yearned for Gerald . . . wished that we could study and pray together . . . wrote a letter to Gerald and received a letter of June 2 . . .* He wrote that *he is sending his medals. I love him so much. God be with him.*"

By the end of the second week of summer school, I *had begun to work on tailoring* the coat *and* had worked some on strengthening the structure of *the chair . . . made 81 and 106 in bowling.* My bowling had improved a little!

Since arriving in Stillwater without a car, I was getting a lot of exercise! *I went to town again to get chair legs and cash postal notes.* It rained again as I *returned home* so I had to *wash and fix my hair.* After that I *had to run to Whitehurst,* a building on campus, *to get my fountain pen which I had lost. I was so happy to find it! Thank God for small blessings!* It was no fun not having a car, but I'm sure the exercise was good for me!

Gerald Beasley in
Brussels, Belgium,
June 6, 1945

I received a v-mail of June 7 and two pictures of Gerald from Brussels, Belgium. I thought *he looked old* in the pictures. Had I forgotten how he looked? Did the war do that to him! It had been too long since I had seen him! I wondered if he had changed! No matter, *I loved him so much!*

Since Gerald had sent me recent pictures of himself, I decided to send him a recent picture of myself. So Saturday, I *was up at 8:00 a.m. and went to Smith's to have a picture made. It rained as I was coming back and I still had to get to the grocery store to buy refreshments for the church party and some groceries* for the apartment; then I had to lug it all back home. *I slept* some; *then worked on my coat. I made sandwiches for the party at the church building. Mabel Ruth and I had a big time at the church party. We walked home . . . studied and to bed . . . wrote a short note to Gerald.* I closed the day writing: *"I love him with all my heart. No letters today."*

Sunday, June 17, *was a beautiful day as* we got *up at 8:00 a.m. and went to church. Mabel Ruth talked to Brother Scott after church about a few* doctrinal *things that had been bothering her.* After that we headed over and *ate a delicious dinner at Sis Best's* (Lydia's mom). *We had a big time with Lydia Mae* who was home from the hospital. *Once home, I wrote letters to Gerald and the Altus Church of Christ;* they may have been looking for a preacher. I let them know of Gerald's interest in the job and inquired about what information they might need from Gerald. *Prayed and to bed.*

June 18, 1945, marked one year of marriage for Gerald and me, but we had had only a little more than two months together.

The popular song "Back Home for Keeps"[*] was playing on the radio, and as I listened, I wondered when Gerald would be home so I could "sweetly kiss the angry years away . . . while the world peacefully sleeps . . . in your welcome arms I'll be back home for keeps."

Despite my loneliness I did what I had to do and kept busy; I *worked on the chair at school, rushed home among the sailors* who were home from the sea and swarming the A&M campus, *ate a sandwich and to town . . . bowled 82 and 116 . . . rushed to class, studied at the library, cooked supper, dressed, and went to the shower at Marylyn Harick's for Ezra Roth.* While at the shower *I had a nice time. Saw Geraldine and David Fultz,* church friends who were now married.

On this *beautiful night,* the late entry in my diary was *"one year ago I married the nicest person on this earth."*

The next day I was back to work. In history class, I *heard a lecture about Japan. It was so interesting;* it helped me to understand Japan's culture and their motives for going to war, though it didn't excuse their attack on Pearl Harbor and declaring war. *I worked on the chair, went to PE and played badminton; then did some studying at the library. I read Adventures on Red River by Grant Forman.*[**] *I ate supper, dressed and went to church . . . walked home, read, studied and wrote a letter to Gerald.* It came a day late, but I was glad when I r*eceived an anniversary card and a long letter from Gerald.*

Though it was raining, Wednesday *was a beautiful day.* I diligently *worked on the coat and chair in class. Rushed home, ate and*

---

[*]   "Back Home for Keeps" was written by Carmen Lombardo and Bob Russell, performed by Guy Lombardo and Kay Armen, and recorded February 23, 1945.

[**]   Adventures of Red River by Grant Foreman; published in Norman, OK; University of Oklahoma, in 1937.

to the bowling alley . . . made 67 and 92—bad. I went to class and to the library, cooked supper and ate too much which I tended to do when I was nervous and stressed. *I wrote cards to Aunt Frankie, Mother, Suffridges, Mrs. Beasley and a letter to Gerald.*

Mr. Suffridge wrote and wanted to know if I would be returning in the fall to teach again. At this point I really did not know and I really didn't want to think about it. I didn't respond right away though I'm sure, he needed an answer.

No letters from Gerald. *Received a bill for A&M fees for $18.90 and paid it. I worked more on the coat.*

Thursday, *I slept until 7:00 a.m.* and *had to rush off to school;* it was getting harder to get up early, so *I worked an extra hour on tying springs* on the chair to try to catch up.

Mabel Ruth was spending the night at the hospital for treatment so I took a housecoat to her. (I don't remember what was wrong with her.)

Since Gerald was seriously considering looking for a preaching job, and/or pursuing further Bible studies to prepare for ministry when he got back home, I had been doing some preliminary work for him. *I wrote letters to several churches asking for information. I wrote Gerald a letter* to let him know what I had accomplished. *I received his April Bond but no letters.*

Got the proofs of the pictures I had made, *but I couldn't decide on which was best.*

Friday was a frustrating and busy day as I rushed and made preparations to visit the in-laws again. After arriving at sewing class, I *had to return* to the apartment *for a key; then later for a sewing box.* It was a good thing that the Straughns did not live far from the A&M campus! Later I ran back to the apartment and *ate; then went to bowl . . . made 92, 128, and 114 . . .* Better scores! *I ordered pictures* at the photo shop, *walked home, packed, and went to the bus stop at 3:40 p.m.* to head to Sand Springs. It had been a rush!

I had so much sewing, upholstering and studying to do, I probably shouldn't have gone to visit them, but I felt I needed to. They looked forward to my visits and Mrs. Beasley was so frail; I wanted to spend as much time as possible with her. I got to the bus just as it was leaving; but no man would be a gentleman and give up his seat for me. *I had to stand up most of the way!*

The Beasleys met me in town. Edgar and Hallie seemed so pleased to see me. *I ate* the delicious meal that Hallie had prepared. As we talked I *told Mrs. Beasley that Gerald had been wounded* in his cheek by shrapnel during the battle in Eilenburg. Apparently, Gerald had not written to tell her because he had not wanted to worry her. She was already so frail. I felt bad. It shocked her and even though the injury was not bad and it was healed, *it hurt her* to hear it.

I took a bath and went to bed at 10:00 p.m. I was very tired. It was hot.

Hallie prepared breakfast Saturday morning so I was *up at 8:00 a.m., ate a lot of breakfast and started a big washing . . . hung it out.* Later *I went to Tulsa* where there were more and better choices *for a few things . . . bought some material to cover the chair. I was so tired* when I got back to Sand Springs! *I lay my head down on the bed* just to rest a bit *and went to sleep until ten.* I hadn't meant to sleep so long. The Beasleys didn't want to wake me; they thought I needed the rest. *I took a bath and went back to bed* too tired to write a *letter.* I was lying on the bed that was once Gerald's and wrote in my diary: *"I could sleep forever. I love my husband with all my heart."*

Sunday, June 24, I was *up at 8:00 a.m., dressed, ate, and went to church with Mrs. Beasley. I had a difficult time keeping awake. I ate a delicious fried chicken dinner, packed and returned to Stillwater by bus, but* this time I *had a seat.* Since I had run around so much, I hadn't spent as much time with Hallie and Edgar as I should have, but I know they appreciated the visit.

I returned to a quiet apartment since *Mabel was still in the infirmary;* it was too late to go visit her. *I dressed and went to church. After church I studied, wrote to Gerald and went to bed.*

The last week in June I spent a lot of time *working on the coat and the chair;* I had so much to do on both and needed to catch up! *I bowled 128 and 99—better today!* In history I had been assigned *to write a term theme about old Greer County* (southwest Oklahoma, the area where I had grown up),so *I did some research, ate and went to the infirmary to see Mabel. While there we worked on a picture puzzle until time for me to leave.*

I ran to the church building and discovered *two letters from my Honey and a paper about the Bronze Star Citation* that he had received. *He had treated German civilians and led them to safety. The official citation was for "going beyond the call of duty." Gerald wrote that Sgt. Gates was missing in action.* He was obviously worried about what might have happened to him! I'm sure there were many other soldiers unaccounted for after the war. *I wrote a letter to my husband* in the heat of the evening with *a beautiful moon.*

The morning of June 25, *there was a big storm and a lot of rain early in the morning. I attended a lecture and a tea in the afternoon. I returned to eat supper and fell on the way to church skinning my right knee.* I was either in too great a hurry, clumsy or very tired. Probably a little of all three!

At church *I saw Theodore Haire,* a former A&M friend that I had dated before dating Gerald. *He came to the Straughns' and we listened to his interesting stories* about his experiences during the war. *I wrote a letter to Gerald* and told him about the visit with Theodore *but received no letters today.*

The following day I *felt very bad and didn't do much.* All my running around in the rain and trying to do too much was wearing me out. I needed to take better care of myself. Though I felt ill, I went to my PE class and *bowled 100 and 101.*

I bought Mabel Ruth a necklace and Ruth (another friend) *a box of candy.* Since Mabel was back at the apartment, we *made ice cream. It was delicious* and so cooling to my throat! *I was very tired* but *we went bowling and I made 121 and 82;* I needed the practice.

I received v-mails written June 13, 16 and 17 from my honey.

Thursday, I *worked on the coat and chair at school,* but after class I felt really bad, so I *came home to bed and slept for a long time.* Later *while sitting on the lawn, I studied; then I wrote a letter to Gerald, cards to Mother and Maxine. I received a check which contained $60.63 from income tax refund. It was a nice surprise! I received two letters from Gerald written June 18 and 20.*

Pauline hitting one a long way.

I worked on the coat all Friday morning, but didn't get enough done—*ate, and went to bowl making 94 and 105. That part* (bowling) *is now finished.* Don't think I did too well! *I came home and read some history and slept for a long time.*

After eating I went to the airport with some friends to tour through two huge bombers. While there I *wrote a long letter to Gerald on the green east of the field-house while the others played golf.* I tried my hand at swinging the club, one of very few golf experiences, and *I did hit one golf ball a long way.*

No mail today. Read and studied.

Saturday, I allowed myself to sleep *until nine and then went to the library to study. Returned at noon for lunch, then returned back to the library* and was there *until five. I returned home and hung out clothes, ate, wrote a letter to Gerald and ironed until twelve* midnight. *I was very tired.*

CHAPTER FIFTY-THREE

I am not saying this because I am in need, for I have
learned to be content whatever the circumstances.
—Philippians 4:11

Gerald's Remembrances—
Mucheln, Germany—July 1945

At first I wasn't very happy when the medical detachment
jerked me back to regimental headquarters in early July. In fact,
I was quite unhappy about it because I had an easy and good life
back at my sunporch office in Querfurt. But headquarters knew
I had clerical experience and wanted me there.

However, I did get to work again with an old buddy, John
Kling. It sounds like a Chinese name, and he looked Chinese,
but he wasn't. I decided, "Well, I'm here. I may as well like it and
really get into the job."

So John and I set up a filing system to handle all the medical
records. Major Leo Litter liked our filing system. Johnny was the
one who had a lot of ideas and was most efficient. I knew some
things and was able to help out.

Anyhow, as a consequence of being at headquarters and
doing a good job, I think I got to head back home a lot sooner
than I might have otherwise. I was grateful for that!

CHAPTER FIFTY-FOUR

There is a friend who sticks closer than a brother.
—Proverbs 18:24b

Pauline's Diary—Summer School— July 1945

With so much to do, I should have cut down on some activities, but church and Christian fellowship were important to me, and I needed breaks for entertainment and visits with friends. I continued to go *to church* most evenings, even *went to the ladies Bible class* some afternoons. I also attended several concerts.

Friends often came to visit us at the apartment. *Lydia Mae came to the apartment for a rather nice lunch* after church Sunday, July 1. Should have been studying, but I hadn't had much of a chance to visit with her and was glad she was feeling well enough to get around. *We sat and talked* that afternoon *until four at which time she had to go.*

I also *enjoyed practicing the piano* when I had a chance.

And of course, back at the apartment *we* frequently *had some good* home-churned *ice cream.* We made ice cream a lot. It was so refreshing on those hot Oklahoma days!

The first week in July, I was back to the grind. I had so much to do! It didn't help that *I overslept* several mornings and had to *rush to class.* I *continued to work on the chair and coat* and I *cut out a suit for my sewing class.* I was behind and *had to sew most of Tuesday.*

We started archery in PE; I was certain I *was going to enjoy it very much.* Thank goodness PE didn't take much time outside of class attendance, except for a little practice.

I had studied hard, so I was encouraged when I got *an A—on a test in history! Not bad! I received the newspapers* from Greer County that I had requested so I *did some studying on the term theme* for history.

There was no school *the Fourth of July, so Mabel Ruth, Lydia Mae and I went to Fair Park. It was a beautiful warm day. We ate so much chicken, sandwiches, pops and watermelon; we were miserable.* Lydia Mae told us she had received a letter from *Lloyd,* her husband, stating that he *would be on his way home soon.* I was envious but happy for her. After *we walked home,* actually we waddled, *I was so sleepy,* but I still *wrote Gerald a short letter.*

It came a big rain, unusual for July. I did not feel very well. I knew I was trying to do too much, but still *had to keep studying* and working. I was *so tired.* For several afternoons that week I *slept a short time; then* pushed myself to *move more rapidly. I did a lot on the chair . . . worked on the coat in the afternoon . . . had archery.*

Squeezed between classes and studies, I had other things to do. I had to *go after* groceries for meals at the apartment and for snacks for the young people's evening services. I *ironed clothes, fixed supper, churned ice cream, washed dishes,* read, and responded to letters from friends, home and Gerald.

The *folks wrote that they were very busy* on the farm. I wished I could be there to help them.

I got a letter from Ms. Blackwell asking if I would be returning to Brinkman in the fall. I still wasn't sure how to answer her and Mr. Suffridge! I didn't know whether Gerald would be back by then or not. I hoped he would! But they needed an answer, so I wrote and told them that I would return to teach at Brinkman in the fall. That done, I returned to the tasks at hand.

Friday, I *worked about seven hours on the coat. It was getting along very nicely. Ping-pong* was then introduced *in PE,* though we still practiced archery.

My day was going along nicely until I discovered that I had *lost a door key.* I had to take the time to look for it. *I was losing and forgetting more things!* My mind was swirling in too many directions!

Bitsy, Regimental Aid Station mascot

There were several letters from Gerald that week . . . *a v-mail dated June 21, a letter written June 22* that said he *was on the move in Europe, v-mails of June 22, 24, and 26.* He sent *a picture of their mascot,* Bitsy, a cute dog! *Gerald was now assigned to* Supreme Headquarters Allied Expeditionary Force (*SHAEF*). Gerald wrote that he would probably be home by the new year. I wrote in my diary: *"I may get to see my sweet before or by the first of the year."*

Saturday was a clear and beautiful day, and it should have been a day of rest, but I *did a lot on the coat.* When I *received two monthly checks, I went to town to cash them and got excelsior* (packing material for the chair) *and some pants for Gerald* that he had requested. And of course, I had to package the pants for mailing.

After I *studied history, Ruth came to practice some archery with me.* It was fun to practice with a friend! Because I didn't remember everything I needed, *we went to the store and to town again.* In preparation for Sunday dinner, I *dressed a chicken, then washed and fixed my hair and wrote a letter to my sweet.*

By the end of the week, I was so tired, I *didn't write a letter to Gerald, but I wrote a long letter later that week* squeezed into my *study of history*

Sunday, July 8, Mabel Ruth and I went to church where *O. D. Duncan gave the lesson.* For Sunday dinner we *had good fried chicken.*

I was able to relax some *after washing the dishes, studying and sleeping some; then we went to church. Joe White gave the evening lesson;* then *Mabel and I went to Midwest for malts* and *enjoyed walking with the Whites.*

That evening *Elsie Mae, Mabel Ruth and I* got together at the apartment and *acted crazy.* It is so great to laugh and have fun with friends! But later I became lonely for Gerald and lamented that *I wouldn't see Gerald until after the first* of the year . . . *It was a long time until then.*

It was cloudy most of the following week as I went to classes! I was making *a great deal of progress on the chair; I worked on the stuffing and started on the arms. I worked on the interlining of the coat; I catch-stitched it down. I enjoyed archery* even though *it was rather warm outside; I arched 36 points. We started badminton.*

I proudly *had all my college records put into the name of Pauline Smith Beasley;* then headed to my upholstery class. However, before I could continue working on the chair, *I had to hurriedly go to town to buy screen wire and to get more excelsior.*

On return I found *a letter from Mrs. Beasley.* I was so worried about her. I knew she was not doing well. I had also received the bill, so I *paid for the x-ray.*

For several days I had had *no mail from Gerald.* I was perturbed with him! The mail had been regular since the ending of the European conflict so why was I not getting mail from him? I decided I was *not going to write a letter to Gerald.* When there was still *no mail* the following day, I *wrote Gerald* anyway. No reason for me to be childish. It probably wasn't his fault!

There was still plenty of researching, upholstering and sewing to do; but I wanted and needed a break. So I *went to a concert* on campus *by Mona Bradford, a contralto. She was very good and I enjoyed the piano-playing too.* Inspired, I spent some time practicing on the piano at Straughns.

Thursday, July 20, *I sewed on the coat until 5:30 p.m. I was very tired—ate, dried dishes and wrote a letter to my honey.* It was a pleasant break when *Sis Reighby came to see us.* Mabel and I *walked her home* in the heat of the evening.

Gerald hadn't forgotten me! *I received Gerald's Purple Heart and Bronze Star and a beautiful linen divan set,* German made, from Gerald! I needed to be more patient!

The summer was rapidly slipping by. There were only two weeks left to finish up all of my projects; I needed to buckle down. *It rained some on* Friday, as I *sewed from 8-12 a.m. and again from 2-5:10 p.m.* I was *getting along rather rapidly with the coat.* Later, *I didn't do badly in archery—out of sixty arrows, made a score of 208.* That evening, *I bowled three games in a tournament—scored 125, 84, and 113.*

Yeah for weekends! I had decided to relax some. It was *hot* as I *put out a wash, washed my hair and went to town to get my pictures. I ate in town.* When I returned *I did some reading and studied until five.*

Sunday, July 15, *was a hot day;* church *services were very good. Afterward I had a very nice time at Leachman's with Lydia Mae.* That afternoon, *I talked with Mabel about the Bible for a long time. After ironing some and studying, I went back to church.*

For the rest of the week my mind was full of finishing *the coat and the chair; the chair was ready to be upholstered.* Monday *was a beautiful, warm day* and I *was very sleepy* as I tried to *study some before classes. In PE we played doubles in table tennis and had archery, which was enjoyable. Tried to sew on the coat, but became very tired. Came home, studied history, read and did some sleeping.*

I received a card from Mr. Suffridge stating that school would start July 23. I did not need any more pressure. I needed a break! So instead of studying like I knew I should, Mabel and I *went to the Helene Druke and Walter Shaw duo-piano concert* on campus. *They were marvelous!*

There had been several days with *no letters* from Gerald! So I was very happy later when *I did receive a letter from Gerald written*

July 7, from Lispenhausen, Germany. It was wonderful to receive his letter! Then *his letter of July 8 said he was working hard* filing at headquarters. *Two* more *letters from my honey written July 5 and 9* lifted my spirits as I renewed my efforts to complete my projects.

July 19, my diary entry was *"Today is Gerald's 25th birthday. He is old. Wish I could spank him!"* Guess I was feeling frisky!

I had previously told the Beasleys that I would visit them in Sand Springs one last time before returning to Brinkman. There was still *a lot to finish on the chair,* and I knew I should not go, but I did not want to disappoint them. So Friday, July 20, I *sewed on the coat all morning . . . Didn't do good in Archery—made 83 on the test.*

I packed and caught a bus to Sand Springs and arrived at 5:45 p.m. Mr. Beasley was there to meet me at the bus station. *I ate such a meal! Wrote a letter to Gerald and actually wrote some on my history report. Studied and to bed.*

Saturday *was a warm day* as *I wrote on the theme paper all day,* except when I took a break to go *to a home garden's meeting with Mrs. Beasley; the lesson was good. Wrote a letter and then to bed.*

On Sunday, July 22, *we went to* the anti*church at Sand Springs.* Mrs. Beasley prepared *all the fish one could eat.* She tried not to show her fatigue, but I was concerned; *Mrs. Beasley seemed so weak!* I hadn't spent as much time visiting with them as I should have, but they understood I needed to work on my theme paper.

I was so glad I had made the visit. I left at *2:17 p.m. and had a seat on the bus.* I returned to the unfinished chair, coat and history theme! *I studied some and went to church.*

I had hoped that Gerald would be back in the states before the summer was over, but since that wasn't going to happen, I had agreed to return to Brinkman to teach. However, school in Brinkman was to start before the summer session at A&M was completed. I had sent a letter to Mr. Suffridge explaining this! Mr. Suffridge wrote back that it was okay if I returned to Brinkman after July 23. My plan was to arrive Sunday, July 29, and start to work the following Monday.

I would have liked to visit my folks, but that was not possible.

The last week of summer school I *didn't feel well, tried to work, but did not get anything done. Mabel Ruth typed my history theme at the church building* for me. What a great friend!

I *worked all day* trying to finish the chair. I was so tired! *I was very far behind—dyed material.* I should have continued working on the chair, but I w*ent to church and talked with Lydia Mae.*

The next day, though I was *very tired,* I *stayed at school all day.*

The evening of Tuesday, July 24, a wonderful thing took place; *Mabel was baptized! I was so happy for her! She was so afraid her parents would object. I wrote a letter to Honey* and gave him the good news. *It was a beautiful, wonderful day!*

Working frantically, I *attended all my classes . . . Had a few final tests . . . Worked on coat and chair . . . Made a poster and worked on the coat until very late.*

Friday, the last day of summer school, I *overslept and went to school without any breakfast. I had to work on the coat until 10:00 a.m.* to finish it. *Then, I worked on the chair until five. Mabel Ruth helped.* Thank God for friends! The coat and chair were finished!

My only reprieve was a *letter from Gerald written July 12; he was still where he was, but expecting to be transferred.* I also *received a letter written July 2.* Here it was the end of July; I wondered why it had taken so long to be delivered!

Those last couple of days as I pushed to meet deadlines took their toll on me. After finishing the chair, Mabel and I *went to town for supper* to celebrate; but I was *suffering a lot, became very ill,* had to come back *and went to bed early.* It was probably just stress, but at the time I wondered if it *might be appendicitis*. I felt better Saturday after a good rest.

It was time for us to return to Brinkman; but I still needed to *pack my things* in boxes for transport. Mabel was ready early; she helped me pack.

We had planned for one last fling, but *I couldn't get ready to leave to go to town until 12:45 p.m.*! *I took my packages to the post office . . . Rested some and went to town to run around. Ruth came to see us* . . . Later we *took baths, studied the Bible and went to bed early.*

We arrived by bus at Brinkman in the early evening of Sunday, July 29. I was to begin teaching the following morning. Because of the whirlwind move, teaching preparations and adjusting back to a teaching schedule, it was more than a week before I wrote in my diary again.

I had survived the summer though it had been very hectic. With the help and encouragement from friends, I finished all my assignments! And I was still sane!

CHAPTER FIFTY-FIVE

Therefore, you kings, be wise.
Be warned, you rulers of the earth.
Serve the Lord with fear and rejoice with trembling.
—Psalm 2:10 and 11

Pauline's Diary—
Back in Brinkman—August 1945

During the closing months of the conflict in Europe, the Pacific battle was still raging. In January of 1945, Krueger's Sixth Army began its siege on Luzon; then took Manila, February 24. Iwo Jima bases were attacked February 19 and taken March 16. The Japanese garrison of almost twenty-three thousand was virtually annihilated. American casualties exceeded twenty thousand.

Fighting on Okinawa started April 1 and continued until the end of June. Okinawa, closer to Japan, was even more heavily defended. The Japanese resisted air and naval bombardment with kamikaze air attacks that sank thirty-three Allied ships and damaged three hundred sixty-eight.

After conquering Okinawa, the Allies launched heavy air attacks on the Japanese home islands between July 10 and July 17. The Japanese navy was no longer a fighting force.

Monday, August 6, started out like any other day, but as the day progressed, radio broadcasts stunned the world! A most formidable weapon, which the general public knew nothing of, had been used by the United States against Japan. Its use changed the world, particularly the war in the Pacific. The impact of this dooms-day devise would be revealed in days and years to come.

On the morning of August 6, 1945, the Enola Gay, a U.S. B-29 bomber dropped the first atomic weapon ever used in warfare on Hiroshima.

America was stunned at the news of the atomic bomb that had been dropped on Japan and the vast devastation reported. That evening, August 6, 1945, *I listened to Truman's* radio broadcast:

> The first atomic bomb has been dropped by a United States aircraft on the Japanese city of Hiroshima. President Harry S. Truman, announcing the news from the cruiser, USS August, in the mid-Atlantic, said the device was more than 2,000 times more powerful than the largest bomb used to date. An accurate assessment of the damage caused has so far been impossible due to a huge cloud of impenetrable dust covering the target. Hiroshima is one of the chief supply depots for the Japanese army.
>
> The bomb was dropped from an American B-29 Super fortress, known as Enola Gay, at 08:15 local time. The plane's crew says they saw a column of smoke rising and intense fires springing up.
>
> The president said the atomic bomb heralded the "harnessing of the basic power of the universe." It also marked a victory over the Germans in the race to be first to develop a weapon using atomic energy.
>
> President Truman went on to warn the Japanese the Allies would completely destroy their capacity to make war. The Potsdam declaration issued 10 days ago, which called for the unconditional surrender of Japan, was a last chance for the country to avoid utter destruction, the President said. "If they do not

now accept our terms, they may expect a rain of ruin from the air the like of which has never been seen on Earth. Behind this air attack will follow by sea and land forces in such number and power as they have not yet seen, but with fighting skill of which they are already aware."

The British Prime Minister Clement Attlee, who has replaced Winston Churchill at Number 10, read out a statement . . . It said the atomic project had such great potential the government felt it was right to pursue the research and to pool information with atomic scientists in the U.S . . . . The statement continued: "By God's mercy, Britain and American science outpaced all German efforts. These were on a considerable scale, but far behind. The possession of these powers by the Germans at any time might have altered the result of the war" . . .

He ended: "We must indeed pray that these awful agencies will be made to conduce peace among the nations and that instead of wreaking measureless havoc upon the entire globe they become a perennial fountain of world prosperity."[*]

The listening audience did not at first comprehend the full meaning of the results of the atomic bomb. It was understood that Japan had been attacked and badly hurt; Japan had been given a chance to surrender but had chosen not to; it was just a matter of a short time before Japan would have to surrender and declare defeat. Civilization was stunned, relieved and grieved that such awful measures had to be used to assure that this war

---

[*]   http://news.bbc.co.uk/onthisday/hi/dates/stories/august/6/ newsid_3602000/3602189.stm

would soon be declared done and over; but hopeful that there would never be another war like this again.

It was a warm day Tuesday, August 7, when I resumed my diary entries. By then I had readjusted to my daily teaching routine. Several years of teaching experience made the job easier. I taught my classes, *enjoyed the home economics class, had a club meeting* and *prepared 4-H demonstrations.* I had not yet had a chance to unpack, so that afternoon I *straightened up the house and put away a lot of things.*

As I was preparing for school Wednesday morning, the news reported *"Russia declared war on Japan today."* Seemed a little late to me. Guess Russia somehow wanted to get a message to the world that as an Ally, Russia was among the victors.

I taught school all day expecting the inspector but he didn't come. Once home I *went to wash, hung out clothes* to dry, *ate, washed dishes and wrote letters.*

The inspector came Thursday. *Mr. Burris was very nice. He liked the system we were using.* His compliment made for a rather pleasant day.

But the very nice day was shattered, especially in Japan, as another atomic bomb was dropped on Nagasaki, destroying most of the city in seconds. I was astonished. Americans were shocked and astounded. This power in the hands of man! Will the destruction ever end?

I was reading Gerald's three letters of July 29, 30 and August 1, when President Truman's radio address of August 9, 1945, was broadcasted:

> The British, Chinese and U.S. governments have given the Japanese peoples adequate warning of what is in store for them. We have laid down the general items on which they can surrender. Our warning went

unheeded, our terms were rejected. Since then the Japanese have seen what our atomic bomb can do . . .

I realize the tragic significance of the atomic bomb . . .

Its production and its use were not lightly undertaken by this Government. But we knew our enemies were on the search for it. And we knew the disaster which would come to this Nation, and to all peace-loving nations, to all civilization, if they had found it first . . .

We won the race of discovery . . .

We have used it against those who attacked us without warning at Pearl Harbor, against those who have starved and beaten and executed American prisoners of war, against those who have abandoned all pretense of obeying international laws of warfare in order to shorten the agony of war, and in order to save the lives of thousands and thousands of young Americans. We shall continue to use it until we completely destroy Japan's power to make war.*

More sobering news! It seemed somehow distant and unreal! But I also knew the bombings had had a great affect on politics throughout the world, the United States, even in my little corner of Oklahoma.

I continued to listen closely to the news throughout the week. It was announced "the Allies gave a reply to Japan's surrender terms!"

Tuesday, August 14, was a historic day! The evening news reported: "Japan has surrendered unconditionally!" My diary entry read: *"Today is the most wonderful day of my life since June 18, 1944. Japan surrendered unconditionally to the four great powers. The*

---

*　www.**famousquotes**.me.uk/**speeches**/presidential-**speeches**/

news came at 6:00 p.m. It may mean that I will be with Gerald soon and get to go to school with him."

It was wonderful for America, but not for the Japanese.

Wednesday, August 15, Emperor Hirohito announced the Japanese surrender. He urged the Japanese people to "endure the unendurable" as thousands of Japanese continued to die from radiation burns. The most destructive war in human history was over. Most Americans were sobered and grieved but rejoiced at the end of the most destructive war in history!

And life went on! School met! Mail service continued! I received mail and wrote letters! Ball games were played! The weather changed! And I was still alone without my true love!

So for the rest of the week, *I rushed to school, gave tests and went to the ball game with Reed. We lost by one point.*

Later it came a rain and there were no lights for a time.

I had a letter from Carmen Woods and a package.

I received my college transcript but was disappointed in a few of my grades.

Saturday *was a warm day* as I slept until *9:00 a.m., crocheted, sprinkled clothes* to be ironed *and listened to the radio* for news. I *went to town, got a haircut and ironed a few dresses.*

The next week *I drove a school bus for the first time . . . worked on a correspondence course . . . slept some while it rained . . . played the piano.*

I spent a lot of time thinking about the future. The correspondence about preaching jobs had fizzled; congregations wanted somebody with Bible schooling and experience. Gerald and I had corresponded about attending Abilene Christian University on a GI bill when he got back to the states. I really wanted to complete a degree in home economics, and Gerald wanted to take Bible and preaching classes. I was looking forward to attending school together.

There were several days in August when I did not receive any communication from Gerald, but I didn't get upset. I did finally *receive letters of July 14, 26 and 28, a letter of August 2 and 4; a card of July 16, and the monthly checks.* But I was especially excited and my spirits soared on Friday, August 17, when *I received a letter from Gerald written August 5* and learned *more men are being moved out of the Sixty-Ninth Division! The Sixty-Ninth was coming home in the next thirty days. I would see Gerald soon!* I floated happily *to church with the Heatleys.* I'm sure everybody got tired of hearing me exclaim, "Gerald should be home soon," but I know many were very happy for me! That night I was so wound up I was unable to sleep, so I *worked on a cushion cover* until very late.

Even with little sleep, I had a burst of energy and stayed busy all day Saturday. *I wrote a letter to Gerald, made the bed, folded clothes, washed dishes, mopped the floors, oiled the floors, washed the windows, sprinkled clothes, worked on a correspondence course and ironed.* Because I hadn't *slept much the night before, I was very tired . . . studied and went to bed early* that evening.

Sunday, August 19, *I ironed two dresses before going to church with the Posts . . . spent the remainder of the day with the Johnsons at Plainview.* Mabel Ruth had not yet returned to A&M so *I got to enjoy time* with the Johnsons . . . *enjoyed it very much . . . returned to evening church with the Moses family.*

With high hopes of seeing Gerald soon, the next week was very pleasant. I *enjoyed teaching very much* even though there was *no mail from my honey.* Each day I anticipated letters with news indicating when Gerald would be on his way home. After I got back home from church, *I wrote to my sweet.* I prayed: *"May he be home soon! God have thy will with him in doing that which is best."* I must have thought God would hear me better if I spoke in the King James language.

I had a letter from Mrs. Beasley; I was glad to hear *she was feeling much better.* I'm sure the news that Gerald would be home soon was an encouragement to her. I think she hung on to life just to see him again.

Tuesday turned out to be a very pleasant day, and life just kept getting better! I was pleasantly surprised and complimented by a report that stated *"Eastview was the only school that had perfect registers last year!"* All that time I had wasted fretting. I had done good work! Even better, I *received three letters from my honey of August 7 and 9! He was still with the Sixty-Ninth,* but there was no word of his coming home, but that did not dampen my spirits. As *school turned out at 3:00 p.m.* and I headed home, it *looked like it might rain* and clean the dusty air. Thank you God for rain!

I wasn't sure how much longer I would be around to enjoy the Suffridges, so I spent as much time as I could with them. *I played with Mona for a long time. Mona was so sweet!* Before heading up to bed I received such sweet affection; *Fred seemed to like me especially well. He came to me and said, "Goodnight moon."* He often said the funniest things!

Wednesday, I *was a bit sleepy at school and therefore cross;* however, *a letter from my sweet of August 10* brightened my attitude. *He was still in the Sixty-Ninth. He sent a picture of Eilenburgh. I worked on the register after school . . .*

I woke up Friday with *a very sore throat, felt badly, but went to school. The boys went to Ocina for a ball game. I let the students take the last hour as an activity. They played volleyball.* Even though I didn't feel well, I went to the Gospel meeting service that evening. *I had a letter of August 12 from honey.* By Saturday I *felt so bad with a cold, I spent most of the time in the bed.* About all I did was *write to Gerald, fold clothes, finish the chair cushion and wash dishes. Mabel came at seven* and helped care for me. *We ate supper, talked and went to bed.*

Sunday, August 26, Mabel and I *went to church at Jester. I ate dinner, washed dishes, slept and listened to the radio . . . wrote to Gerald and read history.*

The last week of August, I still *felt rather badly but taught all day. We had an assembly at school to hear the Baptist preacher; he took advantage and preached a sermon.* I could tell the students were restless and bored. After school I went to the s*tore, graded papers, recorded them, and went to bed and prayed, "He is wonderful. God be with him that he may come home soon."*

By Tuesday, I *felt rather well. I had no letter from my honey,* but my hopes were lifted the following day when I *received a letter from Gerald written August 20. He said, "Only four old Sixty-Niners are left in the medical division." I prayed: "God be with him that he may come home. He seems to have hopes. I am a bit excited. I love you, Gerald."*

I was very excited when *Retha and Gladys* (students) came and *ate supper with me. I enjoyed eating with them.*

I wrote a letter to Gerald and studied on the correspondence course.

A letter from Gerald written August 21 had no mention of his coming home.

It pleased me that evening when *Mabel Ruth came home with me. The morning was very warm as Mabel cooked breakfast. It was good. I went to school and enjoyed teaching very much.*

I had determined to attend a Gospel Meeting with Brother Spiney as many evenings as possible. It started on a *warm* Sunday, August 12, at the Mangum church of Christ. Mabel Ruth went with me several times. Each evening *the singing was good!* Praising God and learning more of his Word gave me peace and strength as I waited for the return of my husband.

The first evening there *came a heavy rain, so there was a small crowd at church.* The evening lesson on True Happiness seemed ironically and symbolically significant to me. I know it is not what Brother Spiney was referring to, but I couldn't help but dream that Gerald would be coming home soon! That was true happiness! I was happy even though I got *no mail* from Gerald.

Each day after school I usually *rested and slept briefly* so I would be able to stay awake during the evening services. I had to get rides with different people. So the next Sunday, I *called the Griffises to get a ride to church, and then ate dinner and spent the day with Mrs. York.* Different evenings I was able to get rides with *the Posts, the Moses and the Heatleys.*

Brother Spiney had good lessons *on* various topics: *True Happiness; Worship of the Church; Humility; Choosing the Best Life; The Beatitudes; The Best Book in the World; Who is Responsible for my Being Saved; Stop, Look and Listen; and The Prodigal Son.*

Ten were baptized during the meeting: Betty Hamilton confessed Christ. Jimmy Rogers was close, but *said, "One foot stepped, but the other one would not move." Mary Beth Scroggins confessed Christ.*

Brother Spiney was very good!

CHAPTER FIFTY-SIX

But those who hope in the Lord
will renew their strength.
They will soar on wings like eagles; they will run and
not grow weary, they will walk and not be faint.

—Isaiah 40:31

Pauline's Diary— Brinkman—September 1945

Friday, August 31, after an Eastview home *ball game* that was *lost by one point,* I *took a taxi and went to Mangum* to go home; the *folks met me at Blair.* After we got home, I *fixed supper while they milked* the cows.

I continued to help around the farm Saturday morning. It was a rather *warm day,* so when *it came up a cloud,* we hoped for a good cooling rain, *but it only sprinkled.* I rather enjoyed helping at the farm. I *washed dishes while the folks picked peas,* and *helped them can peas all day. I milked a cow for the first time in a long time.* My hands were really weak and felt stiff by the time I got finished!

That evening the family *listened to* President *Truman's speech of* September 1, 1945, *on the radio:*

> My fellow Americans . . . the Japanese have just officially laid down their arms and have signed terms of unconditional surrender . . .

Four years ago, the thoughts and fears of the whole civilized world were centered on another piece of American soil, Pearl Harbor. The mighty threat to civilization, which began there, is now laid to rest. It was a long road to Tokyo . . .

We shall not forget Pearl Harbor . . .

To all of us there comes first a sense of gratitude to Almighty God who sustained us and our Allies in the dark days of danger, who made us to grow from weakness into the strongest fighting force in history, and who has now seen us stop the forces of tyranny that sought to destroy His civilization.

God grant that in our pride of the hour, we may not forget the hard tasks that are still before us . . . Our first thoughts, of course . . . go out to those of our loved ones who were killed or maimed in this terrible war . . . No victory can make good their losses . . . Only the knowledge that the victory, which these sacrifices have made possible, will be wisely used, can give them any comfort. It is our responsibility—ours, the living—to see to it that this victory shall be a monument worthy of the deaths it took to win it. We think of all the millions of men and women in our armed forces and merchant marine all over the world who, after great sacrifice and hardship and peril, have been spared by Providence from harm. We think of all the men and women and children who during these years have carried on at home, in lonesomeness, anxiety and fear . . .

This is a victory of more than arms alone. This is a victory of liberty over tyranny . . . It is the spirit of liberty which gave us our armed strength and which made our men invincible in battle . . .

Now let us set aside V-J Day as one of renewed consecration to the principles which have made us the

strongest nation on earth and which, in this war, we
have striven so mightily to preserve . . .

Victory always has its burdens and its responsibilities
as well as its rejoicing. But we face the future and all its
dangers with great confidence and great hope . . .

God's help has brought us to this day of victory.
With His help we will attain that peace and prosperity
for ourselves and the world in the years ahead.[*]

The family gave a collective sigh when Truman's speech
was over. His words reflected my thoughts and feelings, and
the feelings of many others on the home front who had been
lonesome, anxious and worried.

But now it was time to move forward and thank and praise
God for preserving the nation and my beloved husband.

The next morning, Royce, Mom and I went *to church at
Warren . . . Eldon came with Royce.* After coming home, eating
dinner and *resting some, Dad, Mom, Royce and I then went after
pears.* I was reminded that on a farm the work was never done. I
admired my parents so much for their hard work! It was good to
be home and help them.

I had to meet Ms. Blackwell at 5:00 p.m.; she took me home. That
evening, *I took a bath and dressed to go to church.*

After *I wrote Gerald a letter,* my last thought before sleeping
was *"I love Gerald with all my heart."*

Brother Michelhoney began a two-week Gospel Meeting on
September 2. I guess autumn was the time for gospel meetings.
Oklahoma sure had a lot of them. I planned to attend as many
of the sessions as possible.

Brother Michelhoney gave very good lessons in the following *evenings
on: A Look into the Future based on the rich man and Lazarus; What*

----

[*]   http://www.trumanlibrary.org/calendar/viewpapers.php?pid=129

Shall I Do to Be Saved?; Faith by Hearing; Love of Christ; Sin Against the Holy Spirit; Building of the Church; How to Recognize the Church; and The Right Way or the Wrong Way.

The next morning, September 3 was a *holiday*—I did have school, but there was *no mail* service! *The wind blew very hard;* the swaying trees and the wind whistling through the branches were a distraction as I *gave tests* to the students. I was late getting home because of *a 4-H club meeting after school.* I must have been really tired because I slept *after school for a long time* and had to rush to prepare to go *to church.* I was *so very happy when three confessed Christ.*

The next day after giving *six weeks tests, part of the school went to Mangum to take typhoid shots.* While I *worked with the 4-H club members at school, the other children had a party.*

Later that week we *had a baseball game with Ocina and won!*

I *graded papers and worked on the register . . . ate dinner with Retha. The fish was most delicious.*

I had not received any recent word from Gerald about his coming home. I got a letter *of August 15,* but this letter had an earlier date than the last one I had received. It had taken so long to arrive. It had no encouraging news. *I was so disappointed* and made a diary entry: *"I pray that Gerald is on his way. I love Gerald with all my heart."*

By Thursday, September 6, I was really wondering, but not necessarily worried. Where is my husband, and why have I received *no letter* from him? *I was so hurt and thought, "Wish I could hear from him or his whereabouts."*

I continued to write to Gerald though I got no letters. I did *receive letters from Mrs. Beasley and one from the Hunters. And I did receive July war bonds.*

Saturday, I slept until *10:00 a.m., then listened to the radio* hoping to hear something of the whereabouts of the remaining Sixty-Ninth Division. No news.

I talked to Mona and Mrs. Suffridge before studying on my correspondence course; then I *wrote Gerald a letter. I cleaned some house and ironed until time for church.* As I prepared for church, the news stated *"the American forces are going into Tokyo."*

Sunday, September 9, *I cooked a lot for the dinner on the* church *grounds. After a very good lesson on prayer,* I *enjoyed talking to the people though it was very windy and dusty. I visited with the Hastons after church.*

The second week in September there were many things that involved my participation and I had a lot to do, but I continued to attend the gospel meeting when I could.

Monday, September 10, *I got a letter written August 30. I was so* excited! *He stated that he was in La Havre, France, and the division would leave for the states soon. This is the happiest day of my life. Gerald is in England, I hope. He sails from England September 14. I am so happy I can hardly sit still. "God be with him!"* He would sail from England four days from receipt of this letter. His movements explained why I had gotten no letters from him; he had been traveling across Belgium and France and into England. I could hardly contain myself when I *went to church* and shared the good news with my friends. That evening I didn't really hear much of the lesson, but I *went to the baptism of the Leoman boy.*

Tuesday, at school more of the students *went to town for typhoid shots at 2:00 p.m. The buses didn't return until late* so I didn't have much class. It was probably just as well; I was high on happiness and wouldn't have been able to concentrate. *I did some grading of papers; then went to church to hear a good sermon.* I didn't know if Gerald would even get them, but I continued to *write letters.*

I had classes part of the day Wednesday and put grades on cards and typed labels. Once I got home after school, I cleaned up the house and washed dishes and fixed the register. After returning from *church, I felt fine . . .* even with *no letter from my sweet one.*

Because of the upcoming 4-H show in Mangum, Thursday, I went *to school to get the 4-H things together; then* I went *to Mangum with Mr. Heatley to set up the 4-H booth. We stayed until all the girls' things were judged and placed in order. I was very tired* when I got *home and rested;* then I *went to church to hear a very good sermon.*

All day Friday, September 14, I imagined Gerald sailing across the Atlantic. It was difficult to stay focused as I *taught school until three;* then I *went to town to see the 4-H exhibits . . . not enough ribbons. We placed third. But the booth was good—a jump from seventh to third was good . . . Returned home, cooked supper, ate, dressed, and to church for a very good lesson.*

That evening the news announced *"part of the Sixty-Ninth arrived home today."* I was confused and thought, "Is Gerald back in the states! If he is, why hasn't he gotten hold of me?"

CHAPTER FIFTY-SEVEN

The Lord has dealt with me according to my
righteousness; according to the cleanness of my
hands he has rewarded me.
For I have kept the ways of the Lord;
I have not done evil by turning from my God.
—2 Samuel 22:21 and 22

Gerald's Remembrances—
Coming Home—September 1945

After the war was over in Europe, high-point men were put into units to come back to the states. Soldiers received points if they had been wounded, received a medal, been overseas for a long time, had done a good job, and various other reasons. I had sixty-seven points. There were some who had ninety or more. I had a few more points than Johnny, but together we accompanied a company full of high-pointers back home.

These men were gathered together, left Germany and went back to La Havre, France. From there they crossed the channel to Southampton, England.

September 14, 1945, I was in the group of high-pointers who boarded the Queen Elizabeth, a huge floating city, crowded with fifteen thousand troops. There were comfortable beds with clean sheets. There were shows on board and a ballroom. A daily newspaper was printed on the ship during the crossing. There were announcements over the speaking system throughout each day. There was good food on board. It's hard to believe they had all those things on a ship.

Of course, when coming from America in convoy to England some ten months earlier, the trip had taken twelve days because of the zigzagging. But coming home on the Queen Elizabeth, it took only six days.

As the Queen Elizabeth neared the New York harbor, September 20, 1945, thousands of American GIs lined up all along the sides of the ship silently and soberly viewing the Statue of Liberty, as first the torch, then the head and shoulders appeared on the horizon. Grown men sniffled and wiped tears as the rest of the statue rose into view. It was an emotional and very moving scene as this floating city passed the statue of the lady who held up the light of liberty. The men were reminded of the reasons they had gone to war, of the women and children and families they had left behind, of the friends made and lost, of the horror and blood and pain and cold they had endured, of the times when they had wondered if they would see their homeland and loved ones again. At the sight of the Lady of Liberty, they knew they were home.

I had reasoned at times that maybe Pauline and I should not have married. It would have been easier for Mom to lose a sweetheart than to lose a husband. But it all turned out okay.

Anticipation rose as the returning men came into New York Harbor and crossed on a ferry over to New Jersey. Pretty quick, they were scattered to various military camps throughout the states.

I had sent letters with information to let Pauline know what was happening, but I had no way of knowing which letters she had received. I called from New York City to let her know that I was in the states before I headed to Camp Kilmer for a brief stay. Then September 22, I sent a telegram from Camp Kilmer to let her know that I was assigned to and headed for, Camp Chaffee in Arkansas where I stayed only briefly.

CHAPTER FIFTY-EIGHT

I will praise you forever for what you have done;
in your name I will hope, for your name is good.
I will praise you in the presence of the saints.

—Psalm 52:9

Pauline's Diary—Anticipation— September 1945

Because of the 4-H show on Friday, *it was late evening before I got home to find Gerald's letter written September 6.* He wrote that he expected to be *heading home very soon.* According to earlier information received, this very day he should already be sailing across the Atlantic. I was so excited! I could hardly contain myself as I got ready to go home to the folks the morning of Saturday, September 15. I rode *with Ms. Blackwell* to *Mangum* where the folks picked me up.

Sunday, the folks were *up at 8:00 a.m., ate, and* while *Dad read the paper, Royce, Mom and I dressed and went to church. The lesson was on Fellowship. I got to see a lot of people* I knew and excitedly told them, "Gerald is on his way home." After lunch, the afternoon went by quickly as I *listened to the radio and read.* Late afternoon, *Ms. Blackwell gave me a ride back to Brinkman.*

Staying in the apartment alone was out of the question. I could not stay still. *I visited the Posts and the Suffridges.* I wrote in the diary: *"It won't be long until I will be seeing him. It is a wonderful night, my sweetheart."*

I was floating on air! To stay busy, I went with the students *at 2:00 p.m. to go to town for shots;* then after returning, I *gathered some books together, played some basketball, listened to the radio, visited with Mrs. Suffridge and the children;* then I *went with the high school* students *to a skating party. We got back rather late, 12:00 p.m.*

As I got ready for bed, I couldn't help but wonder where Gerald was on the Atlantic. I knew he would be in the states soon, so I decided, *"I am not going to write him anymore."* Lord willing, we would be seeing each other before he received them anyway.

September 19, Tommy came up the stairs to tell me I had a phone call. I was confused and thought, "Is it Gerald? He's supposed to arrive the twentieth! Maybe, it's Mabel! What if it is Gerald?" I'm surprised I didn't fall and break my neck as I flew out the door and down the stairs.

It was Gerald! The glorious day had finally arrived! He was in New York! Traveling home from the east he had gained a day.

"Hey, Pauline. I'm back! I'm in New York City," Gerald said.

Choking on tears, I croaked, "Oh, Gerald. It's so good to hear your voice. I love you so much." I sobbed as I tried to hold back my tears.

"Hey, don't cry. I love you too! I'm back and I'm safe. Hey, I've got to make this quick, so listen. I'll be heading to Camp Kilmer first, then to Camp Chaffee in Arkansas. Did you get my letters explaining all this?" He asked.

"Yes. Okay. So where do I meet you? When should I come?" I exclaimed.

"I'll have to let you know. I want to be with you too, but the government still owns me. I'll arrange a furlough as quick as I can once I get to the camp and let you know when to come. I'll go to Mom and Dad's first, then you can head north by bus, and I can meet you in Sand Springs."

In a daze, I sighed. "I can hardly wait." Aloud but more to myself I said, "I'll have to let them know I can't continue teaching. I'm just so excited. I'll take care of some things here then head to the folks' this weekend. You'll have to call me through the neighbors and they'll come and get me. I don't know their phone number. I'll have to let you know. Oh, Gerald, I can hardly wait to be with you. I've missed you so much."

"I've missed you too, but we have a lifetime to make up for lost time. Pauline, I'll send you a telegram when the furlough is settled, should take only a few days. I've got to go now. My time has run out, and I have no more coins. I love you! Wait for the telegram. We'll be together soon. I'll call you shortly. Love you!" Gerald hurriedly said.

"Love you too. See you soon, sweetheart!" I clung to the phone briefly before setting it back in the receiver. I took a deep breath and sighed and then walked into the next room to tell Mrs. Suffridge the good news.

The Suffridges had politely left the room so I could have some privacy. I was beside myself and as I came into the living room and told Burnice. *Gerald came to the States on the Queen Elizabeth! I am so happy! I love him so much!* Burnice and my little friends were excited for me. I received such sweet hugs from all of them.

After returning to my apartment, I kept circling around my apartment in confusion as I tried to determine what to do first. When I finally settled down, I began in earnest and anticipation to make plans to get ready to leave Brinkman. I could hardly stand the wait; word from Gerald would come in a couple of days, then I could head northeast to meet him.

The next morning with mixed emotions, I spoke with Mr. Suffridge and Ms. Blackwell; I ceased my teaching and 4-H responsibilities immediately. In my excitement, I would not have been able to concentrate anyway. They were very understanding, though my leaving would put them in a bind. I felt bad about that, but I was going to be with Gerald! Nothing was going to stop me!

For the next couple of days I was up early, *cleaned the house, did some mending on clothes, sprinkled clothes, ironed, washed dishes, visited Mrs. Suffridge to sew on her machine, and then studied* on the correspondence course to finish it! *I went to church to hear a good sermon on Are You Drifting?* I was certainly drifting in a dream; I didn't really hear much of the lesson!

I wrote a letter to Aunt Frankie to give her the good news. *I had a letter from Lydia* to answer; now *we could both rejoice that our husbands were home!* I had to let Mom and Dad know that Gerald was back, and that I would be coming home the coming weekend.

I knew I would miss my friends. They had been so good to me. I spent what time I could with them. At the school, many students said their good-byes and gave me hugs. *Ruth Suffridge (sister to Mr. Suffridge) came to the schoolhouse where I was packing up my things and I went with her for a ride. Later, I rode in the car with Mrs. Suffridge to get milk;* I took every chance I could to *talk with Mrs. Suffridge.* I enjoyed *Mona who now had two teeth and was so sweet.* Bernice gave me *pictures of the Suffridge children.* I was going to miss the Suffridges!

Friday, a *storm came up and tore the roof off the Eastview schoolhouse.* I was glad I was not there. I'm sure they had a tornado drill, so all were safe in the basement. I'm sure it was frightening!

Since I had done a wash and couldn't hang the clothes outside because of the rain and wind, *I had to hang some clothes in the hall* to dry.

I prepared for, and then attended Retha's wedding shower. Retha received many nice things.

Saturday, I was *up early to pack and clean the house* and to get ready to go to the folks' when *I received a telegram from my sweet from Camp Kilmer!* He was heading to Arkansas and would *call me from Camp Chaffee. It was wonderful!* He was so close yet too far away! *I was so happy that I would see him soon!* I sent a telegram in reply telling Gerald that I would be at the folks, and gave him a number where he could call and ask for me.

I was to ride to Mangum with *Mr. Suffridge who had to leave for town early, so I had to rush.* In Mangum *I met Ms. Blackwell, ate lunch at her house; then* she drove me *to Altus to the fair where I met the folks.* I could hardly contain myself! They were so happy for me!

Royce sold his pig at the fair *for $40. He was happy.* I was so happy for him! We were all happy!

Mom, Royce and I went *to church* Sunday, September 23. I managed to sit through and *enjoyed the lesson very much . . . ate dinner and slept.* It was work, but fun as all of us took *the tractor and wagon to get pears; I enjoyed picking them.* The activity kept my body busy as *I could think of nothing except Gerald and how I would be with him soon!*

Next morning we were *up at 7:00 a.m.* Mom began to clean, cut and can pears. *We sent Royce to school . . . washed dishes.* I helped Mom some, but *I mostly read until 12:30 p.m.* when *Rainer Farmer came* to our farm *to tell me I had a call from my husband.* I was so grateful to Rainer for taking the time to come get me. *I went* back with him *for the call.*

Gerald stated, "Pauline, it's me. I'm heading out from Camp Chaffee to the folks. Once there, I will pick up my car, and I can meet you at the bus station in Tulsa. I've already checked, and a bus leaves from Hobart in the morning, about 11:00 a.m. You should arrive in Tulsa in the evening about 7:00 p.m. I'll be there to meet you."

"Okay. I'm looking forward so much to being with you," I stated.

"Tomorrow, Pauline. Tomorrow we'll begin our lives again."

Once again I had to struggle to hold back tears. "Okay, I'll see you tomorrow about seven. I love you!"

The Farmer's farm was near the school, and school was almost out for the day, so *I stayed at the schoolhouse and rode the bus home* with Royce. Guess there was still some teacher in me—*I taught Royce his lessons* that evening. *I packed* a bag of clothes and cosmetics and a few other things. I *went to bed* thinking, *"I am going to meet Gerald at Sand Springs! Just think, tomorrow I will see him after almost eleven months! That has been a long time!"* Surprisingly, I slept very soundly!

Epilogue

In the summer of 2006, Neva, Dad and I drove over to the Brinkman area for a look-see.

Over twelve miles of rugged, rough, unpaved road, we drove northwest from Brinkman to the Plainview school where Mom had taught during the 1943-44 school year.

Plainview School, 1943

Since the closing of the school, the building had been used as a meeting place for the Odd Fellows and various other groups. But in 2006, it was a condemned building. The building was not necessarily safe as we carefully stepped over, around and through the mess. A lot of the outside brick walls were still standing, but there were places where structural bricks had fallen; the windows were broken; the inside walls were in disarray with graffiti all over them; holes were punched through the walls, ceiling and floor; there was a lot of trashy debris, including broken beer bottles throughout the inside; black-and-white keys and the wooden frame of a dilapidated old piano were recognizable; and the old gym was recognizable with its higher ceiling, broken and missing wooden floorboards, and a stage that had been enclosed in a mesh of wire, possibly for the protection of band players when bottles were thrown. There was evidence that this old building had been used as a gathering place for teenagers who were probably up to no good.

Only a cement foundation was left of the teacherage where Mom had lived.

The small farming community of Brinkman, established in 1910, had been a major railroad and shipping center for first cotton, then later wheat. It had had a bank (moved to Mangum in 1927), cafes, barbershops, doctors, a telephone and water system, hotel, stores, two large grain elevators, and four cotton gins. But not anymore. There were only a couple of grain elevators and one building.

In the mid-1930s, the town's population began to decline because (1) many left to seek employment because of the drought and depression in 1929; (2) State Highway 34 bypassed the town one mile east in 1930; (3) the cotton crop failed in 1936 due to lack of rain; (4) the farm laborers were forced to seek employment elsewhere; (5) the better roads and cars in rural areas made it possible for the population to drive to larger towns where prices and selections were better; (6) many sought employment at defense plants or entered service during World War II; (7) wheat replaced cotton, so fewer hand laborers were needed; and (8) tractors allowed farmers to farm more land.

A three-story school building was build and opened in 1911. In the 1920s, the school in Brinkman had 450 students who came in from the surrounding farm areas. But in 1934 the building was condemned as unsafe and a new one-story school building was build and opened in 1936. By 1946 (the year after Mom left), the Brinkman School could not maintain thirty students in daily attendance in the high school to get state aid, so the high school students were bussed to the Eastview School. After three years, the Eastview School closed and most of the students came back to the Brinkman School where the facilities were better. However, in 1957, the state required that each high school must average fifty students in daily attendance to receive state aid, so the Brinkman School was forced to close. Most of the students then went to Mangum, Granite, Reed or other surrounding towns.

The ghost town of Brinkman, Oklahoma

In 2006, the town of Brinkman was a ghost town. Few buildings were left standing, but some foundations could be seen on the north and south sides of the road that stretched east and west.

There were no longer noises of human habitation: the whistle of a train, the honk of a car, the shouts of children at play, or friendly calls of neighbors. Only the whoosh of the wind in the grasses, the chirping of crickets, the cawing of crows, and occasional whirring of vehicle tires on the black-topped road broke the silence.

The Brinkman School no longer existed. The field where the school had been was overgrown with little debris left. Across the road, the teacherage foundation was recognizable. There were some large stones about, but the vacant overgrown field lay fairly flat and clean. The old bus barn still stood. Apparently, it was still being used to store the current buses that traversed the area picking up farm youth to bus them to schools in surrounding towns.

The Eastman School was in ruin. There were some large sun-bleached stones still stacked, but many more were strewn about haphazardly making it difficult to walk around without turning an ankle. We had to step through tall weeds and up

Eastview School—1944

and over stones to get closer to the building site. Within the dilapidated structure, a large area was evident where the gym had once been, placement of classroom walls were less recognizable, but toward the back side of the building's foundation we could see a long narrow basement with benches on the long sides; this had to have been the storm cellar.

The guffawing of students' laughter and complaints of too much homework; the slipping sounds of metal locker doors opening and the bangs of the locker doors closing; the affirming and scolding statements of concerned teachers; the scratching of white chalk on black boards; the shuffling of pages being opened and turned and books banging shut; the cheering of spectators; the bouncing of balls and shuffling of feet in the gym; the singing of choirs and songs of marching bands were heard only by the ghosts of the past and the imaginations of the curious visitors.

Plainview, Brinkman, and Eastview schools were no more.

By Carmen (Beasley) Lewis

PART FOUR

Together Again

CHAPTER FIFTY-NINE

How beautiful you are, my darling!
Oh, how beautiful! Your eyes are doves.
How handsome you are, my lover!
Oh, how charming! And our bed is verdant.
—Song of Songs 1:15 and 16

Together Again

Pauline's Diary

Tuesday, September 25, I was *up early* to prepare to leave and pack the car. The folks then *drove me to* Hobart about thirty-one miles north on HI 183, so I could *catch a bus to go to Sand Springs*. Mom, Dad and Royce all hugged me and said in turn, "Pauline, we're so happy for you. Keep in touch. We love you." They stood together waving as the bus pulled away, then turned to their car. The work on the farm was waiting.

A late-afternoon rain obscured my view of the landscape as I stared out the rain-streaked window watching the dripping and dreary countryside race past. Normally the hum of the bus and the rhythm of the rain would have lulled me to sleep, but my anticipation and thoughts kept me awake.

The rain had ceased by the time the bus drove into the station. I *was a bit tired* and stiff from seating for such a long time. *I got on the bus at 11:25 a.m.*, and because of the many stops, *I did not arrive until 8:12 p.m. It had been a long day!*

I felt disheveled and wished I could refresh myself as the bus pulled in at the bus stop. The other passengers seated in front seemed to take their sweet time as they gathered up their bags and belongings. I had to temper myself to remain calm and not push them out of the way. When my chance came to stand up, I gathered my things and moved down the aisle toward the door. My eyes moved in all directions as I tried to look out the dirt and rain streaked windows to locate Gerald. My stomach churned, my mouth went dry, and my thoughts raced, "Will I recognize him? His picture made him look older! What if he hasn't arrived yet? What if he is disappointed when he sees me?"

Gerald's Remembrances

I had been anxiously waiting for the arrival of the bus since 7:00 p.m. As the bus arrived late, it was quite loaded with women who started getting off. I was filled with anticipation and some uncertainty. I sighed and whispered to myself, "Gerald, just calm down." My nervousness betrayed my thoughts, "Maybe I won't recognize her! Maybe she won't recognize me! What if I grab the wrong lady? That would not be good!"

However, I didn't grab any female prematurely. As Pauline appeared in the bus door, I did recognize her and rushed forward. At first sight of her I thought, "She is as beautiful, even more beautiful, than I remember!" As she exited, I could tell by the way her eyes opened wide that she was startled in her first brief glimpse of me; I had picked up several pounds in muscle. In fact, I was quite a bit heavier!

Pauline's Diary

Our eyes met! I recognized Gerald, and my eyes opened wide; I was *much surprised* and thought, "*He is so large and muscular; much more muscular than I remember!*" Though not prone to be publically demonstrative, *I walked into Gerald's arms as I stepped off the bus. It was wonderful!* We embraced, and our lips touched in a lingering kiss. I spoke in whispered sobs, *"I love you beyond words! Thank you, God, for bringing Gerald back to me!"*

Gerald's Remembrances

I swallowed my tears as my throat tightened, but I managed to respond, "I love you, Pauline." We clung to each other and kissed. All I cared about was enveloping her in my arms. While in the embrace, I couldn't help but notice her hair was shorter, but I drew in a sigh and thought, "Her hair still smells real good!"

It was a tearful and joyous reunion. After several minutes of clinging and crying, we finally let go of each other and gathered her bags. Since I had several weeks of leave, we rode to my folks' home in True Love; I held and kissed her hand over and over. We snuck in kisses as I tried to keep my eyes on the road.

We stayed with my folks for a while.

Mom was frail but had lived to see me, her only son, leave and return home from the war. Dad, Mom, Pauline and I had a great time together celebrating life and love.

CHAPTER SIXTY

Come away, my lover, and be like a gazelle,
or like a young stag on the spice-laden mountains.
—Song of Songs 8:14

Forty-Four Days of Furlough

It seemed to me that we were in *a dream . . . walking around* together. We had a lot of loving to make up. Our first evening at the folks' we visited briefly, then retired to the bed that had once been Gerald's, but we now shared as husband and wife. Slightly apprehensive, but eager, we trembled to gentle kisses and caresses, drowning out the past loneliness with complete sweet union.

We were both tired the next morning (can't imagine why) but did not want to ignore our hosts. So slightly embarrassed, we were up *at 8:45 a.m., dressed, ate, and* helped *wash dishes.* But the next couple of mornings, with the *rain falling and rather cold weather outside, we slept late and ate breakfast at 11:00 a.m.*

We were now able to do many things together—things that we had done separately for eleven months. First we planned to spend time visiting with and helping Gerald's folks around the house. Each day I *did some general house cleaning* to help Mrs. Beasley; I cooked, *washed dishes, dried the dishes, put them away,* and dusted. Gerald helped move furniture around and did minor repair jobs.

We *were otherwise lazy* and just relaxed. *I did some crocheting.* We were so grateful to be able to relax together again . . . go to church, pray, walk, shop, visit old friends, and meet with other Beasley relatives. During the day *we read;* it was comforting to *read, go to sleep on Gerald's shoulder,* and wake up to find him gazing lovingly at me. We were especially thankful to be able to *study the Bible and pray together before going to bed.*

Some relatives came by the Beasley's home, but later, we specifically drove to visit others.

We counted our blessings. It was a rainy Wednesday as I wrote in my diary: *"I can hardly believe that Gerald is here, but he is and I am happy. I thank God for his protection over my sweet."*

After making a call, Gerald found out that the *church at Tenth & Rockford Street in Tulsa* was having a gospel meeting, and we determined to attend. So starting Wednesday, September 26, we would eat *an early supper and* then *go to hear Brother John Bannister speak.*

For the next two weeks the weather continued to be *rainy and very cold,* but we attended the *church at Tenth Street to hear Brother Bannister speak* most evenings. Gerald was especially hungry for Christian fellowship and the Word. Most of the time we drove True Love; but when it began to sputter and spit and have problems, we *rode the streetcar to church, went window-shopping, and then rode the streetcar back home.*

We heard various motivating lessons: *Messiah, the Lord; Our Responsibility to the Church; Why Christ was Crucified; Rightly Dividing the Word of Truth; The Blood of Jesus; Is Your Name Written In Heaven?; The Eunuch and How to be Saved; The Church and Jesus; Repentance; and Confession.*

Hallie, Gerald's Mom, went with us some evenings *to church in Tulsa.* Edgar stayed home; he rarely went to church.

At church we saw many acquaintances. After the services on different evenings, we went to the homes of various friends for visits.

One evening we *went home with the Montgomerys to eat watermelon.* While there *Gerald talked of his war experiences.* I was already privy to many of the stories but listened attentively as he retold them.

After returning home and retiring, Gerald told me *of the evil women living on the streets of London;* how he disapproved and was repulsed by their course language and behaviors. I could tell *he was so sour on them.* As I listened quietly, I tried to imagine how he must have felt as he watched his comrades give into temptations and ungodly practices; how Gerald must have felt isolated and alone and different, sometimes even criticized. When he was through talking, we *prayed, and then . . . the most wonderful loving!*

Though it was still slightly chilly Saturday, the skies had cleared, so *we went to town. Later we dressed and dashed to Donna Jean Marg's wedding at four and attended the reception. The wedding and reception were very nice.* I couldn't help but *wish that our wedding had been shared with our friends;* but no matter, I *just wanted to be the best wife possible for my very wonderful husband.*

After the wedding and reception, we *ate at Ike's and went to church.* That night *we set the clocks back one hour.* An extra hour for *such sweet loving!*

It rained most of the day Sunday, September 30, a busy day. We were *up at 8:00 a.m., dressed and to church at Tenth Street in Tulsa. It was a very good service.* After hearing *the lesson on Our Responsibility to the Church,* Gerald was more determined to learn more Bible and prepare himself for ministry.

After *returning to Sand Springs, eating and washing dishes,* the Beasleys *had company.* Word had gotten around that Gerald was back from Europe and was home. *Edgar Beasley's brother, Tom, and his wife Flora* came for a visit—the first of many Beasleys and their relatives that I would eventually meet. It was a happy reunion.

The first week in October, *we were* both *so lazy* and *it was 10:00 a.m. before we arose* most mornings. *The sun came out* and continued to *shine beautifully* for several days. *It was a beautiful sight to see* the sun! With no job to prepare for or go to, it was so different for me . . . no classes, meetings, or grading of papers. But the respite was welcomed! We both *did some reading. I crocheted on a scarf most days . . . finished the scarf* by the end of the week.

Since the sun was *out, for several days we did a big wash and hung wet clothes out* to dry. *Gerald did most of it.* Nothing like the fresh smell of clothes dried in a clean fall breeze.

It was raining some again Thursday, but after hearing that some friends were in Stillwater, we got *up at 10:00 a.m., dressed,* and left *to visit Jerry and David Fultz; but we were too late.* They had already come and gone by the time we got there. So since we were already in Stillwater, we *went after a typewriter.*

It was time to get serious about the future. Gerald wished to write various congregations inquiring about preaching jobs, and/or complete the applications to attend Abilene Christian University. I wanted to complete my degree in Home Economics and Gerald wished to work on a Bible/Ministry degree.

While we were out, we *ate at a cafeteria and then just drove around* to revisit friends and to see familiar places. *We went out to see Helen Beasley,* Gerald's aunt. We got lucky; *Inez and Jerry were there* at Helen's. Returning home, *as we drove out on a country road,* I remembered the romantic places *where we had stopped* to make out *before we married, but we didn't stop as in our courting days.* (God forbid that our future children should know of these romantic episodes when we had driven in True Love to remote locations on moonlit nights.)

The remainder of the week, we were *up at 10:30 a.m. I prepared* to attend *the ladies Bible class* with Mrs. Beasley; *they had a very interesting study over the book of Esther.* Since True Love was not running smoothly, while the women were attending the class, *Gerald took the car to a garage.*

After returning to the house, I felt ambitious and *washed dishes while Gerald studied* the Bible . . . *made hot rolls which didn't turn out to be so good. I had a bad cold,* so later I just sat around . . . *crocheted some . . . pestered my sweetheart.*

Even though I did not feel well, we took the streetcar and *attended church that evening. While returning, we walked by a brawl at a beer joint where someone was hurt.* Gerald protectively and quickly ushered me away. He had seen enough drunken brawls and unseemly behavior while in the service, and he did not wish to get into the middle of this one; and he did not want to expose me to it.

While at the Beasleys, I continued writing daily comments in my diary: "*Many times it seems that I am living a dream when I see Gerald walking around the house . . . It is hard to believe that it is not a dream but real! It is wonderful to have Gerald in my sight. I have the most wonderful husband on this earth. I love him with all my heart . . . I was extremely mischievous this afternoon and pestered him so much, for which I in turn received a beating, in fun, of course. We said our prayer and did some studying* in the Bible. *We thank our heavenly Father for such wonderful blessings.*"

Sunday, October 7, was a special day. We were *up at 8:00 a.m., dressed, and left early for church at the Sand Springs church. Gerald gave the morning lesson, They Know Not What They Do.* Surely the idea came to him as he remembered hearing and watching his fellow soldiers flirting with and giving into temptations while believing it didn't matter since they would probably not live anyway. Gerald was somewhat nervous, but I thought his lesson was very good and *enjoyed it very much.* His mother was very proud! Too bad that his grandfather, Samuel Beasley, had not lived to see his prophesy fulfilled, that Gerald would be a preacher.

Later that same day *at 5:00 p.m.,* I had the opportunity to meet *more of the Beasleys.* In the evening we *went to church at Sand Springs* with Hallie, *then,* Gerald and I hastened *to the Tenth and Rockford church in Tulsa with Mr. and Mrs. Berry,* Gerald's aunt and uncle.

Later, *it was a beautiful night as we took exercises* and walked around the streets in Sand Springs.

While he was overseas, Edgar had used Gerald's car to drive to work; but now, since Gerald was back, Gerald usually drove his dad to work so we could use it to get around. *There was a strike going on at the oil refinery* where Edgar had worked for many years. This was likely to affect Edgar's employment. On October 3, it was *raining when Mr. Beasley came home early because of the strike.* He talked some about it, but Gerald was a bit worried about what his dad would do if he lost his job. His dad wasn't getting any younger, and employment opportunities were limited. A couple of days later, *Mr. Beasley* left the house *and didn't return* until late. Gerald became even more worried! However, Monday, the eighth, *Gerald arose early to take his dad to work;* his dad still had a job.

After some discussion, we had decided during his extended furlough to spend some time with my folks. I had written *a letter to mother* to let them know we would be arriving at the farm on October 11 for a brief stay. So Monday, the eighth, *a cool but beautiful day,* we made preparations for the trip to southwest Oklahoma. *We ate, washed dishes and washed clothes until noon.* Gerald had taken True Love to a garage for repairs, so *Gerald went to town to check on the car. I ironed clothes until about 4:30 p.m. and typed the numbers of our bonds for Mr. Beasley.*

Though it had been great to attend the gospel meetings and visit with friends, I was relieved and thought *it was nice to be at home and not go anywhere* that evening. After preparing for bed, Gerald and I prayed, *"God, be with us on our journey tomorrow and always."*

Another precedent was set for our marriage and family; we prayed before setting out on any journey.

We had been with his parents' for fourteen days from the evening of September 24 thru the morning of October 9, 1945.

Before heading southwest, we first went to Stillwater to visit school acquaintances. We were *up at 8:00 a.m., ate, cleaned up, and packed . . . left for Stillwater about 3:00 p.m. We arrived in time for* the young people's *church, a singing service.* The singing was great! Seating side by side, Gerald sang bass and I sang soprano, our worlds and voices blending in sweet harmony.

We were able to visit with many acquaintances after the services; *it was nice to see old friends again.*

We stayed the night *with the Straughns, a swell couple. After drinking cocoa, we went to bed.* The next morning, we were *up at 7:30 a.m. I fixed breakfast at Sis Straughn's and washed the dishes. I called Lydia Mae and Mabel Ruth* and then *visited both.* After that we *visited the Scotts, Ezra and baby, and Sis Best.* We went to say thanks and good-bye to *Sis Straughn and* then headed out of town toward southwest Oklahoma.

In Oklahoma City we roomed at the King Kade Hotel, our one extravagance.

While there we took the opportunity to contact an old friend. Gerald had heard that his friend, Forest Sweet, and his wife Ruth were attending the Tenth and Francis Church in Oklahoma City, where Yater Tant was the preacher. So Gerald phoned the church to ask if indeed Forest Sweet was attending there.

Gerald asked the church secretary, "Is Tator Yant there?"

The secretary laughed and said, "It's Yator Tant." (A potato-head he ain't.) ☺

It turned out that Forest was indeed attending there, so Gerald was able to get the phone number and contact him. That evening we *attended church at Tenth and Francis* and *were overjoyed to see them.* Afterward we had a good visit. *Forest and Ruth Sweet had a baby girl.*

Forest related the story of how he had made the national news. "Well, after getting into the navy, I went to the Pacific and became secretary for an admiral in the navy. Meanwhile, Ruth was home, pregnant. I managed to get a furlough and flew to California on a military flight, then on to Oklahoma City. I *arrived home only an hour before* my *9 lb.* daughter's birth; I got to the hospital just as Ruth was wheeled into delivery. The news media got hold of the story and decided that I had walked the floor farther than any father in history."

Before leaving, Gerald spoke to Forest, "You really need to attend Abilene Christian College on the GI bill." Forest eventually did.

Thursday, we arose about 8:00 a.m., dressed, and ate breakfast in a cafe near the hotel. It was nearly 10:30 a.m. before we were prepared to leave for the rest of the trip to *southwestern Oklahoma.* We *drove rather steady at 40 mph. At Chickasha we picked up a soldier who had had too many drinks.* Gerald was concerned about picking up strangers while I was with him, but he just couldn't drive passed a soldier without stopping to help. He knew what it was like to have no means of transportation and want to get home to family and loved ones. God was with us; the soldier didn't throw up in the car and he gave us no trouble. In fact, *he slept most of the way.*

He was grateful for the ride to Blair. "Thanks, guys, for the ride. It is greatly appreciated." By then he was more sober.

Gerald had never met my family. He had introduced himself in a letter. He was a bit nervous. On the way out to the farm, we surprised and *picked Royce up from school and took him home.* As Royce stepped out of the schoolhouse, he was startled to see his sister standing beside a car with a stranger. Royce eyed Gerald and knew he had to be my husband.

"Hey, what are you doing here?" Royce exclaimed as he gave his sister a hug.

"We just got here and knew you would be getting out of school, so we decided to come by and get you. Now you won't have to ride the bus home." Turning to Gerald I said. "Royce, this is my husband, Gerald."

Royce shyly lowered his head, extended his limp hand, but responded, "Hi! Nice to meet you."

"Nice to meet you, Royce," Gerald replied. Royce was quiet on the ride home, but he warmed up to his brother-in-law over the next couple of days.

Once at the farmhouse, Gerald met my folks. "Mom and Dad, this is Gerald."

Shaking hands all around, Maggie and John were impressed with their daughter's choice of a husband and somewhat awkwardly in their countrified way said, "Nice to meet you."

Mom had prepared *an enormous supper* and during supper the group *talked for a long time.* I helped clean up the dishes while Gerald continued to talk with Dad in the sitting room. Gerald asked my parents if they were interested in *attending church at Warren* . . . but the older folks had late chores to do, *so we went to church . . . went to bed* shortly after returning to the farm.

This time, the sweethearts shared what had once been my bed.

I had left the majority of my belongings at the teacherage, and I wanted all my Eastview friends to meet Gerald, so on Friday, we were *up at 7:00 a.m. and prepared to go to the Eastview* School. We visited briefly with the students and teachers. I glowed with pride as I introduced Gerald; all seemed impressed with him. It was emotional for me as we drove away from the school; I would miss the job, the students, and the teachers.

Then we headed to Brinkman and *talked to Mrs. Suffridge for a time.* It was good to see her and the children again. Burnice prepared, and *we ate a lunch* with her; then we *began to pack my things* from the apartment. *It took all afternoon to get the dishes packed and loaded in the car. It was dark before we could clean up and get started back to the folks.* I sighed

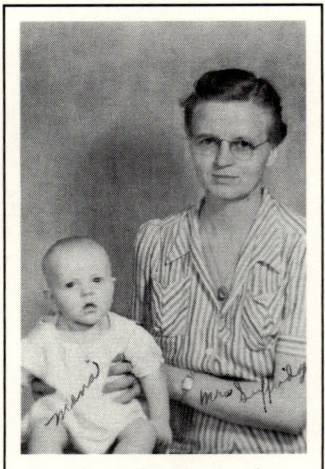

Mona Carolyn and
Burnice Suffridge, '45-46

as we got into the car and headed home; the day had been emotionally and physically draining.

The car generator wasn't charging, but we managed to find a man to fix it in Mangum. Since it was late, we picked up some food and *ate along the way. We were rather tired* when we got back *and went to bed immediately.*

Tommy and
Fred Suffridge '45-46

Saturday, we were *up at 7:00 a.m., ate and again headed to Eastview* to finish packing up everything. This time *Mother, Dad and Royce* brought their car and *went to help us. On the way we stopped in Mangum* at the bank *to get our money and run a few errands.*

Once we got to Eastview, *I went to the school board members (Mr. Drake, Elmo Heatley, Mr. Sherman and Mr. Fauck) to* officially *resign. I hated to leave, but to be with Gerald was so much more important.*

I was able to *see Lynn and Katherine's baby boy* before we left town.

It was late before everything was packed. The tired crew *drove home* to the farm *to eat.* Gerald and I *studied* the Bible before going *to bed.*

Sunday, October 14, we *went to church* in Blair. Afterward, Maggie and Royce headed back home, but Gerald and I *went to Brother and Sis Weldon Curry's for dinner. Brother Nesbott was there also;* everybody *ate so much!* We *enjoyed being with them.*

Another of many precedents in our marriage had begun— *Visiting with people is a wonderful part of life.*

Later that afternoon we *went to Altus to the young people's meeting and returned for night services* in Blair *for a good sermon on Heart Felt Religion. Then we went home and to bed.*

The weather was *cloudy* for a few days with *part-time beautiful sunshine,* so during our stay, we both worked outside. We knew that work on a farm was never completed and wanted to make a contribution. For a week, we were *up at 7:30 a.m., ate* and worked. We did the usual farm chores—gathered eggs, milked the cows, lead the horses, fed the livestock, and whatever jobs Dad and Mom directed us to do. *Monday, we helped load two calves* into a trailer. That was an experience! We hadn't done that in a while.

We did not see it, but had a laugh when Royce told us, "*Daddy fell off the horse." That must have been fun to see.* He wasn't hurt.

I got some relieve from the physical labor when I *took Mother to the store to get some groceries.* Later, *I went to the cow pen just so Royce could squirt me with milk.*

We were not used to getting *up at 7:30 a.m.* or heavy manual labor, so *we felt like the morning after the night before;* we were stiff and sore.

We decided to unload excess baggage and *cleaned up a few things.* We *burned some letters* (the letters we had written while separated?). I don't remember what the rationale was behind that decision. Perhaps it was symbolic of putting the horrors of war and the pain of separation behind us? Had the letters been kept, they would have told quite a story. *We stored some* of my *packed-up items* in the back room at Mom and Dad's house.

We dressed and went to Mangum to sell the portable *stove* that I had purchased for the teacherage; it was heavy and bulky, and we decided it was not needed anymore. After finding a buyer, *we ate dinner with Ms. Blackwell and enjoyed it very much. We returned home, rested, slept, ate supper and talked.* I wrote in my diary: "*I pestered Gerald so much. He is so wonderful. I love him with all my being. We cleaned up, read, studied, and to bed for love play."*

We did have some idle time while at the folks. *We walked to the mailbox to get the mail and then went to do the wash in town and to get some groceries.*

We continued each day to head over to pick up Royce from school. One day when we picked him up, we found out that

Royce had had a fight with Bobby Bagwell; he didn't want to talk about it, so not much was said in the car.

Royce enjoyed the extra attention from Gerald and me. Most days after he got home from school, I *boxed with Royce;* he seemed to crave the attention.

The last day of our visit, everybody took time out from work and *prepared to go on a wiener roast. Everybody had a big time pestering John* (Dad). The family had a great time! Especially Royce! *We ran, jumped, wrestled, and a bit of everything—even hide-and-seek. Everyone was exhausted. Bed was very welcomed.*

We had stayed with my folks for a week, from October 11-18 before we *returned to Sand Springs.*

Thursday, the eighteenth, we left *at 11:00 a.m., stopped to eat at Hobart, and had to flush the radiator in the car.* We took a side trip *through Norman to see the campus and town. In Oklahoma City we stopped and visited Forest and Ruth Sweet again* and *left the city about 9:00 p.m.* (much too late) *and arrived in Sand Springs at 1:00 a.m.* the following morning. On the way, *I pestered Gerald* to help keep him awake *by pinching, biting, kissing, and singing; but later I went to sleep.*

During our second stay at the Beasleys, we *removed more things from the car and put some books on shelves.* We took care of some personal matters . . . *went to town to buy bonds and did some banking and got groceries. It took us a long time downtown.*

We had determined to help Gerald's folks out around the house, but we also took time for pleasure. It was obvious that Hallie was just too weak to do really thorough cleaning; so we were *up at 8:00 a.m., ate breakfast, washed dishes, and cleaned up the house a bit. I washed* clothes *part of the afternoon and Gerald helped. I scrubbed the kitchen floor on my knees and was very tired afterward. We changed springs on the bed and cleaned some of the dirt out of the house. I sprinkled clothes to iron and then spent the afternoon ironing while Gerald was listening to football games on the radio.*

It felt so refreshing after a bath.

Later that afternoon, Gerald brought out a photo album, and we *looked at* family *pictures.*

Since it wasn't functioning very well, Gerald got out some tools, worked on what he called the du-ma-flicky inside the hood and *finished working on the car.*

I told Gerald, "I don't think you know what you are doing."

He responded, "I resemble that."

Another day we *drove out north of town to visit the Bowmans* (the former Baptist neighbors of the Beasleys), *drove through Tulsa and by Lover's Lane.*

For several evenings, with *such beautiful moonlit nights, we took long walks up the big hill and around it.*

While Gerald continued *picking Mr. Beasley* up from work, I took some time to w*rite a letters to Margie and Carmen Wood.*

I continued to write in the diary: "*I love my wonderful husband so much. He is so sweet. It was a beautiful day and moonlit night. Gerald tried to sleep, but I wouldn't let him sleep . . . It was love games with wrestling for hours. I am blue all over. I will have to grow up before I can whip him . . . I love Gerald so much. I was a sour puss today.*"

Sunday, October 21, I *got up at 7:30 a.m. to mix rolls and jello. We dressed and went to church* in Sand Springs *to hear Brother Cotton preach on Giving. After eating* Sunday lunch*, we washed and dried the dishes and then went to church* in Tulsa *at 5:00 p.m. to hear Brother Tinius speak on Modern Versions of the Great Commission.*

We had learned that another gospel meeting was starting *at Forty-First Street Church* in Stillwater; so for two weeks, we drove to Stillwater in the evenings. On different occasions we took different friends with us to hear Brother Hill as the gospel meeting continued. *Mrs. Beasley and Mildred Jiles* often *went with us to church.*

It was good to hear Brother Hill speak on the following topics: *Life of Saul; Ignorance; Church Work for Women; Sin; Noah, a Type of Christ; The Church; How to Recognize the True Church; The Prodigal*

Son; and The Great Physician. Five were baptized, and two came confessing unfaithfulness. We went to the baptisms.

While attending this gospel meeting, we were able to visit with a number of friends and were invited over for dinner several times. We *saw David and Jerry, Dale and Evelyn, Charles and Margaret, J. A. Montgomery, Paul Johnson and his wife, and Chester and Ruby Lee Hill who had a little girl.*

Before the evening services on Wednesday, October 24, we went to *Sis Everett James's for dinner. The meal was so very good. We had a lot of fun with Brother Hill, teasing him about eating.*

The next evening, *Brother Hill came home with us and ate ice cream and talked.*

Friday, November 26, *we took Brother Hill to Tulsa to meet Brother Tinius by playing a trick on him . . .* took him to *Sis Crutcher's for a fine meal . . . Sis and Brother Tinius were* already *there.* Brother Hill was surprised to see them.

Wednesday, November 31, *I fixed a fine meal for Charles Tinius at the Beasleys'; then,* Brother Tinius *had an excellent class* in Sand Springs that evening *with eleven present.*

On various evenings after the gospel meetings, Gerald and I would stop for ice cream. I craved ice cream; I enjoyed the cool, smooth treat.

One evening I asked, "Can we get some ice cream?"

But Gerald responded, "You've had enough ice cream for a while."

I was surprised at his negative response, turned my head to him in disbelief, and responded defensively, "Do what now? *I have had only one this week!"*

Gerald didn't get it for me! Guess he was concerned I would get fat.

The week beginning Monday, October 29, was to be our last week in Sand Springs, so we got busy trying to finish up several projects around the Beasley's house. *I cleaned out more shelves, washed dishes, washed and waxed four floors; I was a bit sore from the washing.* The dust gave me a *nosebleed. I felt bad and slept some. I did a big ironing . . .* In the meantime, *Gerald put* some new *roofing on the house and started painting* around the house.

I was very tired and *lazy* on Thursday, December 1, *a beautiful, warm day.* I decided to take it easy, so I *crocheted and sewed. Afterward,* Gerald and I *took a long walk* before he w*ent to the refinery to get Mr. Beasley.*

Time with the Beasley's was running out as I *washed the dishes, slept a short time, wrote the Hunters and Mother, fixed part of supper and ate hamburgers*—they were *good.* I wrote: "*It was wonderful to be able to stay home and read with my husband across the room from me. It is wonderful for him to be in the States. I must always be thankful to God. I love Gerald dearly"* even if he wouldn't get me ice cream!

By November 6, I seemed to be very tired and *very slowly ironed most of the day. My back was very weak* and hurting, so *Gerald helped out* with the ironing *toward the end of the day. After supper, washing dishes, and listening to the radio . . . We had a rather lengthy discussion about my being pregnant. I doubted it even though my period had stopped.*"

Wednesday, November 7, our last day at his folks, *Gerald fixed breakfast. After cleaning house and ironing some, I rested . . . fixed lunch. I went to town with Gerald.* After we got back, *he took a bath, shaved, and went after his dad in Tulsa.*

We dressed and *went to* midweek *Bible study at Tenth Street* in Tulsa, *had a good lesson on Job. Jerry, Inez's husband, was baptized. We went home, packed, and then to bed.*

For forty-four days we had enjoyed being together and with our families. We had worked, relaxed, and rehoneymooned during Gerald's long furlough, knowing inevitably we would have to return to reality.

CHAPTER SIXTY-ONE

Then Joshua blessed them and sent them away,
and they went to their homes . . .
After a long time had passed, the Lord had given
Israel rest from all their enemies around them . . .
—Joshua 22:6; 23:1

Military Discharge—November 1945

So on November 8, we got *up at 7:00 a.m.*, loaded the car and drove in a repaired True Love from Sand Springs to Camp Crowder near *Neosho, Missouri.* We had *packed* only clothing and household items that we would need for, hopefully, a brief stay. Driving north through Tulsa, we *stopped at Claremore to go through Will Rogers Memorial; it was interesting. It rained as we arrived at Vinita*, Oklahoma, *about 1:00* where we got a bite to eat before continuing northeast into Missouri. From Neosho, we headed south a few miles *to Camp Crowder to see about* Gerald's *orders.*

After we *visited the PX* and found an advertisement on a bulletin board, they *found a room at 111 Colar Street* where we stayed for a brief time. It didn't take very long to carry our few belongings in and unpack. After *eating*, with nothing else to do, we headed *to the USO* to kill some time; we played *Chinker Checkers.* Guess I wasn't very good; *I won two games out of a dozen.* We then *walked home and to bed.*

Early Friday morning, we were *up at 8:00 a.m., dressed, and went to town to eat; then Gerald went to the camp about 10:00 a.m.*

to find out what was expected of him, and to check into what he needed to do to expedite his discharge from the army. I remained at the room and *crocheted and then went to the library, which was close by, and read most of the afternoon.* After I *came home,* I *had an attack of indigestion* and *wrote cards to the folks and Gerald's parents. It was 6:00 p.m. before Gerald came in.* I had had a long day by myself, and I was very happy to see him. There was little to do; so we *went to the library to read, walked home and prepared for bed. It was cold* as we cuddled up together.

We had hoped to get the discharge finalized quickly but were told it might take *all of* the *next week.*

Up early on Saturday, *Gerald left for camp at 6:00 a.m. I remained in bed until 9:00 a.m. then ate breakfast and crocheted until Gerald came in at 12:00* noon. *We ate lunch, read, and listened to the* Oklahoma *A&M vs. LU football game that ended 12-6 in favor of A&M. It was a hard-fought game.* With little else to do, we walked to and *ate supper in town, then studied at the library. After walking home,* I made a diary entry: *"I love Gerald with all my heart. He is a wonderful husband. I am sure I am pregnant!"*

Gerald had checked around and found a church nearby, so we *walked to church* Sunday, November 11, and *enjoyed both the Bible school and church. We ate downtown, walked home, read the paper and took a short nap.*

A daily pattern developed as we *walked around and up to the USO to play Chinker Checkers* again; I *won a few games. We walked home, drove to the grocery store, bought wieners and roasted them along a roadside in the hills.*

Again, a simple precedent was set early in our marriage that would continue for the reminder of our lives with our children and grandchildren—we would gather up the makings for hotdogs (or hamburgers) to be roasted over an open campfire, all would sit around the campfire to enjoy nature and God's blessings. Such simple pleasures!

Later that evening we w*ent to the young people's class and church* and e*njoyed both very much.* It was especially enjoyable because there were *many soldiers* who *attended there.* Gerald had known and worshipped with a few Christian soldiers in Europe, but he appreciated knowing there were other fellow soldiers on American soil who were concerned about spiritual things.

Monday, since we were not a great distance away, we were *up at 8:00 a.m. and drove to Mount Vernon,* Missouri, *to see Gerald's uncle, Sid Morris* (Hallie and Gerald had visited them when he was a child). I had *felt rather sick at the stomach* but felt some better after we *ate lunch at 1:00.* I worried that *I did not make a good impression,* but was assured by the time we left that both his aunt and uncle understood why I felt sickly. They were happy about the expected child, though the pregnancy had not yet been confirmed by a doctor.

Heading back to Camp Crowder, we *got lost on the way as it rained a lot;* we had trouble reading the signs. We *drove through Aurora, Cassville, Monett, and back to Neosho, totaling about ninety miles.*

We went to the young people's meeting at church again *and had a very interesting study. We met a number of people.*

Tuesday, Gerald got up early again and *went to camp at 6:00 a.m. I did sleep well until he left,* then *felt sick,* so I *ate a bit of breakfast. I walked to town with Mrs. Aires and Thelma,* wives of other soldiers. It was good to have lady friends; otherwise I would have been alone most days. After returning from town, I *felt bad and lay on the bed for a long time.* There was little for me to do, and I didn't know when Gerald would return from the camp, so later I *washed and fixed my hair, went to town to eat—had a large appetite,* and went *to the library* to read.

At 4:00 p.m., Gerald walked in a bit exasperated with the army and said, "Nobody seems to know what is going on. Nobody is doing anything. We just sit around all day doing nothing. I wish they would get their act together and get the discharges under way!"

We *came home, ate, and walked to the library* again. We *stayed until 9:00 p.m.* since there was little else to do.

To the camp, to the library, to town, to church in the evenings and time spent with new friends became the daily routine. There were *other soldiers* being assigned and *leaving* to new stations to complete their tours of duty, but Gerald continued to wake up early to leave *for camp* where he did nothing constructive while waiting for a discharge. He would stay on base as long as he could stand the incompetence; then between *3:45 and 5:00 p.m. he would head for the library where he would find me.*

In the mean time, I usually *slept until 10:00 a.m.* I had good and bad days; some days my *stomach wasn't so upset* and I *felt much better;* other days, even though I *ate, I didn't feel so well.* I tried to keep busy at the room—*ate breakfast, changed bed linens, wrote cards to Lydia Mae and the Suffridges* to let them know I was pregnant, *cleaned up the room, and crocheted until one or two.*

A new acquaintance, *Helen Nichols,* came by for several days and *ate lunch with me.* Helen was upset and appreciated having a friend to talk to; *her husband was being shipped out* soon.

After Helen left, I *went to the library,* the only place within walking distance where I could pass the time and not feel so isolated and locked away. I *read a book on George Washington Carver* who *was born, lived, and attended school* near Neosho. It was interesting.

It was wonderful to see Gerald when he arrived at the library. Together we *read the Hygiene Magazine about prenatal care and childbirth.* We were both *looking forward to next July a great deal* though it might put a cramp in my academic plans.

Again True Love wasn't running smoothly, so Gerald *had a few things done to the car* in town. When the car was running again, we drove to and *met Brother Porter at the Stark City church,* about eight miles to the east of the camp. I thought his mustache *looked as though he had tobacco running out of each corner of his mouth.* Not a pleasant picture! However, *his lesson was very good.*

The next evening, *we found some people* from the camp *to go with us to hear Brother Porter.* He gave *a good lesson on the Unknown God.* After the services, we *went home with Brother and Sis Jimmie Jones to play rook.*

Another precedent was started—playing rook and forty-two with church friends.

While waiting to be discharged, the GIs, including Gerald, did not really have any kind of job on base. They were just sitting around while waiting to be processed. It was boring and frustrating. Every day Gerald would go to the base where the only thing being done was processing GIs for discharge from the military. Lots of paperwork was involved, and it seemed to be getting done awfully slowly.

Some of the guys complained to the IG, inspector general, and he began to look into the matter. He found out that the personnel who were supposed to be doing the paperwork for the discharges were coming out to the base, working for a little while, and then going back into town to be with their wives and/or families. Well, when the IG found that out, he really galvanized them into action and things began to pop.

So finally, Gerald got his "honorable discharge." It had been a hassle! It had taken fifteen days of waiting.

At the time of his discharge, Gerald was classified as Clerk General 055, and his papers showed that he had received decorations and citations including (1) a Good Conduct Medal, (2) a Bronze Star Medal, (3) a Purple Heart, (4) a World War II Victory Medal, and (4) an EAME Ribbon.

On Friday, November 23, my diary entry read: "*Gerald received his discharge today. I am so very happy.*"

One concern was taken care of, but another took its place. *I had another shot in my arm* to help alleviate morning sickness, *which made me very sick for a few minutes.* However, *I* soon *felt much better* and was able to enjoy the *beautiful but cold day.*

The next morning *we drove back to Sand Springs and arrived about 8:30 p.m.*

Afterthoughts on War

When the right button is pushed, I can remember some details of long-ago military connections. I know that I studied, meditated and prayed about the "War Question" as a babe in Christ. Seems to me there are inconsistencies on both sides of the question. I suppose I examined most of the well-known arguments on both sides.

In the early 1940s I registered in the draft as a conscientious objector, requesting to be in the medical corps. I guess I couldn't see myself aiming and then pulling the trigger at another human being.

I had to fight to get in the medical corps. After being drafted in the fall of 1942, I was sent to the AAATC band at Camp Hulen, Texas. I immediately went and explained to my commanding officer, "I want to be in the medical corps." He wanted another clarinetist in the band, so I was there more than a year.

From Camp Hulen I was transferred to Camp Shelby, Mississippi, placed in an infantry company and issued a rifle. I explained to my new commanding officer about my conscientious status. He was angry, disrespectful, and stated he would give me "noncombatant service." He put me on permanent K. P. One of the captain's sergeants, who had been present when I talked with the captain, came to me privately and told me, "You can have the captain court-martialed. He can't do that to you." Of course, I didn't do that.

Finally, I was transferred to a Medical Detachment in Camp Shelby. There I did clerical work—a lot of typing—and other work in the dispensary.

However, while in combat overseas, I was a medic attached to an infantry company. The guys in the company called me Doc and Deacon. I think I was respected by all. I gave first aid to American and German soldiers as well as civilians and others who may have been Polish "slaves."

Some men possibly claimed conscientious objector status because they were scared, maybe cowardly. I was plenty scared more than once! But I was willing to service my country, just not carry a gun and shoot another human being. As a medic I could help people and hopefully save lives.

One day in January of 1945, those in the company saw a small group of civilians coming from the German side toward our lines, escaping, I suppose. The ground was snow-covered, and the Germans were shelling (mortar fire). Black dirt exploded on the white snow. An old man in the group was hit, and the rest huddled around him. I went the few hundred yards to the group to aid. A shell exploded nearby. My automatic reaction was to fall against the old fellow knocking him down, but no further damage was done to his leg wound. When things quieted, other GIs came with a stretcher. After doctoring him as best I could, I saw the man no more. Because of this experience, sometime later I was awarded the bronze star. I was told that the company of enlisted men went to the company officers and recommended that I receive the medal. It was a total surprise to me.

There was also the question of GIs sustaining injuries on purpose to avoid combat duty. Should a GI stick his foot out of his fox hole, hoping for an injury that would take him out of combat?

My company was billeted briefly in a small town in the Siegfried Line area. Some of us slept in the basement, others on the first and second floors. In the wee hours one night I was awakened by a gunshot from upstairs. I heard the cry for the medic and went to help. It seems a propped, loaded rifle fell and went off, and the rifleman was wounded in the thigh. I did my thing and then he was jeeped to an aid station. Some days later a judge advocate officer looked me up and asked questions about the GIs wounding. I simply related the facts I knew. I don't think he asked for my opinion. Apparently, some felt the rifleman may have shot himself purposely. I never learned the outcome of the matter.

After VE Day I was yanked back to regimental headquarters to do clerical work.

I was among thousands of returning GIs on the *Queen Elizabeth* who thrilled at the sight of the Statue of Liberty as the big boat headed for docking. Quite a sight!

I serviced my country with pride. I am pleased that things turned out for me as they did. I'm genuinely thankful that the American military allows the status of conscientious objector. I think I could recommend such a course of action to any Christian young man.

I *know* I can recommend that "supplications, prayers, intercessions, and thanksgivings, be made for all men; for kings and all that are in high places . . ."

(1 Timothy 2:1-3).

Gerald Austin Beasley
(November 2012, at age 92)

CHAPTER SIXTY-TWO

And now, O Israel, what does the Lord your God ask
of you but to fear the Lord your God, to walk in all
his ways, to love him, to serve the Lord your God with
all your heart and with all your soul . . .

—Deuteronomy 10:12

Preparing to Serve

Pauline's Diary

We had discussed what would be the best way for Gerald to prepare to become a preacher of the Gospel. He had written several letters inquiring about several preaching positions before his discharge, but congregations preferred to hire those who had Bible and preaching schooling or credentials. So we had reached the decision to attend Abilene Christian College in Abilene, Texas, on the GI bill. As the wife of a soldier, I could also take college classes on the GI bill.

Before heading south to Abilene, we drove back to Sand Springs for a brief visit with Gerald's folks and to collect our things. Saturday, November 24, *was a beautiful day* as we got *up at 7:00 a.m. and first went to Tulsa where Gerald bought a new brown suit* (preachers need a good suit), *and was he happy! He looked like a kid that was given a big piece of candy.*

We then returned to Sand Springs about 2:00 p.m., bought some *groceries, and fixed lunch. I was starving.* Hallie and Edgar were given the good news that I was pregnant. They were both very happy! Hallie had already guessed, but it was now confirmed. *I was very tired* after I *helped put out a washing,* so I *rested* before *baths and prepared for bed.*

Sunday, we *went to the "anti" church* in *Sand Springs* with Hallie. *Brother Cotton was in charge* of the service. *It was a fair lesson.* After eating *dinner about 1:15, we* then *went to sing at the North Main Church* where there was *good singing.* Later we *attended church at Tenth Street* in Tulsa. *We visited with the Montgomerys* and later *had a nice time with Jerry and Inez.* Our hearts were warmed by the fellowship on this *cold but beautiful day.*

Monday *was a beautiful day* as we were *up at 9:00 a.m.* to prepare to head to Abilene, Texas. Clothes were *sprinkled and ironed for most of the late afternoon and then folded and packed; Gerald's pants* were *fixed. Gerald* even *ironed his clothes* when I *was sick part of the day.* After *supper and some packing,* both of us were *a bit tired.* I *felt much better* and appreciated Gerald's attentiveness; *he was the sweetest person in the world.*

The next morning, we headed south toward Abilene by way of *Warren, Oklahoma,* to my folks where we stayed briefly and picked up some of my things.

Wednesday, *we went to Mangum* for a quick *visit with Ms. Blackwell; then* later we drove *the folks to see Uncle Bob at Clinton,* Oklahoma, about sixty miles north on HI 183.

Thursday we relaxed on the farm *with the folks.*

Early Friday, November 30, we *traveled to Abilene* where we had no luck *finding an apartment.* So we *stayed with Sis Conoway,* a member of the church, who was kind enough to open her home to us.

Saturday, December 1, we *found an apartment* with Mrs. Higginbotham *at 2024 Swanson Street.* It was *our first real home.*

Our first Sunday in Abilene, *it was snowing and raining and cold. We attended church at the College Church of Christ* in the morning, *but attended night services at North Main* even though I was *feeling sick.*

That first week in our first real home, I was quite sick and *went to Dr. Sherman for my first physical exam.* The doctor said I was *in good condition. Gerald* said he *wants a boy.*

I love him so much and we are happy to be together.

Gerald went to find work. He got a job with a construction company that was putting in a building at McMurry College. After starting the job, he *was gone most of the day.*

He did hard manual labor. To get ready to pour the foundation, the ground crew had to dig ground that was as hard as concrete. Frozen, dry, and very hard! The men had to use picks and shovels. They'd pick a bit, then get a shovel full, and shovel it out.

The next morning he rolled over and tried to move off the bed, but *he was very stiff* and groaned, "I can't bend over. Don't think I can get my socks and shoes on."

"Just lay back. I'll help you get them on." So for several days I *rolled his socks up* and pushed them on, then *put his shoes on for him.*

The company had professional steel tiers, but Gerald tied steel and probably got paid a third of what the "professional steel tiers" were paid.

He also handled concrete: On the ground below, a wheelbarrow was filled with concrete; the elevator took the wheelbarrow up to the second story; the wheelbarrow was guided on fixed boards; then the concrete was dumped into the appropriate place.

Later he also worked on the old science building on the campus at Abilene Christian College.

Gerald did this construction work from November into the middle of January.

I missed him so much when he is gone.

I continued to be very sick, so I *went to the doctor for shots* that were supposed to help with the nausea. The shots helped some. Throughout the first half of December, *it was cold and snowing* as I continued to stay *in bed.*

I told him, "Gerald, I'm still so *sick and keep losing my food.* I don't think I can handle going to church!"

"That's okay, you stay in bed." *Gerald was so tired and sore from working so hard,* but Sunday, December 9, he *went to church to all services* by himself while *I stayed in bed.*

I kept *losing all my food* and I thought, *"I must see Dr. Sherman again."* Even though *he gave me a shot,* I still couldn't *keep food in my stomach* and wasn't able to *sleep well at night.* I hoped *to get well soon* but was unable to get up to do much.

Gerald worked his job, and took care of me and the apartment. Working out in the cold outdoors was having its effect on him; he wasn't feeling well either. *Gerald was doing a nice job caring for me and keeping house though he had a bad cold and felt bad. He was precious.* The landlady felt sorry for us and helped us some. *Mrs. Higginbotham gave me a gardenia corsage. They spoiled me.*

Still, *we were so happy.* Later *I felt much better, and I was moving around as I went to the doctor* again.

By late December, I was *feeling much better* and really wanted to go out with Gerald but *still* needed to stay *in bed. Gerald went Christmas shopping* alone. We both were happy about the baby but weary of my illness.

On Christmas day, *I spent all day with Gerald. I was ill most of the day, but we did take a ride.* I wrote: *"I am so happy to be with Gerald. Our first Christmas together! May the Lord grant us many more!"*

My diary entry on New Year's Eve, 1945 was: *"This year ends very happy for me. I am with Gerald and that is all that matters. He is the most wonderful husband on the earth. He will make a wonderful father. It seems strange that I will be a mother next year—June. All the past days I have been in bed ill, but I am much better. Thank God for the many blessings of this year."*

Gerald enrolled as a student at Abilene Christian College for the spring semester of 1946.

The college had several little 18X18 hutments on the grounds on the northeast edge of the campus. Since the rent was less and covered utilities, we moved into one that was in the extreme northeast corner of the plot. It had a little kitchen, a dining area, a bedroom and a bath.

The GI bill paid us about $90 a month for living expenses, as well as, covering the cost of tuition, books and fees.

Hutment at Abilene Christian College

I was feeling better by the time we made the move to the hutment. At the hutments, we met and became good friends with several of the neighbors. The Bill Coiners lived in a hutment next door to the west, and the T. Pierce Browns lived in a hutment just south of us.

In the Spring Gerald dug up a small piece of ground just outside the kitchen window of the hutment and planted a small vegetable garden. More than once, as he straightened up from digging, he would bump his head on the open window that protruded out from the building.

This little garden set another precedent for the Gerald Beasleys—much bigger garden plots at future homes.

Gerald's Remembrances

Forest Sweet and his wife did move to Abilene where Forest attended Abilene Christian College. Ruth, an RN, became the college nurse. Unfortunately, sometime later Ruth became involved with a doctor. She and Forest ended up getting a divorce.

It's not really an excuse, but when Ruth was quite young she had seen her parents killed by a fellow with an axe. She had some mental instability that probably contributed to her unfaithful behavior.

Forest later married a widow in Hutchinson, Kansas. They ended up in Florida where he became a grade school principal. Dwayne Eggleston, his brother-in-law, who did some work with Oklahoma Christian University, kept us informed of Forest whereabouts.

I did experience some post-traumatic syndrome, but it was not debilitating. I dreamed and relived some of the unpleasant memories of the war; I had a lot of nightmares, flashbacks, of being in the middle of battle. My worst dreams were of being drafted into combat again. Even years later, when living in Montana with six children, I dreamed of being drafted again. That seemed pretty unfair to me. An old married man conscripted into the army.

In the summer of 1946, I was on the campus of Abilene Christian College just before the Fourth of July holiday. When a firecracker went off, I reflexively made the move to hit the ground, but caught myself before landing face down. Embarrassed, I quickly stood back up and looked around; nobody had noticed my movements.

A retired military man spoke at Abilene Christian College. He said, "Atomic warfare will never be used again because it was two-edged. If we bombed somebody, they could bomb us back."

That discussion didn't relieve my dreams much.

I did some preaching while attending Abilene Christian College. Twice a month Pauline and I drove to Hope, Texas, where I preached for the small congregation at Boyd's Chapel.

On alternating weeks, we drove to Blair, Oklahoma, where I preached twice a month. Granny Smith and Royce would usually go to church with us. Grandpa Smith never went. According to the odometer on the car, the trip to Blair was exactly two hundred miles. The pay wasn't much, but the experience was invaluable, and we were able to stay and visit with Pauline's folks.

Once while crossing the Abilene Christian College campus, a faculty member approached and asked if I could go speak at the Sunday church services in Wink, Oklahoma. Apparently, Don Morris, the ACC President, was scheduled to speak but could not keep the appointment. So I rode the bus to the Monahan service station where a man met and drove me to Wink. The congregation was quite disappointed that the president could not make it.

After speaking, the gentleman drove me back to the Monahan station. Apparently, the bus sign was not properly displayed, or the bus driver did not heed the signal to stop, or maybe the bus driver "winked" and did not see the signal to stop. Anyhow, the bus roared past without stopping. We hopped into the car and chased the bus at 80 mph to get ahead of the bus to flag it down. It did stop, so I was able to get on the bus to return to Abilene.

Chapter Sixty-Three

We will not all sleep, but we will all be changed.
—1 Corinthians 15:51

1

Gerald's Remembrances—
a Child Is Born

On July 14, 1946, Hoyt Terrell Beasley was born to Pauline and me at Hendricks Hospital in Abilene. It was hot in July, with no air-conditioning at the hospital. I first saw Hoyt through the glass at the nursery. Lucky for us, Uncle Sam paid Hoyt's hospital bill since he was conceived while I was still a soldier.

Pauline and I had known a Hoyt at the 10th and Rockford Church in Tulsa; and we knew a Hoyt Bailey, a preaching student at Abilene Christian College. When Pauline had

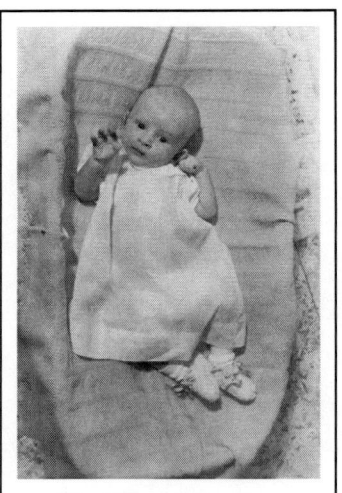

Hoyt Terrell Beasley,
8-14-1946

taught school in southwest Oklahoma at Plainview, she knew a boy in the school named Terrell. We liked the two names together; we decided to name our son Hoyt Terrell.

Since we had no washing machine, Hoyt's cloth diapers and garments were rinsed out at the hut, and then Pauline took them to a do-it-yourself laundry near the campus. Of course, Hoyt had to be changed frequently; but our lives were also changed. Sleep became a luxury.

I was very proud of my son and often would sit and talk to him, "Talk to me, friend! Talk to me, son!" Later, after Hoyt began to talk, I was soon ready to tell him, "Be quiet, friend! Be quiet, son!"

Miracles do happen! From the time that Mom came down with tuberculosis in 1935, everybody was sure that she would not live very long; but she lived to see me graduate from high school in 1938, though she wasn't there for the graduation. She lived to see me graduate from Oklahoma A&M in 1942, and she lived long enough to see me back from war in 1945. Miracle of miracles, she lived long enough to see her first grandchild, Hoyt!

One of Uncle Tom Beasley's daughters, Audrey, who thought an awful lot of Mom, expressed more than once that it was miraculous that she had lived so long.

Money was tight, but Pauline, Hoyt, and I made several trips from Abilene to Sand Springs to visit my folks so Grandpa and Grandma Beasley could see their grandson. However, Mom wasn't doing very well; she had great difficulty breathing and was so weak. We were sure she would not be with us much longer, so we made an effort to spend as much time in Sand Springs as possible.

Hoyt was just over three months old when my mom, Hallie Elizabeth (Morris) Beasley died October 19, 1946, in Sand Springs, Oklahoma. Of course, her death saddened us though there was some relief in knowing that she no longer suffered. She was now in a better place.

Dad and I had batched together for several years after Mom's initial diagnosis of tuberculosis. Those times had been real rough on both of us, but Dad never spoke much about how he had felt during her illness or how he felt after her death. Obviously, he was saddened, but I'm not aware of any bitter feelings he might have had. If Dad had been bitter, I would have known.

Dad was lonely after Mom's death; in his haste to remedy his loneliness, he made some bad decisions.

One time, Pauline and I drove from Abilene to Sand Springs. Our late arrival was unexpected. When there was no answer to our knock at the door, we just went on into the house and found a woman in bed with Dad. That was a very uncomfortable moment. Of course, Dad and this woman had been living together for a while. Dad and Evelyn did marry eventually, but divorced after a bit, and then they got married again. It was a rocky relationship.

Evelyn was an alcoholic. She had even spent some time in the state sanitarium in Vinita, Oklahoma. I'm sure Dad found her difficult to live with; I know it was difficult for me to deal with her. Visits to Dad's became rather uncomfortable. Under the influence of alcohol, she was not always very hospitable. During various visits she cussed me out a number of times.

I believe Dad tried to treat Evelyn right, but he did on occasion, while we were there, tell her to stop her verbal abuse and/or leave.

In her sober moments, she could be a good housekeeper and a good cook. I remember the house being in reasonable order. As the years passed, she made attempts to be cordial and nice to our children when we visited, but the tension was apparent. It was a real sad situation.

My dad, Edgar, was able to relax some after he retired; he did a lot of fishing at Keystone Lake, and he had more time to visit us. On a few occasions, Dad visited us in Abilene. He would attend church with us; probably the only times he ever went to church. He did on occasion state that, "Hell is on earth!" Of course, he was latched on to Evelyn at that time. I know he wasn't happy.

I attended Abilene Christian College from the spring semester of '46 thru the summer semester of '47. But I dropped out of school before obtaining a degree in Bible. I had finished around sixty hours of Bible, Greek, and speech.

Because working to support a family and going to school was too demanding, I sought and found my first full-time preaching job in the small community of Davenport, Oklahoma.

I answered the call to serve and preach the Word for the glory of God.

After returning from the war, I continued for a number of years to use the journal book, not so much to record my thoughts, but to keep a record of the Gospel meetings I conducted, various Christians I met and those I baptized.

PART FIVE

I Sang Bass;
Momma Sang Soprano;
The Kids Harmonized

CHAPTER SIXTY-FOUR

Go into all the world and preach the good news
to all creation.

—Mark 16:15

First Full-time Preaching Job
Ministry in Davenport, Oklahoma

In the spring of '47, I bumped into Floyd Schubert during the teacher's workshop on the Abilene Christian College campus. He spoke to me about coming to Davenport, Oklahoma, to be their pulpit preacher.

So in August of 1947, Pauline, Hoyt and I moved to Davenport where I preached for a small church of Christ. I had traded in my '35 Chevy, True Love, for a jeep station wagon when new cars first became available to the public after World War II. The engine had some problems, but since it was under warranty, I took it in and the manufacturer rebuilt the engine. It ran smoothly after that. So we loaded down the jeep with all our belongings. As we drove down the highway from Abilene, Texas, toward Davenport, the front end of the car tilted up and the back end down, so at night the headlights shined up into the trees. If I had had my gun, I could have gone coon hunting.

In Davenport, I preached at this small congregation for $200 a month.

We rented a house. It did have electricity and gas, but it did not have indoor plumbing. The outhouse was out in the alley. Very inconvenient! We had to purchase an oblong tub to use in the kitchen for baths.

With a small baby, we needed a refrigerator badly, but none was available for purchase that soon after the war. Freezers were, so we bought one, thinking that it could serve as a refrigerator if the temperature was turned to the warmest setting. But that didn't always work out very well. We would put a watermelon in to get it cold, but it would freeze solid. As soon as refrigerators became available, I drove to an appliance store in Chandler, Oklahoma, and bought one.

We very much wanted to find a modern house with indoor plumbing, so we weren't in this house very long. Now, I had been advised by several church members, "Do not rent from Mr. Bean." But against their advice I did anyway.

This rascal soon began spreading the rumor, "The preacher is not paying his rent." I spoke with Uncle Johnson, a church member, and he replied, "Consider the source and go on with your life. If you mess with a mule, you'll get kicked." He was probably thinking, but did not say, "I told you so."

However, news of his gossip went all through me. I produced evidence of my integrity and went to Mr. Bean's house. He was not there, but I stated quite emphatically to his current wife who answered the door, "I have the canceled checks that I paid the rent with, and they have Mr. Bean's endorsement on the back which shows that he cashed them. He better not spread anymore rumors that I don't pay the rent!"

Later, on reflection, I felt guilty for taking my frustration out on his wife, who may have been innocent and unaware of what her husband was doing. I'm sure she didn't deserve the rebuke. In fact, the community was well aware that Mr. Bean had a practice of going to the courthouse, checking death records and then pursuing recently widowed wives who had come into an inheritance. This particular wife, I'm sure, had been one of his "victims."

I'm not sure what effect my confrontation had on their marriage, if any.

I probably should have gone back and talked with Mr. Bean, but I didn't. He was a rascal!

While in Davenport, we got to know several church members quite well. Mr. Floyd Schubert was the Davenport superintendent of schools, and his wife, Nancy, was a very prim and proper schoolteacher. Joe, their son, was around nine then. I spent quite a bit of time at their house playing Carom with Joe.

Uncle Bob Johnson (everybody called him Uncle) was the treasurer for the church. I remember him and his wife quite well.

Ed and Minnie Blankenship were middle-aged members that I remember fondly, and there were others.

The Floyd Richardsons, members of the church, had three boys, Donnie, Bob and Bill. Bill had always been a very active young man.

When he was about fourteen, he took a dive head first from a bridge into a shallow riverbed thinking it was deeper than it was. He broke his neck and was paralyzed from the neck down. It was such a tragedy! Bill had always been very active.

Shortly after the accident, he got pneumonia and nobody thought he would live; but he survived.

I stopped by to visit, stuck my head in the door, and said, "Hi."

Bill replied, "You thought I was a goner, didn't you?

He had a positive attitude though I'm sure he felt depressed, discouraged, and bored at times. I would bring agricultural tapes and films from the veteran's classes I taught. He really enjoyed watching them; they kept his mind busy and active.

Bill was a real inspiration. For years from his bed, he counseled people with their problems, marital and otherwise. He even practiced hypnosis and helped people with smoking and weight-loss problems.

(Even after we moved from Davenport, if we drove through the area, we would stop to visit him. His body shriveled, but he lived to be about fifty years old. He was a real inspiration!)

Floyd Richardson, Bill's dad, was a creative mechanic. He built a vehicle out of an old Oakland frame and parts from other cars; it had no top, two seats, and a motor with four gears. When he went fishing, he pulled a boat with a detachable motor behind his redesigned Oakland.

I had never been before, but Floyd invited me to go *noodling* with him. Hanging on to the bars in this roofless, makeshift form of transportation, we bounced our way south of Stroud, Oklahoma, to the Deep Fork River, where we backed up to the shore and put the boat into the water. I then found out what *noodling* was.

We removed our clothes to prevent them from getting muddy and stained. I grew up skinny-dipping, so this was not so unusual for me. However, I'm sure sunburn was involved.

As we got in and out of the boat, Floyd showed me how to find the dark, sheltered places under the rocks and overhanging edges along the shore where catfish were most likely to lay their eggs. He explained that one had to blindly extend ones arms, reach into these hidden places, feel around, and grab the catfish by the mouth. The disturbed catfish was likely to clasp on to the intruding appendages with its teeth.

I was a bit anxious about sticking my hand into these holes; the idea of a fish catching me had no appeal! So Floyd did the catching; I would not stick my arm in! I did help him by hanging on to the slippery, flopping, fin-slashing, tail-slapping catfish, and stringing them through the gills and mouth to tie them to the brush along the shore.

We also caught carp and buffalo fish on a stringer with hooks which was tied on to a branch of a tree on the shore. Before leaving for home, we would skin and clean, then put the fish on ice in an ice chest.

Now, Floyd had lived in Davenport for a long time, so he was known and knew everybody in the area, even the black folks. White folks usually would not eat carp or buffalo fish because they were very bony, but Floyd was thoughtful and caring and planned to give the carp and buffalo fish to his black friends.

I went *noodling* with Floyd several times. One time we got so many catfish, many which were quite large, up to thirteen pounds, so Floyd arranged and oversaw a community "fish fry" at the Davenport City Park where gas burners were available. I helped by cutting the meat into pieces, rolling them in batter, and dropping and retrieving the fish from the fryer. The ladies brought potato salad, coleslaw, and other side dishes.

I'm sure the blacks were invited, but I'm not sure they came. However, they were welcomed.

When the community found out that I had a degree in agriculture, I was asked to teach some courses to veterans. A lot of veterans took these classes that the GI bill paid for. I also received a monthly check for my teaching.

I was a Veterans Agriculture Training Instructor. Since there was no veterinarian in Davenport, the veterans would come get me at all hours of the day and night when one of their cows or animals was sick. I treated several sick animals in the pastures. Quite often the cows had "milk fever," so I administered calcium gluconate.

On one such venture, I was showing a client how to get a blood sample from his cow to test for Bang's disease which can cause undulant fever in humans (flulike systems that can be treated with antibiotics, otherwise it can lead to more serious illnesses).

As I had my arm around the cow's neck, the veteran told me, "You better be careful, she swings her head pretty hard."

At that moment, the cow slung her head, and her horn hit my mouth, clipping off the end of four front teeth. It didn't knock the teeth out. It didn't even hurt, but when I returned home and walked into the house, I couldn't help but smile (I had a strange sense of humor). Momma, a name I had begun to call Pauline, saw the gaping window in my teeth and she started to cry.

"I'm okay! It doesn't hurt. Don't cry!" I stated. But that wasn't her concern.

"Where have you been? How did this happen?" She sobbed.

As we talked, I came to understand that she thought I had been in a fight, and it scared her.

I had to get gold caps on those teeth so my clarinet playing days were over.

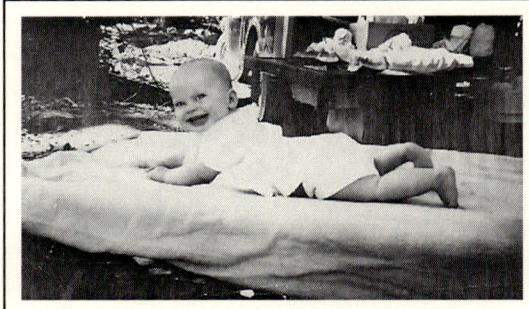

Sheba age four-and-a-half months, taken 06-05-1948

Hoyt and Sheba, taken 09-05-1948

I actually received better pay for teaching than I did for preaching, so the church decided I was not a full-time preacher and my salary was cut some.

Sheba Beth was born to us on January 16, 1948. Guess Momma decided to reverse the Bathsheba of the Bible and named her Sheba Beth. She became a rather chunky child.

I remember an incident when Sheba got hold of and drank several shallows from a bottle of cough syrup. She became intoxicated! It was funny to watch her wobble and sway as she toddled along; then she slid to the floor and fell soundly asleep.

Momma hardly had a chance to catch up on her sleep before Reba Nell was born on December 22, 1948, eleven months later. Reba might possibly have been an abbreviated version of Rebecca.

Anyhow, both girls were born in the Stroud Hospital.

I usually went with Pauline when she went to her obstetrics doctor. During each examination he always repeated, "Uh-huh, uh-huh, uh-huh." Don't know what it meant, but he always repeated, "Uh-huh, uh-huh." (Many years later, we were in Lawton, Oklahoma, to visit Granny Smith, Pauline's mother, when she was in the hospital with cancer. Going down the hall of the hospital we heard, "Uh-huh, uh-huh, uh-huh," coming from a

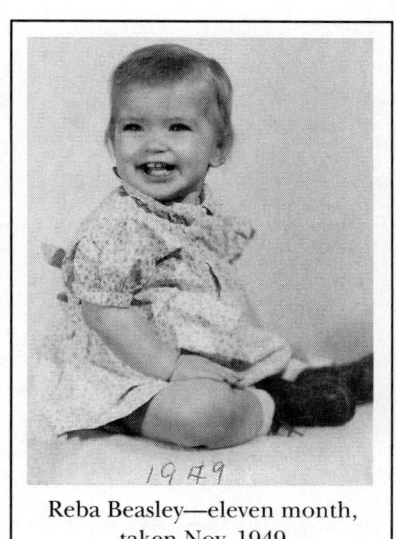

1949

Reba Beasley—eleven month, taken Nov. 1949

room. We both looked at each other and thought, "Surely not." But it was the same doctor who had been her obstetrics doctor. We had a good visit with him.)

Anyhow, because of our growing family, we decided to buy a newer little house that turned out to be rather cheaply put together, but we were glad to move out of Mr. Bean's house.

Before returning to the states while in Germany, I had picked up a leather German navy uniform. I traded it for a chicken coop which we set up near the house. We were able to get eggs for consumption as well as raise chickens for meat.

However, Momma had befriended one of the pullets; it had become her pet.

When the day came for slaughter, I was out chasing chickens. As I grabbed her pet, she started to cry. I felt bad, but we did butcher and freeze the pullet.

Momma gave me the cold shoulder for a while.

During this extremely busy time, I was wearing myself out trying to teach and preach. It was usually late Saturday night before I got around to studying and preparing for my Sunday sermons. I also drove my station wagon early Sunday mornings and evenings to Kendrick, Oklahoma, to pick up people to bring them to church. In addition, I taught a Bible class on Thursday nights in a little congregation in Stroud, Oklahoma, which was a short distance from Davenport.

I wasn't available much to help Pauline who was left alone much of the time to care for three small children, all under the age of four. She never complained, and she always put the kids first, but I'm sure she wished for more help.

So something needed to change; I was worn out and overwhelmed.

I realized I was trying to do too much and needed to give more time to Bible study. So I began to shop around and learned about a job opening in a small mission church of Christ in Manhattan, Kansas, supported by the Southside church of Christ at Lincoln and Emporia in Wichita, Kansas. (At that time, Ted Norton was the preacher in Wichita.) I was invited to preach in Wichita and the elders at Southside hired me for the Manhattan preaching job.

CHAPTER SIXTY-FIVE

Children are a heritage from the Lord,
offspring a reward from him . . .
Blessed is the man whose quiver is full of them.
—Psalm 127:3 and 5a

Ministry in Manhattan, Kansas

We had been in Davenport, Oklahoma, for about two-and-a-half years, when in the fall of 1949 we moved to Manhattan, Kansas. The small congregation met in an old residence on Poyntz Avenue along a main street which went through the city. Some walls had been knocked out to make a small auditorium where a baptistery had been put in. Though they had a meeting place, the congregation was not self-supporting.

We made this move before our house in Davenport had sold, so we rented it out for a time.

Later that fall, we drove back to Davenport to paint the house for upkeep. As I was balancing high on a ladder painting the east side of the outside of the house, Momma was down below pulling up Bermuda grass. (Momma was pregnant again at that time.) Well, the ladder wobbled, and a bucket full of white paint tipped and dropped splattering paint all over Pauline. She was obviously very startled when the wet, sticky, thick goo suddenly splashed onto her. The bucket did not hit her, but she received quite a baptism in paint.

Thankfully, Pauline had a good sense of humor, and after apologies, we had a good laugh. There isn't much else she could have done.

It did take several days for her to wash all the paint out of her "prematurely" grey hair, so for a brief time, she was a painted lady. ☺

We were finally able to sell the house and were glad to be rid of it.

In Manhattan, we purchased a three-bedroom one bathroom house with plumbing, an indoor toilet, a gas stove, and electricity. We shared the house with Nellie Jacobs, a member of the church, who shared expenses with us.

In the front—Sheba, Carmen, Hoyt & Reba, Pauline and Gerald Beasley—1950

Carmen Lee was born at St. Mary's Catholic Hospital, a very dinky hospital in Manhattan, Kansas, on Sunday, June 25, 1950, at 7:07 a.m. Carmen was named after Carmen Woods, a church member that Pauline and I knew while I was stationed at Hattiesburg, Mississippi. Of less importance, the day was also noted as the day the United States officially declared war on Korea.

Nellie, a very faithful Christian and a great lady, helped Mom take

Carmen—age one year, taken at 453 S. Tulip, McPherson, Kansas

care of Carmen and the other kids. Though Nellie was older than Pauline, they became great friends.

During the summer that Carmen was born, we had put in a real nice-looking vegetable garden in the backyard of the house. But there came a terrible hailstorm that just beat the garden into the ground, knocked some holes in our roof, and even broke some windows in the house.

Insurance wrote a check for just over $300; but instead of hiring repairmen or roofers, self-sufficient as I was, I replaced the windows and got on the roof with some black goop and doctored the holes to stop the leaking.

While living in Manhattan, I found out that Floyd Hixon, my college roommate during my second year at Oklahoma A&M, was attending Kansas State where he was continuing his studies in poultry for a doctorate. I contacted him and we had a nice visit.

However, he was having trouble with the committee that read his dissertation and interviewed him toward getting his doctorate. He felt that they were dragging their feet, stalling and being unfair. He may have been "eggsaggerating". ☺ Sad to say, he was quite unhappy and bitter. And that's the way I left him. I haven't seen him since.

In Manhattan, we got to know and often visited the Ray Keens, members of the church, who had kids about the ages of our Beasley tribe. Their and our kids liked to run up and down the stairs at the Keens old two-story big stone house on the north side of Manhattan located on seventy to eighty acres of land. (This area was later developed and the sale of the land probably made Ray rich.)

Ray was a professor of horticulture at Kansas State. The care of trees was part of his curriculum. He taught caution to avoid "free falling" and "loss of limbs" by instructing his students on how to rope themselves onto a tree, and to make sure they did not sit on the outside away from the trunk when sawing off a large branch. ☺

The experience in Manhattan was somewhat a disappointment. The congregation did not feel that the growing Beasley family was right for the work there, perhaps because there were so many little ones underfoot. Carmen made four. We were just growing our own congregation! Anyhow, we were there only about one year.

Nellie was sorry to see us go. She and Mom had become quite close. Nellie remained in Manhattan working on the university campus as secretary for a fellow who was a PhD in the Botany department. She had worked for decades in that particular job. (Some years later, she retired and the department had quite a blowout for her. She received honors that were written up in an article in the newspaper.)

After our move, Momma corresponded with Nellie, who occasionally visited us at our new location. On occasion, we returned to Manhattan to visit her.

Well, we sold the house in Manhattan to a mail carrier; we carried a second mortgage.

The following summer of '51, a real bad flood filled the basement to within four inches of the main floor. This flood was on the news; it was a bad flood. Many houses were flooded. The house next door owned by a very nice black couple was built several inches lower than ours and was filled with water which ruined their furniture.

I figured the buyer/owner would not be able to make the monthly payments that we had arranged on the equity, but the purchaser didn't miss a payment and eventually paid it off.

I returned to Manhattan shortly after the floodwaters had gone down. There was silt everywhere. As it got hot and dry, cars would kick up the silt causing it to fly up and cover houses, trees and everything. It was a mess!

CHAPTER SIXTY-SIX

These commandments that I give you today
are to be on your hearts.
Impress them on your children.
Talk about them when you sit at home and
when you walk along the road,
when you lie down and when you get up.
—Deuteronomy 6:6 & 7

Ministry in McPherson, Kansas

In the fall of 1950, the Beasley family moved to McPherson, Kansas.

The McPherson church of Christ was larger than the Manhattan church with about seventy-five members. The church met in an old building downtown on the north side of the main drag. It had been known as the Polson's church. Grandma Polson was still living when we arrived, but her husband, a successful wheat farmer, was deceased. He had put a lot of money into the building many years earlier.

Down in the basement was an old coal-burning furnace with arms going out in all directions "all over the place around here" to feed heat to the rest of the building. This old furnace had been converted into a gas furnace. I had to laugh when I first saw the old furnace because it reminded me of the children's book,

Mike Mulligan and His Steam Shovel,* that I had heard Momma read to the children. In this story, after digging itself into a hole, Mike's steam shovel was converted into a furnace with arms going out in all directions "all over the place around here." ☺

Anyhow, I set up my study in a basement classroom where I moved in an old table to serve as a desk, and I had a book shelf on a table next to the wall. Using the old mimeograph machine that was there, I wrote, edited, and printed a church bulletin.

For a while, I attended McPherson College on the GI bill because I liked to learn but also because by taking college courses I could receive a monthly GI check for living expenses. I took courses mainly pertaining to business administration, philosophy, economics and accounting.

Pauline often told me, "I mostly see you from the back of your head as you study at the table."

I had to quit because I had taking Bible courses at Abilene Christian College. Apparently, I wasn't supposed to change majors.

Anyhow, I took these courses to augment my salary situation. The church wasn't paying much.

To supplement, Pauline and I hand-shoveled and hoed a large vegetable garden in the backyard. We visited surrounding farms and hauled manure to fertilize the soil. We grew a variety of vegetables, and Momma did a lot of canning and freezing.

Tomatoes produced especially well. Using what Momma called *psychology* and appealing to their vanity, we told the girls "eating tomatoes will make you pretty." It did motivate them to eat more.

---

*   Story and pictures for *Mike Mulligan and His Stream Shovel* was by Virginia Lee Burton and published by Houghton Mifflin Company, New York, NY, in 1939.

While in McPherson, we had numerous social opportunities to get to know church members. There were many Sunday potlucks at the church building, and we occasionally had members over to our house.

One time we had a large church group over on the Fourth of July for a hot dog roast. Everybody brought a covered dish to share. There were adults and children "running around all over the place around here."

Now, the Beasleys never spent much money on fireworks, but we would get a few firecrackers and sparklers for the children. Other members spent more and contributed various other fireworks for the big display.

We often got together with the McNallys and the Musselmans to play forty-two and/or dominoes.

The Aubrey McNally family had four or five children, can't remember just how many. Aubrey was in business with his dad selling tractors. (He started his studies at Oklahoma A&M after I did, and he actually dated Pauline before she and I became engaged. He jokingly stated, "She walked too fast for me. I had trouble keeping up with her.")

In those days, the preacher's family was often invited to the homes of members of the church for a visit and a plentiful family-style meal. The Beasley family was fed well! We numbered six then, so the gathering around the hostess's table was usually pretty snug, or sometimes the kids sat at a separate table. Often a telephone

Hoyt, Sheba, Carmen, Reba, taken 8-1953 at 1117 N. Elm, McPherson, Kansas

book or the Montgomery Ward catalog became a booster seat for the smaller children.

During these sumptuous meals, I would often push back from the table and say, "Pardon me while I loosen my belt." Then, I would loosen my belt and continue to eat.

After the main meal, the hostess would bring in a dessert and ask, "Anybody have room for dessert?"

Very rarely did any Beasley refuse any dessert. I would answer, "I could handle some *ober-globber in the slobber.*" Now, the Beasley children had heard this expression from me at home many times, but the hostess would be temporarily confused and not know whether to feel insulted or complimented; but they soon learned of my peculiar idiosyncrasies and strange sense of humor.

After eating, probably too much, I would pull back from the table and state, "Sorry I was sick, or I could'a really 'et'!"

We were often invited for dinner at the Musselman's. They lived in Lindsberg, Kansas, just north of McPherson. Sister Musselman was a strong Christian and an avid Bible student. Charles, her husband, a railroad boss, was not baptized; but he attended church with his wife and their eight children.

Their big two-story house had stairs going up on one side of the house and down on the other side. The children liked to climb up one side and bump down the stairs on their bottoms on the other side. Visits at the Musselmans were lively and noisy; with so many children of their own, the Musselmans were used to and tolerated rambunctious childish play.

Now, I usually had a brief children's Bible drill just prior to the Sunday evening services. One time, while holding up a clue card with the letter L, I remember asking the question, "What was wrong with the church in Laodicea?" Young Russell Musselman blurred out, "It was lousy!" ☺ (The correct answer was, "It was lukewarm.") Of course, the congregation laughed, and I'm sure he was embarrassed, but his parents got a big kick out of their son's blunder.

I spent time fishing with Charlie. We got to know each other pretty well. He was a nice guy. Some years later, just before we moved to Panhandle, Texas, Charlie showed up at the church building and came down the stairs to my office crying. He was sad that we were leaving, but he had actually come to ask me to baptize him. I was honored to do it. In fact, later when he prayed for the first time at services, I became emotional, choked up, and almost cried. (Years later, he died on the job. It was never proven, but the family believed he was murdered by a disgruntled crewman who had it out for him.)

Momma had been *barefoot and pregnant* about two-thirds of the time from 1946 till October of 1951. During this time, she was kept busy taking care of the children. That was four children in five years!

However, on October 23, 1951, a baby boy was stillborn. That was hard on both of us, but especially on her. Her hormones, I'm sure, were all messed up, but she continued caring for the children and household needs.

Pauline was a great mom. She felt she was doing an important job as a housewife and mother; she knew raising the children to be honest and moral servants of God was an honorable profession. But I'm sure the care of four children and the house was taxing on her, and at times, she probably wished she could have had more time for herself. I'm sure she took advantage of naptimes. Raising *real* children was much more difficult than dealing with the *pretend* children she had imagined as a child.

> When I was quite young, I came up to Mom where she was outside hanging clothes on the clothes-line to dry. She was crying. When I asked her what was wrong, she responded, "Oh, I'm just feeling sorry for myself."
>
> I was too young to understand, but I gave her a hug and told her, "I love you, Mom." I hope it made her feel better. (Carmen)

She was a busy lady. She worked hard to keep the eclectically furnished functional house clean and orderly, but over the years that became less important to her. She enjoyed working in the garden which became a kind of retreat for her. And she still found time to sew, crochet, can, and freeze produce, as well as, study for and prepare materials to teach children's Bible classes. In fact, she built up quite a file of Bible story materials. She was a hard worker and sacrificed for me and the children.

Since I was an only child, and Pauline was about ten years older than her brother, both of us basically grew up alone. We had always wanted a large family so our kids could grow up and play together.

Our wish was granted because Neva Ann was born July 22, 1953, in McPherson, Kansas. She was named after my cousin, one of the daughters of Uncle Richard and Nancy Yokum, and because we decided to continue the rhyming pattern (Sheba, Reba, Neva; Carmen was the odd one). (Aunt

Neva and Gerald Beasley—1953

Nancy was my father's sister. The Yokums had a bunch of kids, ten or twelve, can't remember for sure how many.)

> Because my name did not rhyme with my sister's names, and because people sometimes told me I didn't have the same nose and profile as the other girls, I did think that, maybe, I was adopted.
>
> However, Mom and Dad did talk about when I was born and how I was named after a friend. I thought, "Okay, I must not be adopted." But I still wondered sometimes.

As I got older, I looked too much like Mom to question my heredity anymore.

Most people talked about how Sheba and Reba were very pretty, and how Reba had beautiful eyes. They usually didn't say much about me. Guess, I felt a little insecure! (Carmen)

With five children, we had many birthdays to celebrate. Partly because we did not want to foster greed, and because having birthday parties cost extra money, we did not have parties with invited guests every year for our children. Can't remember for sure, but I think we had *invited guest parties* when each child turned five and ten.

Annually for birthdays, we did have a family celebration with a cake, we sang "Happy Birthday" and gave one gift; and if individual siblings wanted to participate, they could also give a gift, usually handmade.

I started a tradition by singing another *uplifting* version of Happy Birthday: "Happy birthday, happy birthday. Gloom and misery in the air. People dying everywhere. Happy birthday, happy birthday." Many times after I sang this version, which had a mournful melody, the birthday child would look at me with an exasperated expression and stated, "Daaad." However, as they got older, the kids began to chime in as the mournful song was sung.

I don't remember them going to a lot of other children's parties, possibly because of the expense of buying presents. I know they went to some.

Of course, Momma spent all day with the tribe and welcomed the help when I got home. Usually before heading home at the end of my workday, I would call home to ask Pauline if she needed anything from the store.

Sometimes one of the kids would answer, "Beasley residence. This is Hoyt."

I would ask, "How do you know? Are you sure?"

"Yes, I'm sure. Dad, it's me. You know who this is."

"Are you sure?" I would repeat.

Most evenings as I came into the house, the tribe would come running to meet me at the door. I would grab up whoever was the baby at the time, and say, "Hello, friend?" Then I would play briefly with all of them while rolling around on the floor. The older kids would jump on my back for a piggyback ride; it sometimes got pretty rough.

Momma would interject, "Be careful with the baby!"

We didn't let them sit for hours watching the boob tube, but the kids did watch some children's shows and cartoons which included: *Popeye the Sailor Man,*[*] *Betty Boop,*[**] *The Roadrunner and Wile E. Coyote,*[***] *The Mickey Mouse Club,*[****] *The Little Rascals,*[*****] and

---

[*] *Popeye* animated cartoons for were based on the character created by Elzie Crister Segar's comic strip in the daily King Features comic strip. Max and Dave Fleischer's Studios developed cartoon shorts for Paramount Pictures (1933-1957).

[**] *Betty Boop* was an animated cartoon character created by Max Fleischer, produced by Fleischer Studies and released by Paramount Pictures in 1930.

[***] *The Roadrunner and Wile E. Coyote* was a duo character cartoon from Looney Tunes and Merrie Melodies cartoons created by Chuck Jones in 1948 for Warner Bros. and written by Michael Maltese.

[****] "The Mickey Mouse Club" television show aired from 1955-1959; was created and produced by Walt Disney; and televised by ABC.

[*****] "The Little Rascals" was a series of American comedy short films about a group of poor neighborhood children's adventures; created by producer Hal Roach at Roach Studio as silent shorts starting 1922; they were converted to sound in 1929 through 1938; then sold to MGM who continued to produce films until 1944.

The Howdy Doody Show* which gave Pauline a break from chasing and corralling them. And I'm sure there were other shows they watched. On second thought, they may have watched more television than I originally thought.

Now, Pauline did occasional manage to sit and watch a few of her favorite TV programs. She especially liked westerns which included *The Roy Rodger's Show,*** and *I Love Lucy.**** She would laugh and laugh as Lucy got herself into odd predicaments.

However, when I got home, I would change the channel on our black-and-white television to the news or sports, and the kids would groan. I often had to say, and I think the kids would purposely stay in my chair so I would *have* to say, "Do you want me to sit on you, friend?" If they still didn't move, I would cup my hand and slap it gently on their leg, making a popping sound. It didn't hurt, just made a noise. Sometimes, they still didn't move, so I would schooch and wiggle my rear end toward the chair, bend to sit and say, *"Xsqueeze me"*. When they finally moved, I would then sit and unwind from my workday.

Shortly, from my favorite chair I would ask Momma with purposefully incorrect grammar, "Are we going to eat ever again?"

---

*   "The Howdy Doody Show" was a children's program created and produced by E. Roger Muir, aired for television from 1947-1960 by NBC; it was first created by Bob Smith on the radio. Buffalo Bob Smith hosted and started each show asking, "Say kids, what time is it?" The kids answered, "It's Howdy Doody time!"

**   "The Roy Rodgers Show" was a cowboy and cowgirl television series that aired from 1951-1957, and featured the singing husband and wife couple, Roy Rodgers and Del Evans.

***   The "I Love Lucy" show was a black and white Sitcom was aired by CBS from 1951-1957; and featured Lucille Ball, Desi Arnaz, Vivian Vance and William Frawley.

We always prayed before each meal. My standard prayer went: "Mindful again, heavenly Father, of your care . . . Be with those who are traveling . . . Bless this food to the nourishment of our bodies . . . Guide, guard, and direct us . . . Be with those who are sick . . . In Jesus name, Amen." Occasionally, as they got older, one of the kids would say the prayer.

After the meal, it was common for me to ask, "Is there any *ober-globber in the slobber?*" I liked desert! I probably had *ober-globber in the slobber* more often than I should have; I did gain some weight.

I didn't want to lose my *girlish figure,* so I remained active by doing yard work and participating in some community sports.

Because I was just a little overweight and because I enjoyed it, I played Santa Claus for the community at the big Christmas shindig. I would dress up; apply the wig, hat, and beard; "Ho-Ho"; and hand out candy to each child who came through the line to sit on my lap. Some of my own kids didn't figure out who Santa was for a while. When they figured it out, it might have confused them; but I think they enjoyed their dad playing Santa.

Just about every evening before bedtime, Pauline read to the kids from a large children's Bible stories book; the kids heard some stories so many times they could repeat them word for word.

As part of the nighttime procedure, the kids would line up and take turns in Mom's lap for a good night hug and kiss. When the kids cuddled in her lap, Momma would often state, "Your bones are going through my bones."

And they would always smile and giggle when I put my lips to their cheek and gave each a blow-kiss that vibrated and blubbered.

When they were in bed, Pauline and I could then relax and have some quiet time alone.

One sign of aging slipped up on me much too soon. By my late twenties, my hair had started to thin and recede, and by the time I was in my thirties, I had a bare round spot on the top of my head which often got sunburned. While mowing the lawn one particular day, I was puzzled when I felt a warm moist sensation on my hairless spot; and it was a cloudless, sunny, hot summer day with no rain clouds in sight. Touching my head with my hand and bringing it down to have a look, I saw grayish matter. I was being used for target practice. Some birds have real good aim! ☺

I tried to be self-sufficient and fix what I could before calling in professional help. Sometimes I would tinker in the garage with the tools working on the car, making house repairs, or in the backyard on the lawn mower. One of the kids might come to watch me work and inquisitively ask, "What'ja doin', Dad? Or "What's that, Dad?"

I would answer, "A cat-fur-and-dog-fur-and-kitten-breeches-with. You want a pair?"

"Dad, seriously. What'ja doin'?"

"Fat, cat, rat."

"Dad!" Exasperated he/she would sometimes leave me alone.

Occasionally, I would be left with the tribe while Momma was out running errands, getting a haircut, or taking care of some business. One of the kids would come up to me and ask, "Where's Mom?"

I would answer evasively, "She took a rocket ship to the moon. Wanna go?"

"Dad, seriously! Where is Mom? You're not funny!"

I would answer back, "I resemble that."

Or they might ask, "What time is it?"

And I would answer, "Why? Are you taking medicine?"

"Dad! Answer me. What time is it?"

"Time to stop asking questions," I would reply.

"Daaaad!"

Now, Momma and I basically agreed on discipline and believed in "spare the rod, spoil the child," but my approach was a bit different. Momma had more patience. She had read Dr. Spock's child-rearing book, The Common Sense Book of Baby and Child Care,* and adhered to his basic philosophy that parents needed to be more flexible and affectionate with their children and to treat them as individuals. She also used what she called *psychology*, taking a positive approach to motivate or encourage compliance. However, if a child did not do as expected, or if there was no response, she would count to two, then at two, the kid knew they better respond. She did sometimes have to guide a kid by the arm, and she did use a belt on occasion.

I would give a command, "Go do . . . ," and expected immediate compliance. I did not tolerate back-talk.

> One daring kid, don't remember which one, dared to talk back to Dad when he put us to work helping clean the kitchen. "Dad, you never help clean and wash dishes! Why do we have to do all the work?" His sharp reply was, "I have done my share of cleaning and KP duty! Don't you question me! Just do what you're told!" We humbly went about our tasks. (Carmen)

We did use a belt, which was frowned upon by some, but if a child was noncompliant or disrespectful, we spanked only on the bottom. And of course, we depended on prayer when doling out discipline.

Often when something was broken, eaten, moved, or missing, we would ask "Who did it?"

When all proclaimed innocence, "I didn't do it," I would state, "Well, I guess Sam did it then." Poor Sam, our next door

---

*   Written by Benjamin Spock and published in 1946 by Duell, Sloan & Pearce.

neighbor, got blamed for a lot of things; the kids were perfectly willing to let a grown man take all the blame until, of course, someone finally 'fessed up.

Our kids certainly weren't perfect, and you can't have that many children without sibling rivalry. Often as the kids argued, pushed and hit, and shot verbal arrows at each other, I would say, "Watch it or you'll get stuck in the syrup and molasses all over the floor." It usually stopped the argument, at least for a while.

> Actually, for a long time I didn't understand what Dad meant by "syrup and molasses on the floor." They belonged on pancakes!
>
> I thought Daddy was just using one of his peculiar expressions trying to be funny.
>
> I eventually got his meaning. (Carmen)

We didn't have a lot of money to spend on family entertainment, but our young and growing family did inexpensive activities together. The drive-in theater had a car-rate, so occasionally; we would load the tribe into the car and go to a drive-in movie. We never bought drinks or popcorn there, but might bring some from home. The kids would try to stay awake, but would often fall asleep in the car before the movie was over; then later we would have to wake them and guide them to their beds or carry them into the house.

Often I would come home and ask, "Who wants to go on a buggy ride?"

All the children would jump up and down exclaiming, "We do! We do!"

Of course, Momma would corral everybody first to the bathroom and then to the car. I would get behind the wheel and drive out into the country.

Amazingly, the young passengers would sit relatively still and quiet in the backseat for most of the ride.

Sometimes we would play the "animal, mineral or vegetable" game while in the car. They had to ask questions that would prompt answers that would give clues; then they would guess what I was thinking about.

Ours was a singing family from the start, so oftentimes we would sing hymns and sometimes secular songs while in the car. We had no car radio, but if we had had one, I think we would have sung anyway.

We would look out the windows as we passed farm country with plowed fields and tanks and count the cows and other livestock. Occasionally, I might see some wildlife or something unusual along the way, point my finger, and suddenly make an unintelligible noise, "Aba-aba-daba-daba-oo-oo-oo!"

The youngsters would voice in unison, "What? What?" And if we hadn't already passed beyond it, they could follow the direction of my pointing finger to locate the thing of interest, usually a deer, antelope, or other critter.

Occasionally, we would stop, get out of the car, and walk around a bit at a particular point of interest, perhaps a *hysterical marker*; but usually we just drove. After all, it was just a *buggy ride.*

Some evenings after church or after a *buggy ride,* we might drive by a Dairy Queen. I could feel the kids' eyes get big and roll toward the establishment and back to me. Sometimes they would wait quietly to see if I would turn in, but sometimes they couldn't contain themselves and would ask, "Daddy, can we get some ice cream?"

If I knew I had money in my pocket, I would turn to Momma and ask, "What do you think, Momma? Should we get some ice cream?"

Since Momma liked ice cream, she would often say, "Yes."

Sometimes I would zip right in for a treat. Other times, I would drive on past; their sighs of disappointment were audible.

Sometimes I was very tricky, but I'm sure the kids thought it was mean; I would turn into the Dairy Queen, drive around the back, not stop, then drive back out to the road and head home without saying a word. The kids would chime together, "Daaad!" I thought it was funny and would purse my lips in a smile. They did not! Actually, I may have realized I didn't have enough money to make the purchase.

As time passed, Momma and I had to start calling ice cream *dairy product*, so when we discussed whether to get some, they wouldn't know what we were talking about. When they figured out what *dairy product* was, we started saying *DP*. After they figured that one out, we just continued to refer to ice cream as *DP*. They were too smart for us! And who did they get their intelligence from?

Other times, I would come home, walk in the door, and inquire, "Who wants to go on a picnic?"

The children—Hoyt, Sheba, Reba, Carmen and Neva—would jump up and down and excitedly chorus, "We do! We do!" The family liked to picnic, especially at Kannapolis Lake.

"Well, Momma, get the food packed up and let's go," I would announce.

So Momma would gather the items needed from the kitchen into a box for our venture: knife, flipper, matches, plates and utensils, raw potatoes, hamburger or hot dogs, *hoyt* (whole wheat) bread (usually sliced bread, not always buns), shortening, a frying pan, and condiments.

After changing into casual clothes, I loaded the fishing rods and food into the car.

After everybody was shooed to dress appropriately and take care of bathroom needs, the family would jump into Ole Bessie, the *after children* name for almost every car we ever owned, and we would head for the lake.

Shortly after settling in the car and driving off, I would ask Momma, "Did you pack . . . ?" and I would verbally go down a mental list of those items that we would need for the picnic. Sometimes, when I named an item, Mom would meekly respond, "Oh, I forgot . . ."

I would semiseriously respond, "Oh, brother. We can't go without that. Horse feather!" By then we were already away from the house. However, I very rarely turned around and went back to the house for anything. I did sometimes go over the list before we drove out of the driveway, which I probably should have done every time.

Sometimes I would have to stop and purchase a few things. Mom and the kids usually waited in the car while I went into the grocery store. I often got marshmallows and Fig Newtons. I loved Fig Newtons and tried to hide them from the rest of the tribe so I could have more for myself.

As we got nearer the lake, the kids would ask, "Are we going to stop and get some *minerals?*" So we would stop at a little creek and catch some minnows for fish bait.

Once we arrived at our destination, the kids would run to gather twigs and sticks for roasting hot dogs, and wood for the fire, or they would run off to the edge of the lake to explore.

Momma made up the hamburger patties or got the hot dogs out, peeled and sliced potatoes; I started a campfire, melted the shortening in the cast-iron skillet for frying the potatoes, and put the meat into the wire fold-over contraption for cooking over the open campfire.

Occasionally, a hot dog or piece of hamburger would slip off into the coals, sizzle and blacken. I would say, "Oh, fiddle, faddle!" Or "Horse feathers!" then try to retrieve it, but usually it was too burned for consumption.

At the lake I would usually help the older children fish where the water was rolling and splashing onto the dam and/or shore. Depending on the weather, the kids would swim near the shore.

Mom was left to clean up and watch the younger children.

Our family enjoyed these impromptu adventures.

In the '50s, parents were more relaxed about letting their children roam the neighborhood. However, *stranger danger* was a concern, but our kids did play across the street, in the alley, and in the neighborhood. We did have rules we expected them to follow, and we did not want them to take liberties. They were to stay close enough to hear Mom's call or my whistle. If they did not respond and return home quickly when summoned, they were too far from home and were likely to get in trouble.

Occasionally, they did go beyond our boundaries.

> I knew there were boundaries, places I was not to go and things I was not supposed to do. I can't speak for the others, but I had temptations that I just could not say no to.
>
> There was one particular building not too far from our neighborhood; I think it was a courthouse or some city government building. I knew I should not go there; but it called to me.
>
> I ventured over to explore this building. I climbed to the top of the cement steps that expanded the width of the front of the building, climbed onto a side ledge, and shuffled around the corner where I was a story up from the ground. It was such a daring adventure!
>
> With windows along the ledge, I'm sure there were eyes inside aware of my presence. Those tattle-tales from inside must have seen me, known who I was, and put in a call; or maybe a sibling told on me.
>
> Mom showed up with her belt. She was not happy! Through tightened lips, she ordered me to shuffle back around the corner and get down!
>
> Once I was off the ledge, Mom grasped my arm and swung the belt at my bottom. (They believed in "spare the rod, spoil the child.") All the way home, I

was told in no uncertain words, that I was never, ever, to return there again.

I don't think I did, but I'm not sure. The call to adventure was such a seductive thing! (Carmen)

Momma and I were very conservative and frugal. We saved reusable items and things that could be repaired. I had my tools and ingenuity and sometimes spent hours welding, rewiring, gluing, and otherwise fixing things. We didn't mean for it to radically influence our children, but I guess it did.

Now, Mom and Dad didn't throw anything away that could possibly still have a practical use. After all, Mom would use worn-out clothing, towels, and sheets as rags for cleaning, patching, straining berry juicy for jelly and many other uses; she even kept Dad's worn-out, de-elasticized briefs and used them for scouring cloths! (They had both survived the Depression, and World War II.)

So as I roamed the alleys behind the neighboring houses, it seemed natural to peek into filled trash cans before trash pickup to see if there were items of value.

More than once I tilted a metal trash can, leaned over to inspect, and then looked up and around for seeing eyes before grapping up discarded treasures.

I would often find almost empty salad dressing, juice, and other food item bottles; pour all the liquid into one container; shake it up; and dare other kids to taste the concoction.

Don't think anybody ever took the dare.

I sure didn't!

On one occasion, don't remember which sister(s) was with me, but we found several unbroken, pristine dolls that were beautifully dressed in southern-bell gowns! They were in perfect condition! They were just lying there on top of the other trash behind a neighbor's house!

Since we had few dolls, we looked around quickly to be sure nobody was looking and took them! But when we got home (we probably tried to hide them because we didn't want our parents to know we had been scavenging) we were discovered.

Mom was quite angry and could not believe that we had found these intact, nice dolls in the trash. She was sure we had stolen them. She made us go back to the house where we found them, ring the doorbell, and explain to the lady what we had done. I think Mom was surprised when the lady stated, "Yes, I threw them away! They can have them!"

I don't remember playing with them, so I don't think Mom let us keep them. She probably hoped to discourage us from scavenging; she did not want us doing it anymore.

Sorry, Mom, but I continued the practice. (Carmen)

Treasure

A scavenger in search of shiny
Treasures amid the scraps,
I search through the trash
At the back of a neighbor's house.
Tossed in the rusty can
Lay scattered playing cards
Still crisp and clean.

Eyes shift, wary of being watched,
I grasp the rim, spring up, climb in;
Then, bobbing like a prairie dog

Peeking out its hole,
Collecting deck in hand,
I disappear to pop up yet once more.

Behind a shadowy window
A mysterious observer stands.
My knees collapse.
I am trapped.
In this smelly place I contemplate the hours
Of solitaire.

A head bob reveals the phantom
No longer there.
So, with loot intact
I scurry out of my burrow.
From this obscure domain
I rise the Queen of Hearts!

Carmen

We didn't spend a lot of money on recreation and/or toys for the kids. More than once, an empty large cardboard box sufficed as a playhouse with windows and a door cut out. The girls had several baby dolls to practice parenthood as they took care of their pretend household. We had a swing and teeter-totter in the backyard for them to play on and a blow-up swimming pool for them to splash around in. We tried to

Hoyt, Sheba, Reba, Carmen, Neva
Taken 7-05-1954, in McPherson, KS

reserve the pool for just our kids and keep the neighborhood kids out, possibly because they usually wore just underwear while swimming.

We also purchased a small merry-go-round toy; it turned round and round when pumped by hand. This became quite an attraction, and neighborhood kids would line up for a turn. It was not real sturdy and got worn out pretty quick, but it was used until it would work no more.

I bought an old piano so Hoyt could take playing lessons. Our neighbor, a piano tuner, tuned it for us. Pauline may have tried to practice on it some, but with so many children to care for, her free time was limited. The piano was sold when we made our next move.

I wrote and entered a lyric-writing contest for a cereal and won a Schwinn bike for Hoyt. I don't

Carmen, Reba, Sheba, Hoyt, and Neva
August of 1955 in McPherson, Kansas

remember the lyrics, and it was not the one used for advertising purposes. Hoyt rode that bike for years and shared it with his sisters.

I fulfilled my responsibilities as pulpit minister, put together and printed a church bulletin, taught Bible classes, visited those sick and/or in the hospital, taught the weekly morning ladies Bible class, and other ministering jobs.

I directed, hosted, and was the song leader for the annual Vacation Bible School. In fact, other churches of Christ in nearby communities would ask me to come and serve as song leader for their Vacation Bible Schools. I usually took our kids with me, so they received double and sometimes triple douses of Vacation Bible School instruction.

On occasion, I was asked to preach a Gospel meeting in other communities.

At every church I ever served, because I was at the church building when transients stopped by, I often helped those asking for assistance as they traveled through town. The church had a limited benevolence fund, and I felt responsible to screen those asking for financial assistance. Some stories the people told were pretty quirky, and it was obvious their stories were not true. I did say no to a few, but I helped most. It was always heartbreaking when children were involved.

Sometimes, I received calls from other churches in Kansas warning me that a certain family would probably be driving through McPherson, and I should not believe their story.

Instead of handing out cash, I would drive them to a filling station and put gas in their car before sending them on their way, and/or take them to a restaurant, order, and pay for their meal, and/or go to a motel and pay for a room. Rarely did I hand over money. There was always the concern that the money would be spent on booze or cigarettes, not on food or shelter.

Sometimes, I would call Pauline, and she would make up a pot of stew to serve a family passing through. Sometimes we fed hobos off the back porch of our home, but we didn't let them enter the house. Most of the time, our *guests* were very gracious and thankful.

Several unpleasant things occurred while we lived in McPherson, but all in all, our time in McPherson was very pleasant.

I coached Hoyt's little league baseball team. One of Hoyt's little buddy's, Mike Harris, lived across the alley. Mike's dad, a captain in the air force based in Saline, Kansas, north of McPherson, was flying into the base during a thunderstorm when his plane crashed and he was killed. Being neighbors and friends, we tried to console the family. That was tough.

While at McPherson, one of the church elders committed suicide. That really disturbed and upset me a lot. I just couldn't understand how a Christian could commit suicide, and I couldn't understand how I and others could have had no idea that he was distressed and/or depressed. We just didn't see it coming.

Of a lesser note, Hoyt got hit with a baseball bat. He had a big knot on his forehead, and we were pretty worried for a while. It did *hoyt* (hurt) pretty bad, and he had bruised, but he was okay! We waited to see if it would knock any sense into him. We waited a long time.

Across the street the neighbors had a big tractor-tire inner tube that they filled with air. Their kids and ours had a great time bouncing up and down and around this improvised circular trampoline, but even fun things can be dangerous.

When I was about five years old, I was jumping onto one side of the neighbor's blown-up inner tube. Sheba, at least I'm pretty sure it was her, followed by jumping onto the opposite side of the inner tube. The air on Sheba's side of the tube was forced aside and replaced the displaced air on my side causing me to fly up, up, and away. Proving Newton's theory that what goes up must come down, I landed nose first onto the sharp edge of a cement brick lining the flower bed.

I ran to the house screaming and crying with blood streaming into my eyes and down my face from the cut on the bridge of my nose. The back end of a moving car flashed passed as I crossed the street. One of the other kids must have reached our house before I did because Momma came running out of the house with a clean white towel.

Mom and Dad took me to the emergency room, and I lay on a table in a green room looking up into bright lights above. A doctor stitched the jagged cut, and I heard him tell Mom and Dad, "If the abrasion on the bridge of her nose had been just a fraction of an inch longer or deeper, she might have been blinded. She may need plastic surgery on her scar."

My nose was swollen, and I was black-and-blue around the eyes and nose, but I remember the comfort of receiving both Mom and Dad's attention.

On the way home they stopped and got me an ice cream cone which made me feel special! While in the car heading home, Neva, just a toddler, fussed because she didn't have any ice cream. The rest of the kids must have remained at the house. Mom said, "Carmen, you'll share some ice cream with your little sister, won't you?"

Not wanting my parents to think me an ingrate and selfish, I shared my ice cream cone, but all the while I was thinking, "Let her go hurt her own nose and get one."

Don't know if my parents could read my body language or not. I hope they didn't.

I did have a scar that embarrassed me, and for years I would let my bangs grow long to try to cover it up. I often thought of myself as the *ugly duckling*. I never had plastic surgery, and the scar is hardly noticeable now. (Carmen)

The kids thought I could heal and doctor all hurts, and I often took care of their bumps and bruises since I had been a medic during World War II. I didn't like to disappoint the kids, so when an injured bird with a broken wing was found in our yard, I tried to doctor it. I used a popsicle stick as a splint and taped its wing.

Now, we were heading out of town on vacation, so I placed the bird with a dish of water and some worms in a large cardboard box in the flower bed by the front door. When we got home about a week later, the bird was gone; there was no evidence of *fowl* play, no feathers, nothing. I like to believe the bird healed and flew away, but it was probably snatched up by a cat.

On occasion, we would visit Grandpa and Grandma Smith on their farm in southwest Oklahoma. It was important to us that the kids know their grandparents.

Sometimes, we coordinated our visits so we were there when the orchard produce was ready for harvest. We were then able to pick and bring home boxes of apples, pears, apricots and peaches. Once we got home, Momma would be busy canning.

Taken August 1955 on Pikes Peak
Hoyt, Reba, Neva, Pauline,
Carmen, and Sheba

Anyhow, our visits were welcomed but meant more work for Grandma Smith. Her meals were always plentiful and varied. Many canned goods added to Grandma's meals: green beans, black-eyed peas, beets, fruits and other goodies. Maggie worked very hard and always served good meals.

She often served chicken; but first she had to catch one, swing the chicken to break its neck, put the dead chicken in a cardboard box where it reflexively thrashed about, cut its throat, and hang the carcass upside down from the top of the front porch to drain the blood, and then *defeather* it.

At that time, we purchased packaged chickens from the grocery store, so as they watched, the kids were both awed and repulsed by this procedure.

The kids liked to follow and *help* Grandpa Smith and Uncle Royce around the farm. Grandpa and Royce would take them to see the cows, horses, pigs and turkeys. The kids enjoyed the opportunity to give a hand with milking, feeding, and scattering hay for the animals. Grandpa even named the cows after the kids; they liked that. Grandpa and Royce would give tractor rides to each child in turns.

The kids *helped* in other ways around the farm. Just so they would have the experience, we took them out into the cotton fields to pick cotton, but they didn't pick much or stick with that job for very long.

Chickens roamed freely until locked up at night, and the kids liked to wander around the smokehouse, garage, and other farm equipment to find and gather eggs.

The area surrounding the old house was not necessarily conducive and sometimes dangerous for children's play. There was rusty farm equipment (spiraling plow blades, parts of tractors, trailers, and various metal pieces from farm equipment) scattered about in the tall weeds and grasses. These were stumbled over causing scratched and scraped knees and shins.

Grandpa Smith's farm in summer of 1956—Back row from the left: Pauline Beasley, Maggie and John Smith, and Hoyt; middle row from the left: Reba, Carmen, Sheba; Neva in the front

We had to warn them to stay away from the old splintery wooden garage and smokehouse where black widow spiders posed a possible threat. There was a small pond up from the house with standing water, so we had to watch to keep them away from there.

The kids didn't like the stickers or cockleburs that grew everywhere, poked them and would stick to socks, shoestrings and clothes; they were hard to pull off and remove.

Hot dry sand surrounded the house and surrounding area.

However, none of these obstacles stopped the kids from playing.

Like their mom did as a child, the girls used their imaginations and pretended to set up house, making furniture of the scattered odds and ends.

The kids would come inside very dirty and sweaty. With no indoor plumbing, water had to be carried from the well; baths were taken in a round metal tub on the floor in the kitchen.

Grandmother's Bathwater by Carmen Lewis

Like a harnessed ox weighted down,
The wooden beam balances
On her shoulders like liberty;
Filled well-buckets on each end
Slosh their contents onto thirsty ground.

With a sun-shielding bonnet bound beneath her chin,
Her five-foot frame is conditioned daily
By stepping and sinking in the Oklahoma scorched sand.
She leans forward as the buckets wobble,
Then tilt and teeter on the splintered pine porch.

She rests, then carries them inside
Handles cutting into her fleshy fingers
To heat water on a wood-burning stove.

A steaming mist releases as a hot stream is poured into
The metal wash tub on the floor.

Each child in turn bathes gritty sand and sweat,
Then stands as wetness slides down small naked bodies;
The last the least clean.
Refreshed and wrapped in thin towels,
Bathers slip modestly past visiting men-folk.

The basin is lifted, hinges groan as she turns and tilts through
And the screen door slams shut.
She tips and tosses the dirty bathwater in a spray
Over startled singing crickets and flying moths,
Cooling and cleansing a portion of the night air.

Grandmother straightens her tired back
While in the back room
The giggles of grandchildren's voices
Slide out from between
Clean sheets.

All the kids slept together on a mattress on the floor in a room between the living room and back bedrooms.

In the summer when the weather was hot, the squeaky screen door allowed the warm Oklahoma breeze to blow through the room where all of us kids slept together on a mattress on the floor.

I was aware of coyotes howling, crickets cricking, the earthy smell of plowed soil, and the gentle rustling of tall grasses and weeds just outside the door.

For nighttime bathroom needs, a potty-bucket was left in the room which would be emptied the following morning.

I avoided using the potty-pot; to make a deposit was unthinkable, especially after someone else's; so I would slink out the screen door careful to not let it slam shut. I would squat and take care of *business* quickly while imagining wild things lingering in the grass ready to snatch a bite of my shiny derriere; mosquitoes, bees, a prowling coyote, or worse, a slinking rattlesnake.

Once, when taking a squat, something pricked me. I jumped up quickly and rushed back inside.

I didn't die, so it wasn't the imagined rattlesnake.
(Carmen)

Our time in McPherson was a good experience, and we stayed there about six-and-a-half years. During our stay, there were some really good times and a few bad times. Most times were good, but the salary I received was not enough to support our growing family, and I didn't have the nerve to speak to the elders about a raise. So I shopped around for a better-paying preaching job.

Hoyt, Reba, Neva (front), Sheba, Carmen ready for church 1956
in McPherson, Kansas

CHAPTER SIXTY-SEVEN

A farmer went out to sow his seed . . . some fell along
the path . . . some fell in rocky places . . . other seed
fell among thorns . . .
Whoever has ears, let him hear.
—Matthew 13:3-9

Ministry in Panhandle, Texas

In 1957, the Beasleys loaded up and moved to Panhandle,
Texas.

After our move, one of the elders from McPherson and his
wife Gertrude (can't remember their last name) visited us, and
he apologized to me for not paying a better salary. I realized
then that had I spoken up, we might have been able to remain
in McPherson.

Anyhow, we had already made the move, so we made the
most of it. Moves are always difficult—packing the house, leaving
friends, unpacking, adjusting to new surroundings and making
new friends. The tedious job of unpacking was mostly Pauline's.
The children probably adjusted more easily than Momma and
me, but even they had to adapt.

The first Sunday after we moved to Panhandle, I
experienced a new procedure and I guess I reacted
inappropriately.

During Bible class for second graders while sitting around a table, the teacher gave a collection plate to the child on my right. As the plate went around to all the children, each put in a coin or two. I was the last one it came to. As it was placed in front of me, I looked at the plate with all those coins, my face lit up, my eyes widened, and I thought to myself, "Boy, they really know how to welcome the new preacher's kid?"

The question, "This is for me?" must have been displayed on my face when I looked up because the teacher promptly removed the plate and said, "I'll take that."

Embarrassed, my eyes immediately fell as I realized it wasn't for me. (Carmen)

The preacher's residence provided by the church was located across the graveled parking lot from the church building. It was a smallish house with only three bedrooms, so the sleeping arrangements were tight. Pauline and I had a room (Neva, the youngest, slept in our room), Hoyt had a room, and the girls had to share a *dormitory-like* room. But the house had indoor plumbing and electricity!

Dad purchased a portable, electric dishwasher for Mom, which she would fill with dirty dishes throughout the day, and turn on in the evenings while she and Dad sat on the couch watching TV, or before they went to bed.

I would snick out of bed with a blanket and pillow, crawl behind the couch and into the kitchen to lie on the floor huddled up next to the warm, humming, vibrating dishwasher; the am biotic sound of water rushing through the cycles was a soothing, relaxing lullaby to me. When the machine finished its cycles, I would usually wakeup and return to bed.

I think Mom and Dad discovered me there once
and told me not to do it again, but I continued doing
it anyway. It was so soothing to me! (Carmen)

There was a chicken coop in the backyard, so we purchased some chicks. Of course, the kids saw them as pets and named them. Neva named the prominent rooster Popeye (one cold winter night, his foot froze and later dropped off, so he hopped around on his one *peg* leg), and she named one of the hens Olive Oyl. I'm sure the others had cartoon names as well, but I don't remember them.

Anyhow, we were able to gather eggs for consumption. Despite potential chicks sacrificed as scrambled eggs, Popeye and his harem increased the chick population. The kids were always intrigued when chicks hatched. Chicks were fun, but once grown, the adult chickens became a liability.

When the barefoot kids stepped out onto our back porch, Popeye, who was very mean, and his submissive and imitative harem would dash over and peck at wormy looking toes. There were many tears shed over injured phalanges. The kids soon learned to wear shoes or avoid going out the back door. And that's no *eggsaggeration*! ☺

During the day, the chickens roamed around the backyard, but retreated to the coop at night which was then latched shut. I'm sure there were stray dogs and coyotes about the rural community of Panhandle that would have loved to *wing it* and take our feathered friends off our hands.

Speaking of injured feet, in McPherson the kids went barefoot a lot in the house and on the cushioned green grass; there were many stubbed toes, but the grass was soft to the foot. However, in Panhandle, thistles and thorns grew prolifically in the grass around the house. Being in the habit of running out of the house without wearing shoes, many times the kids would step a few feet into the lawn, get punctured by thorns, and stop in their steps unable to step backward or forward without causing further injury. With tears of anguish, they would stand still and cry out for help, then a shoed parent or older child would have to rescue them, carry them to the porch, and help remove the offending spears. Most of the kids learned to take the precaution of putting on protective shoes.

Anyhow, animals were intriguing to the kids, but we had no dog or cat. Momma had her hands full caring for children and did not want or need any animals to care for. However, we did have some unusual pets while in Panhandle.

> I think they might be rarer now, but little horny toads (by today's reckoning that might be an inappropriate expression.) used to be abundant and "ran around all over the place around here" (as Daddy would often say) in the open field next to the house, in our yard and by the church building.
>
> We liked to catch them, hold them in our hands, run our fingers over their bumpy backs, watch them open their mouths with their tiny tongues flicking and the under skin of their chin hanging down panting as though they had difficulty breathing.
>
> We would bring them into the house to keep as pets, but Mom explained, "They need to live free and run around outside. They would not be happy cooped up in a box and would probably die if you try to keep them. You need to take them back outside and let them go." (Neva)

Once while driving out in the country to visit members of the church, we spotted several baby jackrabbits by the side of the road. It seemed that the mother rabbit had abandoned them, or maybe she had died. I shouldn't have done it; but I stopped, picked them up, and brought them to the car.

We found and took several baby jackrabbits home, and for a while they were soft furry pets. But soon it became clear that they were not doing so well; they were sick. Dad tried to care for them, but really didn't know what to do. I think he was afraid they might have a disease that we might get, so he said he would take them back out into the country. He probably "bobbed them on the head" rather than leave them sick and helpless. (Neva)

On another visit out into the country while picking corn in a field belonging to a member of the church, Hoyt found and caught several big hairy tarantulas that he kept in a quart jar. They appealed to him, but not to the girls. They survived for a while.

The kids were pretty good about entertaining themselves in the backyard on the swing set and teeter-totter and were sometimes able to participate in some special activities.

They played together in the gravel parking lot between the church building and the house. They would expend much energy and time pushing gravel with rakes, shovels, anything that could be used to move the stones to form trail ways that turned, intersected, and circled about. These paths were destroyed each Sunday morning and evening, and Wednesday evenings when cars were parked for church services, and had to be remade.

They didn't have sit-on pedal-pushing toy cars; they had to share one tricycle and Hoyt's bicycle; or using their imaginations they practiced their driving skills while holding a pretend steering wheel and walking. They made engine noises, stopped at stop signs, held their left arm out to indicate a turn, and drove many miles through a pretend town.

Often during the day while studying and preparing a sermon, I would be entertained when several of the kids would come into the unlocked church building and play church in the auditorium. They would take turns leading hymns, praying, passing the communion (pretend) and preaching, the coveted position.

I heard arguments about who got to be the preacher. If Hoyt was involved in the play, he would state, "I'm the boy, so I will do the preaching." I heard some pretty good little sermons.

The song leader would mimic what had been heard and observed while in church. "Please, turn to song # 391. We'll sing the first and third verses. That's 391," then wave an arm to lead the song. These were probably the only times when a female presided in our church building!

I was amused, and I'm sure God was pleased with their innocent worship.

Hoyt would go to the city pool by himself to swim.

For modesty's sake, though the general public probably thought we were fanatical, most men and women of the churches of Christ did not participate in mixed public swimming. Therefore, a once-a-week, early morning time was arranged during the summer months when just women and girls could go to the city pool to swim. Momma took the girls. They enjoyed the cool experience.

Even when the girls were very young, to protect their virtue, Momma and I would not allow them to wear short skirts and/ or low neckline clothing. I'm sure there were times when they felt like "aliens and strangers" (1 Peter 2:11) among their peers, especially when popular styles of clothing became really short and revealing. Nevertheless, Momma and I did not bend our standards on this issue.

Occasionally, I would preach on modesty. However, sometimes there were some present in the services who didn't appreciate my conservatism on modesty.

To fill idle time and because she wanted her girls to learn, Pauline spent time teaching and supervising creative arts-and-crafts activities. Hoyt probably participated too.

> Momma taught us the basics of crocheting. With four girls of varying ages and skills, it must have tasked her patience. First we had to master how to cast on. I would cast on until the length of my chain was many feet long. Then, she showed us how to turn around on the chain, put the hook through the chain, catch the thread and pull it through, then catch the thread again and pull it through all the loops on the hook to make the next row. We eventually learned to make square potholders and the more ambitious crotchetier made scarves.
>
> She also cut square pieces of muslin and had us do fabric painting and embroidery on tea towels.
>
> Mom purchased a kit that had a metal square with prongs sticking up on all four sides, precut stretch-fabric circular bands, and a special hook for weaving the bands to make woven potholders. We learned to use this. When the kit's fabric bands were all used up, Mom would cut the ankle part of worn-out socks into circular bands to weave more potholders.
>
> When we got old enough, Mom taught each girl how to layout a pattern, cut fabric and sew simple things like aprons. We all learned to sew using an old treadle-sewing machine. (Reba)

At the time of our move to Panhandle, all but Neva were in school. Hoyt was in sixth, Sheba was in fourth, Reba was in third, and Carmen was in second grade. With only one child at home during the day, Pauline had a nice break.

The school system in Panhandle was into the arts. All-grade plays and/or operettas were commonly performed and presented to the community.

> I think I was in second grade when my grade performed a musical of *Alice in Wonderland*[*]. I was one of the three finalists for Alice, but I didn't get the part. I was so disappointed. I was put in the chorus instead and can still remember the lyrics and melodies of many of the songs that the chorus sang:
>
> "I'm Tweedle Dee, I'm Tweedle Dum, bumpity boompity boo", and "The Walrus and the Carpenter went walking hand in hand."
>
> Funny how one can remember lyrics and melodies from songs heard and learned ages ago! (Carmen)

We got to know and spent some time with different members of the church. Again, we were often invited for dinner at various members' homes.

We had invites to the Cecil Cumming's farm. One such visit, their and our kids went exploring around the pond on their land not too far from the house.

> We came running into the house very excited and fearful to report seeing giant footprints in the mud by the water. We were convinced a giant was roaming around looking for small children to snatch up.

---

[*] *Alice in Wonderland* was a novel written by Lewis Carroll in 1865, a musical play based on the novel was written by H. Saville Clark with music by Walter Slaughter and performed in 1886 at the Prince of Wales Theatre in London. Musicals and operettas were very popular in the early 1900s.

> The adults showed no interest in our discovery, continued with their game, and did not go investigate.
>
> I was quite frustrated with their lack of concern, but went back outside to play. (Carmen)

We visited with the O.D. Smith's, an elder at the church. He was a good guy, but it always bothered me that he would never say a prayer or teach a Bible class.

> During visits at the Smith's house, I remember playing on a toy John Deer peddle-tractor. I just loved peddling around on it and had trouble sharing. I never wanted to leave when it was time to go.
>
> Mrs. Smith had a ceramic tea service play-set, as well as, a miniature set of ceramic dishes that all of us girls admired and got to play with. Sometime later, she presented those to us as a gift. We played with them for many years; some were lost or broken. (I think Treva has the surviving pieces.) (Neva)

I remember leaving our kids with the Parks for several days while Pauline and I went to the Abilene Christian Lectureship and Teachers Workshop. Mr. Parks was a lineman for the electric company; he drove a company truck, climbed, and shimmied up the poles to work on the electric wires. The parks had two children, a boy and a girl, about Hoyt's and Sheba's ages and lived around the corner near the church building.

> While staying with the Parks, we slept "all over the place around here"—some on beds, some on couches; it was like a big slumber party.
>
> In the evenings, we played long games of monopoly. Sometimes the games went on forever, but we had a good time.

The adults and the older kids would talk and joke. I mostly listened. I remember a comment made about how Momma made and served cornbread and beans at least once a week. (We also had liver and onions about every week. They were cheap meals that went far to feed our large family.)

Everybody was joking and laughing about beans causing gas: "Beans, beans, the musical fruit. The more you eat, the more you toot. The more you toot, the better you feel. So let's have beans at every meal!"

I laughed so hard, my eyes started to tear up. My tears were misunderstood, and Mrs. Parks came over, put her arms around me, and said, "Oh, honey, we weren't making fun of your mom. I'm sorry we hurt your feelings."

Well, everybody looked at me. The attention then made me cry more. I was so embarrassed! I couldn't stop crying and then I didn't know how to tell them that my eyes had teared up because I had been laughing so hard.

Actually, I think the mention of Mom made me homesick, so maybe I really was crying. (Carmen)

The kids had some freedom to roam about the neighborhood, but again, they had some restrictions. However, there were always discipline issues.

Shortly after moving into the house, a garage and basement were added on to the house just outside the back door. Later a panel within the garage caught on fire; one of the kids started it. The fire, which was limited to one small spot, was put out quickly, so the garage did not burn down.

I had to have been only about three or four years old, but one day, I climbed up onto the stove to get some matches. I knew I shouldn't get them, but I liked to strike the matches and watch the flame! So I was playing with the matches in the garage when the wall caught on fire. I tried to smother it by piling scrapes of wood blocks and a pair of rubber boots on top of the licking flames.

Dad came out into the garage and saw the fire. I tried to blame it on the neighbor boy I played with sometimes, but Dad knew better. He put the fire out, then picked me up by my arm, and paddled my bottom good while scolding me and removing me from the garage.

I was lucky the garage and house didn't burn down.

Once the fire was out, his temper cooled. (Neva)

Sometimes natural consequences were the best punishment for disobedience.

I guess I must have been a rascal. I seemed to do things that I had been told not to do, but would do anyway, get caught, and punished.

There was a single-story house (it might have been a trailer) behind our house that was easy to climb. I had been told not to climb onto its metal roof. The occupants had probably complained to Mom and Dad. But it was intriguing, so I continued to shimmy up the water pipe to sit and walk on top.

However, the same afternoon that Mom and Dad were to host a church gathering at our house, I climbed up, slipped and slid down the water pipe, and sliced my right little finger from tip to palm on the metal edge. I ran home bleeding and screaming.

First Dad, washed my cut, applied some stinging red mercurochrome, and wrapped a thick wad of gauze and tape on my little finger.

Of course, I was again told to stay away from that house, but I was surprised that I did not get a spanking. Guess he thought my injured finger was punishment enough.

Well, at the taffy-pulling party that evening, my bandaged finger hurt; and threads from the gauze kept getting in the candy making it inedible. I didn't have much fun.

I don't think I climbed that house again.

We had been told to not play in the car, but of course, I did anyway. One time I shut the car door on my foot. I screamed and cried!

Dad came out the back door into the garage to see what was wrong and found me in the car.

I'm sure his first impulse was to spank me, but when he opened the car door and realized my foot was smashed, he removed my bare foot. What he saw was black-and-blue toes. He doctored and consoled me and probably said, "If you had stayed out of the car like you were told, this would not have happened."

I did get a scolding, but I didn't get a spanking. The naturally consequences hurt enough!

It was difficult to walk for a while, and the toenail on my big toe eventually fell off. Gross! (Carmen)

The Beasley children were not perfect; even members of preacher's families make mistakes and are tempted. So it took more than going to church and playing church to teach our kids to be honest and moral.

When I was about four, I had taken money from the collection tray in church. I don't know if Dad actually saw me take it, but I lied and told him I found it. He suggested that I put it in the collection plate.

Boy, was I disappointed and relieved at the same time. Even as young as I was, I realized that he knew I was lying. I was ashamed and disappointed in myself.

Another time, like so many kids, I gave into temptation. I had taken candy from the store near the house and Mom found out. She took me back and had me return the stolen candy to the man behind the register.

He said, "That's okay. She can keep it."

Mom responded, "No, it's not okay. She can't have it."

Mom and Dad tried to instill the virtue of honesty in us and did not want me rewarded for wrong doing.

Since I'm confessing, I sometimes took coins from a leather pouch that Momma carried in her purse. I don't know if she ever knew that. (Neva)

I guess money must have been an issue and a temptation for me and at least one other sibling. When Dad would come home, he would empty his pockets of loose change and place it on the dresser in Mom and Dad's bedroom.

I have to admit that my conscience did bother me, but I would look around and quickly snatch up a nickel or a dime. It was never very much, but I don't think they were aware of my theft.

I would then go to the corner store to buy bubble gum or candy. I continued to do this for many years.

Sorry, Dad! If all the others were doing this too, you must have been shorted a lot of money! (Carmen)

Sometimes, our kids would repeat unacceptable expressions and/or words that they had heard on TV, in school, or while out in the public. When that happened, we talked to the offender(s) and explained that the Bible taught that "your speech should be 'yea' and 'nay'"; that you should say what you mean and mean what you say, extra flourishes were unnecessary; "you don't swear by heaven or earth"; and you should "not take the Lord's name (in any way, shape or form) in vain." We did not even allow "gosh," "golly," "gee," or "shucks" to be used because they were simply a derivative of the inappropriate words.

Occasionally, a slang word might slip out of innocent mouths, but the kids were pretty compliant.

> We took Mom and Dad's instruction seriously but sometimes took advantage of opportunities to tweak our language to sneak in "worldly" expressions.
>
> The family went to a church friend's farm to pick a supply of corn from their field. After returning, Mom put all of us kids to work outside to remove the shucks so she could prepare the corn for eating and/or freezing.
>
> I remember sitting outside in a circle with other siblings tearing the outside covering off the corn cobs and repeatedly saying, "We've got to 'shuck' this corn." "There's a lot of 'shuckin' to do." "Keep 'shuckin' until it's all done." "This 'shuckin' is hard work."
>
> We thought we were getting away with something really evil. (Carmen)

We continued to supplement my salary and save money anyway we could. We didn't really have a spot for a garden; but we were often allowed to pick corn, tomatoes, green beans, and other vegetables on farms belonging to various members of the church. We kept our shelves filled with canned goods and our freezer full, and we continued to go to Grandpa and Grandma Smith's farm for fruit from their orchard.

Momma sewed matching dresses of varying sizes for the girls, usually with full gathered skirts made from yards of fabric. She would even use the scrapes to make purses and hats to match. Don't know how she found the time, but I guess it was cheaper to make than to buy dresses, plus she liked to sew. As each girl grew too big, her dress became a hand-me-down to the next smaller girl. The dresses were passed down several times and got plenty of wear!

Hoyt had no brother to hand down to.

She kept all the remnants from the many clothes she sewed over many years. Some pieces she used to make doll clothes, others she used in quilts. Many fabric remnants were stored in several large Rubbermaid trash cans. She didn't throw any of it away.

For Christmas, we usually purchased a small Christmas tree, but made the ornaments. We strung popcorn, glued paper strips into connecting circles for chains, and used ideas that Momma found in magazines to make ornaments out of aluminum foil, construction paper, and other available materials. Any ornaments that the kids made in school, especially those that had their picture, were saved and hung on the tree in succeeding years.

One Christmas we purchased twelve-inch grown-up dolls for Sheba, Reba and Carmen. Neva was just a toddler, so she got a baby doll.

Sometime later, with saved cereal box-tops, Sheba acquired a Linda Cartwright doll that was advertized on the Danny Thomas Show.[*]

> We named our adult dolls using movie-star names: Sheba's doll was named Shirley Temple, Reba's was named Patti Page, and Carmen's was named Loretta Young.

---

[*]   *Make Room for Daddy*, starring Danny Thomas, aired 1953-57 on ABC; 57-64 on CBS. Wikipedia, the free encyclopedia.

Now, Momma didn't really like Barbie dolls because she thought their physique was too perfect. She was concerned that her girls would grow up thinking that they should have a figure like Barbie, but would be disappointed when we did not develop into curvy female specimens. We never received any Barbie dolls. (Reba)

I wore dress shirts to worship services, for funerals and weddings; and Pauline starched and ironed my shirts for me. There were cleaners around, but it was expensive; I did sometimes take my suit(s) to be cleaned.

As a preacher, Dad always wore a dress shirt and/or suit to church. Dad liked his shirts starched. Actually, I think the starch helped them look crisp, smooth and wrinkle free.

Momma went to a lot of trouble to prepare his shirts. First she washed them, and prepared the right consistency of dry starch in hot water, not too thick, not to thin. While holding each washed shirt by the collar, Dad didn't like his collars starched, she dipped the rest of the shirt into the light blue, warm liquid. After lifting each dripping shirt, she twisted the fabric and rung out excess liquid starch back into a large bowl. She next hung the shirts on the outside line to dry. Once dry, she used an improvised water bottle with a squirter or holey lid to sprinkle each shirt till slightly damp. Then, she would hold the shirt by the collar, its full length hanging like a limp duck, and roll the shirt up like the dough of a cinnamon roll. These rolled-up shirts were stuffed into cleaned emptied plastic bread bags and put into the freezer. Then, when she had the time, she brought them out of the freezer and ironed them.

We got to, or had to, help with the ironing. For practice we started out ironing square cloth dinner napkins and Dad's cloth handkerchiefs, which we then folded several times into rectangles and stacked.

I never quite understood why the handkerchiefs needed to be ironed; they were just going to get nasty when Dad blew his nose.

We graduated to Dad's shirts; the frozen shirts would crinkle as they were unrolled and sizzle and steam when the heated iron slid smoothly over the fabric. (Thank God, they now make permanent press!) (Sheba)

My dad, Edgar, visited us in Panhandle several times and would attend church with us. The kids were aware of his smokers' voice, smokers' cough, and smokers' smell.

I remember one time when Grandpa Beasley visited us in Panhandle. Several of us walked with Grandpa to the little store a short distance from the house. He bought real cigarettes for himself, but candy cigarettes for us.

I thought it was so cool to pretend to smoke like the beautiful, sexy women in the advertisement pictures. He did tell us, "Now,

Hoyt in the back, Sheba, Grandpa Edgar Beasley, Reba, Carmen in middle row, and Neva in front of Grandpa—1957 or 58.

you need to eat the candy cigarettes before we get back home. I'm not sure your parents would appreciate me getting these for you."

I don't know if Mom and Dad ever knew we pretended to smoke with Grandpa Beasley. I'm sure they were concerned that we might be influenced to someday smoke real cigarettes.

I did try smoking once. While crossing the street in front of the church building, I saw a smoking cigarette butt in the middle of the street, picked it up, and took a puff. It was awful! I coughed and coughed. That experience killed my desire to smoke. (Carmen)

We had vacationed some in Colorado while we lived in McPherson, but now in Panhandle, located in the north-western corner in the Panhandle of Texas, we were closer to New Mexico and Colorado. So while living in Panhandle, we participated at Blue Haven Bible Camp near Las Vegas, New Mexico, and our family often vacationed in the Rocky Mountains.

Mom and I taught Bible classes at Blue Haven Camp so Hoyt could attend for free as one of the campers. Of course, the other kids were with us, but they were actually too young to sleep in the dorms and participate with the other campers. They had to stay with us, and we had to keep an eye on them.

On one of the trips, our car sputtered and spit and barely made it up the mountain to the camp grounds. Later, with help from another adult, I got the car back down the mountain to town where a mechanic took a look at it.

I just knew the repair was going to take hours and cost me a fortune, but in just a couple of minutes, the mechanic came out and stated, "Your car's ready."

I was surprised! I asked, "How much do I owe you?"

"Nothing."

I was pleasantly surprised! He said there was a loose valve, and all he had to do was tap and tighten it. He did accept a tip from me for his trouble; I think I gave him twenty dollars.

Blue Haven Camp had not been established for very long. In fact, it might have been its first year since Hoyt was recorded as the first camper to be baptized in 1957.

While living in Panhandle, Hoyt attended the camp for two years; Sheba attended once.

We camped in the mountains of New Mexico and Colorado or sometimes stayed in economy motels. Sometimes after driving till late in the evening, I would stop and go inside to inquire about the cost of a room while the rest of the family remained in the car. If the price was too steep and they would not barter with me, I would return to the car and drive some more to find a room with a reasonable rate. The kids would sigh and were usually pretty restless and/or in need of a bathroom break.

They would ask, "How much farther?" or "Are we there yet?"

And I'm sure Mom was ready to get out of the car as well, but our trips were made on a budget. I would pay for only one room, so we had to double and triple on the two beds. Some kids had to sleep on the floor. The youngest may have slept in a drawer on top of a pillow.

Eventually, since we made a number of trips to the mountains, Momma and I devised a system where the entire family could sleep in the station wagon while we parked in free camping sites. We custom cut thick plywood to fit in the car to make bunk beds. One child slept on the front seat, another slept on a board that fitted over the hump in the floor of the backseat, another slept on the backseat, and then Hoyt slept on a board that rested perpendicular on top of and across the front and back backrests. Mom, Neva (the youngest), and I slept in the back of the station wagon. It made for cozy comfort and blanket-wrapped warmth.

There were a few roll-over and roll-off incidences during the nights, but we survived. By morning, the car windows were fogged over from all that close breathing, and everybody was really in need of a bathroom break in the available outhouses.

When Hoyt was older, he and I sometimes slept out in the open in sleeping bags. On one occasion, we woke to discover a porcupine on a limb above us. We were glad he didn't make a point of dropping in for a visit! ☺

> One family vacation, we went to the Seven Falls in Colorado. We hiked up the mountain to the memorial to Helen Hunt Jackson,[*] but on the way back down, a cloudburst opened up with hail and rain that beat down mercilessly. Our family and many others huddled together under a pavilion along the trail. The frozen stones hit the tin roof beating a loud un-syncopated tapping ruckus, and the mixture of rain and melting hail flowed down the slopes in wide rivulets.
>
> It got very cold! Dad took his shirt off (he still had on a T-shirt) and wrapped it around Neva, who was still quite young.
>
> The storm eventually passed, and when we got back down the mountain, many cars were covered with mud from a mud slide. Ours was located in a save spot, so it was not covered. (Sheba)

We stopped at numerous *hysterical markers* and read the history of the areas that we passed through. Our intent was to "raise no ignorant children."

While twisting and turning on the winding mountain roads of New Mexico, Colorado, and later Wyoming and Montana, I retold the following story that I had made up:

> A brave Indian chief, Swift Eagle, was married to an Indian maiden, Yellow Flower. They had a son. Their

---

[*] Helen Hunt Jackson, who lived October 18, 1830, to August 12, 1885, was an activist for Native Americans and wrote *A Century of Dishonor* in 1881 about how the actions of the government had adverse effects on Native Americans.

son was a strong, sturdy, and tough baby who seldom cried; so they named him Rock. They loved their son very much.

Rock learned to walk at a very early age, but he would often fall as he stumbled over the uneven ground around the tipi and along the rocky streambed near the camp. The parents would say, "Rock has fallen." So they began to call him Fallen Rock.

One day Yellow Flower was crouched by the water washing clothes, and the toddler was playing near his mother along the banks of the stream. Yellow Flower gazed back at her son to find him gone. Frantically, she ran up and down the banks of the river yelling his name and looking for him. She did not find him. She ran into the forest calling for Fallen Rock. There was no answer.

When Swift Eagle returned from hunting, he gathered all the other braves, and they searched in the woods and along the brooks and rivers for many days; but Fallen Rock was not found.

Swift Eagle and Yellow Flower were saddened by the loss of their son, but they could not give up hope that someday their beloved son would be found.

Their love was so great that even to this day signs can be seen along mountain roads asking travelers to "Watch for Fallen Rock." ☺

While traveling, we seldom stopped for food at a restaurant or for prepared food from a fast-food place. Usually, we packed perishable food from home in a cooler. We brought *hoyt* (whole wheat bread was healthier than white) bread, a slab of bologna and chips, and would pull over at a roadside picnic table or at a scenic view, cut slices of bologna, and slather on some mayonnaise to make sandwiches. When we stopped to camp, we would grill hamburgers or hot dogs over an open campfire and, of course, marshmallows.

Occasionally, while traveling, we might run into a long line of backed-up cars due to road work or a long caravan of army/military vehicles hindering our travel and impeding the flow of traffic. I would state, "Brother! It's Coxey's Army." I didn't like it when we were prevented from moving forward.

I guess the kids thought the expression "Coxey's Army" originated from my experiences during World War II when long military caravans were traveling through Europe, but that's not the case; so when asked where the expression "Coxey's Army" came from, I didn't know.

Now, at home whenever the kids would ask me a question, I would tell them to "go look it up in the encyclopedia." So I did likewise.

I educated the kids by relating my research: Jacob Sechler Coxey was the leader of a group of unemployed men during the depression of the 1890s. He urged a huge road improvement program to create employment, and organized an army called Coxey's Army of five hundred men to attract national attention. They marched out of Ohio to Washington in May of 1894. So that's Coxey's Army.

(In fact, for years whenever my golf buddies and I would go to the golf course and there were quite a few people ahead of us, I would say, "Oh brother, it's Coxey's Army.")

Anyhow, the vacations were enjoyable and made for pleasant memories. Of course, extra clothing, food and other items had to be packed carefully and sparingly and were usually carried on the top of the car, so we could have more room for sitting and sleeping inside the car.

While living in Panhandle, I heard about a new Bible camp, and mission opportunities in Montana. In 1957, a group of Christians had purchased the Bow and Arrow Dude Ranch in the Absaroka Range in the Gallatin National Forest just north of Yellowstone National Park near Pray, Montana. They named the camp Yellowstone Bible Camp.

I guess I had a bit of the adventurer and pioneer in me, and Pauline was a willing companion; so in the summer of '59, the family loaded up and traveled north through Colorado, Wyoming, and Yellowstone National Park to this camp to check it out.

The trip through Yellowstone National Park was interesting. The kids said the geysers stunk, but none of us had ever seen or smelled them before.

Back then, bears would congregate on the roads, go right up to the cars, stand, and scrap their paws on the car windows begging for food. Travelers were warned not to open their windows or doors, not to feed the bears, and not to get out of their cars; but many people did anyway to take pictures. We didn't! However, the family was quite fascinated to see Yogi bear up close and personal.

We also saw Bullwinkle the moose, buffalo, Bambi the deer, elk, and other wildlife.

When we camped in the park, the females all slept in the car on our improvised beds. Hoyt and I slept outside in a pup tent.

One night, some roaming bears came into the campground and literally tore into latched coolers that other neighboring campers had left outside of their vehicles! Sleeping near to a roaring stream, Hoyt and I did not hear the ruckus; we were "snug as a bug" and sound asleep in our sleeping bags. I guess the bears moved away from the campsite on to better pickings.

Other campers related the story the next morning. Pauline and the girls were glad they had slept in the car. Hoyt and I were glad we were not bothered.

Yellowstone Bible Camp was located in a beautiful rustic mountain setting among tall scented pines and wildflowers. The camp had a large log Lodge and several scattered rugged log cabins located in a valley between mountains. Bordering the south and east perimeters of the land, two mountain streams with rushing rapids formed a Y where a log bridge crossed on to the grounds. Baptisms took place under this bridge.

(In 1992, this bridge was featured briefly in the movie, *A River Runs through It*. In fact, the movie crew, including Robert Redford, slept in and used the camp's cabin facilities during filming. Later the toilet seat that Robert Redford used was auctioned off, and the purchaser had it framed and displayed in the Lodge with a plaque stating, "Redford sat here.")

Three cabins were located on the west bank of the Old Mill Stream, which flowed north and eventually into the Yellowstone River. Deer could be seen in the early mornings drinking in Mill Creek.

The Mule Barn, then designated for the male campers (Hoyt, who was about thirteen years old, slept there), was located slightly to the west at the foot of a logging mountain where bears were often seen coming down from the mountains.

Momma and I and the girls stayed in the Honeymoon Cabin. Yeah! Some honeymoon with five children!

The roar of the rapids outside the cabin sang our tribe to sleep each night.

Breaking through the roaring cadence of the stream, the clang of the large bell located by the Lodge rang its wake-up call early each morning, throughout the day to announce activities, and at night for lights out.

The family camp session at Yellowstone Bible Camp was enjoyed by our family. We made the memorable hike to the falls up the logging road from the camp. Some of us went up T-shirt Mountain across Mill Creek. Hoyt and I spent some time fishing. The kids delighted in jumping from one big rock to another around the circle drive in front of the Lodge, and traipsing around in the frigid waters of the stream. The Bible classes and worship services were inspiring. And we loved the scenic location!

On August 17, 1959, within several weeks after returning from our trip to Montana, the news reported an earthquake that measured 7.5 on the Richter scale in southwestern Montana, an area just west of Yellowstone National Park. We had just traveled through this valley sightseeing.

I read that the earthquake caused the side of Sheep Mountain to slice off and slide down to form a dam on the Madison River. Huge rocks hit the bottom of the valley and bounced hundreds of feet from their points of impact. The landslide, 80 million tons of rock and dirt, traveling downward at an estimated 100 miles per hour, created strong winds that snapped trees, shot them as if from a bow, and embedded them like arrows into other trees and structures. Twenty-eight people who were camping along the Madison River were killed, many literally buried under the debris, others drowned as the dammed river waters rose and washed their campsites away.[*]

This news had a profound effect on my nine-year-old psyche. I thought, "Boy, God must have a plan for me and my family. He let us leave the area and return home before allowing this earthquake to happen!" (Carmen)

The churches of Christ in Montana were in need of missionaries who were willing to live in the less settled, expansive, but beautiful lands of the big blue sky country. So we returned to Panhandle, Texas, with plans to move to the mission fields of Montana.

---

[*] **Retrieved from en.wikipedia.org**/wiki/1959_Yellowstone_earthquake. Wikipedia the free encyclopedia.

We had to sell the chickens; we couldn't take them with us. The kids got pretty upset. Despite pecked toes, they were attached to their feathered friends.

A member of the church agreed to take them off our hands—the chickens, not the kids. The kids made Mom and me promise that the chickens would not be eaten. We crossed our fingers behind our backs and told them, "They will not be eaten."

The last Sunday before we set out, all was going well until the purchaser jokingly stated when all were present, "Those chickens made a really good fried chicken dinner." If looks could kill, Momma and I would be dead. We had to console, dry tears, and gain back their trust.

Gerald and Pauline, Sheba, Hoyt behind;
Carmen, Reba, Neva in front
1959 at 209 E. 4th, Panhandle, Texas

CHAPTER SIXTY-EIGHT

As the deer pants for streams of water,
so my soul pants for you, my God.

—Psalm 42:1

Ministry in Lewistown, Montana

In October of 1959, about two months into the school year, the Beasley family packed up and headed north to Lewistown, Montana, to work in the mission field where the churches of Christ were few and far between, and membership was limited. Because of limited contributions, this congregation was supported by churches in New Mexico.

On the trip north Pauline had a harrowing experience. I drove the moving van with Hoyt as a companion, and Momma drove the station wagon with the girls. Driving north on HI 25 through Colorado, we ran into a snow blizzard. While watching through my rearview mirror, I observed *Ole Bessie* make a complete spin-around on the highway. There were few cars out, so there was no collision. When we stopped a little farther up the road, I found Momma pretty rattled and all shook up.

As we continued the trip, we did run into more snow but continued on our journey safely. The crew was glad when we finally got to Lewistown.

Members of the church had arranged to rent an older two-story house located at 911 Spring Street. The kids were delighted when we pulled up in front of a house with two very tall evergreen trees, one growing on each side of the front sidewalk. (The kids would spend a lot of time climbing those trees.) Before unloading, the kids ran into the house to lay claim to their territory.

Of course, Momma and I helped them figure out where they would sleep. Upstairs, Sheba and Reba shared a bedroom on the west side, and Carmen and Neva shared one on the east side. Over time, sometimes, because of sibling rivalry, the girls had to be switched around. Hoyt had his own strange little room by the stairs between the other bedrooms that was accessed through a very narrow hallway. The kids shared the upstairs bathroom.

Mom and I had our own bedroom and bathroom downstairs; the living room, kitchen, utility room, and a screened-in back porch were also downstairs.

This old house was intriguing to the kids with crawl space in the eaves of the slanted roof, a dirt basement and a back porch with crawl space under it. We told them black widow spiders lived in the basement and under the porch (which was probably true) so that scare kept them out of those places most of the time. However, they would sneak into the crawl space through an opening in the upstairs bathroom closet, crawl into the narrow spaces looking for left-behind treasures or bodies hidden around the corners. Momma got after them time after time saying, "Don't go back there," but the temptation was too great; they kept sneaking in there for *secret club meetings*. I'm surprised they didn't fall through to the main floor.

The elementary, middle, and high schools were located within reasonable walking distance from the Spring Street address. At the time of the move, Neva was in first, Carmen in fourth, Reba in fifth, Sheba in sixth, and Hoyt in eighth grades.

Reba ended up having Margaret Latham, a member of the church, as her teacher. (That particular year, Margaret piloted a program to teach the New Math and used the *open classroom* concept.)

I'm not sure, but I think my fourth grade teacher's name was Mrs. Reardon. I'm not sure of her name, but I do remember her language.

I just knew that if Mom and Dad heard her they would be concerned for my innocent ears. Throughout the day, she would repeat over and over to the class, "Shush," instead of "Sh-h." I thought it was a cuss word, an unwholesome derivative of Sh-h and something I shouldn't say or hear. (Carmen)

The kids soon experienced the cold winter walks trudging through feet of snow. They shivered and complained some, but wrapped in several layers of clothes, they faired okay.

There was a railroad track that passed thru the neighborhood on the east side of the house east of ours. When weather permitted, the kids would crush pennies on the tracks and walk down the track to the high trestle that crossed above a small valley. They would gingerly step from plank to plank, glancing through the spaces at a small creek below. Trains usually came through at night, but should a train whistle a warning during the day, they would anxiously hasten to the end of the trestle to get out of the way.

In the spring, the entire valley down from the backyard overflowed with rushing mountain snow water, and the creek under the trestle became a roaring river. It was dangerous! We warned the kids to stay away from and not step into the water. They could have been washed away.

In the summer, after the mountain run-off had decreased, the kids enjoyed exploring the creek under the trestle, and fishing around the two small ponds down in the football-field wide valley.

Hoyt once caught a really *big one* while fishing at the pond in the valley down from the house. As he was swishing his fishing line back and forth to cast it into the middle of the pond, I came up behind him. On a backward swish, the hook caught in my cheek (not the one behind my back, the one by my nose). He gave a jerk, and puzzled as to why it did not swish back.

His eyes went wide as he looked back and heard the *big one* scream.

He released me and let me go. (Carmen)

After a summer rain, the kids would often gather in the front yard after the sun had gone down to catch night crawlers for fishing. Like the big sky overhead, Montana grew big night crawlers!

Night Crawler by Carmen Lewis

Standing stooped,
silent and still
after a spring shower
with flashlight focused
on the damp lawn,
I grab as a pointy head appears.
I hold on as the slimy cylindrical form
expands and grasps
onto tunneled sides of earth,
retracting strong and slippery
through my fingers
back into the ground.

I regain my statuesque pose
so no movement will vibrate
a sensory warning
to the brainless creature
who soon reappears to breath dry air.
Holding firmly, I pull up slowly
so as not to break and spill guts.

My long trophy loses the struggle,
curls and twists,
tickling the palm of my hand
instinctively searching
for its natural habitat.

I briefly ·
contemplate
how I might feel
after eating
through a dark dirt world
to the surface
to be manhandle.
I consider letting it go,
but callously resolve
to imprison my catch
in my can
for fish bait.

During the brief growing season, Momma planted vegetables on the rocky, sloping side at the Spring Street address. Gooseberries and rhubarb were already growing around the house, so Mom harvested and froze bunches.

Deborah, Bill Jr., Big Bill, and Brad Tidwell
Taken at the City Park at Lewistown, Montana
Summer 1963

The church attendance vacillated, numbering up to as many as forty or forty-five. Some members of the church lived in town: the Lathams, Kolars, Demillos and Tidwells. The Muirs drove a pretty good distance from

Harlowton for worship services. Edward and Mammie Billadeau drove in from the hills west of town. Several other members attended sporadically.

The Tidwells later moved to Stanford, Montana, where Bill Tidwell Senior owned and operated a grocery store; but when weather permitted, they continued to drive to Lewistown to church.

Other families came and went. Because missile silos were being built all over Montana, occasionally, a nomadic military family might attend church until transferred to another base. We occasionally had some Mennonite families visit our worship services.

Due to inclement weather, there were times when our family was the only one in attendance; at those times, Hoyt and I would conduct the services, and our family would sing and harmonize the hymns with all four parts.

The Lathams, Kolars, Muirs, Tidwells, and Beasley families were the staple members. These families took turns cleaning and maintaining the church building and grounds located across and on the east side of town.

Our family took our turn cleaning and taking care of the church grounds. During the summer, Dad would load our lawnmower and rakes in the back of the station wagon and all of us kids would go with him to the church building. I'm sure there were times when we begrudged this task, but I have fond memories of the times when we worked together.

There was a large vacant lot next to the building that had to be mowed, and the grass raked and bagged. The kids usually took turns pushing the mower; it was more fun than raking. I think Dad hauled the clippings back to the house to the garden.

When it was our turn, on Saturdays, we went with Dad to clean the church building. We dusted the pews, used a big dust broom and mob for the upstairs and downstairs floors, straightened the song books, and scrubbed the bathrooms. None of us really liked the latter job. One person poured and prepared the communion trays.

There was a really heavy rainstorm one time and the basement of the building was flooded. We had to carry tables and chairs up the stairs and pile them to get them out of the water. It was a big job to mop up, squeeze out water, and carry filled buckets up the outside stairs to empty the water on the lawn. I'm sure doors and windows had to be left open so the basement could dry.

The Beasleys probably did more than their share of the maintaining and cleaning; we filled in when others could not. (Reba)

While sitting around the dinner table one evening, I announced, "There is going to be an addition to the family." It got real quiet. Mom looked at the kids to read their responses; the kids looked at us, and then their faces lit up.

Neva, the youngest, may have wondered about the new one taking over her position as the baby of the family, but all seemed excited and pleased. (There was about eight years difference between Neva and the new one.)

This incident prompted the question, "Where do babies come from?" I'm sure we were somewhat evasive with our answer, "When a man and women are married, God gives them babies." Dinnertime was not the time for an in-depth discussion.

So while living at the old house on Spring Street, Treva Kay was born early in the morning the day before Mother's Day, May 13, 1961, in the Lewistown Hospital. That particular Sunday morning, I left the kids sleeping while I drove Momma to the hospital. I was grinning widely when I returned home, woke them, and announced that they had a new baby sister.

After attending church, we went to see Treva in the hospital.

And yes! Now as we continued the rhyming scheme, it became an even bigger challenge to use the correct name when trying to summon a particular daughter. It was common for Mom or me to become flustered and say, "Sheba, uh, Reba, uh, Carmen, Neva, Treva, whoever you are, come here."

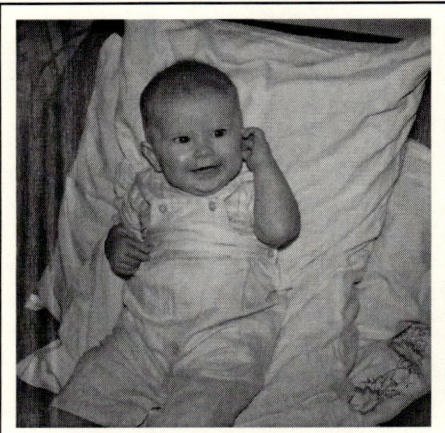

Treva Kay Beasley—Four-and-a-half months old Lewistown, Montana—born May 13, 1961

Floyd and Frankie Lou Reeves lived and worshiped with us in Lewistown for a while, as well as the Jim Coales. They were educators and lived in Lewistown for a couple of years. (Pat Coale was one of Carmen's teachers at the Junior High School.) Treva, the Coale's surrogate child, received a lot of attention from them until they had Lane. I think Treva was confused, but intrigued with the newcomer.

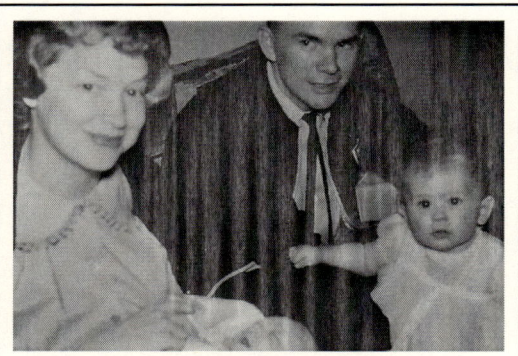

Pat, Jim, and Lane Coale with Treva Beasley about 6 months old— Lewistown, Montana—October 1961

For recreation we sometimes went to movies, but we were pretty protective about what shows and movies the kids could watch. The movies had to be rated G, usually Disney movies. However, I have often wondered sometimes about the themes of violence, hatred, and anger in *Snow White, Cinderella,* and other Disney movies.

> I wonder what my parents would have thought had they known about a cowboy movie that my entire school went to see.
>
> It had Dean Martin in it, and there was one scene when an Indian maiden undressed from behind a bush, then dived into the river. My innocent eyes opened wide at the image. Though the water obscured the diving figure, it was obvious that the maiden was in the nude.
>
> Had my parents known, I would not have been allowed to attend. In fact, they probably would have voiced an objection to the school system. (Carmen)

Our family enjoyed the outdoors. Picnicking, camping and hiking became our favorite recreations. We enjoyed traveling and exploring the mountain ranges in central Montana surrounding Lewistown: the Judith, Little Snowy, Moccasin, and Little Belt Mountains.

Often as we drove along watching the scenery, one of us would start humming or singing and the others would join in. I sang bass, Momma sang soprano, and the kids harmonized. We sang our way down the highway and into the mountains in harmony with each other, nature and God. (Realistically, though we did sing in harmony, there were fights and fussing amongst the siblings, and I did have to raise my voice on occasion and stop the car to discipline them.)

Shortly after moving to Montana, I had purchased a large used tent that would accommodate the entire family in close quarters. However, the tent was the only luxury; we did not use propane gas for heating or cooking, nor did we use fancy camping equipment. We gathered and used dead wood for an open campfire; we used a fold-over contraption for holding the meats and a blackened cast-iron skillet for frying potatoes over the campfire.

When we headed to the mountains to camp, *Ole Bessie,* our station wagon was piled high on top with the tent, cooking materials, food and clothes, and blankets for warmth. We had a couple of sleeping bags, but mostly, we packed several duffel bags with blankets from the house for these trips.

In fact, on one such trip, my old army duffel bag stuffed full of blankets flew off the top of the car, unbeknownst to us. When we got to our destination, we looked for it and thought we must have forgotten it. So like wrapped tamales lying side by side in a pan, we huddled close in the tent for warmth, sharing what blankets we had.

After returning home, we received a call from the gas station on the corner of HI 87 and 191; someone had found the bag along the side of the highway with our name on it and had left it at the station. We were glad to get the blankets back.

A cool dip in Crystal Lake

We made many trips to Crystal Lake in the Little Belt Mountains. The narrow gravel road was cut into, wound around, and clung to the edges of the mountains. As the car ascended, passengers on the right side of the car could look straight down the steep slope of the outside ledge into the valley below; the thought of falling over the edge caused concerned passengers to hang on tight to their seats. Later on returning, the right side passengers had a close view of the rugged rocky mountain walls.

Sometimes we camped at the lake, but more often, we picnicked for the day, floated, and often fell from a log raft into the cold water at the lake. We also hiked up various less traveled trails, or followed the trail that climbed to the top of the mountain next to the lake where we found and collected sea-creature fossils in the stratified rock.

Sometimes, usually on a Sunday afternoon, we took nonfamily, usually the youth from church, with us.

Most of the time, we drove up during the warmer summer months, but occasionally we attempted to reach Crystal Lake when the snow still covered parts of the road. We would drive as far as we could and stop only if the snow prevented us from going further.

> Because I was the oldest and a boy, Dad would allow
> me, an independent spirit and adventurer, to trek over
> the snow and venture ahead on the road, possibly to
> see if the road was clear further up. I never went very
> far ahead, but enjoyed the quiet solitude. (Hoyt)

One early June, the family headed up to Crystal Lake right after school let out for the summer. We got all the way to the lake, apparently the road had been plowed, but once at the lake, there were snow drifts taller than our car.

We pitched the tent, gathered a lot of firewood, and romped around the lake and over the snow drifts in several thicknesses of clothes. It was cold, but the family slept side by side like sardines in a can sharing body heat all warm and cozy.

Dad purchased a toboggan that would accommodate all of the family. In the winter, we would locate a good hillside near Lewistown, load on and race down the hill; then pulling the toboggan back up the hill, load back on again and race back down. We'd keep going up and down until we were too tired or too cold to go anymore. It was a "cold time in the ole town" for us. We had some great times!

Summers, we often traveled to and camped in the Rocky Mountains in northern, western and southern Montana. We explored Glacier National Park, the Flathead Range, the Big Belts, the Teton Mountains, and other ranges reading *hysterical* markers as we traveled.

Beasley family tobogganing
near Lewistown, Montana

We found and explored old gold, sapphire, and silver mines. Of course, we had to warn and watch the kids to make sure they did not go where they might break through rotten timbers and fall into deep mine shafts.

At the sapphire mines, there were small specks of sapphires imbedded in rocks "all over the place around here;" but it would have been difficult to crush the rocks to get them out, and they probably had little value.

On one occasion, we tried panning for gold with the Muirs, but with little success.

On our many camping trips we would sit around the evening campfire and roast marshmallows and eat s'mores.

Later in the evening, we would have a worship service, sing hymns, have communion, and quote from the Bible. A couple of our favorite songs were "How Great Thou Art", "As the Deer Pants for the Water," and "I Come to the Garden Alone." The words spoke of communion with God and nature, and were so meaningful to us.

I come to the garden alone,
While the dew is still on the roses;
And the voice I hear falling on my ear,
The son of God discloses.

He speaks, and the sound of His voice,
Is so sweet the birds hush their singing;
And the melody that he gave to me,
Within my heart is ringing.

I'd stay in the garden with Him,
Though the night around me be falling,
But he bids me go; thru the voice of woe
His voice to me is calling.

And he walks with me, and he talks with me,
And he tells me I am his own;
And the joy we share as we tarry there,
None other has every known.[*]

Many times on the following mornings, other nearby campers would let us know how much they had enjoyed our beautiful and harmonious singing. Some had come closer in the dark, had sat, and joined in.

We went anywhere and everywhere the station wagon would go (likely messed up the suspension, brakes and other parts of the car); we went a few places where only jeeps should go.

I remember Dad's spirit of adventure which I think rubbed off on the rest of us. While living in Lewistown,

---

[*]   Words and music by Austin Miles in 1912; it is now public domain.

Montana, we went on many family picnics and campouts; and it didn't have to be in the summertime!

One winter adventure, we had a picnic, went sledding and tobogganing somewhere in the mountains. We just dug a hole in the snow down to the ground, loaded in gathered firewood for a fire, roasted hot dogs and boiled water for hot chocolate. It was cold outside, but our hearts were warm!

Dad's spirit of adventure came into play when he would find less traveled dirt roads in the mountains. If they weren't too muddy, overgrown or extremely rocky and bumpy, it was likely you would find *Ole Bessie* and the Beasley clan headed up and down one of them. Some of the roads were pretty rugged and I think Mom and some of us were pretty nervous; but we pressed our lips together, held on tight and went along for the ride.

The family would usually pile out of the car when the car could go no further, and we would hike along a marked trail or an animal trail.

One time near Crystal Lake, we arrived at an ice cave near the peak of a mountain!

On another such adventure, we counted one hundred deer. Dad was probably wishing it was hunting season and/or wishing he had his gun.

Of course, Dad loved fried potatoes (still does). We never left the house without an iron skillet, a sharp knife, a sack of potatoes, shortening, salt, and, of course, matches. (Sheba)

The small Lewistown congregation had several "all church" campouts, usually headed up and planned by the Virgil Muir's. Some of the younger campers would load up in the back of a large truck with wooden sidebars, along with the food and camping equipment. Others of the forty or so campers drove in other vehicles. These campouts were great adventures with lots of food, fishing, fellowship and fun.

Sometimes, other church families from other scattered congregations in Montana joined and camped with our church group. The Clint Brazel family joined us once in the Belt Mountains. They had several girls and boys about our children's ages. Their girls interested Hoyt; their boys interested our girls.

The campsite was in a forested area just off a narrow dirt mountain road by a stream that flowed cold and rapid over rounded rocks.

The campfire was the focal point in a small clearing. The various families set up their tents on the perimeter beneath the tall pine trees surrounding the campfire.

However, the teenage girls chose and set up closer to the stream in a spot away from the rest of the tents. They draped a large canvas over several standing trees to form a V-shaped tent. There was a relatively flat cut, wide tree stump in the middle that served as a cosmetics table. They thought they were so clever!

I was not yet a teenager and was disappointed when I did not qualify to sleep with them. I had to sleep in the family tent.

During the day, those who chose went fishing, others hiked. A horse-shoe toss was set up, and various card games were played during more restful times. Some relaxed with a book in lawn chairs. Some crazy campers were brave enough to swim in the chilly rocky rapids.

Meals had been planned and the food was usually prepared over the campfire by Virgil and Leola Muir. It was great to wake to the smell of cooking bacon and pancakes!

In the evenings, we had a worship service around the campfire. Scriptures were quoted, hymns were sung and prayers of thanksgiving rose and dissipated with the smoke through the tops of the pine trees to mingle with the sparkling stars in the heavens.

Well, there were no outhouses; the necessary had to be taken care of in the privacy of the woods. I woke in the middle of the night desperately needing to relieve myself. Stepping into my shoes, I quietly unzipped the door and crept cautiously behind the tent. For modesty's sake, I gingerly stepped over twigs and branches, and moved into the woods. I did not want anyone to see me in a state of exposure.

In the dark foreboding shadows of the surrounding trees and brush, I took care of my business.

It was dark! I quickly headed back the way I had come. I could see only the dark shapes and shadows of the tree trunks and the swaying canopy of branches above outlined by the moonlight and twinkling stars. I could see no shapes that looked like tents.

Suddenly alarmed, I heard a girl's scream off to my right. It must have come from the girl's tent! The sound gave me a direction to go to find my bearings; so I turned right and headed toward where the scream had come from. After going a brief distance, I was suddenly alarmed again! A girl's scream came from my left. Now I was really scared! Desperate to get out of the woods, I turned left. Then a scream came from above. Two yellow eyes shined down on me! The eyes suddenly leapt forward coming directly at me!

I screamed and woke up! (Carmen)

After returning home from one of the all-church fishing-trip campouts, the church had a potluck fish-fry after Sunday morning services in the city park.

Many other Sundays, we had potluck dinners at the church building and/ or at the park. We usually sent someone ahead from church to reserve several picnic tables because many other picnickers would be there to take advantage of the large spring-fed public swimming pool at the park.

Our kids didn't swim there. Instead, they took

Church picnic at the City Park in Lewistown, Montana

advantage of the swings, slides and other play equipment. The grownups visited in the relaxing atmosphere under the shade of the park's trees.

To accommodate those members who traveled distances into town for church, we eventually changed the Sunday evening worship service to an afternoon service, right after the potluck at about 2:00 p.m.; that way the travelers could return home during the light of day at a reasonable hour. However, after eating a good potluck dinner, it was sometimes hard to stay awake and be alert for those afternoon services.

Though we were more likely to participate in outdoor activities, we did watch some television. The kids especially liked to watch *Bonanza** that was broadcast Sundays about 5:00 p.m. Before evening services were changed to the afternoon, we had to leave the house in the middle of the show to get to evening church. The kids didn't like that. Sunday evening church

---

*   *Bonanza* was a popular western television series aired by NBC from 1959-1973. It was one of the first shows filmed and shown in color.

interfered with "Hoss and Little Joe," but when we changed to two in the afternoon, the kids got to see the whole program. In fact, the Kolars had won a color TV (colored TV was relatively new then and only the more well-to-do people had one) in some contest, and sometimes we would drive to their house to see the show in color.

Before the first winter freeze, the spring-fed pool at the city park was drained of all but a few feet of water that would then freeze for ice-skating. With secondhand ice-skates we had purchased, the kids would sometimes walk to the park to ice-skate.

Other times, the kids would carry shovels down into the valley to the pond and spent hours clearing the frozen rough surface. After shoveling for a long time, they were often too cold and tired to ice-skate for very long.

Yellowstone Bible Camp became a very important part of our lives while we lived in Montana. The family usually attended several sessions each summer. We participated in the early summer "cleanup" session right after school was dismissed for the summer to help prepare the cabins, kitchen, and grounds for the upcoming weekly summer sessions. We also went to a family session where I sometimes got free admittance for the family by serving as camp manager and Momma usually taught a children's Bible class. And once old enough, the kids started to attend the appropriate youth sessions. On occasion, I was camp manager at these sessions, so they could get free admittance. Then, in the late summer, the family participated in the "close-up" session to help close down and prepare the camp for the winter.

Sometimes it was just the family that headed south from Lewistown toward Livingston to go to camp, but we often provided rides for several other church children (the Kolar, Tidwell, and Knapp kids).

In fact, I remember one time in particular when the station wagon was loaded beyond capacity with fourteen passengers besides me. Outside, the top was piled high with luggage and sleeping gear covered with a tarp that was tied down to prevent anything from flying off.

Driving south we were riding the rollercoaster hills of HI 191; our stomachs seemed to push down as we reached the top of each hill and then float weightless as I put the car in neutral and coasted to the bottom.

People in other cars would stare at us as they passed, amazed to see a car so top-heavy and with so many heads inside. The kids finally wrote "there are fifteen" on a sheet of paper and held it up to the window at passing cars.

After reaching Livingston, Montana, we continued south on old highway 540 thru Paradise Valley, the last leg of the trip to camp. In unison, the entourage would read the sequentially spaced Burma Shave advertisement signs along the highway: "The monkey took / one look at Jim / and threw the peanuts / back at him. / He needed / Burma-Shave." These signs with varying messages were posted along the edges of highways from 1925 to 1963 in most of the states. During that time "If you / don't know / whose signs / these are / you can't have / driven very far."*

At these camp sessions, we met many members from the scattered churches throughout Montana and many Christians from out of state. We met the Clint Goben family from Livingston; they had a good-sized family like ours—the Clint Brazel family and many others.

These sessions had daily meals, Bible classes, recreational activities, a canteen where soft drinks and candy could be

---

* Retrieved from en.wikipedia.org/wiki/Burma-Shave, Wikipedia, the Free Encyclopedia.

bought, worship services and evening campfire assemblies for entertainment.

As camp manager, I was expected to plan activities. I was in charge of setting up and assigning rotating KP duty teams. At the end of the week, the cooks judged which team cleaned and served the best, and had the best attitude. It was a common practice for the cleaning teams to sing and/or "whistle why they worked." The winning team was honored and usually got to share a specially prepared pie or other treat at the end of the week.

I also planned recreational activities which included horseshoe tournaments, baseball games, hiking and fishing excursions.

The falls up the logging road from camp

I also conducted cabin inspections.

I signed up talent for the Friday evening campfire entertainment; there was usually some singing, joke telling, skits, and storytelling.

Sheba, Reba, Carmen and Neva sometimes sang the song, "I feel pretty. Oh, so pretty."*

I often participated by telling or acting out various stories, including, "It's a Long Way to Tip a Rary." I performed "The Dying Soldier," a one-person skit with a scarf as a prop.

---

* The song "I Feel Pretty" is from the 1957 Broadway musical *West Side Story* based on the book by Arthur Laurents, music by Leonard Bernstein, and lyrics by Steven Sondheim; filmed in 1961.

On one knee with a scarf draped over my head and held under my chin, I would speak using a high-pitched voice pretending to be a female nurse. I would say, "Soldier, soldier, tell me your name."

Taking the scarf off my head, I would then lie on the ground, cover my chest and face with the scarf and cough. "Hack, hack, hack."

Rising, I would become the nurse again and repeated, "Soldier, soldier, please, tell me your name."

Again the scarf was removed, I lay down and played the dying soldier, "Hack, hack, hack."

Up again, as the nurse I pleaded, "Soldier, soldier. Tell me your name."

Once again on the ground, I would cough, "Hack, hack, hack. Why do you want to know my name?"

Finally, the nurse stated, "Soldier, I want to tell your parents."

On the ground, the coughing soldier would reply, "Hack, hack, hack. My parents know my name." ☺

I also told the story "Thnap, Thnap" with hand gestures.

There was a young boy who wasn't very intellectually bright, but he had very quick physical reflexes. Every day he would sit very still on the porch of his house with flies buzzing around him, suddenly flash his hand through the air, catch a fly and say, "Thnap." (I would pretend to catch a fly with my hand.) He never squeezed and crushed the critters. Each time he would open his hand (I would open my hand) and release the fly. It would buzz away.

He "thnapped," caught, and released flies all day long, day after day.

One day in the spring when the honeysuckles were in bloom, he was passing time in the usual way. He heard the buzzing of the flies, but did not distinguish the bees that were also buzzing around him. He sat still, flashed his hand, said, "Thnap" (I would pretend to catch with my hand) and caught a bee.

Almost immediately, he opened his hand and said (I would quickly open my hand.), "Unthnap, unthnap, unthnap." ☺

Reese Bryant, a preacher from Searcy, Arkansas, was a speaker at one of the Yellowstone Bible Camp sessions. That week, a stomach virus was going around, and Reese Bryant and his son-in-law, Phil Burrows, both came down sick. Since I was the manager, to emphasize the need for cleanliness, I put up a sign by the mess hall, "Warsh your hands," and watched to make sure each camper did just that.

At that camp session, the various boys' and girls' cabins competed against each other for the award for the cleanest cabin. An inspection was made each day, and each day's winner was announced; then at the end of the week, an award was given to the cabin deemed the cleanest all week.

For the inspections, Faye Brazel made an exaggerated extra large white glove for me to use. I ran that glove over log walls, above the

The campfire at Yellowstone Bible Camp with the Honeymoon Cabin and Mill Creek in the background

doorframes, everywhere. The competition became very intense. Campers really worked hard to dust and sweep, straighten bed coverings, hang clothes evenly in the closets, place flowers in vases, and keep shelves with luggage and cosmetics neat and orderly.

All the cabins' occupants went overboard; the girls lined the paths to their cabins with rocks; the boys planted flowers at the Mule Barn. It became very difficult to make a judgment as to which cabin was the cleanest and most attractive.

Of course, I don't remember now who won.

The churches of Christ were few and far apart in Montana, so there was often a sharing and exchanging of preachers. At one time, I went to Libby, Montana, to conduct a Gospel meeting.

Phil Burrows, the preacher from Libby, later conducted a winter Gospel meeting for us in Lewistown. Now, Phil was six-foot ten-inches tall, and when he stayed at our house, Momma sewed sheets together to cover him and pushed the sofa to the end of a bed to accommodate him.

We took him tobogganing with our family up into the mountains, dug a hole in the snow, piled in wood for a campfire, roasted hot dogs and made hot chocolate.

Phil went sliding down the hill sitting all crunched up on a small sled, holding up his cup of hot chocolate.

Hoyt and I also took Phil deer hunting.

Phil's father-in-law, Reese Bryant, the preacher from the College Church of Christ in Searcy, Arkansas, later came to Lewistown to conduct a Gospel meeting. He had been told by his counselor/psychiatrist to participate in sports and exercise activities for relief from pressure and stress; so Reese, Hoyt and I went golfing at the Lewistown golf course.

Besides Bible camp, there were opportunities to meet with other Christians for spiritual encouragement and instruction. At least once a year, one of the larger congregations (Bozeman, Helena, Great Falls, or Anaconda) in Montana would host a youth rally. I would take a car load of youth from Lewistown to these gatherings. We met with various Christian families and youth throughout the state.

After settling into the old house for almost two years, the landlady decided to increase the rent, but we did not want to pay more or sign on for another year. We had been looking into building a house that would accommodate our family using a GI loan. This loan was in my name, but with the idea that the house would belong to the church.

We needed temporary housing until the prefab house we ordered was ready for assembly. We ended up renting a duplex on the north side of town.

Shortly after moving into the duplex, I overheard the mother from the next door duplex state, "Oh! Those beasties are driving me crazy."

I became very concerned that the Beasleys should step carefully and make an extra special effort to show our best behaviors. I instructed the kids accordingly.

I heard and learned later when she repeated "Oh! Those beasties are driving me crazy" that she was referring to her own children. I was relieved, but I still wanted our children to behave.

This duplex had a kitchen, living room, bathroom and one-bedroom for Pauline and me. Treva was just an infant, so she slept in our room. In the basement, Hoyt got the one walled-in bedroom, and the four older girls arranged their beds and dressers in the larger open basement area. They were all the time rearranging beds and drawers and hanging drapes (usually old bedspreads) to divide the area into smaller rooms.

A ping-pong table was set up on one end in the basement area and the kids had competitive tournaments.

This old duplex had a coal-burning furnace, so we had to order and have coal delivered during the winter, and we had to shovel the coal into the furnace and be careful to keep the black dust off our clothes.

The new house was being constructed on Carroll Trail on the south side of town near the Lewis and Clark Elementary

School; so we enrolled Reba, Carmen and Neva there. Sheba was in junior high and Hoyt was in high school.

Though Lewistown wasn't a huge community, the kids had to walk to school from the north side to the south side of town, a pretty good distance. On really cold and snowy weather days, I would drive them.

While sides of our ordered house were being assembled at the manufacturers, the male members of the church worked together to prepare the foundation. Virgil Muir, an experienced contractor, was in charge of directing and instructing the men as the foundation was laid. Karl Kolar was also involved in the construction process. Hoyt, then about fourteen, helped.

It took a little longer than we thought, but the prefab sides of the house were finally ready in early spring of '62. As the younger girls arrived at Lewis and Clark Elementary one morning, they could see only the foundation on the hillside; but when they headed home after school, they were surprised to see a whole house with all four outside walls and a roof setting on the foundation. Cranes had lifted intact walls and roof structures from the bed of a large trailer, set them on the foundation; and the walls and roof were secured.

The inside of the house was still incomplete, so all Beasley members old enough to help were involved in the work to finish the inside. We put up insulation, sheetrock, plastered, sanded and painted.

The men from church installed the plumbing, electricity, doors, windows, tile floors, cabinets, sinks, toilet and bathtub.

The summer of 1962, the house was ready to move into. We now had a house with enough bedrooms and space to accommodate our numbers. Upstairs there were four bedrooms, one bath, kitchen, numerous closets, and a living room; and there was a full basement with a utility room and extra space yet to be divided into rooms.

Sheba and Reba shared a bedroom, Carmen and Neva shared a bedroom, Hoyt had a bedroom, and Pauline and I had a bedroom. Treva slept in our room for a while.

Shortly after moving into the new house, while jumping and flipping on the bed, I landed a solid hit with the heel of my foot on the wall, making a perfectly round small hole in the wall. We had been told not to use the bed as a trampoline, so I moved the furniture around, and placed a chest in front of the hole to cover it up. I never jumped on the bed again.

It was years later when we packed up to move that my parents discovered the hole. I heard them say, "How did that happen?"

I quietly and guiltily slipped down the hall and never said a word. I think they had their suspicions but they never asked me about it.

In the winter when the furnace was on, I would crawl out of bed and lay on the floor with a pillow and blanket by the air vent. The humming of the furnace and blowing warm air would lull me to sleep. I was warm and cozy, but probably kept the heat from reaching my roommate. (Carmen)

Eventually, a bedroom, and a half bath with a shower, sink and toilet were built in the basement for Hoyt. Treva then had a nursery room upstairs.

To save money on landscaping, we drove into the forest, dug up small pines, and brought them back to plant around the house. There's probably a law forbidding that now. At Momma's request, however, I purchased some lilacs.

The church was not self-supporting and had sponsoring congregations in New Mexico, so the family drove south several times to visit and report to these congregations.

Money was tight for us; we had to supplement. I drove a school bus for $90 a month.

The kids had to wear hand-me-downs, and we sometimes received boxes of used clothing. The girls would excitedly go through them hoping something in the box would fit them. Sometimes, there were arguments over who got what. There were disappointed exclamations, "Oh. It doesn't fit me!" and/or happy announcements, "Yes! It fits!"

We put in a large vegetable garden in the backyard, so we had fresh vegetables. Sometimes, if the siblings were arguing, which happened frequently, they were sent out into the garden to hoe or pick green beans or other vegetables.

> Carmen and I had a brilliant idea. We were going to build a dam in the backyard at the bottom edge of our yard where the garden was, and then run water from the hose to create an ice-skating rink. Then, we wouldn't have to haul shovels clear down to the pond and spend our time and energy clearing paths on the frozen lake.
>
> We were so proud of our ingenuity.
>
> When the gardening season was over, we shoveled, sweated, and piled the dirt at the lower end of the garden to form a dam; then when we heard there was to be a freeze, we ran the water. It looked like it was going to work; but when we checked the next day, the water had broken through the dam and run downhill into the neighbor's backyard. We were disappointed!
>
> I've always believed the scripture that states, "Faith can move a mountain." The dirt we moved for this project, and the dirt we have moved during our lifetimes doing yard and garden work has to have been a mountain's worth! (Neva)

We sometimes were given or able to pick cherries and other seasonal fruits, so Mom did a lot of canning and freezing. We made a couple of trips to visit Pauline's folks in Oklahoma and brought back apples, peaches, pears and apricots for canning and freezing.

Mom had a washing machine but no dryer. I'm sure money was an issue, but I would have gotten one for her if she had requested it. She said she preferred to hang the clothes outside so they would smell fresh. I bought and put a turnaround clothes line in the yard. She even hung clothes outside in the winter, or, otherwise, hung and draped them on lines in the basement.

> I would hear Momma singing as she worked in the garden or hung clothes on the outside line. I would often go out to help her and hand her the clothespins as she draped and clipped the clothes on the line.
>
> One time when I went out, she was crying. "What's wrong, Mom?"
>
> "Oh, I'm just feeling sorry for myself," she replied.
>
> I felt bad!
>
> Looking back, I think she was sometimes overwhelmed with taking care of all of us; and as the older girls became teenagers, their hormones made them pretty defiant and difficult to deal with. Or, perhaps, she was worried about money. Maybe she was just tired; she worked so hard. (Neva)

We didn't have a lot of money to spend on Christmas gifts. We had to be practical; so the kids always received socks, sturdy shoes, underwear, and maybe a few inexpensive, frivolous items. Momma usually made handmade gifts.

The first Christmas after moving into the house on Carroll Trail, we gave the kids a large broom and dust pan as a gift. Don't think they were impressed.

> Mom made doll clothes for us, and I especially remember the red and white dress she crocheted for

my twelve-inch adult doll. I think she must have added on more stitches than the directions called for, because when I tried to lay it flat, the skirt billowed with waves there was so much fullness. It must have taken her forever to make it. This dress was see-through, so it needed an undergarment.

I still have the doll and dress; they're very special to me. The dolls hair is a mess, but I'll never get rid of the doll or the dress. (Carmen)

One Christmas, Pauline and I purchased a whole bolt of light green corduroy fabric (probably on sale) for the girls. By strategically placing the pattern pieces on the uncut roll, the fabric went further, there was less waste, and more clothing items could be made.

By then the girls knew how to use Momma's Singer sewing machine or the old treadle sewing machine and could make their own clothes.

I guess it might have looked kind of funny for all the girls to have clothing made from the same fabric, but it didn't seem to bother them. In fact, they seemed excited to be able to make some new clothes. Each used different patterns making their clothes look different.

A neighbor two houses away on the Carroll Trail cul-de-sac, Mrs. Thayer (who had a girl about Neva's age, and a boy about Carmen's age), must have been aware of our financial situation. Mrs. Thayer was Carmen's sixth-grade teacher at Lewis and Clark Elementary and later Carmen's physical education teacher in junior high. When school let out for Christmas breaks, she would give us the tree that had been in her classroom. (The Thayer's had a house in town but spent their Christmases on their ranch somewhere up in the mountains.)

We would not have bought a tree. We used saved ornaments and sometimes made new ones to decorate.

Our family of eight drank a lot of milk. We purchased milk from Mr. Bowman, who had a dairy farm on the east side of town close to the church building. Mr. Bowman had to meet certain standards in producing and bottling his milk, and the State inspected his dairy barn regularly. Occasionally the cows would eat certain weeds that made the milk taste bitter, but most of the time it was real good milk.

We would wash gallon jars and reuse them on return trips. We bought up to as many as eight gallons of whole milk per visit. This sounds like a lot, but with six kids, we went through it fast. (We drank tea sometimes, but did not purchase soda.)

Now, this was certified raw milk. It was not homogenized, so there was always some cream that would settle at the top. Sometimes, it seemed there was more cream than milk. We would skim the cream off the top into other containers, and the kids received a scientific lesson on how to shake the cream to make butter. I liked to drink the buttermilk that was left after removing the clumps of butter, but the kids would not drink it.

Mom often used buttermilk or sour milk or cream to make pancakes, chocolate cake, and other baked goods. Very seldom did any milk or cream go to waste—waist maybe, but not waste. ☺

I went hunting for deer, antelope, elk, and even bear with some of the men from church, most frequently with David Latham and/or Virgil Muir.

In the winter deepfreeze, it was a common sight to see a deer carcass hanging high from the kids' swing set in the backyard, high enough so stray dogs and other critters could not reach it.

I obtained a book of instruction on how to butcher and saved money by doing some of my own butchering, wrapping and freezing. Our freezer was usually full in the winter but getting empty in the summer.

If I found a sale on ground beef, chicken, or other meats, I would purchase some; but otherwise, we ate mostly game meat.

Occasionally, I found a sale on frozen nine-inch potpies and would buy a bunch and freeze them. The family really liked them, and it saved Pauline the trouble of having to plan and prepare a meal. All she had to do was pop them into the oven. When the children were small, we could give each half of a pie, but as they got older, they wanted a whole pie.

Speaking of pies. Before Treva was born, when there were only seven in the family, it was difficult to cut a dessert pie into seven equal pieces, so we cut our pies into eight pieces. I thought as Dad I should get the extra piece and often claimed it. However, there were many not-so-pretty disputes among the siblings about who should get the extra piece.

To make a point and show them how selfish and unreasonable they were being, I took an aluminum pie pan, measured and divided the circumference of 360 degrees by seven, and then measured and marked 51.4 degrees around the edge of the empty aluminum pie pan. Then we could place a cooked pie into the premeasured pan and use the markings to cut seven equal pieces.

They still argued! It was hard to find and cut from the middle of the pie, so the pieces were unequal. They didn't get the point.

I resumed eating the extra piece until Treva was old enough and made eight.

Anyhow, back to hunting, several of the children would come with the men on hunts. Hoyt went quite often. Reba also liked to go hunting with us. The other girls preferred to remain inside the warm house, so they didn't go very often. The children learned to walk behind the men carrying the guns.

We often came home empty handed.

The Shame of It All by Carmen Lewis

Dad walked ahead,
The children cautiously behind.

The recent warmth had wetted the snow
That refroze in the night,
And feet crunched through white crust.

Our roving eyes searched for victims,
But fell silent
On the only prey seen that day.
Our skin chilled beneath our buttoned coats
As we stood before the elk buck with eight points.

This magnificent creature stared blankly;
One leg had caught between two barbed wires;
It had snared while hurtling,
Then twisted, entangled and snapped.
Melting snows revealed cold eyes and bitten tongue.

We stood momentarily silent.
Shaking his head Dad said,
"The shame of it all."
With gun shouldered,
Dad guided us back to the car.

We were game to try for anything. On a few occasions after Sunday morning church, all the kids would go rabbit hunting with the men. The adults shot, and the kids dug into the snow drift for the rabbit carcasses.

The rabbits were cooked soon after returning home, didn't have much meat, and tasted a lot like chicken. They were hare that day but gone the next. ☺

Several of us would go rabbit hunting with the men in the winter. We were instructed to always follow behind the men.

The rabbits scurried so fast across the snowy white fields and into their burrows, I don't know how the men could get off shots fast enough to shoot any.

After they shot, we were allowed to go ahead of them and dig through the snow drifts to find the rabbits; the drops of red blood on the white snow gave a pretty good clue as to where to find them.

The rabbits were gutted right then and there. I was grossed out and wrinkled my nose as the slit was made on the underbelly from the neck to the tail, the entrails were removed and the fur was pulled off. But I was fascinated when I scooped up a handful of snow with the tiny, pinkish, still pulsing heart in my gloved hands. It amazed me that the isolated heart could still be beating!

I felt pity for the poor rabbit.

Though Dad sometimes took us out into the woods and let each kid take some target practice with a .22 rifle, I could never seem to get the hang of how to aim. I tried to look through both eyes. I learned later that's not how you're supposed to do it.

I was not too keen on traipsing around in the cold, cold woods, and I always saw each deer as a Bambi; so I seldom went hunting. (Carmen)

Reba was the only girl who consistently accompanied the men on hunts.

Some of my fondest and most vivid memories are from our life in Montana.

Venison was a main staple on our dinner table bagged by Dad and maybe even Hoyt. On occasion we were given some elk and bear meat.

I had the opportunity to go with Dad on many occasions after obtaining my hunting license. I remember tracking over quite a few mountains with Dad and others, which often included Virgil Muir and David Latham.

Dad drove a school bus to help supplement his income. His route took him past our house on Carroll Trail quite a ways up into the foothills and mountains west of Lewistown. Sometimes I would ride with him on the bus, or Mom would drive me up to the end of his route, and then Dad and I would hunt until dark.

One particular afternoon, we were driving through a valley when we sighted two bucks grazing on the side of the hill. A farmhouse was ahead, so we drove up to it and asked for permission to go back to "bag the big one."

Dad and I hiked back what seemed like miles, but probably really wasn't, to where the deer had been sighted. They were still there.

Apparently, Dad had bagged his limit, so I was the lucky one to get to shoot. Dad immediately looked for a limb to balance and steady my aim. No limb was in sight, so Dad got down on all fours and whispered for me to steady the rifle on his back.

Out of breath and riding high on adrenaline and anticipation of shooting my first deer, a buck no less, I followed his directions. I shot and missed both deer. Of course, the shot scared both deer back into the timber. I was so disappointed!

We talked about it later. Dad stated that we should have rested first so I could catch my breath and steady my aim. Maybe, just maybe, the outcome might have been different. (Reba)

I remember an incident when Reba went hunting with David Latham and me. Returning back to town in David's pickup, we slipped on ice and slid into the ditch by the side of the road. There we were in a pretty good slant, gravity pulling us down against the passenger side door, the piled-up body weight making it difficult for us to move and climb out of the driver's door. We sat there all squashed-up discussing what to do.

On the bottom of the pileup with the weight of two other bodies squishing me, I stated, "*Exsqueeze* me, but I would like to get out of here."

Finally David said, "Hold on, guys. Let me try to pull myself up, then I can help you out."

After much squirming and twisting around, David was able to get up, step on us—squashing me into the passenger's door—get the driver's door open, and pull himself up and out of the car.

"Okay! Reba, give me your hand, and I'll pull you up," David instructed.

Well, she squirmed, twisted, and stepped on me; then, I got her feet into my hands and pushed her up so she could get out.

David then said, "Gerald, give me your hands so I can pull you up." They both then helped me out of the car.

Once out, we walked some distance before we found a residence where we made a call for someone to come get us.

As we walked, I asked David, "Do you have tow insurance?"

"Well, yes. Once we get into town, I'll call the insurance company."

Well, we finally got home. Reba had remained quietly listening during all this time, trusting in us to take care of her. After we got home, she very innocently asked, "Did someone hurt their toe?" ☺

We didn't get any bounty that trip, just bumps and bruises, and a laugh.

Another time, I went hunting for antelope by myself, which I probably shouldn't have done. I didn't plan very well because I ran out of gas in the middle of the plains east of town. Fortunately, I was able to walk to a ranch that I remembered passing some distance away. The rancher greeted me warmly, and while he helped by giving me a ride back to my car and giving me some gas, we were able to visit a bit.

The rancher was very pleased to tell me that he listened to my radio sermon that was broadcast from Lewistown. I was pleased to know that my weekly trip to the radio station to record a religious message was touching peoples' lives. It's a small world!

While living on Carroll Trail, the kids liked to ride their bikes around the neighborhood. Hoyt had a three-speed hand-brake bike that he sometimes shared with the girls, and the girls had a one-speed foot-brake bike that they had to share, so only two could bike ride at a time.

> I think, unbeknownst to Mom and Dad, Neva and I would sometimes ride bikes out west of town along the school bus route that Dad drove.
>
> Neva often expressed concern that we had been out too long, had gone too far and should head back. After all, if Dad gave his "whistle" and we did not hear it, and if we didn't return home quickly, we could get in real trouble.
>
> Well, I was tenacious and not one to give up or quit. I always wanted to keep going, so I would say, "It's okay. We can still go farther." We went pretty far out at times but never as far as I wanted to go.
>
> Don't know if Mom and Dad ever knew we took that route out into the foothills.

Another time, Neva and I were riding in the neighborhood. We coasted down a hill with the wind blowing through our hair having a wonderful time until—

Flesh and Stones by Carmen Lewis

Bicycles with thin tires do not function safely on dirt roads.
I know because my sister and I
Were speeding toward an intersection
Where cars were zipping perpendicular to our zooming.
The wheels of the three-speed bike wobbled
When hand-brakes were applied.

Metal bikes are more durable
Than human flesh.
I know because as I squeezed the brakes again
I found myself sliding on gravel
And the bike
Riding atop me.

My broken and scrapped skin
Bled from the mess made
Of my face.
Red trickled down as we knocked at the house
Where the stranger stood in shock,
Then rushed to help me.

Summoned by a phone call
Mom then rushed me to the emergency room
Where a nurse cleaned
And bandaged my wounds.
Neighborhood friends later filed by the bed
Where I lay bloodied.

Fingering my forehead I felt
A bump beneath healed flesh.
I know the ease with which the doctor
Made a slight incision to extricate tiny stones;
But I wonder how the lady fared.
Did she as easily remove the bloodstains from her towel?

Momma told me,
"I always knew you had rocks in your head."

We had some really good times in Montana, but "he causes his sun to rise on the evil and the good, and sends rain on the righteous and the unrighteous" (Matthew 5:45).

Hoyt developed a kidney infection. Don't know for sure, but the infection may have developed from a bad cold and sore throat that Hoyt acquired while helping with the construction of the house in the cold weather. He was pretty sick and had to be transferred to the hospital in Great Falls, Montana. Pauline went with him initially, and I hitchhiked to Great Falls immediately when told of his condition.

Hoyt was eventually able to come home but had to remain bedridden for quite a while. He continued to be in and out of school, and in and out of the Lewistown hospital.

We had no health insurance, but were able to take care of the bills using the money we had saved from the sale of our house in McPherson.

Hoyt missed a lot of school, but kept up with his studies at home. He was smart and actually read algebra and trigonometry books for fun. He loved to learn!

The high school teacher who taught German took the time to come to the house to work with him. She was very kind.

During this illness, Hoyt had a difficult time not only physically but emotionally. He was angry! As a young teenager, he couldn't understand why God would allow this to happen to him.

That time was hard for the family too!

While he was bedridden, Treva, a toddler, would sit by him as he read his textbooks aloud. She retained a lot of what she heard. Hoyt actually taught her to count, write numbers, and some math; and he taught her the alphabet and how to read. Because of this, Treva had a head start by the time she started to school. (Years later when we lived in Wichita, Kansas, she attended a school for advanced students.)

Hoyt's condition eventually developed into ulcerative colitis, which was to cause him physical problems for the rest of his life.

Mom and I wished we had been aware sooner of how sick he was. Maybe we could have prevented the infection, but the past couldn't be changed. We had to leave it was in God's hands.

One advantage for Hoyt, because of his health, he was not drafted to serve in the Vietnam War.

All of our kids were musically talented. Hoyt and various girls played the clarinet in school bands using my old clarinet. It got a lot of use. I could help them with the fingering of keys and I did repairs on the instrument. Carmen took piano lessons for about nine months while we lived at the Spring Street address until the landlady removed her piano and gave it to the Christian Church. At one time or other, all of them participated in school choruses and ensembles.

And some of them participated in school plays and musicals.

> While in Junior High I had an acting and singing part in a musical about Robert Burns, the famous Scottish poet and lyricist. I played a flirtatious lassie and sang a modern, version of "Coming Through the Rye: "Every lassie has her laddie . . . Ney they say have I . . . Yet all the lads they smile at me when coming through the rye . . .

> Mom made my costume, a red plaid cotton kilt-skirt,
> Scottish-looking cap and a shoulder sash. She made
> the skirt longer than I thought it should be; I wore the
> skirt (but not the cap and sash) some to school after
> the play, but I rolled it up at the waist band. She usually
> noticed and told me, "Pull your skirt down." Couldn't
> pull anything over on her. (Carmen)

All over America the Red Scare, the potential of the Russians coming over and bombing America, caused great concern. Missile silos were constructed and scattered all over Montana, so some military families attended church until transferred. Virgil Muir, a member of the church, worked as a contractor for the military during this time.

At one of the schools in Lewistown, quite an audience gathered to discuss the matter of bomb shelters and the right kinds of food to store in them. Many in the general population put in bomb shelters. We did not.

Radioactive fallout was discussed, and the population was advised not to eat the snow.

Schools planned and practiced air raid drills; students were instructed to get under their desks and put their hands over their heads. Like that would help.

I had dreams of hearing airplanes overhead and concluding that the Russians had come. I even dreamed that I was drafted again. I thought, "How very unfair to draft a man with six kids."

Several college students from Lubbock Christian College came to do mission work in Lewistown; Jerris Bullard and I worked together quite a bit. That summer, the two of us went ahead to make preparation for a camp session at Yellowstone Bible Camp. While there we went upstream behind the Mule Barn, caught a number of trout, cooked and ate them. We enjoyed each other's company.

He dated Sheba once or twice while in Lewistown. She had turned sixteen, so she was allowed to date. I trusted Jerris to treat Sheba honorably, but they never had a serious relationship. (Years later, Jerris and his wife became part of a mission team from the east coast that went to India.)

Don Armstrong was another student who came to Lewistown. While there, he worked on Spring Creek, which flowed through town, at a dairy to support himself. His parents were divorced, and he was upset. I spent a lot of time talking to him. He was a confused and messed-up young man. (Years later in the state of New York, he became enamored with the writings of a female philosopher, Ayn Rand.)*

Wally (Wallace) Bradberry, a college student, also did some summer mission work in Montana. He later moved to and became a preacher in Billings, Montana.

There were also a couple of college girls and a male student from India, all from Abilene Christian College, who were involved in the mission fields in Montana; but I don't remember their names.

Our family really enjoyed all the acquaintances and experiences while living, working and playing in Montana; we had many pleasant memories; but in 1965, I accepted a preaching job in Winfield, Kansas.

The decision to move was made for several reasons. Pauline and I lived quite far from our parents who were getting older and not in great health. My father in Sand Springs, Oklahoma, was quite ill. We needed to be nearer to all of them. Mom and I were

---

* Ayn Rand was writer and philosopher from Russia who had come to America in 1926. She believed in *objectivism*, the philosophy that an individual should be preeminent over the state and collective action and that enlightened selfishness and capitalism are the purest forms of individual freedom.

also concerned about financial issues. Hoyt had been attending York College in York, Nebraska, starting the fall of 1964; and the girls, starting with Sheba, would soon be heading to York College. How were we going to provide funding for college tuition and other related expenses? And with three teenage girls still living at home, we thought a church with more teenagers would be socially beneficial. They were close to dating age, and there were few Christian young males in Lewistown.

We made the announcement to the kids, "Guys, I have accepted a preaching job in Kansas, so we will be moving this summer, and I don't see how we can afford to attend camp this summer."

They did not take the announcement very well.

They liked living in Montana and did not want to miss attending Yellowstone Bible Camp. Mom and I felt bad, but I think we made the right decision to move.

The Lewistown radio station had a daily money-winning Bingo game. From Monday thru Friday, only so many letter/numbers were called, and each day there was no winner, $10 was added to the "pot." If after ten days no one had won and the pot was at $100, then letter/numbers were called until there was a winner.

I thought, "If I can win the $100 playing Bingo, then we'll have the money to go to camp." (I also thought, "I'll have enough to buy me some new clothes.")

So for two weeks I prayed fervently that nobody would win, and they didn't! I knew God was listening and answering my prayers. I also prayed that I would win the $100.

Well, the day arrived and the big game started. However, I began to worry as the game progressed. Many letter/numbers had been called, but few were on my card. I prayed again silently. I knew that God had and would continue to answer my prayers.

However, when a caller phoned into the station to say, "I have a Bingo," I just knew it had to be mistake, but it wasn't. The caller won.

I was so devastated! I had had faith that would move a mountain. I had believed that God had heard my request and would give me what I had asked for. I was so upset! I didn't speak to God again for weeks.

Ironically, the family did get to go to camp. Dad probably volunteered to be camp manager so we could go for free.

It was a hard lesson, but it took a while in my immaturity to realize that God did answer my prayer, just not the way I expected him to. (Carmen)

With reluctance, we packed up again and moved. As a parent, it was hard to watch the kids looking out the back window of the moving van and the car as we drove east out of Lewistown. It was obvious they would miss many things about Montana.

Chapter Sixty-Nine

He loads the clouds with moisture;
he scatters his lightning through them.
At his direction they swirl around over the face of the
earth to do whatever he commands them.
—Job 37:11 and 12

Ministry in Winfield, Kansas

We moved to Winfield, Kansas, in the summer of 1965. At that time, Winfield had been identified nationally as one of the safest, best communities in America for raising kids. It was a nice town.

However, the family really missed communing with the pine-scented mountains with their abundant wildlife, cold running rivers and streams, and the big blue sky of Montana. It was hard not to make comparisons between Montana and Kansas. The Kansas landscape was relatively flat with some low rolling hills, wheat fields, manure-smelling farms and warm water lakes; but it was so different from what we had been used to.

It wasn't the wisest thing I ever did, but after moving to Kansas, all I did was talk about Montana and how great it was. So much so, that one of the teenage girls from church, got pretty upset and rebuked me rather strongly. "If you like it so much, why don't you just go back?"

> Humbled, I had to learn to hold my tongue and
> appreciate the virtues of all God's creation. (Carmen)

At the time of the move, Sheba was a senior, Reba a junior, and Carmen a sophomore in high school. Neva was in junior high. Treva was four years old and not in school yet. Hoyt was attending York College.

The church had a couple hundred members with several elders. Of course, I preached and had other ministerial duties.

There were thirty-plus high school students who attended church, but the church didn't have a youth minister; so we worked with the Kings, Moodys, and other families to plan activities for the youth group.

There were several young men about the ages of our girls, and some interest was shown, but no romantic entanglements occurred. Actually, Momma and I weren't really ready for them. The girls did date some while in Winfield but nothing serious.

Daryl and Beverly Moody, Pat and Bernice King, and the Beasleys often planned and had a number of fun youth activities in our homes and/or devotionals at the church building. The elders were approached about using the newly build, attached educational building for youth gatherings; but there were too many members who felt it was inappropriate to use the church building for entertainment purposes.

Mrs. Moody, who was active in Girl Scouts, often had the girls over for overnight sleepovers. I never understood why they called them sleepovers when nobody slept, but the girls enjoyed the overnighters.

One time, Pauline and I allowed a bunch of girls to sleep in a tent in our backyard. I had to shoo the church boys away. Their showing up made me very unhappy as I endeavored to protect the virtue of our female charges.

The church planned some area wide youth activities, and we made sure our church youth had the opportunity to attend. About once a month, there was an evening reserved at the roller-skating rink.

> Roller-skating was my all-time favorite, especially when the girls got to ask the boys to skate.
> Church members from as far as Wichita would come to Winfield. (Neva)

There were various Bible camps available in Kansas, but our girls didn't seem interested in attending them. Part of it was because they started working to earn money, but I suspect, in their minds they compared them to Yellowstone Bible Camp and found them wanting. Though we encouraged them to go, they didn't attend.

Pauline continued to attend the weekly ladies Bible class and prepare for and teach children's Bible classes. Sometimes our girls helped her. In fact, I was having difficulty finding enough teachers for Vacation Bible School, so several of our girls agreed to teach a class.

> I helped Mom in a Wednesday evening children's Bible class for a while. She usually did the lesson, but I remember singing a song as I galloped around the room with the children. I got weary of it, but the little ones wanted to do it over and over again.
> "I like to share my pony, come and take a ride.
> Galloping, galloping, galloping, galloping.
> Whoo-o-o! Thank you for the ride!"
> One summer, I taught a Bible class during Vacation Bible School. I don't think I had a helper. I guess I did okay, but was relieved when the week was over. It had

been a lot of work and showed me how little I knew about dealing with young children. (Carmen)

We were often invited over for meals with members of the church. Sometimes the older girls went with us; but sometimes it was just Pauline, Neva, Treva and me.

As we got to know the members and their needs, we tried to be impartial and "respecters of persons."

Momma and Dad, but especially Mom, had always been very sympathetic toward any underdog or less likeable person.

Lucy was an unusual older single woman who would approach others after church with a toothy smile, showing her misshapen and discolored teeth.

Mom and Dad were always very kind to her, but she just didn't know when enough was enough. She would stand right in front of their faces and visit even when they were trying to greet others; and after we got into the car and tried to leave, she would walk along beside our moving car, bending at the waist looking in the window as she continued to talk.

I felt sorry for her. She must have been lonely, but it seemed that after every church service, she sought me out. I tried to be kind, but got rather exasperated after multiple "in your face" experiences.

Mom and Dad even invited her home for Sunday lunch once. That was an enduring experience!

Mom and Dad were great examples of compassion as we later discussed her situation.

Tex Stewart, an older church member, would frequently drop by to visit at our house. Mom always welcomed him in. He loved to talk and sometimes brought goodies. He wore a very large cowboy hat and had lots of stories under his belt.

One year he took me to the county fair. I still have the giant toothbrush I won at a booth! (Neva)

After the worship service, I always went to the front entrance to the church building to greet and shake hands with the members as they were exiting. I also took great pleasure in greeting my own children as they exited.

Daddy didn't always say much, but he had his own way of reaching out to us.

I would always get in line so I could shake Daddy's pinky with my pinky. He would smile quietly as we crossed pinkies. I always thought that was cool!

I thought I was the only child Dad did this with, but apparently, as I learned later, he did it with all of us. And I thought I was the only special one! (Treva)

After Sunday evening services, we were usually among the last to leave, probably to lock up the building.

One evening we came out of the building and headed to where our car was parked, only to find the car was gone.

Dad said, "Oh, me!"

I'm sure he was very disturbed, but he tried to make light of it as he went back into the building and called the police to report the situation. They arrived to investigate.

The car next to ours was a relatively new Cadillac with the keys left in the ignition, and we were driving a blue station wagon. There was much discussion as to why our car was stolen but not the nicer car parked next to us.

It was surmised that some college students had
more than likely taken ours so they wouldn't have to
walk the several miles back to the campus.

Sure enough, the car was found the next day and
returned to us. (Treva)

The Winfield church had a small preacher's house on the
east side of town. It was pretty snug for our family. Sheba and
Reba shared a room, Carmen and Neva shared another, and
Treva slept in the room with Pauline and me.

The house we lived in was across the street from
the Christian Church building. I spent some time on
their grounds walking and riding my bike.

One evening when the folks were gone, as I was
walking, I saw a cat and said, "Here, kitty, kitty." As it came
running toward me, I noticed a white strip down its back.

I *hightailed* it home and observed it through the
window walking on our porch and around the house.
Instinct told me to stay inside. (Neva)

There was only one bathroom in the house, so there were
problems, especially mornings, taking turns as everybody got
ready for the day. Since I was usually the first in the bathroom,
a female would often knock on the bathroom door while I was
shaving. I would mutter, "Brother!" (I should have said "sister")
as I stood in the hallway with shaving cream all over my face
holding my razor because someone had to use the restroom.

There were times when he was angry because the
females took too long getting ready for church.

Sheba was always very slow and often pushed the
limit. One Sunday morning, she was taking too long to
get dressed, so she was left at the house.

I know Daddy was perturbed, but I appreciated him
sticking to his guns. However, I was mortified that she
was going to miss church, and she wasn't even sick!

I don't think that happened again. (Treva)

Of course, Momma put in a garden on the north side of the
house, so there were always lots of vegetables for meals.

Because it was cooler than in the house, the front
porch became a gathering place for snapping beans,
shelling peas and shucking corn. Everyone that was
available was expected to contribute and help.

I hated to shell peas but loved to eat the fresh peas
out of the pods. And I wasn't much help, but I did help
some with the canning process.

We also churned homemade ice cream on the
front porch; the anticipation was great as we took turns
cranking the handle until the sweet cream was frozen
"just right." (Treva)

Once the older girls became involved in school activities
and/or work, sometimes Treva and Neva were the only ones
home in the evenings for supper.

Momma always said, "If you're not at the table when dinner
is served, then you get what is left over. If there isn't anything
left, you are out of luck"; so if the older kids came home later in
the evening, they often had to fend for themselves.

Sitting around the table in the kitchen for meals
was a special time for me. I liked it when the others
were home for lunch and dinner. Otherwise, I was
home alone with no child to play with.

Mama started babysitting a brother and sister who
were about my age. I can't remember their names, but

their mother would drop them off early to go to work. We would walk to school and then back to the house together.

Mama probably babysat them partly to earn a little money, but also so I would have someone to play with.

I do remember Mama purchasing a new tricycle for me with her earnings. That was special! (Treva)

Mornings, I usually drove the girls to the high school and then picked them up at a designated spot and drove them home for a quick lunch and then back to school.

After school, the girls usually walked home or to work. The street they walked home on was lined with magnificent trees that formed a shaded canopy. On bad weather days, they walked home briskly; or sometimes they would come to the church building which was near the school, and I would drive them home.

One by one as the girls turned sixteen, Momma and I had to accept the fact that they were of driving age. On occasion, we reluctantly allowed them to use the car. We did ask that they pay for and contribute gas.

They watched *Happy Days*[*] on TV and thought it was important to be seen cruising. I think Mom and Dad thought it was pretty silly and a waste of gasoline, but occasionally they would allow the older girls to use the family car to cruise downtown.

Sometimes, they would allow me to go drag Main Street with them. (Neva)

---

[*]   *Happy Days* originally aired from January 15, 1974, to September 24, 1984, on ABC and was created by Garry Marshall. The TV series portrayed an idealized vision of life in the mid-1950s to mid-1960s. en.wikipedia.org/wiki/Happy_Days, a free Wikipedia encyclopedia.

The older girls began working part-time after school and weekends as soon as they turned sixteen. Reba was the first to work at an old folk's home. Several of the girls also cleaned houses for extra money.

>With Reba's recommendation, I worked at the same old folk's home where she worked. I actually started work at age fifteen but did not receive my first paycheck until after June 25 when I turned sixteen.
>
>My starting wage was $.50 per hour, but thanks to the federal government, soon after I started, the minimum wage was increased to $.75 and later to $1.00 per hour. It seemed like big money to me!
>
>I began buying my own shoes and clothes. (Carmen)

>Shirley Scrivner's wife was killed in a car accident. She had been a particularly meticulous housekeeper; so soon after her death, Shirley hired me to clean the house and iron shirts for him and his son, Larry.
>
>I was under sixteen, but Mr. Schriver paid me generously; perhaps, he saw me as the daughter he never had.
>
>The Scrivner's had a stereo and many albums of various musicals. I especially liked *The Sound of Music.* I would get the music playing as I worked and then sing and dance along with flourishes and gestures as I pretended to be like Julie Andrews.
>
>I also cleaned for Bernice, a widow who worked at a bank on Ninth and Main.
>
>I played matchmaker. I often teased Shirley about Bernice, "Isn't she pretty!" And I talked to Bernice about Shirley, "Isn't he handsome!"
>
>They began dating and were engaged within a brief time, only about a month, before I even knew they had

found each other. They told me that I was responsible for them getting together.

They asked the Beasley girls to sing at their wedding, and we did.

After they were married, I then cleaned their house. (Neva)

The motivation to earn money taught the girls responsibility. They were good workers, but working hendered them from being as responsible with their homework. Momma usually encouraged and/or helped the girls to complete their homework, but occasionally I assisted.

I had a writing assignment in which I was to express my opinion about a certain topic (don't remember the topic). I did not know where to begin, what to do, or what to write.

Mom referred me to Dad, the former editor of his high school paper, but by then I was crying tears of frustration.

With furrowed brow, he asked, "What are you supposed to do?"

Through my sobs, I stated, "I'm supposed to write my opinion about (this topic) and I don't know what to write!"

Confused at my emotional state of mind and with furrowed eyebrows, he replied, "Well, tell me what you think about (the topic)."

To which I sobbingly rattled off several ideas.

Perplexed at my ineptness but with obvious concern, he stated simply, "Well, just write what you just told me."

I sat in momentary silence. An "aha" clicked in my brain as I realized, "So that's what writing is about! Writing down what I think!"

Until that moment from what poetry and literature I had read, I had perceived much of the written word as flowery, obtuse expressions to be grasped and understood only by those who were uniquely gifted and intellectual. Obviously, I didn't see myself as one of those people.

In previous written assignments, I had basically plagiarized, writing what others thought but never giving any value to my thoughts.

My writing skills developed at a slow pace. Teachers had failed to teach me to write "stream of consciousness," but Dad, in that brief gentle moment, helped me to begin to understand the simple concept of thinking and writing words to express those thoughts. Duh!

Thanks, Dad!

My writing assignments continued to receive only average grades, but in my sophomore year I did receive one small award which boosted my ego. My literary contribution was published in the Winfield High School's *1965-66 English Echoes*:

Once there was a shy knight. One day as the King rode through the village, all the villagers bowed before him. However, the timid knight trembled, froze in his stance and did not bow down. In a rage, the King exited his carriage, stood in front of him and demanded the knight to get on his knees. The knight stood there frozen in fear. The angry King ordered the knight shot by the firing squad.

The moral: Silent Knight, Holey Knight. (Carmen)

Instead of the long cold snowbound winters and the short summer season of Montana, Kansas had long hot summers, thunderstorms, and seasonal tornados that welcomed the spring and continued through the summer into early fall. On more than one occasion the family had to gather in the hallway as a tornado touched down in and around Winfield.

Tornado by Carmen Lewis

Standing by the screen door
I watched the moody sky change complexion.
I was fearful, but fascinated,
Hoping to see a funnel form.

Huddled in the hallway
Dad called for me to join them.
As the house shivered sturdily,
Adrenaline sharpened my wide-eyed senses.

Unseen by us, the twirling tongue tasted the earth.
Blackness bumped and bruised northeasterly;
Then, gradually the southwest horizon
Began to bleed blue splotches on grey.

Fingers of light pierced the threat of danger
As tension relaxed into relief.
With false bravado I mused,
"I could have faced this foe, this wonder of nature."

We continued trying to have family outings at surrounding lakes to cook fried potatoes and roast hot dogs. However, as the older girls became more involved in school and work, they seemed less interested in going with us. Pauline and I often called them *old stick in the mud.* It became harder for all of us to do things together which was disappointing. We spent more time with Neva and Treva.

Neva and Treva were also more likely to go with Pauline and me to visit other members of the church.

> I enjoyed visiting people with Mom and Dad. I often asked Dad if I could go with him. This gave me the opportunity to talk to him and ask questions.
>
> He always put a lot of thought to my questions before answering. I would wait for Dad to respond because he would think it over, but he would forget to tell me his answer. When I asked again, he would respond, "What? Oh!" and then he would answer.
>
> This is an example of the thought Dad always put into his responses. He didn't talk just to talk. (Neva)

In 1966 after two years at York College, Hoyt came home for the summer. He had majored in music, but had been active in the theater acting in Shakespearean plays. We had driven to see some of them. His plan was to transfer to Harding College in Searcy, Arkansas, in the fall to continue to work on a music degree.

In the house not suited for our numbers, we moved the washing machine out into the garage and converted the utility room into a bedroom for Hoyt.

He got a job on the night shift at a funeral home across from the church building where he washed the cars, made rounds, and had other duties.

> One night as I made the rounds, a corpse lying in its casket reflexively moved. It about scared me to death! I had nightmares following that incident.
>
> Since I worked nights, I slept during the day, and everybody had to be quiet, which they didn't particularly like. (Hoyt)

The church would often put together a group of singers to sing at a funeral, the old folk's home or weddings. Different Beasley girls often sang with the group, and if Hoyt was home from college, he would sing as well.

Hoyt took his education seriously and would often go around the house singing and practicing the scales, seconds, thirds, and fifths. I think he was pretty proud of his beautiful baritone voice.

Across from the church building was the funeral home, and we girls sang for many funerals. I recall getting paid on occasion and rather liked that. Most of the time, however, we sang because Dad asked us to, for free. (Neva)

Once Hoyt returned to college, the washing machine was moved back into the utility room, but during the summer, Momma did her washing in the garage. She still did not have a clothes dryer, so she hung the clothes on the outside clothesline, and she was still starching and ironing my shirts.

Sometimes I would be outside when Momma was hanging clothes on the line. She would give me instructions on the proper way to hang clothes to utilize the existing space.

I can remember coming up to Mama and finding her crying and talking to herself while hanging out the clothes. I felt "funny" and bad for her. I asked if she was okay, and of course, she said she was fine.

As an adult and a mother, I can speculate as to why she was crying. Raising teenagers was difficult, and I don't think she received much appreciation like she deserved.

I know she and Dad sacrificed a lot to give us the necessities. Mama went without new underwear and new clothes so her children could have them instead. She gave so much to us.

I know we didn't have much, though I didn't have to do without as much as the older siblings.

I had a happy childhood and felt loved, not only from my parents, but my siblings as well. (Treva)

On a few occasions, Mom and Dad would go visiting and leave me at the house with Treva who was only about five. One time, driving the extra car, I drove with her out into the countryside (I liked the isolation and getting away from civilization). She just sat looking around all happy and pleased to be with her older sister.

I had not asked permission to use the car and thought, "What if I have an accident or flat tire or get lost? They would not know where to start looking for us. Or, what if Mom and Dad get home before we do? I guiltily returned home. I was relieved to get back before my parents did.

I wonder if they noticed the gas tank was depleted?

Treva had happily gone along for the ride; she seemed to have no second thoughts about the venture. She trusted her older sister to take care of her. I'm glad nothing bad happened.

I wonder if she innocently related the incident to Mom? Ugh! They never said anything to me. (Carmen)

Sheba graduated from Winfield High School in the spring of 1966 and attended York College in the fall.

In the summer of '67, both Hoyt and Sheba were home for the summer.

Hoyt liked to watch the stars, so one summer Sunday night he decided we needed to drive out into the country for some stargazing. Hoyt, Sheba, Sally McNally (a friend of Sheba's from York College), and I plotted the night's adventure.

Mom and Dad were in bed, so we waited until we were sure they were sound asleep. Hoyt, Sheba, and Sally were still in their Sunday "going to meeting clothes"; but I was in my nightgown and robe.

Well, we put the car into neutral, pushed the car out of the driveway and into the street and away from the house, then we started it up.

We were off! The night was clear, and we chose to find the highest point around Winfield (the land was pretty flat, so it couldn't have been too high). Just outside of town, we turned onto a dirt road and headed up the hill. We had traveled a short distance, when suddenly we became stuck and came to an abrupt halt.

Apparently, a hog farmer had cleaned his pig pins and dumped his "cleanings" in the middle of this dirt road. After a recent rain, we found ourselves stuck in this nasty mess.

We sat for a few minutes discussing how we were going to get out of our predicament, and came to the conclusion that our only choice was to get out of the car and push our way out.

So we pushed, slipped, and slid and finally got out.

Our next thought was, "How are we going to get home and clean up without waking Mom and Dad?" Being as quiet as possible, we drove into the driveway, got inside, and cleaned up a bit; but with the "mud" all over the car, we knew we were going to have to "fess" up.

We were so grateful for parents with a great sense of humor.

You know! We never got to look at the stars that night! (Reba)

Reba graduated from Winfield High School in the spring of 1967 and attended York College in the fall. Sheba and Reba were together for a year at York College.

Carmen graduated from Winfield High School in the spring of 1968 and attended York College in the fall. Reba and Carmen were together for a year at York College. Sheba had transferred to Harding College in Searcy, Arkansas.

We certainly did our share of supporting York College and Harding College; they arranged thousands of dollars of government grants and NDSL loans for our kids. With my income and multiple dependents, they qualified for several grants.

We had four children in various colleges in 1968.

Now, only Neva and Treva were living at home, so they each had a bedroom of their own. The others did come home from college for holidays, and sometimes summers; so we would have to temporarily tweak the sleeping arrangements.

I believe the church was having trouble finding a janitor, so when Neva heard me talking about the job, she state, "I would like to have the job." I asked the elders, and they were willing to give her a try.

She was offered an amount, not an hourly rate, and took the job. She was a hard worker, though, perhaps, a little slow and easily distracted.

> When I was a freshman or sophomore in high school, I was hired as the janitor at the church building. I really appreciated the chance to earn some money.
>
> Occasionally, I would let Treva come to the building to help clean with the promise of a toy. She seemed pleased and was a good little worker.
>
> One of my jobs was cleaning the glass communion cups. One time, I put the cups in water to soak with plans to wash them later, but I did not clean them for

several days. An elder's wife came to the building, saw them soaking and growing mold; she cleaned them herself. She then talked to Dad about her concern that I was not being responsible.

I felt she should have come to me. It angered and embarrassed me; it made me feel small.

I had a particularly embarrassing moment one day as I paused in my duties of dusting and vacuuming in the auditorium. I went to the podium and began leading an imaginary congregation in song. I was singing rather energetically and loudly, thinking what a fine song leader I would make when Dad came through the auditorium and down to the front to reach his study.

He had been standing with a suppressed smile for a while before he politely cleared his throat, probably to warn me of his presence. I stopped abruptly. He probably had to suppress a boisterous laugh after he reached his study. (Neva)

We still sometimes went on vacations to Colorado and/or New Mexico, but sometimes the older girls stayed home because of summer jobs.

Dad was packing the car the night before heading out for a vacation. The plan was to leave very early in the morning, at 3:00 or 4:00 a.m.

At that time, I did not understand why Mom and Dad would want to leave so early in the morning. Now that I have experienced traveling with my children, I understand this reasoning.

I was pretty young and not much help in the packing process, but I was outside playing and trying to help. Daddy started laughing. I went over to see what was so funny. He leaned over and showed me the top of his head. A bird had pooped while in flight, and the droppings had landed smack dab in the middle of his bald spot.

Of course, he then went inside to share his misfortune and laughter. Everyone got a big kick out of the bird bomb. (Treva)

We had moved to Winfield to be nearer Grandpa Beasley. He was not doing so well; he had emphysema from a live-time of smoking. Hoyt, Sheba, Reba and Carmen were off at college; but Neva and Treva were still living with us, so they went to Tulsa with us to visit him in the hospital.

> While Grandpa Beasley was in the hospital, he had to wear an oxygen mask. We were allowed five-minute visitations. I had left the room, but Dad sent me back in. Didn't know what I should say, but I did find something to talk about.
>
> During this visit, while lying on his hospital bed, Grandpa asked Dad to baptize him. I'm sure Dad wanted to do just that, but Grandpa was not in any shape to get out of his bed and be immersed in water. (For liability reasons, the hospital probably would not have permitted it.) So the baptism did not take place.
>
> Grandpa did get better and was actually able to go home for a while. However, he did not ask again to be baptized.
>
> I believe it was two weeks later that he passed away.
>
> I know Dad regretted not baptizing him. (Neva)

When my dad asked me to baptize him while he lay so ill in the hospital bed, I was afraid that getting him out of bed and lowering him into the water might make his physical condition worse or kill him, so I didn't follow through with his request. I wish I had. However, God is a gracious God and knows a man's heart. Like the man who hung on a cross next to Jesus, God can say, "Today, I'll see you in paradise." I clung to God's mercy.

My Dad, Edgar Beasley, died December 28, 1968, in Sand Springs, Oklahoma. He had been a chain-smoker and died of emphysema.

I had planned to preside over his services, but at the last minute I choked up and just couldn't keep my emotions in check and backed out.

All the older kids had come from their scattered college locations and were at the funeral, so I asked all of them to sing at the funeral. They choked up some but sounded like angels. I know my dad would have appreciated their gesture.

Since my dad did not have a Will and the law perceived his live-in wife, Evelyn, as the inheritor, I received nothing from his belongings. It saddened and hurt that she would not even let me have his old radio. She gave me nothing!

The kids all got together, came home, and really pulled one over on Pauline and me. They had a surprise twenty-fifth anniversary shindig for us on June 18, 1969.

Gerald and Pauline's twenty-fifth
anniversary, June 18, 1969, at 1311
Mansfield, Joe Sears's home

We planned a surprise twenty-fifth anniversary for Mom and Dad and invited the whole congregation. Mom was especially shocked.

Joe and Libby Sears opened their home to us and got them to their house on false pretenses; they had invited them over for dinner.

The siblings pooled together and bought a silver tray; since Joe was a jeweler, he probably gave us a special deal.

The congregation collected and gave Mom and Dad twenty-five silver dollar pieces displayed in a special made holder. Mom held on to the coins for a long time, but they were eventually sold to cover some expense. (Neva)

I had been working on-the-side selling "Success for You" course tapes, which I had some success at, but I needed a part-time preaching job so I would have more time to spend on this endeavor. So in the summer of 1969, I accepted a part-time preaching job at Forty-Seventh Street Church of Christ in Wichita, Kansas.

Reba, Sheba, Hoyt, Neva, Carmen in the back and Treva in the middle; Gerald and Pauline Beasley in the front. Taken January 4, 1969, in Winfield, Kansas

CHAPTER SEVENTY

Find wives for your sons and give your daughters in
marriage, so that they too may have sons and daughters.
Increase in number.

—Jeremiah 28:17

Ministry in Wichita, Kansas

In the summer of 1969, Pauline, Neva, Treva and I moved to
work with the Forty-Seventh Street church of Christ in Wichita,
Kansas, about sixty miles northwest of Winfield. Our other
children were scattered to the four winds: Hoyt was finishing
up his music degree at Harding College; Sheba was working in
the business office at Harding College; Reba was at Oklahoma
Christian College; and Carmen was at York College.

The preacher's house was located by and to the south of
the church building under a big shade tree. There was a front
porch on the south side where we could sit outside and look at
a plowed field. What a view!

An air-conditioning unit in the window on the
front porch dripped water into a pan placed under the
cooler. Frogs would visit this pool of collected water.
I would pet them with a paint brush because I had
heard touching frogs would give you warts. I didn't
want warts!

For several years I would pet my friends and wonder
if they could be the same frogs returning year after
year. (Neva)

Though I was only hired for part-time preaching, I was
involved in many church activities; I preached, taught Bible
classes, continued with visitations, and dealt with transients.
The family participated in many church activities.

While at Forty-Seventh Street, one of the things
we did as a church group was to meet on a Friday
or Saturday evening to roll newspapers to be sold
for packing material. The boxes filled with the flat
newspapers were opened. We removed the newspaper
and rolled them and then bound them to be sold to
financially support the church.

Of course, whenever the group met, we had to
have a meal together. It was actually fun despite the
work involved. It was a great time of fellowship.

Daddy and Mama vigorously contributed to this
project as they did with all things pertaining to the
church.

One of the ways that Dad and the church used to
reach the community before Vacation Bible School or
a gospel meeting was to canvas the neighborhoods by
knocking on doors, inviting people or registering kids
for VBS. This was a task I did not enjoy.

One time, I was with Daddy under protest and
complaining as we walked up and down the streets.
"It isn't fair! Just because I'm a preacher's daughter, I
shouldn't have to do everything."

He was getting quite fed up with my whining and
attitude. He told me, "This is something that needs

to be done, and you are capable of doing it. This is something we can do to help spread the gospel."

The way he said it made me feel great shame for my behavior.

I still think of that day when there is something that needs to be done, and I really don't want to do it. In fact, I have often told my own kids, "This is the right thing to do!" (Treva)

The auditorium had air-conditioning, but my office at the building did not. I often wore what Treva called wife-beater shirts to go over to the church building to study. I would set up a fan or two to stay cool.

Once when by myself, I was probably ten or eleven, I was in the auditorium "playing church." I did the song leading, prayed and preached. I was preaching away and did not realizing that Daddy was in his office at the back of the auditorium.

The door opened quietly, and Dad skulked out into the adjoining men's restroom. He apparently had waited for a while but couldn't wait any longer.

He apologized for interrupting and went back into his office.

I was mortified that he had heard me. Church services ended abruptly. (Treva)

Pauline was always involved in attending the weekly ladies Bible class and teaching children's Bible classes. She continued to add to her Bible teaching materials.

Mama spent numerous hours developing her Bible class lessons. She enjoyed teaching the younger kids and was diligent to make things that involved "hands on" activities.

She used songs to teach. One I remember is "The Bible, the Bible, I love the Bible. It is God's word. Please don't throw (cut, tear, color) it. Please don't . . . it. It is God's word."

She accumulated many lessons that she would use again and again in the different congregations Daddy preached at. (Treva)

There was a vacant lot to the north of the church building where Momma turned the soil, added manure, and planted a vegetable garden. She was an organic gardener and emulated her parents' methods of feeding the soil.

Mama was always environmentally conscious. I often told my children that she was a "hippy" in some aspects because of organic gardening, natural treatments/cures and recycling. She was into "save the environment" before it became popular, and had been doing it for many years.

I have to admit, the containers left on the cabinets where she saved vegetable scraps and peelings were not too pleasant, especially since she let the contents sit for several days before emptying it into the garden. The flies and gnats could get pretty pesky!

Mama, of course, had a huge garden on the north side of the classroom wing of the Forty-Seventh Street church building. She spent a lot of time out there.

I didn't enjoy going out there in part because I knew she would deliberately put snakes that she found out there to keep pest away.

Her gardening efforts provided us with plentiful fresh vegetables.

There were only five houses on the part of Forty-Seventh Street where we lived, and the neighbors had gardens and orchards with varying fruit trees. I remember sharing going on among the neighbors.

Two of the houses had two older women living in them. Mama was always good about checking in on them and providing veggies to them.

One summer, Mama spread manure on the yard between the house and by the church building. It sure messed up playing for quite a while. I was disgusted and in an overly dramatic manner would hold my nose to run to the church building for church.

However, it did the grass wonders. (Treva)

Along with gardening, sewing, canning, and involvement in church work, Pauline worked part-time at the elementary school on Seneca Street where Treva attended third grade.

Mama and a neighbor, who had a girl that I played with, would car pool and work as lunchroom attendants and playground supervisors at my school. Their hours were 11:00 to 1:30ish.

The first year she worked there, the school had actual cooks who prepared home-cooked food. The dinner rolls were great! But the next year the lunches were pre-made and in aluminum containers.

Mama collected food that the kids did not eat and would bring it home (she could not let good food go to waste) as well as many aluminum containers that she washed and reused for freezing food at home.

Ironically, I generally took my lunch. (Treva)

For fourth through sixth grades, Treva went to a special school for "high performance" students, along with a neighbor boy.

> I attended Stanley Elementary, what would today be called a magnet school, for fourth through sixth grades. The school was about five miles from our house and out of our district, so I had to be driven. There were a couple of other children in our area who also attended there, so Mama and the other parents carpooled.
>
> I know it was a hassle, but it proved to be a very good educational experience for me. Mama voiced the advantages and didn't complain about the drive though there was an added expense for gas. (Treva)

Neva attended South High School in Wichita located near the elementary school on Seneca and graduated in a class of over nine hundred.

> One day I got off the school bus on Forty-Seventh Street and walked past the garden where Mom was usually at work. However, this time, Mom was not in the garden.
>
> When I got to the house, I called, "Mom." but there was no answer. I looked throughout the house, even in the closets and under the beds as I called out to her.
>
> Mom was always home when I got home, so I was worried. I was getting frantic and went to the church building. She was not there. So I looked in the garden again.
>
> There she was, working in the garden. As I had come around the front of the church building, she had gone from the house to the garden behind the church building. I'd just missed her. (Neva)

I don't think Pauline and I had many disagreements in front of the kids. We talked in the privacy of our bedroom. We always tried to be calm and positive. So I was surprised one day at Pauline's vehemence and determination to save the old tree by the preacher's house and church building.

> The only serious disagreement I witnessed between Mom and Dad wasn't very serious, but interesting. The men of the congregation had decided in a business meeting that they were going to expand the parking area by cutting down the old huge tree between the preacher's house and the church building.
>
> When Dad mentioned this to Mom, she became quite angry and very expressive, "That is a stupid idea! They are not going to cut down that tree! They can find another place. There is plenty of room on the other side of the building to expand the parking lot!" She was quite unhappy!
>
> Dad tried to calm her, "But, Momma, let's be reasonable."
>
> "That tree is not going to be cut down! I'll willingly give up my garden space. If they have to have more parking spaces, they can use that area!" she exclaimed.
>
> I sort of remember agreeing with her and saying so. This tree was close to my bedroom and it was special.
>
> The tree wasn't removed, but I'm not sure we influenced that decision. (Neva)

With only two children living at home, discipline was sometimes still necessary, but much less frequent. The street where the church building and our house was located was a short street that dead-ended after a turn to the west where there were a few other houses. Sometimes the girls would wonder off across the open field or down the street, so one evening when Neva was not to be found, I went looking for her.

>Dad demonstrated his fatherly concern one night when I walked down our road at Forty-Seventh Street. Stan, a neighbor, was rebuilding the engine on his car. He was distracted when it didn't work. I didn't realize how terribly late it was until Dad drove up in his car looking for me in his bathrobe.

>He was worried, but sweet, even though he was quite aggravated and muttering to himself "brother" and "horse feather."

>I was told not to go out without telling Mom or Dad where I was going. (Neva)

>I was a pretty good kid growing up, but I did receive some well-deserved spankings from time to time. I don't ever remember Mama raising her voice, but I knew punishment would be swift and fair.

>Once, I decided I didn't need the deserved spanking, so I ran from her. After taking chase for a short distance, she called after me, "I will catch you eventually, and you will be much sorrier."

>Being the relatively intelligent kid that I was, I took her to heart and ceased running and took my punishment. (Treva)

Like a boomerang, our girls kept coming back. Usually it was for a brief time, coming home between college semesters and/or to work to earn money to pay for a wedding.

Reba left Oklahoma Christian College and came to live with us briefly. Maude Carpenter Children's Home was searching for house-parents. They preferred married couples but had no promising applicants. When Reba expressed an interest in the job, they were hesitant to hire a young single female, but they gave Reba a try. It was a pretty overwhelming responsibility overseeing and dealing with children who had emotional and behavioral issues.

She hung in there for a while, but later moved back in with us while she determined what to do with herself. Reba decided to take courses in medical transcribing; she was quite good at it.

Wichita was in "tornado alley," and there were a few times we had to take shelter. At least once, we went under the house through the hole in the floor in the back bedroom closet. Other times we went to the end of the street to Stanley's house where they had a cellar. The women and children would go down into it, but the men generally stood outside watching.

> Once when we were in the Stanley's cellar, and the men were standing outside watching, I asked Dad, "Why aren't you getting into the shelter!"
>
> "I want the children and women to be safe. Right now it's pretty crowded. The men will come down if it becomes necessary," he replied.
>
> The men were being big and brave.
>
> There were a couple of times while living in Wichita when tornadoes passed close to our location. Mr. Lundgren told about an earlier time when a tornado had flown over the field in front of the houses. (Treva)

The spring, summer and fall weather in Kansas was usually warm to hot with mild winters. However, occasionally a winter storm would bring chilling temperatures and snow.

> After an unusually big snow fall for Kansas, with two or three inches covering the ground, Reba, Treva

and I built a twelve-foot tall snowman by the big tree by the house. We rolled balls of snow from "all over the place around here" picking up and using the snow all around the house and church building. Our snowman was so tall that we had to get a ladder to *plaster* the head onto the top with more snow.

That evening we watched the TV evening news show other snow creations from all over Wichita. We wished we had called in our sculpture.

The temperature turned warm the next day and it melted quickly. (Neva)

Pauline, Treva, and Gerald in front;
Neva, Sheba, and Reba in back.
Taken in Wichita, Kansas

Hoyt had graduated from Harding College with a degree in music and took a teaching job at Crowley's Ridge College in Paragould, Arkansas, so he did not come home to live again.

He met and married Brenda Kaye Erwin, a student at the college, in Cardwell, Missouri, on June 5, 1970. Most of the family drove and attended the wedding.

After two years at York College and one year at Harding College, Carmen came to stay with us in Wichita for the summer of '71. She had plans to marry in August and wanted to earn enough to pay for a wedding. Jobs were hard to find, so she worked cleaning motel rooms for several months.

I tried to always remain calm and speak positively about my work with the church and people I encountered. However, one time after Pauline and I had gone to visit a lady, I came home rather upset and expressive. We had met the lady's husband. I saw nothing redeeming about the man and spoke aloud that he was an evil man. I guess Carmen was shocked to hear me speak that way.

> Dad usually spoke positively about everybody and everything; very rarely did he speak negatively about anybody. He'd always find something good to say.
>
> However, one evening Dad and Mom came home after visitation and I heard him say, "That was an evil man. He had no redeeming quality."
>
> I was shocked! But I realized the man must have been really bad for Dad to say that. I'm sure he was concerned for his soul. I know he felt compassion for the lady. (Carmen)

Carmen married Michael Lee Lewis on August 13, 1971, a Friday the thirteenth, at the Forty-Seventh Street church of Christ in Wichita, Kansas. They hauled all their wedding gifts in Mike's car to Abilene where Mike attended Abilene Christian University and Carmen went to work at K-mart.

> The summer I got married, jobs were hard to find in Wichita. I ended up cleaning motel rooms across town.
>
> I worked days, and Neva worked nights at a donut shop, so we shared one of Dad's cars to get to work. I would get home late afternoons, and Neva would head out to her job. Our work schedules made it difficult to spend time together. I missed her camaraderie.
>
> Mom and Dad had always said that if we wanted a church wedding with the "fixings," we would have to pay for it. So I found fabric, netting, and all I needed on sale or clearance; and I made my wedding dress. I spent about $300 altogether on my wedding, which included a few flowers.

A man from church told me he had just spent
$5,000 for his daughters' wedding dress, not counting
the thousands more he had spent for everything else.
He said there was no way I could have a wedding for
$300. But I did! Granted, it was a simple wedding.
(Carmen)

In the fall of 1971, Neva attended York College for only one
semester where she met Mike Russell. They became engaged.

Neva came home to work and plan her wedding.

Mike actually dropped out of college and lived at the house
too. It was not the best situation, but he slept on the sleeper
couch. We watched them very closely. Mike wanted to save
money, so Mom and I agreed to let him stay.

Mike and I went walking in the field near the house
one day. He was carrying a bee-be gun. Somewhat
playfully, he aimed at a bird that was quite far away.

I objected to his killing it just for the fun of it.
"Don't aim at that bird. It never did anything to you."

He replied, "I can't possibly hit it." He shot anyway
and hit it. He was surprised as it fell to the ground.

I was upset and not very happy with him.

That spring, Mike worked in Wichita selling
Volkswagens. He was told that if he sold a certain
number of cars, the company would provide a free car
for our honeymoon.

Dad told Mike if he sold the remaining number of
VW's minus one, he would purchase one.

Well, Mike sold shy of one car, so Dad bought a
Volkswagen. Mike was shocked that Dad would do
that. (Neva)

True to his word, when Mike called from the car dealer's and said he had one more car to sell, Daddy, Mama, and I went to buy a 1972 baby blue Volkswagen Beetle which I named *Herman*. There were *no* extras! No radio, no air-conditioning, pretty much seats and a steering wheel.

I want to say Daddy paid about $2,200 for the car. I'm sure it was somewhat of a financial burden, but I hope the savings in gasoline helped offset the expense of the car.

Daddy seemed so proud to have the car. We drove that car many, many places crammed full of people and camping supplies.

Later during my sophomore year of college, Daddy sold the car for around this same amount. We had driven it for about nine years.

I still find myself looking at baby blue Beetles, and I have heard Daddy comment when seeing one, "I wonder about *ole Herman*." (Treva)

Neva married Mike Edward Russell on May 27, 1972, in Wichita, Kansas. They drove a new Audi to Colorado on their honeymoon. However, they had a problem with the car. During a heavy rainstorm, Mike turned on the windshield wipers, but when the rain stopped, the windshield wipers would not turn off. Mike had to disconnect a wire to stop them.

After we returned from our honeymoon, Mike continued selling cars until the fall when we returned to York College in York, Nebraska.

I tried taking twelve college hours while also working at a bank in York, but working and going to school was too much. So I quit school and worked while Mike finished his two years at York College. (Neva)

John Earl and Maggie Lillian Smith in front of the "new" farmhouse built about 1965

Grandpa, John Earl Smith, died of a heart attack in October of 1972 in Warren, Oklahoma.

Most of our children drove to attend the funeral. Once again we were together, and of course, though it was a sad event, we sang.

Uncle Royce was there. I don't think he understood how we could sing joyfully at his dad's funeral.

Pauline and I always believed that our kids should spend time in pursuit of spiritual things, so we were willing to send our children to Bible camps and go to Christian youth rallies even if we had to drive them.

Daddy was always willing to drive me and other teenagers from church to various high school days at Christian colleges, youth rallies, and to church camps near and far.

I can only imagine how tiring it must have been to drive from Wichita to Oklahoma Christian College, and then drive home that same evening, and get up the next morning to preach.

Mama and Dad were such proponents of our getting together with other Christian young people and being exposed to a Christian college environment. (Treva)

Sheba had moved back home from Searcy, Arkansas, and was living in Wichita with us when she met and later married Larry Dean Thomas on January 25, 1974. They eventually went to the Bear Valley Preaching School in Denver.

Once again I was surrounded by the female gender. They must have brought out a bit of orneriness in me. There were always girls in the house with long hair, and where there was long hair, there were rubber bands to hold the hair back.

> I honestly think Daddy visually scoured the floors looking for misplaced rubber bands that he could pick up and shoot at whoever was near. With a twinkle in his eye and a little smirk, he let the recipient know he had kind of enjoyed doing it. (Treva)

I guess the old black-and-white television must have gone kaput because for a while we did not have a TV. However, I still enjoyed listening to football games on the radio.

> Daddy always enjoyed football! I can remember when there was no television, he would set every radio in the house on different games and walk from room to room keeping up with what was happening.
>
> We had no television at the house, unless one of the girls moved back home, usually before they got married, and brought one with them.

> Without a television to watch when sick, Mama sometimes let me sleep in her bed. I don't know what her logic was, but I felt very special being in their room. It was the "holy of holies." They usually kept the door closed and even going into the room to use the restroom when the other one was occupied was a real honor. (Treva)

I guess we got to watch Reba's TV when she moved in with us, and Mike Russell had one during the spring when he lived at our house and slept on the couch until he and Neva married in May.

While raising six children, Pauline did not really want the extra work of caring for a dog or cat, so for years we did not have any pets.

> Pretty much the only time we got a pet was when a stray cat adopted Mama, not Mama adopted a stray. Once one came around, she didn't have the heart to turn it away.
>
> Or one of the girls got one and then didn't take it with them when they left home. Neva acquired Feisty, the cat.
>
> The house in Wichita had wood floors, so Mama had placed some rag rugs around to save wear on the floor. Like any respectable cat, Feisty would sit on these rugs instead of the wood floors. Daddy would come through the room with a twinkle in his eye, see the cat on the rug, grab a hold of the end of the rug, swing it, and proceed to give the cat a ride. Feisty would extend his claws into the rug and hold on for one of many rides of his life. I don't know if Feisty enjoyed it, but Daddy sure seemed to get a kick out of it. (Treva)

At one point, I got "down in my back." Guess lifting those heavy water barrels, tossing feed to the animals, and moving heavy milk jugs in my younger years finally got to me. As I got older, sometimes, lifting and moving heavy objects would throw my back out of whack. I recall keeping a chair by my bed so I could hold on to it to help me get out of bed, and I preached more than once sitting on a stool because of back pain. It's no fun getting older.

CHAPTER SEVENTY-ONE

Watch yourselves closely so that you do not forget the
things your eyes have seen or let them slip from your
heart as long as you live.
Teach them to your children and
to their children after them.
—Deuteronomy 4:9

Ministry in Electra, Texas

Once again I sought a full-time preaching position. Pauline, Reba, Treva and I moved to Electra, Texas, during the Christmas break in 1974, when Treva was in eighth grade. She was not very happy about the move.

We left Wichita, Kansas, on a Saturday morning, and I was scheduled to preach in Electra the following day on Sunday; but the rented moving van broke down. It was rather embarrassing to miss my first appointed preaching assignment at my new position.

We did finally get to Electra with all our stuff. I remember being very tired. Typical of a small town, as we unloaded, people would drive by and stop to see who was moving in. The two sons of Kenneth Dye were among the many members from church who helped us unload.

The preacher's house was located right next to the church building. There were three bedrooms, so Momma and I had one, and Treva and Reba each had their own room for a while.

There wasn't much yard space, but Pauline did utilize what space there was and put in a garden. Okra grew well so we had lots of okra for frying.

Our family quickly became involved in the church work. I kept busy with my ministry responsibilities as I continued preaching, teaching, and giving assistance to transients who came through on HI 287 that ran east and west just north of town. Momma, Treva and I would go with a group of members to the nursing home occasionally on Sunday afternoons for devotionals. We were also involved in visitation groups. I continued to have a children's Bible drill just before the Sunday evening worship services.

Many mornings I would go down to the Diary Queen to drink coffee to get to know the men from town.

Momma continued to attend the weekly ladies Bible class, and she continued to prepare teaching materials for children's Bible classes. She became friends with many of the neighbors; she was so good about taking care of the little old ladies close by; there were many neighbors who were members of the church.

The Electra congregation was active in the mission fields in Malaysia.

It was also active in the community with a successful bus ministry program with Tom Daugherty in charge. There were many willing workers. I think we purchased five buses.

I recall that the mother of one of the bussed children was baptized. She was crippled, so Leon Brown carried her piggyback up to the elevated baptistery.

During our time with the Electra church, a Sunday morning attendance goal was planned; we worked hard to reach five hundred in attendance. I recall reaching a little over four hundred, a pleasing number.

Soon after we moved in, the church hired a youth minister, Larry and Aleta Tittle. They were a welcome addition to the church staff, and I feel that Larry and I worked together very well. We were especially glad since Treva benefited from their mentoring.

Interestingly, another applicant for the youth minister position was named Tuttle. I suggested to the elders that perhaps, we should wait to see if a Tattle or Tettle might apply. ☺

Again, we were invited to the homes of various members of the church for meals. My stomach recalls delicious catfish meals at Tompie (an unusual name) Huffman's home just north of Electra.

Treva had a difficult time for a while after the move; but she soon adapted, made new friends, and became involved in a number of activities at her school and at the church.

> I was devastated to be moving from friends and school, especially right in the middle of the school year. I *tried* to be miserable until school started after the holidays. I was nervous about starting at a new school.
>
> When the school doors reopened, Daddy took me to school to get me registered with the principal who was also the basketball coach.
>
> Because I was a bit taller, the coach was excited at the prospect of a new basketball player. Unfortunately, I was not very good and can remember fumbling and making many mistakes that were very embarrassing; but the coaches must have seen potential because they continued to work with me, and I eventually became a decent player.
>
> I'm sure I would have been a much better player if I had had more confidence. Later, I discovered my skills were not so bad while playing intramurals in college. (Treva)

To help Treva with basketball, I put up a basketball goal on the carport in the driveway. My shoulder would bother me, but when Treva would challenge me, I would shoot some baskets with her. I did pretty well for an old guy. Momma even came out and shot every now and then.

Reba had moved to Electra with us, and she got a job as a medical transcriber at a hospital in Wichita Falls about twenty miles east of Electra. She lived with us for a while; then moved into a trailer until she came down with mononucleosis. Unable to work and pay the rent, she moved back into the house with us. She later went back to work at the same job.

As the preacher's family, we lived in a *glasshouse*. We were often scrutinized and criticized, so to avoid providing reasons for criticism, we had set very high standards for our children. We continued to emphasize humility, modesty and purity with Treva. She didn't always like it, but we never let her (or any of our daughters) wear short skirts, shorts or low-cut bodices. Some church members allowed their children to dance, but we did not.

Sometimes Treva may have balked at our standards, but she was not defiant. She was a pleasant and easy child to discipline.

> I'm sure many children experience the "go ask your mother/father" phenomenon. At Electra the preacher's house was next door to the church building. When I would ask Mom if I could do something, I got the patent "go ask your father." So I would go next door and get the "go ask your mother" response.
>
> This went on back and forth a couple times until I got smart and called the church building so Mom and Dad could talk over the phone.
>
> It saved me lots of steps.

We had a piano. I think Mama played it some while I was in school, and occasionally I would sit down and play a few tunes. Since the churches of Christ sang a cappella during worship, Mama never wanted me to play hymns on the piano in case someone came to the door and heard. She was always so cautious about things being misconstrued by someone.

I thought that was so silly and played them anyway. Sorry, Mom! (Treva)

Treva adapted quickly to the changes and grew to appreciate the smaller school and the activities she could be involved in.

The Electra Junior High school's curriculum was not as advanced as the Wichita school's curriculum where I had previously attended. I basically became a teacher's aide in Math and helped the other students because I had already studied what they were learning.

I was in the orchestra in Wichita, but Electra did not have an orchestra, so my violin playing days were over.

I did grow to appreciate the smaller school. The school in Wichita was so large I had been just a little fish in the big ocean and did not feel like a *somebody*. However, in Electra, I began to feel like *somebody*.

I felt accepted despite my *big city* and *foreign* ways. When my new friends asked if I wanted a Coke, I would say, "No, thank you, but I would like a Dr. Pepper." Of course, they were referring to a nonspecific soft drink and thought it was funny when I would ask for a *pop*. (Treva)

We went to some of Treva's basketball games. We were quite a bit older than her peers' parents, so we didn't develop any close friendships, but we were cordial. Once Julie Durbin got into high school, we usually sat with her parents, Al and Pauline Durbin—members of the church. Reba also came to some of Treva's games.

Since Tuesdays were visitation nights for church and many of my basketball games were on Tuesdays, Mom and Dad were not always present at sporting events. I know there were other students who would have been mad if their parents weren't there to watch them, but I wasn't bothered by it.

Dad usually didn't say much at ball games, but I do remember one particular game when he actually yelled at the refs. It is weird how one can manage to hear and recognize the voices of one's own parents over the noise in the gym. I was amazed that he had said anything.

For modesty sake I was not allowed to wear shorts in public, so I remember feeling somewhat self-conscious in the basketball uniform when Mom and Dad were there. In fact, I was surprised that I was allowed to wear them! Mama did emphasize that I should not wear them outside of the gym, but since it was a uniform, it was okay for the games.

Kind of along that same line, I never tried out for cheerleading because I didn't think Mama would let me wear the uniform, kick up my legs, and jump which would have revealed my legs and more. However, as an adult when I mentioned that, Mama said we could have worked something out. Again, I was a little surprised.

I also told her that I had always wanted to learn to tap dance. Mama said, "You should have said something." I guess the use of the word "dance" made me figure it wouldn't even be a possibility. (Treva)

I did sometimes assist Treva with school assignments. She would ask me to proofread research papers and other assignments.

> I wanted Daddy to tell me what needed to be corrected, make suggestions and changes on my research papers; but for the most part, he would read them, then just ask, "What do you think would make this paper better? Are you happy with it?" Guess he didn't feel it was his place to redo my work; maybe he felt that it would be cheating to help me too much; or maybe, I was so brilliant, nothing needed to be changed! (Treva)

In 1976, Grandma Smith was diagnosed with ovarian cancer. After visiting her in the Lawton hospital, she came to live with us in Electra so Pauline could take care of her. Maggie had made Momma promise that she would not put her in a nursing home.

Because she had been living with Maggie, Jerrie Ann—Uncle Royce's daughter—came to live with us as well.

Taken 1976 before Maggie became sick—Pauline Beasley, Myrtle (Eddins) Wampler, Maggie Smith, Theda Wampler Allgood, and Jerrie Ann Smith

It was a difficult time for all of us, but especially for Pauline; she was very busy, stressed and overwhelmed. Maggie required a lot of care and attention at the house. Pauline had to drive Maggie to Altus, Oklahoma, for cobalt and radiation treatments. Sometimes, Grandma had to stay overnight in the Altus hospital.

Treva, I'm sure, felt neglected as she had to share Mom's attention with Maggie and Jerrie Ann; but Pauline felt a strong responsibility to take care of her ailing mother.

Reba had to give up her room; she and Treva then shared a bedroom. Reba did eventually move out and back into the same trailer.

> Grandma Smith came to live with us when I was about fourteen. I think I was a freshman in high school. Jerrie Ann also lived with us.
>
> I know Mom was torn between taking care of Grandma, being there for Jerrie Ann, and being a wife and mother.
>
> As time went on, I think she somewhat regretted her promise not to put Grandma into a facility, but however difficult it was, she was very dedicated to Grandma.
>
> It had to have been so hard on Mama to watch her mother decline.
>
> Sometimes, Grandma would get out of bed and forget where she was going. One day I found her just standing by a bookshelf. More than once she would urinate and be standing in a puddle when Momma found her. Of course, Mama would have to clean up the mess.
>
> Grandma expressed concern for Jerrie Ann. I selfishly felt left out and jealous because of the attention that Jerrie Ann received. As a result, Daddy talked to Reba and me in the kitchen. He chastised me for my words and actions toward Jerrie Ann, and for complaining that Mom wasn't being a mom to me.
>
> Unfortunately, I can't take back my stupidity, but I do feel bad about it.
>
> Grandma only lived with us a couple of months before she died, but Mama seemed to age about ten years during that time. Her hair turned from dark brown with speckles of grey to all grey. (Treva)

Maggie Smith died the spring of 1976 at the Altus hospital.

It had been a difficult time for all of us. Pauline was very weary. I had endured the stress silently as I tried to be supportive. Jerrie Ann had helplessly watched her grandma suffer and die. Treva had expressed feelings of neglect, but had been busy with school activities so she was gone a lot. Reba tried to remain quiet.

With God's help, we survived.

After Grandma's death, Jerrie Ann stayed on with us until she finished that school year. Jerrie Ann had a difficult time adjusting to Maggie's death. Grandma was the only mom she had really known since her real mother had left when she was a baby. Uncle Royce was an absentee dad who drove a truck for a living, though he occasionally dropped by.

Jerrie Ann had been used to being the center of attention and was understandably needy and very insecure. She would often proclaim to be sick and whine, vying for attention. Many nights, she would come into our bedroom to Momma and wake us up in the middle of the night crying in distress. Pauline tried to remain patient, but after many interrupted nights and lack of sleep, her patience was wearing down.

> Mike and I were visiting shortly after Grandma Smith's death. Jerrie Ann was holding her stomach and saying, "Oh, my stomach is hurting!"
>
> I said, "Oh, I'll fix you some chicken noodle soup."
>
> She asked, "Why should I eat chicken noodle soup?"
>
> "Well, that's what Momma would fix for us when we didn't feel well."
>
> She looked at me with creased eyebrows, but she ate the soup.
>
> Later, when dessert was brought out, Jerrie Ann was excited and wanted some, but I said, "Oh, but you're sick. You can't eat that."

"But I feel better now."

"I'm sorry, but dessert would upset your stomach," I stated.

She was not very happy, but she did not get any dessert. (Neva)

I'm sure Grandma had indulged Jerrie Ann, but Mom was not a spoiler. Momma's idea of raising kids was very different from Grandma's, and Jerrie Ann did not always react to the changes well. In fact, to indicate that she did not have to do what Mom said, she stated more than once, "You aren't my mama!" I'm sure that really hurt Mom's feelings. (Treva)

Jerrie Ann was baptized while living with us in Electra. She may have done it to please us, but I hope she really understood and took God into her life. She had attended church in Blair with Grandma Smith while they were still living on the farm, so she had had previous exposure to the Bible.

There were some disagreements between Pauline and Uncle Royce over who should be caring for Jerrie Ann, and how much financial support was needed. Royce had been providing $50 monthly for Pauline to care for Jerrie Ann, but that was not nearly enough to cover her expenses.

There were also conflicting issues over the inherited distribution of the Smith property and farmhouse in southwest Oklahoma. There was a falling-out between Pauline and Royce; there were some hurt feelings between Pauline and Royce and Jerrie Ann.

Jerrie Ann went to live with Royce.

It was a relieve for Pauline, but we continued to pray for Jerrie Ann's well-being.

I have purposely looked her up and visited with Jerrie Ann some over the years. She seemed to be doing fine.

Several years later when Jerry (my husband) and I were attending a singing worship in Vernon, Oklahoma, I saw a nice-looking young lady across the room. I thought, "She looks so much like Jerrie Ann!"

So I went over and asked if she was Jerrie Ann, and it was her!

We had a good visit. She seemed to be doing well.

Last I heard, Jerrie Ann and her husband, Nathan Hill, lived in Altus, Oklahoma, and Jerrie Ann was working as a dispatcher for the Altus police department. (Reba)

After caring for her mom, Pauline needed relaxation and relief from stress, and a much deserved break from additional responsibilities.

After raising six children, Momma told us, "When you have children of your own, don't bring them to me to raise them."

She wasn't being mean, and we didn't take it offensively; she had spent her adult life devoting herself to us, and she deserved a rest from being responsible for somebody else's children.

However, I'm sure, if it had become necessary or needful should something happen to us, she would not have neglected her grandchildren. (Carmen)

Pauline inherited the farmhouse and surrounding land, so we rented out the house; the rent money covered property taxes. Royce inherited the north and some bottom-land acreage.

Pauline and I would periodically drive the 120 miles to Blair to work and do repairs on the farm. Treva sometimes went with us. We mowed, built fences, trimmed fruit trees, picked fruit in season, worked on the water pump, and tore down the abandoned, condemned old house.

Daddy drove the tractor to mow the fields. I wanted to drive it but wasn't allowed to.

Daddy also used a chain saw to clear brush and trees. I felt sure I could do it, but Daddy wouldn't let me. He emphasized the danger. As a result, to this day I am fearful of them.

We put a fence between the property that Mama inherited and Uncle Royce's property to the north. We dug the fence post holes the *good ole fashioned way* with hand shovels. Ugh! It was hard work and not much fun.

I was thrilled when we tore down the old farmhouse. Since I was part monkey and really enjoyed climbing trees, I got to climb up on top of the old house to take up the boards. Of course, I was instructed to be careful, but it was fun.

We eventually tied a rope or chain to the frame and attached it to the tractor to bring down the shell of the house.

The cellar had caved in, so we had to dig down to get the canned goods down there. Mom and Dad warned me to be aware of snakes. Ugh! That deterred me from wanting to be near the cellar. We did retrieve a number of jars, full and empty.

I really enjoyed working with Mom and Dad. Because of the extent of the projects, it was sometimes difficult to see results, but the hard work was fulfilling.

We looked for antique *treasures* in the old barn and surrounding grounds, stacked and stored the boards from the house in the barn, rode on the tractor (an antique which Dad worked on to keep it running) to the orchard, and picked peaches, apricots and apples in what was left of the orchard.

However, being a *modern* child, I was anything but excited about having to potty in nature.

Once while helping to clear out locust trees, I was stung by a wasp; my hand and arm became like a club. The swelling continued for several days, so Mama took me to the doctor where I got a shot. (Treva)

Al and Pauline Durbin were members at the church; Al was an elder. Their daughter, Julie, though she was younger, became a good friend of Treva's. Once Julie was in high school, they did a lot together.

Momma and I always tried to encourage Treva and Julie to participate in spiritual activities: Bible camp, youth rallies and meeting with the other church teens.

Mom and Dad drove Julie and me to Blue Haven Bible camp in New Mexico several times for several years.

We also went to the Quartz Mountain Christian Camp near Lone Wolf, Oklahoma, where the Durbin kids had grown up attending. We became acquainted with many teenagers in that area; but we became particularly close to several teenagers from Burkburnett, Texas.

At sixteen, I began driving *Herman*, my baby blue Volkswagen Beetle (actually, they just let me drive it a lot, so I called him mine). Mom and Dad let me drive with Julie to Burkburnett about twenty miles northeast of Electra on Sunday evenings for church and a youth devotional. I wasn't allowed to drive distances after dark, so I drove only during the summer months.

I remember thinking that was so stupid, but guess what I later told my own kids, especially my daughter!

Herman was even pictured in the school yearbook. I was messing around with the yearbook staff as we were putting pages together, so a picture was taken as I lay across the top giving him a big hug.

Julie and I also attended Lubbock Christian College's music camp for several summers. Al and Pauline Durbin would drive us and stay to visit with their son Jimmy and his family.

I know there was expense with all the camps I went to, but Mom and Dad wanted me to be exposed to any and all spiritual influences available.

Thank you! Thank you! Thank you, Mom and Dad! (Treva)

Reba married Al and Pauline Durbin's son, Jerry, on March 19, 1977. They lived about four blocks away. We did not wish to intrude or butt in on their affairs, so we didn't call them up or drop by their place a lot.

I think maybe Reba might have felt forgotten; she would comment to me that she never saw Mom and Dad. (Treva)

When Treva got parts in school plays, Mama would sometimes help by reading the script lines with her and suggest that Treva read her lines aloud. And Pauline was more than willing to sew whatever costume Treva needed.

My junior and senior classes put on plays as fund raisers. I got the lead female part both years; I was a mom in one, and a dumb blonde in a comedy. It wasn't necessarily because of my acting ability, but more because the sponsors/directors knew I was smart enough to learn the lines.

I was dramatically inexperienced. Since none of the rehearsals were in front of an audience, I wasn't prepared when the audience laughed and I thought, "Did someone's pants fall down or something?"

Of course, Mama and Dad came to the plays; Reba may have come too.

I was proud because I had grown up watching my siblings participate in plays in high school and college and even community theatre while in Winfield. (Treva)

So in 1977, all of our offspring, except Treva, were married. At that time, Hoyt and Brenda Beasley had three children, Martha Kay born in 1971, Mary Beth born in 1974 and Terry Austin born the summer of 1977; Sheba and Larry Thomas had one child, Shawn Allen born in 1976; Carmen and Mike Lewis had two children, Samantha Joy born in 1975 and Shane Tucker born in 1977; and Neva and Mike Russell had one son, Matthew Edward born in May of 1977. Additional grandchildren were to come later.

Our offspring often came with their children to visit, and we sometimes went on vacation with some of them.

During one visit to Electra, Reba, Jerry, Mike and I went on a picnic with Mom and Dad to the Red River. I think Treva went with us or she may have been at a camp. I can't remember for sure.

Reba had just found out that she was pregnant.

Mike, Jerry and Dad went fishing; the females were watching from the shore. The men caught some big fish, but one fish got hung up on a line in the water. Mike wasn't about to let it get away, so he waded into the water up to his neck to untangle the line. He bagged his fish!

We were in Utah the week of August 16, 1977, when we heard over the radio that Elvis Presley had died. Mike and I, with our three-month-old son, Matthew, had driven from San Rafael, California.

We met Mom, Dad and Treva at Bryce Canyon National Park west of Cedar City, Utah, to camp. That first night we camped and cooked over an open campfire. However, during the night it rained and rained, creating a creek that basically flowed under our tent. It was wet and quite cold.

Mom, Dad and Treva left their tent and went to their car; Mike and I with the baby left our tent and went to our car where we tried to sleep, but with little success.

The next couple of days, all of us stayed in motel rooms in Cedar City and drove into the mountains during the day.

Treva got an earache, probably because of the cold, but also from changing elevations while driving through the mountains in the area.

We enjoyed meeting with Mom, Dad and Treva, but were glad to leave Utah to the Mormons. (Neva)

In 1979, after completing their training at the Bear Valley School of Preaching in Denver, Larry and Sheba moved in briefly with us in Electra while Larry was looking for a preaching job. They had two children, Shawn and Mandy (just a baby), and Sheba was pregnant again. The house was once again crowded. It was not the best situation, but Larry did eventually get a preaching job.

Another time, Mom and Dad, Sheba and Larry, and Mike and I went together on a vacation to Red River, New Mexico. Treva had been dropped off at Blue Haven Bible Camp.

After picnicking by the stream, Dad, Mike and Larry went fishing. The fish were being elusive and were swimming around each man's fishing hook nibbling at the bait having a good laugh at the guys.

Dad was quite frustrated with the fishes' lack of cooperation. He deliberately tried to hook a fish in its side. He quickly yanked the line as a playful fish was consuming his bait. To his surprise, he hooked it and brought it out of the water.

He laughed and laughed as he retold his story over and over again.

I laugh just thinking about him laughing. ☺ (Neva)

While living in Electra, I would drive to Wichita Falls to visit sick church members in the hospital, and while there, would take care of errands.

Sometimes I would go with Daddy when he went to visit in the hospital. Sometimes, Mama came.

Dad was usually pretty quiet during the twenty—to thirty-minute drive; but it was a comfortable quiet.

I don't know what my motivation was to go, we didn't shop, but we would generally eat in the inexpensive hospital cafeteria. I guess my going with Daddy was equated with a father/daughter date, or maybe, I just wanted a change of scenery.

I know by watching him, I learned about conversing with the sick.

If Mama went with us, we usually stopped at the fabric store. Daddy would remain in the car, but would come in to cool off since *Herman* didn't have air-conditioning. I'm sure he wished we would hurry, and sometimes he was not happy. He would mutter "horse feathers" or "brother." (Treva)

Electra was in tornado country, so we had to seek shelter on several occasions. The F4 tornado on April 10, 1979, referred to as Terrible Tuesday, hit Wichita Falls and caused massive damage. That same day, other tornadoes touched ground along the Red River Valley.

> I remember Daddy standing out in the front yard, or in the church parking lot watching for tornadoes during watches and warnings. When the big one hit Wichita Falls, Texas, he was very watchful of the skies. I wanted to see a tornado first hand; but when I asked if I could climb on top of the church bus to look, Daddy wouldn't let me. (Treva)

Northern Texas didn't usually get much snow during the winter, but when it did, schools were usually closed. Now, Mama liked to do jigsaw puzzles and sometimes a puzzle was left out on the dining room table (we usually ate at the kitchen table). If there wasn't already a puzzle out, we would get one out on bad weather days.

> On snow days when there was no school, Julie Durbin would spend the night. We would drag out a puzzle and stay up pretty much all night working on it. It was so aggravating for Mama to walk in the next morning and immediately find the piece that we had been looking for! (Treva)

Treva graduated from Electra High School in 1979. We learned by reading the paper that she was valedictorian of her graduating class.

> I had a successful high school career. I made good grades, was involved in many activities, and seemed to be liked by my peers.

I know Mom and Dad were proud of me, but they didn't necessarily say "I'm proud of you" a lot.

Humility was something that Mama and Daddy taught all of us kids as we were growing up; so I didn't brag about my accomplishments. So when I found out I was valedictorian and chosen by the student body as "most typical girl," I didn't mention it to them because I felt like it would be bragging.

After reading it in the paper, Mom approached me and asked why I hadn't told them. I guess I didn't want to call attention to myself. (Treva)

In the fall of 1979, Treva headed off to Lubbock Christian College.

After Treva had finished high school and was off to college, Pauline and I moved to Silverton, Texas, in the Panhandle of Texas. This location was closer to the farm so we were able to drive the shorter distance more often to maintain the grounds.

We were empty nesters. Treva did come home during holiday and semester breaks. And our other children, with their children, did come to visit.

More grandchildren were to be born. The family continued to increase.

(In the nineties, I was invited back to speak at an Electra church homecoming. It was a very pleasant experience.)

CHAPTER SEVENTY-TWO

You will again obey the Lord and
follow all his commands I am giving you today.
Then the Lord your God will make you most
prosperous in all the work of your hands and
in the fruit of your womb.

—Deuteronomy 30:8 and 9

Ministry in Silverton, Texas

In the summer of 1979, we moved to Silverton, Texas, to begin work with the Silverton church of Christ. Ironically, it was the best salary we had ever received, and they provided a very nice preacher's house with three bathrooms. And there was only the two of us! It was nice and spacious for when the kids came to visit.

Pauline and Gerald Beasley.
Taken 07-06-1982
at Silverton, Texas

Possibly because of the strenuous work of packing and moving heavy boxes, Momma pinched a sciatic nerve. She was really hurting when we got to Silverton and had to get around in a wheelchair, so unpacking was very difficult for her. Neva came to help her unpack.

Silverton's population was only about seven hundred, so the church membership consisted of local citizens and farmers and ranchers in rural Texas. There were a number of young couples in the congregation with small children, so we had a great children's Bible drill.

The church had occasion to work with several deaf persons in the community, so we contacted Bob Anderson at the Sunset School of Preaching in Lubbock, Texas. He was skilled in teaching sign language and came to Silverton frequently to help us.

Apparently, the church was expected to open their doors to service all kinds of needs. I recall being in the office at the church building one day and hearing a loud scratching coming from the classroom section. I went to check it out and found a prairie dog trying to get in at the glass door into the classrooms. Showing "respect of persons" I chased it away.

Two young men from the church, Dwin Davis and Dwight Rampley (a pharmacist), attended the Sunset School of Preaching. Dwight eventually did mission work in Australia. We were proud of our homegrown missionaries.

The first Thanksgiving after the move, we had a family reunion in Silverton. Most of our offspring and their small children were there. The house had plenty of room to accommodate the bunch.

Momma was still in the wheelchair so the girls had to do most of the cooking.

There was a finished basement where the grandchildren especially liked to play. They would be playing outside or in the living room and state, "Let's go down to *the area* to play." It was cool with lots of space. They really liked the basement.

When she was able to get around the next spring, Momma put in a garden behind the wooden backyard fence; it took several years of adding humus to build the soil up. She had to keep a watch for vandals. Young community children thought it was *entertaining* to pull up and destroy her vegetable plants. One day she positioned herself by the gate; when some children, probably the culprits, came near, she stepped out and said to them, "Could you guys help me with something? Somebody has been pulling up my plants, and I need you to help me keep an eye out for them." She may have paid them something, but I'm not sure. However, her plants were left alone after that.

She also planted many flowers around the house, especially in the backyard, including multiple colored tulips.

She had already begun to collect and write down genealogy information, but while in Silverton, Momma went to the courthouse and looked up her grandparent's names, William Riley and Rosa May Smith. From the courthouse records, she was able to pinpoint the location of the ranch where her ancestors had worked and lived near Quitaque, Texas. We drove to and were able to find the old rugged house where they had lived in the Palo Duro Canyon.

While at Lubbock Christian, Treva met and married Steve Vogl on November 27, 1981. She had not finished her BA. She did finish it several years later; then with teaching credentials, she taught junior high subjects for a number of years.

We were in Silverton for about six years.

(Several years ago I was invited back to Silverton for a Gospel meeting. It was a delightful experience. The return visit to the Silverton church seemed particularly homey to me; the Silverton ladies displayed a profusion of beautifully colored flowers for my benefit using the flowering plants that Momma had planted while we lived there.)

CHAPTER SEVENTY-THREE

For what we preach is not ourselves, but Jesus Christ
as Lord, and ourselves as your servants for Jesus' sake.
—2 Corinthians 4:5

Ministry in McLean, Texas

Pauline and I worked with the church of Christ in McLean, Texas, very briefly in 1985. It is a bit interesting that the McLean church has had about five preachers who did college work at Oklahoma A&M, including myself.

Each of our moves got us closer to the Smith farm. It was probably unrealistic, but Momma thought we might retire and someday actual live on the farm.

The McLean church seemed to have a high percentage of older members.

We moved into the church's very nice preacher's residence that had four bedrooms. And only two people to live in it.

I appreciated the spacious office in the church building.

Not long after our arrival in McLean, I received a phone call at the house; a male voice advised me that "you will be blown to hell." I had never been greeted that way before. It was a little unnerving. I called one of the elders, and he was dumbfounded as well. I reasoned that it was probably a teenage boy and wasn't a real threat. We didn't get blown up!

Much more pleasant was getting acquainted with brethren in their homes and "contending earnestly for the faith."

The church's garden spot had very rich soil. We put in a garden soon after the move and were able to take quite a few garden vegetables to the Westview Boys' Home in Hollis, Oklahoma, across the Texas border on HI 62.

For various reasons, we did not remain in McLean for very long.

I still pray for congregations that we have worked with. Some are thriving. Others are limping.It is good to know that the Lord is in the helping business (Hebrews 13:6).

CHAPTER SEVENTY-FOUR

A wife of noble character who can find?
She is worth far more than rubies . . .
Her children arise and call her blessed;
Her husband also, and he praises her.
—Proverbs 31:1 and 28

Ministry in Geary, Oklahoma

Pauline and I moved to Geary, Oklahoma, in December of 1986. The congregation was quite small and we received only part-time pay. We signed up for and started to receive social security.

We bought an older brick house in Electra.

The membership had only a couple of families with small children, a few husband and wife teams, and a number of widows. It was a good loving group of Christians, and we were warmly welcomed.

For a number of years, Pauline and I had continued to travel north to attend Yellowstone Bible Camp—sometimes with the families of some of our offspring.

In the summer of 1990, we attended camp with Sheba and Larry's family.

When we arrived at the camp, Pauline wasn't feeling well; she was in a lot of pain. She tried to endure but finally said, "I think I need to see a doctor." I took her to a doctor in Livingston,

Montana. The doctor diagnosed gallstones, but suggested she would probably be more comfortable if she had the surgery in Oklahoma City nearer to home. So Momma and I drove back to Oklahoma before the camp session had ended.

Momma had the surgery at Deaconess Hospital in Oklahoma City. When Reba heard about the surgery, she came north from Electra to be with us. She had been working in the Wichita Falls hospital as a medical transcriber where she had seen lots of things. When she saw Momma's jaundice-yellow coloring, she suspected something more serious than gallstones.

When the doctor came out from surgery, his face told a serious story. He said, "I don't know what to say. I went in to do routine gallstone removal, but her gallbladder was inundated with stones and was basically mush. I'm sorry, but I need to send for an oncologist. I'm so sorry!"

Reba called the siblings and explained the situation. By the time Momma was out of recovery and in a hospital room, other family members had arrived, and others were on their way to Oklahoma City.

Carmen had driven up from Houston. Since Reba had been the only sibling there when Pauline went into surgery, Momma was surprised to see Carmen and asked, "What are you doing here?"

"I came to be with you and Dad," was Carmen's reply.

Neva and Mike had been on vacation with their family in Colorado and had stopped at Salida, Colorado, to visit Sheba's family. Sheba got the call while the Russells were there, so she rode with them to Oklahoma.

Treva and Steve, and Hoyt and Brenda showed up later at the hospital with their families.

We were devastated when the oncologist informed us in the hallway that Momma had gallbladder cancer, a very rare cancer.

"It has spread to the bile duct. Her gallbladder is metastasized to her liver, and the cancer will soon affect her liver. Radiation and chemo probably won't help, but it is the only option we have. It might extend her life some. She will probably live only three to nine months."

I went into the room and spoke with Momma as soon as she was awake enough to understand and told her of the doctor's diagnosis. I gently touched Pauline's face while looking into her eyes. It was the hardest thing I had ever done, telling her she had cancer. "Momma, were going to beat this. We are going to fight! We can't give up!"

> I can visualize Dad as soon as he saw Mom after her surgery and told her the doctor's findings. He had his hand on her face and his face so near to hers. He stayed with her while she was in the hospital and appeared rather hesitant to leave her side when he did.
>
> Dad was a devoted, loving husband as he cared for Mom in her last few weeks. He would wake up at night routinely to give Mom her medications, bath her, sit and hold her hand. It demonstrated the tremendous love he had for Mom, an unconditional love. His devotion was very apparent.
>
> For this care and love, I thank him. (Reba)

As the other family members arrived, small groups took turns entering to visit Mom in the hospital room. Pauline was still in shock; she was very quiet sorting out her thoughts and feelings.

I continued to stay at the hospital every day until she was ready to come home. I had just combed Momma's hair and propped her up with pillows, when a new nurse came into the room, looked at Pauline and exclaimed, "You're beautiful!" I'll never forget her reaction and comment. She was right! Pauline was beautiful!

Several of the girls drove west to Electra and stayed at the house to clean and make preparations for when Momma finally came home to Geary.

It was probably a bit overwhelming for Pauline with so many at the house, but pretty quickly they began to head home to resume their other responsibilities. Before leaving, the girls made plans and arrangements to stagger visits to help and spend time with their Mom.

After several weeks of recovery, Momma started radiation treatments, so she entered the Baptist Hospital in Oklahoma City. The kids' extended families drove to Oklahoma City and gathered at the Baptist Hospital for a visit. We wanted to sing for Momma and got permission from a nurse to crowd into her room, "Yes, I think it will be okay, but keep it brief. I'll let you know if the singing disturbs other patients. If you see she is in distress, you know to stop."

About thirty family members crowded around Momma's bed, and the entire group sang and recorded hymns on a tape recorder. It was such beautiful singing; the angels in heaven must have envied the harmonious voices of our children, grandchildren, daughter-in-law and sons-in-law.

We thanked God for all his blessings and prayed that he would heal our grandmother, mother, mother-in-law and wife.

After leaving Mom to rest, we all gathered again in the hospital chapel where we continued to sing and record. The grandchildren sang and recorded some simple children's songs. We gave the recordings to Momma so she could listen to them in our absence.

After she came home, Pauline had a hard time. Nothing tasted good to her; she ate only little bits at a time; though medicated, she was in pain; her hair began to fall out; she had no energy. I kept telling her, "Don't give up! We have to fight this!"

Neva had contacted Pauline's estranged brother, Uncle Royce Smith, about her diagnosis even though Momma said she did not want us to contact him.

At first Royce said, "I'm sorry, but I have nothing to say to her." But after giving it some thought, he called back and asked if he could come see her. It was tense and awkward, but he returned for several visits. Brother and sister were reunited, and some wounds were healed.

I took Pauline to Oklahoma City for a treatment. While there she had heart failure, was revived, but went into cardiac arrest and passed away on October 4, 1990, about six weeks after her surgery.

The celebration of the life of my beloved Clara Pauline Beasley's life was on October 7, 1990, at the Geary church of Christ. She had chosen the scripture to be read, Phil. 4:4-7, and the following songs to be sung: "Jesus Loves Me," "No Tears in Heaven," "Jesus Is Mine," "Count Your Many Blessings," "When We All Get to Heaven," and "Let the Beauty of Jesus Be Seen in Me."

Her obituary summarized her life:

> Pauline Beasley was born March 15, 1924, in Cold Springs, Kiowa County, Oklahoma, to John and Maggie Smith. She departed this life last Thursday at age 66 in Baptist Medical Center, Oklahoma City.
>
> Pauline graduated from Warren High School, near Blair, Oklahoma, in 1941, and then attended Oklahoma A&M in Stillwater where she met Gerald at church. She and Gerald Beasley were married June 18, 1944, in Meridian, Mississippi, while he was stationed at Camp Shelby, Mississippi. During World War II when her husband was in the service and overseas, Pauline taught in the Brinkman and Plainview Schools in the Mangum School District.

During school days at Warren, she was very active in 4-H work. Both Pauline and Gerald attended Abilene Christian College after the war. She also enrolled in extension courses from Eastern Montana College of Education in Billings, Montana.

During decades of Bible class preparation, she accumulated many shelves full of teaching materials. Gerald and Pauline have served churches of Christ in Oklahoma, Kansas, Texas and Montana.

For years she has been faithfully involved in the exalted occupation of HOME-MAKER.

Survivors include: Husband, Gerald of Geary; One son, Hoyt of Morrison, Colorado; and Daughters: Sheba Thomas of Salida, Colorado; Reba Durbin of Electra, Texas; Carmen Lewis of Houston, Texas; Neva Russell of Lucas, Texas; and Treva Vogl of Paris, Texas. Seventeen grandchildren include ten grandsons and seven granddaughters. One brother, Royce Smith, lives in Blair, Oklahoma, and two nieces. Pauline's family definitely includes her one daughter-in-law and her five sons-in-law.

She was preceded in death by her parents.

Burial will be in the Blair, Oklahoma cemetery at 5 p.m. today.

We had been in Geary about four years, and Pauline had become good friends with the ladies at church. One of the dear ladies wrote the following to me after her death:

Dear Gerald,

It will soon be Pauline's birthday. I rejoice that she was born and that God brought her to Geary, where I could share a part of her life.

I believe that she was one of the worthy daughters spoken of in Proverbs 31:29 & 31.

I miss Pauline. And I am strengthened as I see your strong faith in making the many adjustments to living without her. You and your family are a part of my daily prayers.

"Now to him who is able to do immeasurably more than all we ask or imagine, according to his power that is at work within us, to him be glory in the church, and in Christ Jesus throughout all generations, forever and ever! Amen." (Ephesians 3:20, 21).

Thank you for the many encouraging lessons you bring us, scripturally sound, and so enlightening and practical for our living in Christ.

Sincerely,
Wilda Rinehart

Momma and I had earlier received the following, meaningful letter which I would like to share:

Dear Mom and Dad,
I've wanted to tell you both what you mean to me. A daughter or son could not have had more concerned parents. I want to make sure that you are aware of your great value as parents, Christians and people in general.
As Parents you (1) loved our souls more than our bodies; (2) wanted our utmost happiness; (3) taught us to be kind to a hurt bird, a taunted child, a hateful co-worker, and deaf old folks; (4) desired that we have more success in our marriages, careers and endeavors of all kinds, even better than what you had; (5) aided us in every way possible to solve problems, unless

wisdom dictated otherwise; (6) were an example of communication accomplished with love, gentleness and understanding instead of malice, strife and conflict; (7) sacrificed hours of sewing, reading, teaching, gardening, raking, washing and preaching to make our stomachs full, our minds knowledgeable, and our bodies clothed; (8) listened to bratty, belligerent, rebellious teenagers criticize and tear down, but you remained sane and stern throughout it all; and (9) didn't give into the whims for shorter dresses, later hours, and freer activities.

I love your dedication to us and our mates. I'm sorry it hasn't been expressed more and oftener. You're both great human beings and God must hold great pride for both of you.

We've always wanted to please you and still need your approval.

It's not hard to honor parents that are as honorable as you are.

I've thought that if something should ever happen to you or me, I would have wished you to know how important you have been and are, not only to the family, but to many Christians and non-Christians in your acquaintance.

I appreciate the qualities you both possess and hope I can obtain them: (1) You rarely utter a critical or harming word for others. (2) You have a calmness and serenity, a peace of mind. (3) You are satisfied with little things. (4) You don't let petty aggravations disturb you. (5) You want the whole world to feel your happiness. (6) You have a wonderful humbleness and quietness.

I thank you!

Neva Beasley Russell

Since Pauline's departure from this world, it has been hard, but I determined to keep busy, and to not lose my sense of humor while continuing to preach in Geary.

A couple of summers later after her passing, Mike Brazel, son to Clinton Brazel who we knew in Montana, invited me to join a group of senior citizens on a bus trip from Springfield, Missouri, to Yellowstone Bible Camp in Montana. I wasn't sure I would like traveling in a group on a bus with a set schedule, but I agreed to go.

I'm convinced that several of the widows on board made moves on me, but I wasn't interested. I had had the best marriage partner and couldn't do any better. I ignored them.

Anyhow, traveling northwest toward Yellowstone Bible Camp while driving from Laramie, Wyoming, to Rock Springs, Wyoming, the bus riders pointed out and exclaimed about the numerous windmill farms on the hill tops. One of the ladies asked, "What do they raise on a windmill farm?"

I answered, "Preachers." ☺

I had played some golf but started to play more often with my buddies. Ray Price, a church member, would call me up and ask, "You wanna go play some golf?"

I would respond, "I expose so." ☺

When I went to the doctor's to receive a shot, the nurse would ask, "Where do you want it, the arm or the buttocks?"

"I expose so," I responded. ☺

On January 2, 1997, the following article appeared in the *Geary Star* which summarized my life to that point in time:

Did You Know? by Iris Warkentin

There has been one friendly and dedicated preacher among us for the past ten years. His church is the church of Christ on the corner of Blaine & 1st Street. His attractive red-brick house overlooks the southwest side of Geary on the corner of Galena and South Street. The Lloyd Randolphs used to live there. No one would envy him that lawn mowing job. And yet, I'm told he has been known to get so engrossed in mowing the lawn to forget a special church camp dinner!

Gerald Austin Beasley was born, raised and had his early schooling in the Sapulpa—Sand Springs area. He was an only child, a farm boy. He graduated from OSU (then Oklahoma A&M) in 1942, with a degree in Agriculture. He wasn't through with school though. He later attended Abilene Christian University, McPherson (KS) College, and West Texas State University.

Gerald served in the 69th Infantry Division, European theatre, during WWII as a Medical Aid. He was also a member of a military band, playing the clarinet. I understand a close encounter with a pesky cow and her horn knocked out some of his teeth and ended his clarinet playing.

In 1944 he married his college sweetheart, Pauline Smith, while stationed at Camp Shelby near Hattiesburg, Mississippi. In his words—it was a tremendous marriage, which sadly ended with Pauline's death of cancer on 1990 in Geary.

The Beasley's are the parents of six children, a son and five daughters. The son and three of his sons-in-law are Gospel preachers.

Their children are: Hoyt Beasley who lives with his family in Nevada, Missouri. The daughters are: Sheba (Mrs. Larry Thomas) who lives in Salida, Colorado; Reba (Mrs. Jerry Durbin) who lives in Electra, Texas; Carmen (Mrs. Michael Lewis) who lives in Houston,

Texas; Neva (Mrs. Mike Russell) who lives in Lucas, Texas; and Treva (Mrs. Steve Vogl) who lives in Gilmer, Texas. There are seventeen grand-children and one great-grand-daughter.

Presently attending college are one daughter, five grand-children and a grand-daughter-in-law.

From preaching at "practice on" churches of Christ in Palacios, Texas, and Hattiesburg, Mississippi, Gerald has been a preacher in churches of Christ in Oklahoma, Kansas, Montana and Texas before coming to Geary in 1986.

From some of his Geary flock, I've gleaned that Mr. Beasley has a wonderful collection of poetry, that he never forgets a friend, and likes to keep in touch with former friends and associates. He's been known to coin a new word, or phrase to fit an occasion, or to get a point across. He keeps his own house, keeps an interest in the farm work on his farm at Warren, Oklahoma, and enjoys keeping up with his large family.

Ray Price has taught him the joys of golfing. His friend Dwight Mowrer of Lariat Creek Christian Camp is also a golfing buddy. A little bird told me he has made a **hole-in-one** a couple of times on the Watonga Golf Course. How about that!

Epilogue

I am ninety-two years old at this writing (October 2012). I still preach for the tiny church of Christ in Geary, Oklahoma. Attrition has reduced our attendance to a handful. Eight or ten present would be a crowd for us. We pray for successful outreach and increased numbers.

I have been privileged to work quite a bit with Lariat Creek Christian Camp near Geary.

I take great pleasure in spending time with my six children (including a widow daughter-in-law, Brenda) and their families. At last count I had seventeen grandchildren and sixteen great-grandchildren. Family reunions are usually well attended, noise and busy affairs.

With some of my children, I have attended family sessions at Bow and Arrow / Yellowstone Bible Camp in Montana. Hopefully, this will continue.

My son, Hoyt, had multiple severe health problems for decades. He departed this life in September of 2012 at the age of sixty-six. Many times in past years, my phone has rung and I've heard four words, "This is your son." At hang-up time, four more words, "I love you, Dad." Hoyt preached for churches of Christ in Oklahoma, Kansas, Nevada, Colorado, and Missouri. It seems unreal that he no longer sojourns among us.

> For I am already being poured out like a drink
> offering, and the time has come for my departure.
> (2 Timothy 4:6)

> I am torn between the two: I desire to depart
> and be with Christ, which is better by far; but it is
> more necessary for you that I remain in the body.
> (Philippians 1:23)

When Pauline died in 1990, I resolved to keep busy in the Lord's work. I've been abundantly blessed.

> The thief comes only to steal and kill and destroy;
> I have come that they may have life, and have it to
> the full. (John 10:10)

Thank you, Lord!

I love the Lord, for he heard my voice; he heard my cry for mercy.
Because he turned his ear to me, I will call on him as long as I live.

The cords of death entangled me, the anguish of the grave came upon me; I was overcome by trouble and sorrow.
Then I called on the name of the Lord: "O Lord, save me!"

The Lord is gracious and righteous; our God is full of compassion.
The Lord protects the simple hearted; when I was in great need, he saved me.

Be at rest once more, O my soul, for the Lord has been good to you.
For you, O Lord, have delivered my soul from death, my eyes from tears, my feet from stumbling, that I may walk before the Lord in the land of the living.

I believed; therefore I said, "I am greatly afflicted."
And in my dismay I said, "All men are liars."
How can I repay the Lord for all his goodness to me?
I will lift up the cup of salvation and call on the name of the Lord.
I will fulfill my vows to the Lord in the presence of all his people.

Precious in the sight of the Lord is the death of his saints.

O Lord, truly I am your servant;
I am your servant, the son of your maidservant; you
have freed me from my chains.

I will sacrifice a thank offering to you and call on
the name of the Lord.
I will fulfill my vows to the Lord in the presence
of all his people, in the courts of the house of the
Lord—in your midst, O Jerusalem.
Praise the Lord! (Psalms 116)

There are, indeed, "precious memories."

—Gerald Austin Beasley

Beasley Clan family reunion near Stroud, Oklahoma—2010

APPENDAGE

A record of the genealogy . . .
Thus there were . . . generations in all.
—Matthew 1:1, 17

Beasley Genealogy

The Beasley genealogy has been validated to the early settlers in Virginia. A number of Beasleys were born in various counties in Lancashire, England, but immigrated to America seeking freedom from social, economic, and/or religious oppression.

Gerald Austin Beasley's lineage was traced through (1) William Beesley Sr., (2) William Beasley Jr. (spelling changed), (3) John Beasley, (4) Charles Beasley, (5) Nathaniel Harrison Beasley, (6) George Washington Beasley, (7) Samuel Porter Beasley, and (8) Edgar Beasley.

1. **William Beesley, Sr.** was born about 1638 in Lancashire, England. He immigrated with a Henry Roach on March 16, 1658, to Westmoreland County, Virginia. Henry had received a land grant of 140 acres in 1657/58 as well as transportation of three persons: William Beesley, John Draper, and Elizabeth Russell. It is likely they were fleeing religious persecution for refusing to comply with the Church of England.

   William married an Elizabeth in about 1658, probably the Elizabeth Russell who crossed the Atlantic with Henry Roach.

William Sr. may have helped work Henry's land at first, but records indicate that he did eventually settle on and work his own land in Virginia.

2. **William Beasley, Jr.** was born to William Sr. and Elizabeth in 1658 (one record said in Lancashire, England, but another source said in Virginia).

   William Jr. married Mary Ripley in 1678. They had five sons, all born in Essex County, Virginia

3. **John Beasley** was born to William and Elizabeth in 1685 in Virginia.

   Around 1705, with some of his brothers, John ventured to Craven County, North Carolina. He worked land under a Lord Proprietor and paid rent and taxes. Later on April 20, 1745, John was granted a patent for two hundred acres on the North Neuse River in Craven County near Cove City and Core Creek. He purchased additional surrounding lands, and his property became known as Beasley Island.

   He married Sara Joann Jenkins in about 1705 in North Carolina, and they had eight children.

   Some Beasley' ancestors may still live in the area of Beasley Island in North Carolina.

4. **Charles Beasley**, the youngest of the eight children born to John and Sara at Beasley Island, was born in 1732.

   Charles married Susanna Allen in 1769. They had six children.

   Charles remained on Beasley Island in North Carolina his whole life.

5. **Nathaniel Harrison Beasley** was born May 19, 1774, on Beasley Island to Charles and Susanna.

After the American Revolution, the new country was suffering from high taxes, crowded conditions on the seacoast and economic difficulties. In about 1795, Nathaniel and his new wife, Sarah Sutton, traveled west through North Carolina into the Tennessee territory with his cousins, William Beasley and Solomon Beasley Jr., along with other neighboring North Carolina friends.

The Nathaniel and William Beasley families settled and remained in Kentucky from 1797 to about 1819 where Nathaniel worked as a surveyor. Both families relocated briefly to North Butler County in Kentucky, then later to Macon County, Decatur, Illinois.

Nathaniel and Sarah had fifteen children, most of them born in Kentucky.

Nathaniel died on March 27, 1835, in Decatur, Illinois, as listed in Byrd Township, Brown County.

Some Beasley' ancestors still live in Illinois.

6. **George Washington Beasley** was born April 26, 1818, the twelfth of fifteen children born to Nathaniel and Sarah in Kentucky. In 1819, as a baby, George traveled with his family as they made the trek to North Butler County, Kentucky, and later to Illinois.

   George married Elizabeth Plaster in 1845, probably in Illinois. Sometime after 1873 they moved to Missouri with their nine children and then later to Oklahoma with some of their children.

   George and Elizabeth both died in 1911 and were both buried in the Wagoner County, Oak Grove, Oklahoma.

7. **Samuel Porter Beasley** was born December 23, 1853, in Illinois, the third of the nine children born to George and Elizabeth. He moved with his parents to Missouri sometime after 1873.

Samuel married Lavina Jan Smith in 1876 in Missouri. From 1878-1898, they had eight children all born on a farm four or five miles northeast of Marion County, Almartha, Missouri. The family took their corn to be ground at a mill near Rockbridge, Missouri. The older children attended Sauder School at Sauder, Missouri.

In about 1900, Samuel and Lavina moved with their eight children, Samuel's parents, George and Elizabeth, and some of Samuel's siblings to Indian Territory in Oklahoma. They settled at Spring Hill east of Haskell near Clarksville, Oklahoma, probably to acquire cheap and/or free land or for gainful employment. At that time, their children ranged in ages from twenty-two to three.

Eddie and Edgar, twins, were their youngest children. Eddie died at age three (possibly of pneumonia) in 1900 and was buried in Clarksville. Lavina died in 1904 and was buried in Clarksville.

Prior to Oklahoma becoming a state in 1906, the Samuel Beasley family moved to Oak Grove, Oklahoma, near Sapulpa.

There is no indication that Samuel remarried, so he probably raised his younger children with the help of his parents and his older children.

Samuel died in 1939 while living with Edgar and Hallie in Sand Springs, Oklahoma.

8. **Edgar Beasley** and his twin brother, Eddie, the youngest of eight children, were born to Samuel and Lavina on September 15, 1897, in Almartha, Missouri. As toddlers, they moved with the Samuel Beasley family to Oklahoma.

Since Edgar's mother, Lavina, had died in 1904 when he was only seven years old, Edgar likely grew up with less supervision. He only attended school through elementary grades.

He met Hallie Elizabeth Morris and married in 1919.

Edgar Beasley died in Sand Springs in 1968.

9. **Gerald Austin Beasley** was born July 19, 1920, to Edgar and Hallie Beasley.

Morris Genealogy

Hallie Elizabeth Morris was of Scottish descend. Her descendants came from Tennessee and had a Pentecostal background.

Early Scottish immigrants first settled together in groups in the eastern Appalachians and later immigrated together to western interior territories, many from Tennessee to Missouri.

Hallie's genealogy has been confirmed from the early 1800s by Helen Holloway, a Morris descendant. Hallie descended through (1) Thomas Franklyn Morris and (2) George Newton Morris.

1. **Thomas Franklin Morris** was born in Tennessee, probably before 1820.

   His wife's name is unknown, but Helen had the impression that her great-grandparents, especially the female "was a terror! And he was no lamb!"

   Thomas Morris and his wife had at least two children, Robert and George.

   Around 1850, the Morris descendants moved west to Missouri. Robert Morris, was probably born before 1850. He later fought in the Civil War for the South. After the Civil War, Rob became a Texas Ranger and was involved in the pursuit of Geronimo in Texas.

2. **George Newton Morris**, the second son of Thomas, was born August 8, 1854, in Shannon County, Missouri.

   George later went to Clarendon, Arkansas, where he met and married Francis Ann Thomas (born October of 1856), probably around 1878.

Francis Ann's family worshiped with the churches of Christ.

George and Francis remained in Clarendon, Arkansas, where Albert Sid was born March 29, 1880. Sometime after 1880, George and Francis moved with their family to Missouri where Florence Valentine, Virginia Vee, Georgia Floyd, Frank, and Hallie Elizabeth were born. Their three older children (Albert, Florence, and Virginia) had married and remained in Missouri.

About 1900, George and Francis then moved with their three younger children (Floyd, Frank and Hallie) to Oklahoma Territory.

Frank died in 1910 of a heart condition while pulling up a fence post in Coweta, Oklahoma. He was only about fifteen years old.

3. **Hallie Elizabeth Morris** was born November 1, 1897, in West Plains, Missouri, the Howell County seat.

Edgar Beasley married Hallie Elizabeth Morris on May 05, 1919, in Sand Springs, Oklahoma.

Hallie died October 19, 1946, in Sand Springs, Oklahoma.

4. **Gerald Austin Beasley** was born to Edgar and Hallie Beasley on July 19, 1920, in Sand Springs, Oklahoma.

Smith Genealogy

Clara Pauline Smith descended through (1) James Henry Smith, (2) William Riley Smith, and (3) John Earl Smith.

The Smith lineage was traced from an Old Settlers list—those full-blooded Cherokee who moved west from the Tennessee area before the forced migration over the Trail of Tears.

1. **James Henry Smith**, a full-blooded Cherokee, was born November 13, 1824, in Missouri.

   He married Lucinda Couch on January 1, 1848, in Van Buren, Arkansas. They had nine children.

   Lucinda Couch descended from:

   i. **Jacob Couch** was born about 1730. Jacob and his wife had ten children.

   ii. **Nicholas Couch**, the eighth of the ten children, was born in Tennessee in 1750.

   Nicholas married Mary Elizabeth Roach on July 26, 1787, in Green City, Tennessee.

   iii. **John Couch**, the third of four known children born to Nicholas and Mary, was born in 1810 in North Alabama.

   John married Ann Ross (born in 1812 and died in 1850). John took a second wife, Matilda.

   iv. **Lucinda**, the second of eleven children born to John and Ann, was born October 8, 1832, in Van Buren, Arkansas.

   Instead of settling in the Indian Territory in Oklahoma, James Henry and Lucinda Smith moved to Grayson County in northeast Texas where they had nine children.

   They later went to Graham, Texas, in Young County, where both died and were buried in the Oak Grove Cemetery.

2. **William Riley Smith**, the youngest of Henry and Lucinda's nine children, was born January 30, 1873, in Cook County, Dexter, Texas, just west of Sherman.

   On February 3, 1893, twenty-year-old William married fifteen-year-old Rosa May Golden in Indian Territory near Norman, Oklahoma.

   Rosa May descended from:

i. **Elijah Golden** married Virginia L. Hammons. Virginia died on May 12, 1882. After Virginia's death, Benjamin W. Hammons, Virginia's brother, raised four-year-old Rosa May and her two other siblings until his death January 14, 1889. Rosa May was eleven years old at the time of his death.

Apparently, Elijah, her father, was alive but was not around. Elijah died in Healdton, Oklahoma, on January 21, 1928.

ii. **Rosa May** was born May 15, 1878, in Graham, Texas, to Elijah and Virginia L. (Hammons) Golden.

Perhaps Rosa's young age and lack of a guardian contributed to her marrying at such a young age. William and Rosa May moved to the west Panhandle of Texas where they ranched cattle on land close to Quitaque, Texas, near the county seat of Silverton, Texas.

Rosa was sixteen when she had the first of eight children:

1) William Carson (Cye) born May 6, 1894, in Quitaque, Texas;
2) Bennie Leon (Bud) born October 12, 1895, in Quitaque, Texas;
3) John Earl born January 28 (or 29), 1898, in Turkey, Texas; and
4) Ada May born February 19, 1901, in Graham, Texas.

Then in about 1902, the Smiths moved from the Panhandle of Texas with their four children to southwest Oklahoma when land became available for homesteading in Old Greer County. Four more children were born in Oklahoma:

5) Imy Mercedes was born July 15, 1904, in Mill Creek, Oklahoma. She died on November 2, 1919, at the age of fifteen;

6) Ida Minnie was born June 24, 1907, in Roosevelt, Oklahoma. She died on May 16, 1915, at the age of seven;

7) Robert (Bob) Roy was born November 6, 1910, in Roosevelt, Oklahoma;

8) Lillian Frances (Frankie) was born July 23, 1916, in Roosevelt, Oklahoma.

William and Rosa Smith eventually settled at Mountain Park, Oklahoma, near the North Fork of the Red River. It was in this area that their children grew up and attended school.

Home of William Riley and Rosa May Smith in Mountain Park, OK

3. **John Earl** was born January 28 (or 29), 1898, in Turkey, Texas.

John married Maggie Lillian Herring on July 26, 1922, in Mangum, Oklahoma.

4. **Clara Pauline Smith** was born to John and Maggie on March 15, 1924, near Blair, Oklahoma.

Herring Genealogy

The Herrings were of Dutch origin. Clara Pauline Smith descended through (1) Jim Herring, (2) Edmond Pinkney Herring, and (3) Maggie Lillian Herring.

1. **Jim Herring** was born about 1850 in Lockesburg, Arkansas. Jim married a Bessie, and they had four children.

2. **Edmond Pinkney Herring**, Jim and Bessie's fourth child, was born September 20, 1870.

    December 5, 1900, thirty-year-old Edmond married eighteen-year-old Willie Crawford Eddins.

    Willie Crawford Eddins descended from:

    i.   **Will (JW) Eddins** was born in 1858 in Tennessee. He married Dora Ann Miranda Black (born February 12, 1856, in Tennessee).

        A United States Census of 1880 registered in Shelby, Texas, listed JW as a farmer. They had two children, Myrtle and Willie Crawford.

    ii. **Willie Crawford Eddins** was born December 24, 1882.

    Edmond and Willie Herring had two girls, both born in Sailes, Louisiana: Myrtle Lavonia born 09-14-1901, and Maggie Lillian born 01-14-1906.

    Edmond and Willie traveled by covered wagon as they moved around, possibly as migrant workers. In 1909 the family moved by covered wagon to:

    1) Hester, Louisiana;
    2) back to Sailes, Louisiana, three years later;

3) south to Cheneyville, Louisiana, for one year;
4) back to Sailes, Louisiana, near Mount Lebanon for a couple of years;
5) west to Elkview, Oklahoma, in Jackson County;
6) to Mountain Park, Oklahoma, for three years;
7) then, four miles north of Mountain Park, Oklahoma, for a year.
8) In September of 1918 they moved back east to Green Forest, Arkansas, for a year and a half.
9) They then moved back to Elkview, Oklahoma, in 1920. All the trips but the last two were made by covered wagon.

3. **Maggie Lillian Herring** was born January 14, 1906, to Edmond and Willie Herring.

Maggie married John Earl Smith July 26, 1922, in Mangum, Oklahoma.

4. **Clara Pauline Smith** was born March 15, 1924, to John Earl Smith and Maggie Lillian.

The Beasley genealogy is based on information researched, collected and recorded by Pauline Smith Beasley.

The above quotes and Morris genealogy information came from Albert Sid Morris's daughter, Helen Holloway, and was written down and recorded by Pauline Smith Beasley.

The genealogy of the Smith and Herring families is limited and based on research that was collected and recorded by Pauline Smith Beasley.

I, Carmen Beasley Lewis, and was able to look up and verify most of Mom's information at Genealogy.com.

Gerald Austin Beasley married Clara Pauline Smith on June 18, 1944, in Meridian, Missouri. They had seven children:

1. Hoyt Terrell Beasley born July 14, 1946, in Abilene, Texas;
2. Sheba Beth Beasley born January 16, 1948, in Davenport, Oklahoma;
3. Reba Nell Beasley born December 22, 1948, in Davenport, Oklahoma;
4. Carmen Lee Beasley born June 25, 1950, in Manhattan, Kansas;
5. Baby Boy Beasley born and died on October 23, 1951, in McPherson, Kansas;
6. Neva Ann Beasley born on July 22, 1953, in McPherson, Kansas; and
7. Treva Kay Beasley born on May 13, 1961, in Lewistown, Montana.

Edwards Brothers Malloy
Thorofare, NJ USA
March 5, 2013